The Diaries of
GEORGE WASHINGTON

Volume IV

1784–June 1786

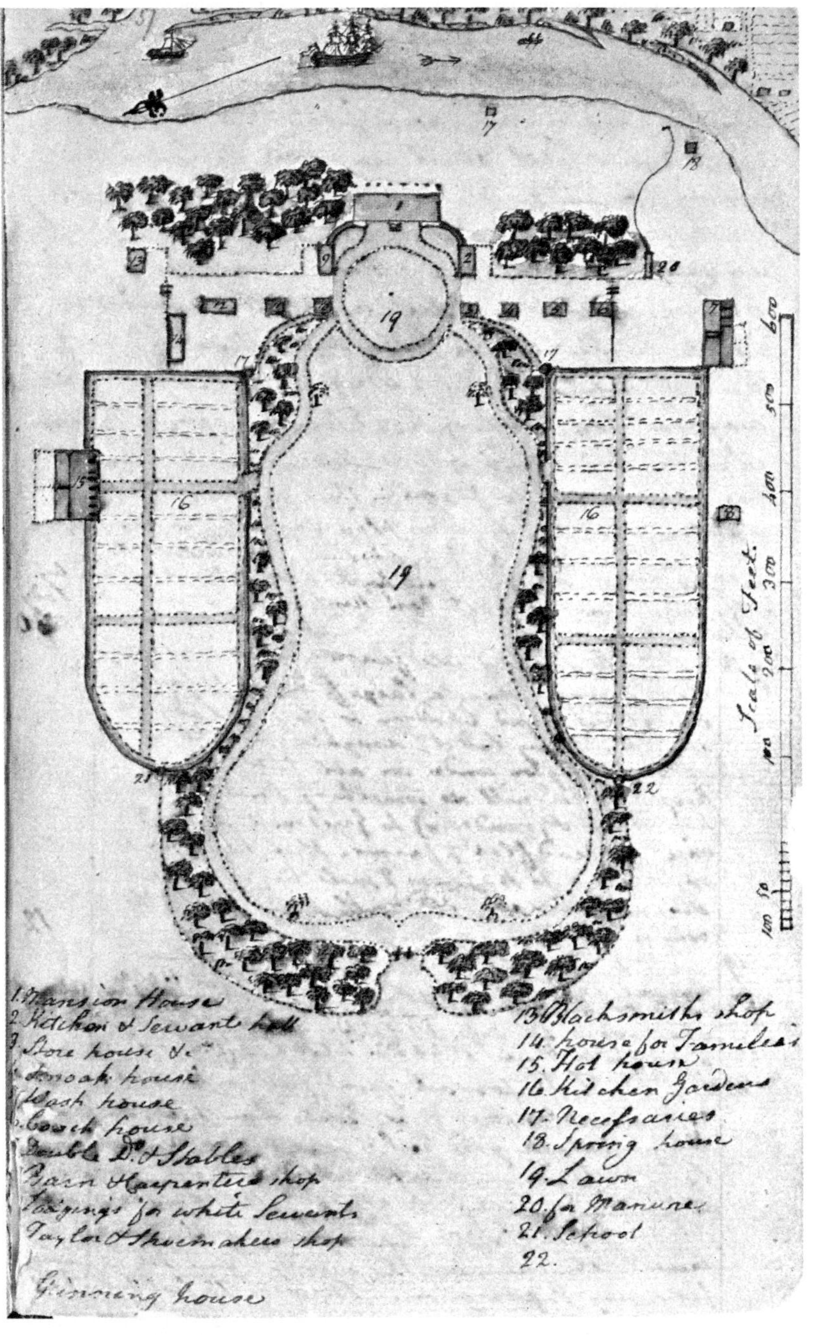
Scale of Feet
1. Mansion House
2. Kitchen & Servants hall
3. Store house &c
Smoak house
Wash house
Coach house
Double D.o & Stables
Barn & Carpenters shop
Lodgings for white Servants
Taylor & Shoemakers shop
Ginning house
13 Blacksmiths shop
14. houses for Families
15. Hot house
16. Kitchen Gardens
17. Necessaries
18. Spring house
19. Lawn
20. for Manure
21. School
22.

ASSISTANT EDITORS

Beverly H. Runge, Frederick Hall Schmidt,
and Philander D. Chase

George H. Reese, CONSULTING EDITOR

Joan Paterson Kerr, PICTURE EDITOR

THE DIARIES OF GEORGE WASHINGTON

VOLUME IV

1784–June 1786

DONALD JACKSON AND DOROTHY TWOHIG

EDITORS

UNIVERSITY PRESS OF VIRGINIA

CHARLOTTESVILLE

This edition has been prepared by the staff of
The Papers of George Washington,
sponsored by
The Mount Vernon Ladies' Association of the Union
and the University of Virginia
with the support of
the National Endowment for the Humanities
and
the National Historical Publications and Records
Commission.

THE UNIVERSITY PRESS OF VIRGINIA

First published 1978

Frontispiece: Samuel Vaughan's sketch of Mount Vernon,
from his 1787 journal.
(Collection of the descendents of Samuel Vaughan)

Library of Congress Cataloging in Publication Data (Revised)

Washington, George, Pres. U.S., 1732–1799.
The diaries of George Washington.

Includes bibliographies and indexes.
1. Washington, George, Pres. U.S., 1732–1799.
2. Presidents—United States—Biography. I. Jackson,
Donald Dean, 1919– II. Twohig, Dorothy. III. Title.
E312.8 1976 973.4'1'0924 [B] 75-41365
ISBN 0-8139-0722-5

Printed in the United States of America

Contents

Illustrations

Editorial Procedures and Symbols

Transcription of the diaries has remained as faithful as possible to the original manuscript. Because of the nature of GW's diary entries, absolute consistency in punctuation has been virtually impossible. Where feasible, the punctuation has generally been retained as written. However, in cases where sentences are separated by dashes, a common device in the eighteenth century, the dash has been changed to a period and following word capitalized. Dashes which appear after periods have been dropped. Periods have been inserted at points which are clearly the ends of sentences. In many of the diaries, particularly those dealing with planting and the weather, entries consist of phrases separated by dashes rather than sentences. Generally if the phrase appears to stand alone, a period has been substituted for the dash.

Spelling of all words is retained as it appears in the manuscript. Errors in spelling of geographic locations and proper names have been corrected in notes or in brackets only if the spelling in the text makes the word incomprehensible. Washington occasionally, especially in the diaries, placed above an incorrectly written word a symbol sometimes resembling a tilde, sometimes an infinity sign, to indicate an error in orthography. When this device is used the editors have silently corrected the word.

The ampersand has been retained. The thorn has been transcribed as "th." The symbol for per has been written out. When a tilde is used to indicate either a double letter or missing letters, the correction has been made silently or the word has been transcribed as an abbreviation. Capitalization is retained as it appears in the manuscript; if the writer's intention is not clear, modern usage is followed.

Contractions and abbreviations are retained as written; a period is inserted after abbreviations. When an apostrophe has been used in contractions it is retained. Superscripts have been lowered, and if the word is an abbreviation a period has been added. When the meaning of an abbreviation is not obvious, it has been expanded in square brackets: H[unting] C[reek]; so[uther]ly.

Other editorial insertions or corrections in the text also appear in square brackets. Missing dates are supplied in square brackets in diary entries. Angle brackets (<   >) are used to indicate mutilated material. If it is clear from the context what word or words are missing, or missing material has been filled in from other sources, the words are inserted between the angle brackets.

A space left blank by Washington in the manuscript of the diaries is indicated by a square bracketed gap in the text. In cases where Washington has crossed out words or phrases, the deletions have not been noted. If a deletion contains substantive material it appears in a footnote. Words inadvertently repeated or repeated at the bottom of a page of manuscript have been dropped.

If the intended location of marginal notations is clear, they have been inserted in the proper place without comment; otherwise, insertions appear in footnotes.

In cases where the date is repeated for several entries on the same day, the repetitive date has been omitted and the succeeding entries have been paragraphed.

Because Washington used the blank pages of the *Virginia Almanack* or occasionally small notebooks to keep his diaries, lack of space sometimes forced him to make entries and memoranda out of order in the volume. The correct position of such entries is often open to question, and the editors have not always agreed with earlier editors of the diaries on this matter. Such divergence of opinion, however, has not been annotated.

Bibliographical references are cited by one or two words, usually the author's last name, in small capitals. If two or more works by authors with the same surname have been used, numbers are assigned: HARRISON [2]. Full publication information is included in the bibliography for each volume. The symbols used to identify repositories in the footnotes precede the bibliography.

Surveying notes and dated memoranda kept in diary form have not been included in this edition of Washington's diaries, although the information contained in them has often been used in annotation.

Individuals and places mentioned for the first time in this volume have been identified in the footnotes; those which have been identified in the first three volumes may be located by consulting the indexes of those volumes. A cumulative index will be included in the last volume of the *Diaries.*

The Diaries of
GEORGE WASHINGTON

Volume IV

1784–June 1786

A Western Journey

1784

September 1784

Having found it indispensably necessary to visit my Landed property west of the Apalacheon Mountains, and more especially that part of it which I held in Co-partnership with Mr. Gilbert Simpson[1]—Having determined upon a tour into that Country, and having made the necessary preparations for it, I did, on the first day of this month (September) set out on my journey.

Having dispatched my equipage about 9 Oclock A.M., consisting of 3 Servants & 6 horses, three of which carried my Baggage, I set out myself in company with Docter James Craik;[2] and after dining at Mr. Sampson Trammells (abt. 2 Miles above the Falls Church)[3] we proceeded to Difficult Bridge, and lodged at one Shepherds Tavern 25 Miles.[4]

[1] Gilbert Simpson, Jr., son of the Gilbert Simpson who for many years leased part of Clifton's Neck from GW, had since 1773 been manager of Washington's Bottom, a 1,644-acre tract that GW owned on the west bank of the Youghiogheny River about 35 miles southeast of Fort Pitt. This land, now site of Perryopolis, Pa., was the first claimed by GW west of the Appalachians, having been surveyed for him in 1768 (William Crawford to GW, 7 Jan. 1769, DLC:GW; see "Remarks" entry for 15 Oct. 1770). In need of a settler to hold the tract against squatters and to begin clearing it for profitable cultivation, GW must have been pleased in the fall of 1772 to receive a letter from the younger Simpson, then living in Loudoun County, proposing a partnership to develop Washington's Bottom. GW, of course, would provide the land; Simpson his personal services as manager; and both an equal amount of slaves, livestock, and supplies. "I Should think it my greatest duty" Simpson told GW, to act in this business "with the utmost Care and onnesty and as the land is so good, for indion Corn and meadows I make no dowt but it would in a five years add Sumthing wo[r]th[while] to your Fortune and a Reasonable Compency of good liveing to my Self" (Gilbert Simpson, Jr., to GW, 5 Oct. 1772, DLC:GW).

Articles of agreement between the two men were promptly signed. However, GW soon had reason to regret it, for the partnership almost from the start proved to be more troublesome than profitable to him. Simpson did clear some land, build a cabin and outbuildings, plant crops, and eventually secure several tenants for various parts of the tract. Nevertheless, he sent to Mount Vernon not profits, but a flood of excuses, a remarkable self-pitying litany of troubles: bad weather, bad health, bad times, and a shrewish wife. Simpson was, in truth, a fickle and careless manager who knew only one art well, that of ingratiating himself with a studied humility and professions of good intentions while feathering his own nest.

Among the earliest engravings of George and Martha Washington were these portraits, done in 1782 by John Norman. (Mount Vernon Ladies' Association of the Union)

Simpson's art, his remoteness from Mount Vernon, and the unavoidable neglect of GW's personal affairs during the War of Independence all combined to stay the day of reckoning for the partnership. However, on 13 Feb. 1784, a few weeks after returning home from the war, GW dispatched a letter to Simpson demanding by 15 April "a full & complete settlement of our Partnership accounts, wherein every article of debit is to be properly supported by vouchers. . . . The world does not scruple to say that you have been much more attentive to your own interest than to mine. But I hope your Accots. will give the lie to these reports, by shewing that something more than your own emolument was intended by the partnership" (DLC:GW). Simpson was not able to give lie to the world's opinion, and arrangements were soon made to dissolve the partnership. On 24 June 1784 GW wrote an advertisement announcing that on 15 Sept. at Washington's Bottom, Simpson's farm would be leased to the highest bidder and GW's part of the partnership effects, including livestock, would be sold. Simpson was allowed to do as he wished with his share of the effects (*Va. Journal,* 15 July 1784; GW to Simpson, 10 July 1784, DLC:GW).

Besides settling the partnership with Simpson, GW was going west to inspect his vacant bounty lands on the Ohio and Kanawha rivers (see entries for 10 Sept. and 4 Oct. 1784). A third main purpose of the trip was to learn about the possibilities for convenient water transportation between the Ohio Valley and the eastern seaboard, especially via the Potomac River (see entry for 3 Sept. 1784).

[2] Besides Dr. Craik and servants, GW was accompanied on this trip only by his nephew Bushrod Washington and Craik's son William, both of whom joined the party at Berkeley Springs (see entry for 8 Sept. 1784). Others

wished to go, but GW declined to invite them. "It can be no amusement," he wrote Craik 10 July 1784, ". . . to follow me in a tour of business, and from one of my tracts of Land to another; . . . nor wou'd it suit me to be embarrassed by the plans, movements or whims of others" (DLC:GW). Craik was invited not just because he was an old friend but also because he had lands near GW's to which he needed to attend after his long service as a senior physician and surgeon in the Continental Army.

GW's baggage included "a Marquee, some Camp utensils, & a few Stores." Each man was to bring his own bedding, a servant to look after his horses, and a gun if he wished to hunt (GW to Craik, 10 July 1784, and GW to John A. Washington, 30 June 1784, DLC:GW; see also entry for 22 Sept. 1784).

[3] Although GW today paid Sampson Trammell £1 6d. for expenses, Trammell's place was not a licensed public ordinary (Cash Memoranda, DLC: GW). Rather, it must have been one of the many "Private houses" that the German traveler Johann David Schoepf found in Virginia about this time. "The distinction between Private and Public Entertainment," Schoepf noted, "is to the advantage of the people who keep the so-called *Private houses*, they avoiding in this way the tax for permission to dispense rum and other drinks and not being plagued with noisy drinking-parties" (SCHOEPF, 2:35). GW had stopped at Trammell's house several times on the way to and from Leesburg 1763–64 (LEDGER A, 166, 184).

[4] "Difficult run," GW informed John Gill 12 Nov. 1799, "is mirey, inconvenient and troublesome to cross at *most* seasons of the year, and in winter *generally impassable,* except at the bridge" (DLC:GW). Shepherd's (Shepperd's) tavern, apparently run by local resident John Shepherd (Shepperd), stood on the south, or Fairfax County, side of Difficult Run bridge. On the north, or Loudoun County, side lay a tract of about 275 acres of land that GW had bought from Bryan Fairfax in 1763 as a way station for wagons going between Mount Vernon and his Bullskin plantation. Because Bullskin had since that time been leased to tenants, this tract on Difficult Run was not now being used for any purpose, but GW had been disturbed during the previous year when someone, probably Shepherd, threatened to preempt a good mill site on his land through condemnation proceedings in the county court (Bryan Fairfax to GW, 4 Aug. 1783, Robert T. Hooe to GW, 23 May 1793, and GW to Bryan Fairfax, 26 Nov. 1799, DLC:GW).

Sep. 2. About 5 Oclock we set out from Shepperds; and leaving the Baggage to follow slowly on, we arrived about 11 Oclock ourselves at Leesburgh, where we Dined.[1] The Baggage having joined we proceeded to Mr. Israel Thompsons & lodged makg. abt. 36 M.[2]

[1] Dinner was at Thomas Roper's ordinary (Cash Memoranda, DLC:GW).

[2] Israel Thompson (d. 1795), a Quaker, lived on a 700-acre plantation in the vicinity of Catoctin Creek in Loudoun County (will of Israel Thompson, 10 Jan. 1795, Loudoun County Wills, Book E, 87–92). His place had been recommended as a stage on the road by GW in 1761, but it was apparently neither a public nor private ordinary, for GW recorded no expenses here today or on any other occasion (GW to Charles Greene, 26 Aug. 1761, ViBCtH).

Brig. Gen. Daniel Morgan, by John Trumbull. (Yale University Art Gallery)

3d. Having business to transact with my Tenants in Berkeley;[1] & others, who were directed to meet me at my Brother's (Colo. Charles Washington's),[2] I left Doctr. Craik and the Baggage to follow slowly, and set out myself about Sun rise for that place—where after Breakfasting at Keys's ferry[3] I arrived about 11 Oclock—distant abt. 17 Miles.

Colo. Warner Washington, Mr. Wormeley,[4] Genl. Morgan,[5] Mr. Snickers[6] and many other Gentlemen came here to see me & one object of my journey being to obtain information of the nearest and best communication between the Eastern & Western Waters; & to facilitate as much as in me lay the Inland Navigation of the Potomack; I conversed a good deal with Genel. Morgan on this subject, who said, a plan was in contemplation to extend a road from Winchester to the Western Waters, to avoid if possible an interference with any other State but I could not discover that Either himself, or others, were able to point it out with precision. He seemed to have no doubt but that the Counties of Frederk., Berkeley & Hampshire would contribute freely towards the extension of the Navigation of Potomack; as well as towards opening a Road from East to West.

[1] In the late 1760s and early 1770s GW leased the lands he owned on Bullskin and Evitt's runs to ten tenants. Collection of rents from those ten-

ants, as well as from ones in Loudoun and Fauquier counties, was much neglected during the war years, and what rents were received were paid mostly in badly depreciated currency. GW could do little about this last circumstance, having given lifetime leases that specified particular cash payments with no allowance for inflation (GW to John Armstrong, 10 Aug. 1779, DLC:GW). Nevertheless, he could collect the considerable balances still due and, being in need of ready cash, was determined to do so. On 28 Feb. of this year, he sent a stern warning to his Berkeley County tenants through Charles Washington: "if they do not settle & pay up their arrearages of Rent very soon I shall use the most efficatious means to do myself justice" (InU). One tenant, Isaac Collet, who held 200 acres on Bullskin, settled in April, but the others still had debts outstanding (LEDGER B, 22, 31, 32, 71, 72, 101, 113).

[2] Charles Washington had moved to the Shenandoah Valley from Fredericksburg in 1780, settling on land on Evitt's Run which he had inherited from his half brother Lawrence. Charles's new house, Happy Retreat, stood on a hill overlooking the run, near the southern edge of present-day Charles Town, W.Va. The town, named for him, was laid out on his property in 1786 (WAYLAND [1], 160–62; HENING, 12:370–71).

[3] Key's (Keyes') ferry on the Shenandoah River, about four miles east of Happy Retreat, had been authorized by the General Assembly in 1748 to run between William Fairfax's land on the east bank and the land of Gersham Keyes (d. 1766) on the west bank (HENING, 6:18). John Vestal, apparently a tenant on Col. Fairfax's land, kept the ferry for many years, and hence, it was often called Vestal's ferry. Humphrey Keyes (1721–1793), son of Gersham, now lived on the west bank and was probably operating the ferry at this time (BROWNE, 313–14, n.18; HARRISON [1], 482, 511, n.124; KEYES, 18).

[4] Ralph Wormeley, Sr., of Rosegill, Middlesex County, was staying at his hunting lodge on the Shenandoah River, Berkeley Rocks, also known simply as The Rocks (Wormeley to GW, 16 July 1784, DLC:GW). Situated near the mouth of Long Marsh Run, about ten miles south of Happy Retreat, this lodge was at the heart of a tract of about 13,000 acres, which Wormeley is said to have bought on GW's advice "many years before" (NORRIS [1], 484; CHAPPELEAR [2], map facing p. 56). The lodge and much of the land were given about this time to Wormeley's son James (ROCKS, 16–17; WORMELEY, 37:84–85).

[5] Daniel Morgan (c.1735–1802), a rough-and-tumble frontiersman during his youth, had emerged during the Revolution as an American military hero and was now one of the most prominent men in Frederick County. Forced to retire from military service in 1781 because of the ill health that frequently plagued him in his latter years, Morgan went home to Frederick County and finished building his house, Saratoga, on his farm between Winchester and Berry's ferry, near present-day Boyce, Va. Morgan shared GW's interest in western lands, east-west transportation, and flour manufacturing. In the postwar years he obtained extensive holdings beyond the mountains and about 1785 became a partner in a large merchant mill near his house (HIGGINBOTHAM).

[6] Edward Snickers today offered to act as GW's agent in leasing 571 acres of unsettled land near Snickers's home which GW had bought from George Mercer in 1774. GW accepted the offer on the following day (GW to Snickers, 4 Sept. 1784, DLC:GW; CHAPPELEAR [2], map facing p. 56).

4th. Having finished my business with my Tenants (so far at least as partial payments could put a close to it) [1] and provided a waggon [2] for the transportation of my Baggage to the Warm springs (or Town of Bath) [3] to give relief to my Horses, which from the extreme heat of the weather began to rub & gaul, I set out after dinner, and reached Captn. Stroads [4] a Substantial farmers betwn. Opeckon Creek & Martinsburgh [5]—distant by estimation 14 Miles from my Brothers.

Finding the Captn. an intelligent Man, and one who had been several times in the Western Country—tho' not much on the communication between the North Branch of Potomack, & the Waters of Monongahela—I held much conversation with him—the result of which, so far as it respected the object I had in view, was, that there are two Glades which go under the denomination of the Great glades—one, on the Waters of Yohiogany, the other on those of Cheat River; & distinguished by the name of the Sandy Creek Glades [6]—that the Road to the first goes by the head of Pattersons Creek—that from the accts. he has had of it, it is rough; the distance he knows not—that there is away to the Sandy Creek Glades from the great crossing of Yohiogany (on Braddocks road) [7] & a very good one; but how far the Waters of Potomack above Fort Cumberland, & the Cheat river from its Mouth are navigable, he professes not to know—and equally ignorant is he of the distance between them.

He says that old Captn. Thos. Swearengen [8] has informed him, that the navigable water of the little Kanhawa comes within a small distance of the Navigable Waters of the Monongahela, & that a good road, along a ridge, may be had between the two [9] & a young Man who we found at his House just (the Evening before) from Kentucke, told us, that he left the Ohio River at Weeling (Colo. David Shepperds), & in about 40 Miles came to red stone old Fort on the Monongahela, 50 Miles from its Mouth.[10]

Captn. Strodes rout to the Westward having been, for the most part, by the way of New river and the Holsten, through (what is called) the Wilderness, to Kentucke, he adds that when he went out last fall he passed through Staunton, by the Augusta Springs, the Sweet springs, &ca. to the New River; on which he fell about ⟨10⟩ Miles as he *was told* above the Fall in that river, that these falls are about 70 Miles from the Mouth, that a Vessel could not pass them tho' the perpendicular fall did not exceed Six feet.[11]

The distance from Staunton to the [Augusta] Springs, according to his Acct., is 45 Miles; between the [Augusta and Sweet]

Springs 28 Miles; and from the Sweet Springs to the New River, 30; in all 103 from Staunton to the New River: from this part of the New River to the place called Chissels Mines, is passable for Canoes & Batteaux with little difficulty; & from thence to the Roanoke where it is as large as the Opeckon near his house is only 12 miles & a tolerable level Country.[12]

[1] While at Happy Retreat, GW received from Thomas Griggs £24 of rent due for 200 acres on Bullskin Run, from Henry Whiting £50 12s. for 600 acres on Bullskin, from Samuel Scratchfield £6 for 113 acres on Evitt's Run, and from David Fulton £10 for another 113 acres on Evitt's Run (Cash Memoranda, DLC:GW; LEDGER B, 199). None of these sums fully discharged the accounts on which they were paid. A few weeks later GW entrusted collection of all his rents in Berkeley, Frederick, Fauquier, and Loudoun counties to Battaile Muse of Berkeley County (GW to Muse, 3 Nov. 1784, DLC: GW).

[2] The wagon was hired from William Grantum, a tenant on 226½ acres of GW's Evitt's Run land. Grantum was allowed £2 2s. on his unsettled rent account in return for use of his vehicle (Cash Memoranda, DLC:GW; LEDGER B, 72).

[3] The small settlement at Warm Springs was officially established as the town of Bath in 1776, but continued to be known also as Warm Springs and Berkeley Springs (HENING, 9:247–49).

[4] John Strode (1736–1805) and his brother James Strode (died c.1795) both lived in this part of Berkeley County and both were called captain. While exploring in Kentucky in 1776, they each claimed 1,000 acres of land near present-day Winchester, Ky. Three years later those tracts were officially granted to the Strodes, and John returned to Kentucky to build a fort or station on his land. After recruiting settlers to defend his station against the British and Indians, he went home in the spring of 1780, and according to one of the settlers, who considered him "pretty much of a coward," he "never came out again for three or four years after" (CLINKENBEARD, 103–5; ALLEN, 68, 95, n.7). John did settle in Kentucky with his family sometime after the war. James continued to live in Berkeley County, where he had been named a justice 1772 and a militia captain 1774. He became a trustee of Martinsburg in 1778 and of Darkesville in 1791 (BERKELEY [2], 29).

[5] Martinsburg, established 1778, was the site of the Berkeley County courthouse (HENING, 9:569–71). It was named for Col. Thomas Bryan Martin.

[6] The Great Glades are natural marshy grasslands amid well-timbered ridges on both sides of Maryland's western border. The Youghiogheny Glades are in the vicinity of Oakland, Md., and the Sandy Creek Glades are near Bruceton Mills, W.Va. (see entry for 26 Sept. 1784). Big Sandy Creek flows into the Cheat River, a main branch of the Monongahela. A short, convenient land route between the Cheat or Youghiogheny and the North Branch of Potomac in their navigable portions could effectively link the Ohio with the Chesapeake.

[7] Braddock's Road, the route followed by Gen. Edward Braddock's army in 1755, began at Fort Cumberland, Md., and ran to the vicinity of Fort Pitt by way of the Great Crossing, the Great Meadows, and Stewart's Crossing. GW traveled part of this road 12–17 Oct. 1770 and 10–12 Sept. 1784.

[8] Thomas Swearingen, of Berkeley County, one of the early settlers of the Shenandoah Valley, lived on the Potomac River near Shepherdstown. For many years he ran a well-known ferry across the river to Maryland and at one time or another served as justice, vestryman, and burgess (HENING, 6:494, 8:263). His election as burgess occurred in 1756 when he and Hugh West were chosen over GW to represent old Frederick County, but two years later GW and Thomas Bryan Martin unseated Swearingen and West (FREEMAN, 2:147, 320; GW to Robert Dinwiddie, 9 Oct. 1757, DLC:GW). During the French and Indian War, Swearingen was a captain in the Frederick County militia and for a time led a detachment of rangers (H.B.J., 1752–58, 458; Lord Fairfax to GW, 1 Sept. 1756, DLC:GW).

[9] The West Fork River, a main branch of the Monongahela, runs near the Little Kanawha in the vicinity of Bulltown, W.Va. (see entry for 24 Sept. 1784). Such a route, if practicable, would shorten the distance to the lower Ohio and could be completely controlled by Virginia.

[10] David Shepherd (1734–1795) left Berkeley County with his family in the spring of 1770 and settled at the forks of Wheeling Creek near present-day Wheeling, W.Va. In 1777 he was appointed county lieutenant of newly formed Ohio County, which he successfully defended against Indian attack throughout the War of Independence (JOHNSTON, 55; DANDRIDGE, 192, 346). The route described by the young Kentuckian must be the one later used for part of the Cumberland or National Road. Red Stone Old Fort became the site of Brownsville, Pa., in 1785.

[11] The common route to Kentucky, first taken by Dr. Thomas Walker in 1750, went down the Shenandoah Valley to Ingles ferry on the New River (near present-day Radford, Va.), then on to the Holston River, and west through the mountains to the Cumberland Gap at the extreme southwestern tip of Virginia. However, in the fall of 1783 Strode apparently followed the alternate route by which Walker had returned from Kentucky, crossing New River farther north near the point where it is joined by the Greenbrier River (in the vicinity of present-day Hinton, W.Va.), and then following nearby Bluestone River west toward Tug Fork, a branch of the Big Sandy River (WALKER, 70–75).

Staunton, established 1761, was one of the major towns of the Shenandoah Valley. Augusta Springs must be Warm Springs, Va., now in Bath County but before 1791 in Augusta County. It was commonly called Augusta Warm Springs to distinguish it from the Warm Springs in Berkeley County (FITHIAN [2], 161). Sweet Springs was in Botetourt County, now Monroe County, W.Va.

[12] Chiswell's Mines, now the site of Austinville, Va., were well-known lead and zinc mines on the banks of the New River about 120 miles upstream from the mouth of the Greenbrier. Discovered by Col. John Chiswell in 1756, they had been a particularly important resource for the Patriots during the War of Independence (W.P.A. [4], 477–78). The New River actually comes closest to the Roanoke River, not near Chiswell's Mines, but farther downstream in the vicinity of Ingles ferry. Strode also overstated the ease of navigating the New River up to Chiswell's Mines, the way being obstructed by falls, rapids, and narrow twisting gorges (SOLECKI, 323). Nevertheless, because the New River flowed into the Kanawha, it was seriously considered for many years as a possible transportation link between the east and west.

5th. Dispatched my Waggon (with the Baggage) at day light; and at 7 Oclock followed it. Bated at one Snodgrasses, on Back Creek and dined there;[1] About 5 Oclock P.M. we arrived at the Springs, or Town of Bath—after travelling the whole day through a drizling rain, 30 Miles.[2]

[1] Robert Snodgrass ran the tavern which his father, William Snodgrass, an emigrant from Scotland, had built on Back Creek about 1740. The tavern site is near present-day Hedgesville, W.Va. (GARDINER, 25, 39).

[2] Bath, despite ambitious plans for its development, had hardly changed during the war years. In the fall of 1783 Johann David Schoepf reported that it was a "little place . . . as yet in poor circumstances, made up of little, contracted, wooden cabins or houses scattered about without any order, most of them with no glass in the windows, being only summer residences" (SCHOEPF, 1:310). With the close of the war, a building boom had begun which would result in 164 houses being erected in four years' time (VAUGHAN, 34).

6th. Remained at Bath all day and was shewed the Model of a Boat constructed by the ingenious Mr. Rumsey, for ascending rapid currents by mechanism; the principles of this were not only shewn, & fully explained to me, but to my very great satisfaction, exhibited in practice in private, under the injunction of Secresy, untill he saw the effect of an application he was about to make to the assembly of this State, for a reward.

The model, & its operation upon the water, which had been made to run pretty swift, not only convinced me of what I before thought next to, if not quite impracticable, but that it might be turned to the greatest possible utility in inland Navigation; and in rapid currents; that are shallow. And what adds vastly to the value of the discovery, is the simplicity of its works; as they may be made by a common boat builder or carpenter, and kept in

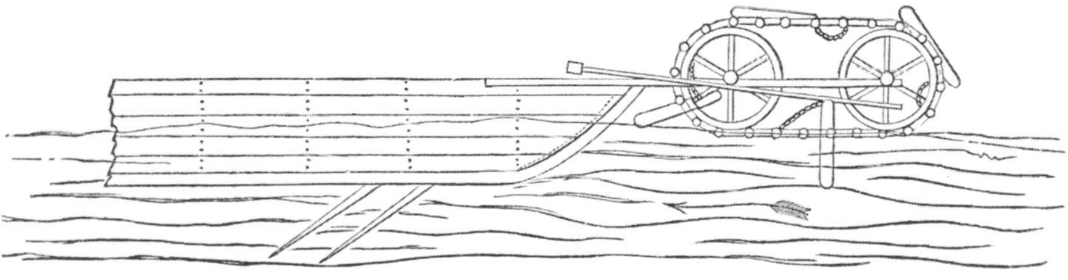

James Rumsey's mechanical boat, from a drawing in Bennet Woodcroft's *A Sketch of the Origin and Progress of Steam,* London, 1848. (Virginia State Library)

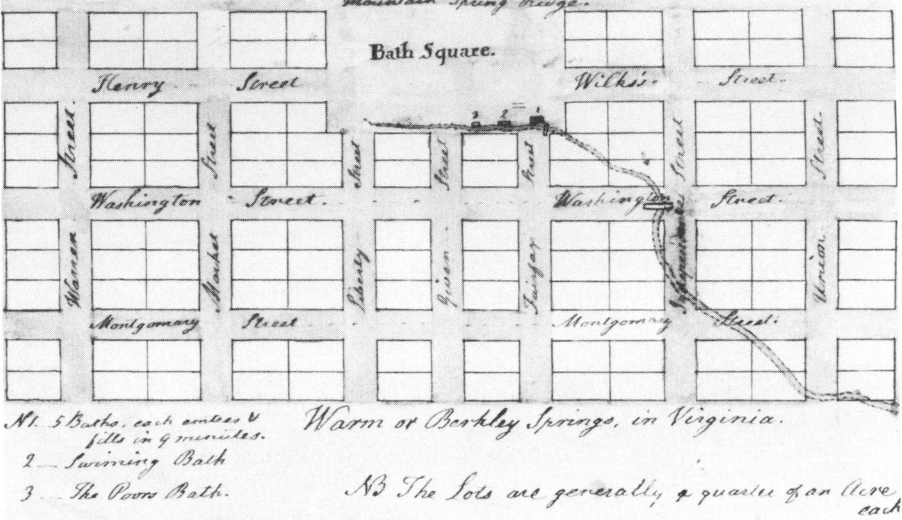

This plan of the town of Bath, or Warm Springs, was drawn by Samuel Vaughan for his 1787 journal. (Collection of the descendants of Samuel Vaughan)

order as easy as a plow, or any common impliment of husbandry on a farm.[1]

Having obtained a Plan of this Town (Bath) and ascertained the situation of my lots therein, which I examined; it appears that the disposition of a dwelling House; Kitchen & Stable cannot be more advantageously placed than they are marked in the copy I have taken from the plan of the Town; to which I refer for recollection, of my design; & Mr. Rumsey being willing to undertake those Buildings, I have agreed with him to have them finished by the 10th. of next July. The dwelling House is to be 36 feet by 24, with a gallery of 7 feet on each side of the House, the whole fronts. Under the House is to be a Cellar half the size of it, walled with Stone, and the whole underpined. On the first floor are to be 3 rooms; one of them 24 by 20 feet, with a chimney at the end (middle thereof) – the other two to be 12 by 16 feet with corner chimneys. On the upper Floor there are to be two rooms of equal sizes, with fire places; the Stair case to go up in the Gallery – galleries above also. The Kitchen and Stable are to be of the same size – 18 by 22; the first with a stone Chimney and good floor above. The Stable is to be sunk in the ground, so as that the floor above it on the North, or side next the dwelling House, shall be level with the Yard – to have a partition therein – the West part

262. September 1784.—

Certificate to Mr. Rumsey—

I have seen the model of Mr. Rumsey's Boats constructed to work against stream;—have examined the power upon which it acts;—have been an eye witness to an actual experiment in running water of some rapidity; & do give it as my opinion (altho' I had little faith before) that he has discovered the art of propelling Boats, by mechanism & small manual assistance, against rapid currents:—that the discovery is of vast importance—may be of the greatest usefulness in our inland navigation—&, if it succeeds, of which I have no doubt, that the value of it is greatly enhanced by the simplicity of the works, which when seen & explained to, might be executed by the most common Mechanic's.—

Given under my hand at the town of Bath, County of Berkeley in the State of Virga. this 7th day of September 1784—

G: Washington

See Vol. 2d. page 222. Letter to Majr. Freeman dated 23d. Sept. 1784.—

Letterbook copy of Washington's certificate to James Rumsey. (Library of Congress)

of which to be for a Carriage, Harness, and Saddles—the East for Hay or Grain—all three of the Houses to be shingled with [ ] [2]

Meeting with the Revd. Mr. Balmain at this place, he says the distance from Staunton to the Sweet Springs is 95 Miles; that is, 50 to what are commonly called the Augusta Springs & 45 afterwards. This differs widely from Captn. Strodes acct., and both say they have travelled the Road.[3]

From Colo. Bruce [4] whom I also found at this place, I was informed that he had travelled from the North Branch of Potomack to the Waters of Yaughiogany, and Monongahela—that the Potomk. where it may be made Navigable—for instance where McCulloughs path crosses it, 40 Miles above the old fort (Cumberland), is but about 6 Miles to a pretty large branch of the Yohiogany, but how far it is practicable to make the latter navigable he knows not, never having explored it any length downwards[5]–that the Waters of Sandy Creek, which is a branch of Cheat River, which is a branch of Monongahela, interlocks with these; and the Country between flat–that he thinks (in order to av[oi]d passing through the State of Pensylvania) this would be an eligable Rout using the ten Miles C[ree]k with a portage to the Navigable Waters of the little Kanhawa; which from report he says, are only 10 Miles apart.[6] He adds that the distance from the North branch to Cheat Rivr. is great–and from the South branch greater, but it is to be observed that most of this information is from report–vague and not much to be depended upon. I therefore endeavoured to prevail upon Colo. Bruce to explore the Country from the North Branch of Potomack at McCulloughs path, or the highest practicable navigation on it to the Nearest Waters of Yohiogany–thence to Sandy Creek, & down that to its junction with the Cheat River–laying the whole down by actual surveys & exact measurement; which he has promised to do, if he can accomplish it.[7] On my part I have engaged, if a Surveyor can be obtained, to run the Water of the little Kanhawa from the Mouth to the highest Navigation–thence across to ten miles Creek on the Monongahela, & up that to the Mo[uth] of Sandy Creek, in order to connect the two Works together, & form a proper plan with observations and even to continue up the Cheat River further, to see if a better communication cannot be had with the Potomack than by the Sandy Creek.

Having hired three Pack horses–to give my own greater relief –I sent my Baggage of this day about one oclock, and ordered those who had charge of it,[8] to proceed to one Headricks at 15 Miles Creek, distant abt. ten miles, to Night, and to the old Town next day.[9]

[1] James Rumsey (1743–1792) of Bath was a handsome and engaging jack-of-all-trades. Born in Cecil County, Md., he moved to the Warm Springs area from Baltimore about 1782, and although a man of relatively limited means and education, he had soon become owner of a sawmill and bloomery, partner in a store, contractor for building new bathhouses, and operator with Robert Throckmorton (Throgmorton) of a new boardinghouse "at the Sign of the Liberty Pole and Flag" (*Md. Journal,* 15 June 1784, 25 June 1784; NEWBRAUGH, 1:15; TURNER, 3–7).

GW lodged at the boardinghouse (Cash Memoranda, DLC:GW), and there probably met Rumsey, whose chief interest, he found, was not business, but mechanical invention. The small model of the mechanical boat that GW saw today was designed somewhat paradoxically to be propelled forward by the force of the current against which it was to move. The "boat" actually consisted of two boats with a paddle wheel mounted between them. As the wheel turned with the current, it operated poles that were supposed to push against the river bottom, making the vessel "walk" upstream (Rumsey to GW, 10 Mar. 1785, GW to Hugh Williamson, 15 Mar. 1785, DLC:GW).

Before leaving Bath, GW gave Rumsey a certificate attesting to the potential value of the invention and his faith in its ultimate success (7 Sept. 1784, DLC:GW). Rumsey promptly had the certificate published in several prominent newspapers, and soon obtained exclusive rights from the legislatures of Virginia, Maryland, and several other states to make and operate his mechanical boat, a necessary step to protect his invention in the absence of any national patent office. A modified full-scale version of the vessel was tried 9 and 13 Sept. 1786 on the Potomac River near Shepherdstown with little success. The poles slipped on the bottom on the first occasion, and the current was too slow to operate the poles on the second one (Rumsey to GW, 19 Sept. 1786, DLC:GW). Rumsey then abandoned this particular invention, having previously decided on developing a steamboat, a decision that led him in a more fruitful direction, but involved him in much controversy.

[2] In 1777 Fielding Lewis had secured lots 58 and 59 in the new town of Bath for GW at a cost of £100 15s. Virginia money (deed of trustees of Bath to GW, 25 Aug. 1777, GW ATLAS, pl. 10; GW to Samuel Washington, 27 Oct. 1777, PHi: Gratz Collection). To maintain title to those lots, GW was now obliged by law to build "a dwelling-house twelve feet square at least" on each one by 1 Nov. 1785 (HENING, 9:247–49, 460, 10:108–9, 11:26). The kitchen and stable mentioned here, being placed on separate lots, would evidently fulfill that minimum requirement, giving GW freedom to locate his main house to best advantage with regard to the terrain. Rumsey never built the main house, because in April 1785 a fire burned his sawmill as well as all the lumber that he had cut for GW's buildings (Rumsey to GW, 24 June 1785, DLC:GW). Fortunately for GW, the Virginia General Assembly extended the deadline for building on lots in Bath to 1 Oct. 1787 (HENING, 12:214–15). Rumsey built a kitchen and stable in the summer of 1786, but little was accomplished beyond satisfying the law, both structures being log cabins 17 by 19 feet, "badly built, and of bad timber" (George Lewis to GW, 25 Aug. 1786, DLC:GW). Rumsey received £73 1s. 4d. for his efforts (LEDGER B, 210).

[3] Alexander Balmain, or Balmaine (1740–1821), was an Anglican clergyman whose past duties had required him to travel widely and often in western Virginia. Born in Scotland, he came to Virginia as a young man to tutor Richard Henry Lee's sons. He was ordained in England in Oct. 1772 and in the following year became assistant to the rector of the extensive frontier parish of Augusta. A staunch Patriot, he served on the committee of safety in Augusta County and during the War of Independence was a chaplain in the Virginia line. He was chosen rector of Frederick Parish in 1785 and served until his death (MEADE [1], 2:95, 285–86, 319; EATON, 23). Balmain's distances to the springs are accurate for the roads of the time.

[4] Normand Bruce served 1775–79 as a colonel in command of a battalion of Frederick County, Md., militia and for a time was county lieutenant (FREDERICK COUNTY, 11:58; MD. COUNCIL, 1778–79, 416–17, 546). On 1 Aug.

1783 the Maryland State Council, acting in accord with a resolution of the General Assembly, appointed him and Charles Beatty of Montgomery County "to examine, and report their Opinion of opening, clearing and making navigable the River Potomack . . . to the Line of this State, the Time the work would take, and the Expences" (MD. COUNCIL, 1781–84, 443; GW's undated notes on their report are in MHi: Jeremiah Colburn Papers). Bruce wrote to GW 13 Nov. 1784 outlining a proposal for a Potomac Navigation Company, to be financed by issuing paper money, circulation of which, he argued, would greatly benefit the general economy (NUTE, 706–10).

[5] McCullough's Path, named for an early Indian trader, was a rough trail running from Winchester to a point near the junction of the Cheat and Monongahela rivers. Crossing the South Branch of the Potomac at Moorefield, Va. (now W.Va.), it went through the Allegheny Front at Greenland Gap and over the North Branch of the Potomac near present-day Gormania, W.Va. In Maryland it crossed the Youghiogheny west of present-day Oakland and then passed again into Virginia, crossing Big Sandy Creek at present-day Bruceton Mills, W.Va. (MCCULLOUGH'S PATH, 297–98; W.P.A. [5], 98). GW traveled most of the northern part of McCullough's Path 25–26 Sept. 1784.

[6] Tenmile Creek in Harrison County, W.Va., is a branch of the West Fork River.

[7] GW later obtained a rough sketch map of this region from Bruce (GW ATLAS, pl. 25).

[8] GW engaged drivers with the horses (Cash Memoranda, DLC:GW).

[9] Fifteenmile Creek flows into the Potomac River in eastern Allegany County, Md. In 1784 the main road to Fort Cumberland crossed the creek near its mouth and continued on 19 miles to Col. Thomas Cresap's Oldtown settlement and then 15 miles farther to the old fort (SCHARF [3], 2:1328; GRIFFITH, MAP).

8th. Set out about 7 oclock with the Doctr. (Craik) his Son William,[1] and my Nephew Bushrod Washington;[2] who were to make the tour with us. About ten I parted with them at 15 Miles Creek, & recrossed the Potomack (having passed it abt. 3 Miles from the Springs before) to a tract of mine on the Virginia side which I find exceedingly rich, & must be very valuable. The lower end of the Land is rich White oak; in places springey; and in the winter wet. The upper part is exceedingly rich, and covered with Walnut of considerable size many of them. Note—I requested a Mr. McCraken at whose House I fed my horses, & got a snack, & whose Land joins mine—to offer mine to any who might apply for £10 the first year, £15 the next, and £25 the third—the Tenant not to remove any of the Walnut timber from off the Land; or to split it into rails; as I should reserve that for my own use.[3]

After having reviewed this Land I again recrossed the river & getting into the Waggon road pursued my journey to the old

Bushrod Washington was a law student in Philadelphia when Henry Benbridge painted this 1783 portrait. (Mount Vernon Ladies' Association of the Union)

Town where I overtook my Company & baggage. Lodged at Colo. Cresaps—abt. 35 Miles this day.[4]

[1] William Craik (b. 1761) studied law and began practice, probably about this time, in Charles and St. Mary's counties, Md. He was chief justice of the fifth judicial district of Maryland 1793–96 and 1801–2 and a member of Congress from Maryland 1796–1801. He died before 1814 (CONGRESSIONAL DIRECTORY, 796).

[2] Bushrod Washington (1762–1829), eldest son of John Augustine and Hannah Bushrod Washington, was long a favorite of GW. After attending the College of William and Mary, Bushrod served briefly as a volunteer cavalryman during the Virginia campaign of 1781 and early the following year went to Philadelphia, where with the help of a recommendation and 100 guineas from GW, he began studying law under politically prominent James Wilson (GW to Wilson, 19 Mar. 1782, typescript from PSC, and 22 Mar. 1782, DLC:GW). His studies were now finished, and he was temporarily "at leisure . . . waiting the arrival of his Law Library" to set up practice in Virginia. Somewhat ill earlier in the year, Bushrod had left his father's Westmoreland County home in July and had gone to Warm Springs in order "to confirm his health and be in readyness" for the western trip (John A. Washington to GW, 8 July 1784 and July 1784, MH).

[3] This 240-acre tract in Hampshire County (now Morgan County, W.Va.) had remained virtually undeveloped since GW acquired it by patent from Thomas, Lord Fairfax, in 1753 (SIMS, 803). In an effort to derive some real benefit from the land at last, GW announced in conjunction with the 24 June 1784 advertisement of his Washington's Bottom property that he would

lease this Hampshire tract for a term of seven years to the highest bidder at Bath on 7 Sept. (*Va. Journal,* 15 July 1784). As GW's actions of this date indicate, no satisfactory offer was received while he was in Bath. The tract apparently was not leased during GW's lifetime, and over the years much timber was taken off it by trespassers.

Ovid McCraken appears in the 1784 Hampshire County census as head of a family of nine whites (HEADS OF FAMILIES, VA., 72). In 1799 Squire Virgil McCraken lived next to GW's land (Isaac Weatherington to GW, 24 Aug. 1799, ViHi).

[4] Col. Thomas Cresap, now about 90 years old, had been blind for several months, but a visitor to Oldtown in May 1785 reported, "his other faculties are yet unimpaired his sense Strong and Manly and his Ideas flow with ease" (MATHEWS, 34).

9th. Having discharged the hired Horses which were obtained at the Springs, & hired one more *only* to supply the place of one of mine, whose back was much hurt, we had them loaded by Six oclock, and was about to set out when it began to rain; which looking very likely to continue thro' the day, I had the Loads taken of to await the issue.

At this place I met with a Man who lives at the Mouth of ten Miles Creek on Monongahela, who assured me, that this Creek is not Navigable for any kind of Craft a Mile from its Mouth; unless the Water of it is swelled by rain; at which time he has known Batteaux brought 10 or 12 miles down it. He knows little of the Country betwn. that and the little Kanhawa & not more of that above him, on the Monongahela.

The day proving rainy we remained here.

10th. Set off a little after 5 Oclock altho' the morning was very unpromissing. Finding from the rains that had fallen, and description of the Roads, part of which between the old Town & this place (old Fort Cumberland) [1] we had passed, that the progress of my Baggage would be tedeous, I resolved (it being Necessary) to leave it to follow; and proceed on myself to Gilbert Simpson's, to prepare for the Sale which I had advertised of my moiety of the property in co-partnership with him and to make arrangements for my trip to the Kanhawa, if the temper & disposition of the Indians should render it advisable to proceed. Accordingly, leaving Doctr. Craik, his Son, and my Nephew with it, I set out with one Servant only. Dined at a Mr. Gwins at the Fork of the Roads leading to Winchester and the old Town, distant from the latter abt. 20 Miles [2] & lodged at Tumbersons at the little Meadows 15 Miles further.[3]

The Road from the Old Town to Fort Cumberland we found tolerably good, as it also was from the latter to Gwins, except the Mountain which was pretty long (tho' not steep) in the assent and discent; [4] but from Gwins to Tumberson's it is intolerably bad—there being many steep pinches of the Mountain—deep & miry places and very stony ground to pass over. After leaving the Waters of Wills Creek which extends up the Mountain (Alligany) two or three Miles as the road goes, we fell next on those of George's Creek, which are small—after them upon Savage River which are more considerable; tho' from the present appearance of them, does not seem capable of Navigation.[5]

[1] Abandoned since 1765, the fort lay in ruins. The town of Cumberland, Md., was laid out here in 1785 and was established officially by act of the General Assembly 20 Jan. 1787 (VAUGHAN, 30; LOWDERMILK, 256, 258–61).

[2] Evan Gwin (Gwyn, Gwynne) ran a well-known tavern on Braddock Run about five miles west of Fort Cumberland near present-day Allegany Grove, Md. (VAUGHAN, 29; WESTERN MD., 290).

[3] The Red House tavern was built at Little Meadows in the 1760s by Joseph Tomlinson (d. 1797) and was taken over eventually by his son Jesse Tomlinson (c.1753–1840). Several travelers refer to the place as "Tumblestone's" or "Tumbleston's," apparent corruptions of "Tomlinson's"; in GW's ledger entry for this date, it is called "Tumblestowns" (TOMLINSON, 69–71, 96; LEDGER B, 200). Traces of Braddock's 1755 camp at Little Meadows were still "easily discernable" as late as 1794 (WELLFORD, 10).

[4] Between Fort Cumberland and Gwin's tavern the main road went over Wills (now Haystack) Mountain at Sandy Gap rather than around the mountain by the longer, leveler route which Braddock's army took through the Narrows of Wills Creek (LACOCK, 6–12).

[5] THE WATERS OF WILLS CREEK: apparently Braddock Run, a tributary of that creek. West of Gwin's tavern the road followed the narrow valley of Braddock Run through the front of the Allegheny Range, passing Piney Mountain on the north and Dans Mountain on the south. About 2½ miles upstream, near present-day Clarysville, Md., the road left the run and continued west to the headwaters of George's Creek in the vicinity of present-day Frostburg, Md., and then over Big Savage Mountain to the headwaters of the Savage River, a tributary of the North Branch of Potomac. Beyond the Savage River the road crossed Little Savage Mountain, Wolf Swamp, and Meadow Mountain, at the western foot of which lay the little Meadows (LACOCK, 12–18; TOMLINSON, 69).

11th. Set out at half after 5 oclock from Tumbersons, & in about 1½ Miles came to what is called the little crossing of Yohiogany—the road not bad.[1] This is a pretty considerable water and, as it is said to have no fall in it, may, I conceive, be improved into a valuable navigation; and from every Acct. I have yet been able to obtain, communicates nearest with the No. Branch of Potomack of any other. Breakfasted at one Mounts, or Mountains,[2] 11 Miles from Tumberson's; the road being exceedingly bad, especially through what is called the shades of death.[3] Bated at the great crossing [of the Youghiogheny], which is a large Water, distant from Mounts's 9 Miles, and a better road than between that and Tumbersons. Lodged at one Daughertys, a Mile & half short of the Great Meadows—a tolerable good House.[4] The Road between the [Great] Crossing and Daughertys is, in places, tolerable good, but upon the whole indifferent—distant from the crossing 12 Miles.

[1] Little Crossing was a ford of the Little Youghiogheny (now Casselman) River about a mile east of present-day Grantsville, Md. This river flows north into Pennsylvania and then west to join the Youghiogheny at Confluence, Pa. (LACOCK, 19, n.44; VAUGHAN, 28).

[2] Joseph Mountain kept a tavern on the eastern slope of Negro Mountain in Washington (now Garrett) County, Md. (WESTERN MD., 291). "Mr. Mountain," reported a traveler in November of this year, "has a Sufficiency of Liquors and Provisions but falls short in the Article of Bedding—he has but three one Occupied by himself and Wife one by the small Children and the Other by the Bar-Maid" (MATHEWS, 27). Another traveler ten years later referred to the place as "Mountain's hovel" (WELLFORD, 11).

[3] Along Braddock's Road there were two Shades of Death, both areas of exceptionally dark and dense woods. The Little Shades of Death, the one most noticed by travelers, lay between Little Savage and Meadow mountains in the vicinity of Twomile Run. The Big Shades of Death, the one to which GW here refers, must have been near the confluence of Big and Little Shade Runs, about a mile west of present-day Grantsville, Md. (HULBERT [1], 195; LACOCK, 17–18). The names apparently were unrelated to the events of the Braddock expedition, being merely descriptions of the natural gloom of the areas (DIARIES, 2:288, n.2). There were also Shades of Death in northeastern and south central Pennsylvania (DONEHOO, 184; W.P.A. [6], 501).

[4] James Daugherty of Fayette County, Pa. (WESTERN MD., 291).

12th. Left Daughertys about 6 Oclock, stopped a while at the Great Meadows, and viewed a tenament I have there, which appears to have been but little improved, tho capable of being turned to great advantage, as the whole of the ground called the Meadows may be reclaimed at an easy comparitive expence & is a very good stand for a Tavern. Much Hay may be cut here when the ground is laid down in Grass & the upland, East of the Meadow, is good for grain.[1]

Dined at Mr. Thomas Gists at the Foot of Laurel [Hill], distant from the Meadows 12 Miles, and arrived at Gilbert Simpsons about 5 oclock 12 Miles further. Crossing the Mountains, I found tedeous and fatieguing. From Fort Cumberland to Gwins took me one hour and ten Minutes riding—between Gwins & Tumbersons I was near 6 hours and used all the dispatch I could—between Tumbersons and Mounts's I was full 4 hours—between Mounts's and the [Great] crossing upwards of 3 hours—between the crossing and Daughertys 4 hours—between Daughertys and Gists 4¼ and between Gists and Simpsons upwards of 3 hours and in all parts of the Road that would admit it I endeavoured to ride my usual travelling gate of 5 Miles an hour.

In passing over the Mountains, I met numbers of Persons & Pack horses going in with Ginsang;[2] & for salt & other articles at the Markets below; from most of whom I made enquiries of the Nature of the Country between the little Kanhawa and ten Miles Creek (which had been represented as a short and easy portage) and to my surprize found the Accts. wch. had been given were so far from the truth that numbers with whom I conversed assured me that the distance between was very considerable—that ten Miles Ck. was not navigable even for Canoes more than a Mile from its mouth and few of them, altho I saw many who lived on different parts of this Creek would pretend to guess at the distance [to the Little Kanawha].

I also endeavoured to get the best acct. I could of the Navigation of Cheat River, & find that the line which divides the States of Virginia & Pensylvania crosses the Monongahela above the Mouth of it; wch. gives the Command thereof to Pensylvania—that where this River (Cheat) goes through the Laurel hill, the Navigation is difficult; not from shallow, or rapid water, but from an immense quantity of large Stones, which stand so thick as to render the passage even of a short Canoe impracticable—but I could meet with no person who seemed to have any accurate knowledge of the Country between the navigable, or such part as could be made so, of this River & the No. Branch of Potomack. All seem to agree however that it is rought & a good way not to be found.

The Accts. given by those Whom I met of the late Murders, & general dissatisfaction of the Indians, occasioned by the attempt of our people to settle on the No. West side of the Ohio, which they claim as their territory; and our delay to hold a treaty with them, which they say is indicative of a hostile temper on our part, makes it rather improper for me to proceed to the Kanhawa agreeably to my original intention, especially as I learnt from some of them (one in particular) who lately left the Settlement of Kentucke that the Indians were generally in arms, & gone, or going, to attack some of our Settlements below and that a Party Who had drove Cattle to Detroit had one of their Company & several of their Cattle killed by the Indians—but as these Accts. will either be contradicted or confirmed by some whom I may meet at my Sale the 15th. Instt. my final determination shall be postponed 'till then.

[1] GW's 234½ acres at Great Meadows were offered for lease on a ten-year term to the highest bidder at Washington's Bottom 15 Sept. (GW's advertisement, in *Va. Journal,* 15 July 1784). The right to patent this tract, which straddled Braddock's Road and embraced virtually all of the meadows, had been bought by GW 4 Dec. 1770 for 30 pistoles, or £35 5s. Virginia currency, a price GW considered high. Due to a variety of circumstances, the patent was not issued until 28 Feb. 1782 (bill of sale from Lawrence Harrison to GW, 4 Dec. 1770, DLC:GW; LEDGER A, 344; GW to Charles Simms, 22 Sept. 1786, DLC:GW; HULBERT [2], 137; UMBLE, 36). Writing to Thomas Freeman about the Great Meadows tract on 23 Sept. 1784, GW noted that "there is a house on the premises, arable land in culture, and meadow inclosed" (DLC:GW), but as his observations here indicate, those improvements must have been small and in poor condition. In a letter to Freeman written 22 Sept. 1785, GW urged the necessity not only "of reclaiming the Meadow" but of "putting the whole under a good fence" and building a dwelling house, kitchen, and stable (DLC:GW).

[2] North American ginseng, *Panax quinquefolius,* was a staple of the China trade, being a common substitute for the oriental variety, *P. schinseng,* roots of which the Chinese used extensively in medicines. While crossing Laurel Hill in 1783, Johann David Schoepf met "a man . . . who was taking to Philadelphia some 500 pounds of ginseng-roots . . . on two horses. He hoped to make a great profit because throughout the war little of this article was gathered, and it was now demanded in quantity by certain Frenchmen [for the China trade]" (SCHOEPF, 1:236–37).

13th. I visited my Mill, and the several tenements on this Tract (on which Simpson lives).[1] I do not find the Land in *general* equal to my expectation of it. Some part indeed is as rich as can be, some other part is but indifferent—the levellest is the coldest, and of the meanest quality—that which is most broken, is the richest; tho' some of the hills are not of the first quality.

The Tenements, with respect to buildings, are but indifferently improved—each have Meadow and arable [land], but in no great quantity. The Mill was quite destitute of Water. The works & House appear to be in very bad condition and no reservoir of Water—the stream as it runs, is all the resource it has. Formerly there was a dam to stop the Water; but that giving way it is brought in a narrow confined & trifling race to the forebay, wch. and the trunk, which conveys the water to the Wheel are in bad order. In a word, little rent, or good is to be expected from the present aspect of her.[2]

[1] Gilbert Simpson's plantation or farm covered about 600 of the 1,644 acres GW owned at Washington's Bottom. Included on it were 152 acres of fenced meadow, "a good Dwelling House, Kitchen, Barn, Stable, and other necessary Buildings, 110 bearing Apple Trees &c." (GW's advertisement, in *Va. Journal,* 15 July 1784). The gristmill stood about a mile from the farm on the bank of Washington's Run, a small stream that flowed into the Youghiogheny River about three-fourths of a mile below the mill.

[2] GW had spared little expense in making this large stone gristmill as fine as possible. Its construction, which had taken nearly two years, cost him between £1,000 and £1,200 (GW's land memorandum, 25 May 1794, DLC: GW), and after William Crawford saw it "go for the first time" in spring 1776, he assured GW that "I think it the best Mill I ever saw any where, tho' I think one of a less value would have done as well" (20 Sept. 1776, DLC:GW). Equipped with two pairs of millstones made of local rock, which the alcoholic but skilled millwright Dennis Stephens deemed "equal to English burr," the mill was supposed to grind "incredibly fast" when working (GW's advertisement, in *Va. Journal,* 15 July 1784). The shambles that GW found today in his first view of the mill should not have surprised him knowing what he did of his partner and manager Gilbert Simpson. "I never hear of the Mill under the direction of Simpson," he wrote Lund Washington 20 Aug. 1775, "without a degree of warmth & vexation at his extreame stupidity" (NN).

14th. Remained at Mr. Gilbert Simpsons all day. Before Noon Colo. Willm. Butler[1] and the Officer Commanding the Garrison at Fort Pitt, a Captn. Lucket[2] came here. As they confirmed the reports of the discontented temper of the Indians and the Mischiefs done by some parties of them and the former advised me not to prosecute my intended trip to the Great Kanhawa, I resolved to decline it.[3]

This day also, the people who lives on my land on Millers run came here to set forth their pretensions to it; & to enquire into my right. After much conversation, & attempts in them to discover all the flaws they could in my Deed, &ca.; & to establish a fair and upright intention in themselves; and after much Councelling which proceeded from a division of opinion among themselves—they resolved (as all who live on the Land were not here) to give me their definitive determination when I should come to the Land, which I told them would probably happen on Friday or Saturday next.[4]

[1] William Butler (1745–1789), of Pittsburgh, was known to GW to be a good woodsman and something of an expert in Indian warfare. Both be-

fore and after the War of Independence, Butler was an Indian trader in the Ohio Valley. During the war, as a lieutenant colonel in the Pennsylvania line, he was assigned by GW to help defend the New York frontier 1778–79. In Oct. 1778 he led a small expedition of Continental soldiers which destroyed a number of Indian villages near Unadilla, N.Y., and the following year he was responsible for wiping out several more Indian settlements in the vicinity of Lake Cayuga. In all Butler served nearly seven years in the Continental Army before retiring 1 Jan. 1783 (BOATNER [1], 152; CHALFANT, 69–70; GW to Continental Congress, 22 July 1778, and GW to John Stark, 5 Aug. 1778, DLC:GW).

[2] David Luckett of Maryland had very recently assumed command of the small detachment of underpaid and ill-clad Marylanders who currently occupied Fort Pitt (FRONTIER FORTS, 2:151–52). Although sometimes addressed as captain, the rank the fort's commander apparently was supposed to hold, Luckett was a lieutenant, having advanced only one grade since entering the Continental Army as an ensign in 1779 (EVANS, 227; Craig Bayard & Co., to Luckett, 27 May 1785, DNA: PCC, Item 163; HEITMAN [1], 271). He requested the War Department on 1 Aug. 1784 to relieve him of his command before 20 Sept.; "I can't," he declared, "think of spending my time and Substance in so trifling a Service as the present without some advantage" (DNA: PCC, Item 60). Nevertheless, he remained in charge at Fort Pitt until after 7 June 1785, when Congress finally permitted him to retire from the army (JCC, 28:435).

Luckett probably came to Simpson's today in response to a letter which GW had sent to Fort Pitt 10 July, requesting the use of public boats there, if any, and "three or Four trusty Soldiers" from the garrison to go down the Ohio (DLC:GW).

[3] The situation, GW explained in a letter to Henry Knox 5 Dec. 1784, did not "render it prudent . . . to run the risk of insult." In another year the Kanawha lands might be usurped by "people who [will] set me at defiance, under the claim of pre-occupancy . . . but as the land cannot be removed . . . I thought it better to return, than to make a bad matter worse by hazarding abuse from the Savages of the Country" (DLC:GW). That danger was real, according to Thomas Freeman. "Had you Proceded on you[r] Tour down the River," Freeman wrote GW 9 June 1785, "I believe it would have been attended with the most dreadfull Consequences. The Indians by what means I can't say had Intelligence of your Journey and Laid wait for you. Genl. [James] Wilkinson fell in their Hands and was taken for you and with much difficulty of Persuasion & Gifts got away. This is the Common Report & I believe the Truth" (DLC:GW).

[4] GW's 2,813-acre tract on Millers Run, a branch of Chartier's Creek, lay in Washington County about eight miles northwest of present-day Canonsburg, Pa. William Crawford surveyed this tract for GW in 1771, but almost from the start Crawford was hard put to keep unauthorized settlers off it. To protect GW's claim he built four cabins on the tract in 1772 and engaged a man to stay there (Crawford to GW, 1 May 1772, DLC:GW). However, he still had to reckon with the wily speculator George Croghan. Miffed because GW questioned his land titles and declined to buy any tract from him, Croghan arbitrarily extended his already overblown claims to include the Millers Run land and urged settlers to move on it. The result was that 10 or 12 persons occupied the tract in the fall of 1773 without purchasing or leasing from either GW or Croghan. "There is no geting them of without

by Force of Arms," Crawford wrote GW 29 Dec. 1773, and such tactics would be of little use, because "they will com back Emedetly as soon as my back is turnd. They man I put on the Land, they have drove away, and Built a house so Colse to his dore that he cannot get into the house at the dore" (DLC:GW).

On 5 July 1774 GW obtained a patent for his Millers Run land from Virginia, which was then disputing Pennsylvania's jurisdiction over what is now southwestern Pennsylvania (Va. Colonial Patents, Book 42, 516–18, Vi Microfilm). Although Virginia gave up its rights to the area six years later, its grants there remained valid, being recognized by Pennsylvania as the price for Virginia's concession (CRUMRINE [3], 521–23). Nevertheless, the people on Millers Run questioned GW's title on grounds that Crawford was not a Virginia county surveyor in 1771; that his survey was registered and the patent granted after they moved on the land; and that the tract was deserted when they occupied it.

Among the arguments GW later made in response were that Crawford did not have to be a county surveyor because the land was surveyed under a military warrant; that most of the *present* occupants did not move on the land until after the date of his patent; that none of them ever took any steps to obtain a patent; that Crawford improved and had the land occupied long before anyone else did; and that the settlers were frequently warned over the years that they were trespassing. In short, he was convinced that the Millers Run people had taken "a very ungenerous advantage" of him (GW to John Harvie, 19 Mar. 1785, and GW to Thomas Smith, 14 July 1785 and 10 Sept. 1785, DLC:GW).

15th. This being the day appointed for the Sale of my moiety of the Co-partnership stock—Many People were gathered (more out of curiosity I believe than from other motives) but no great Sale made. My Mill I could obtain no bid for, altho I offered an exemption from the payment of Rent 15 Months. The Plantation on which Mr. Simpson lives rented well—Viz. for 500 Bushels of Wheat payable at any place with in the County that I, or my Agent should direct. The little chance of getting a good offer in money, for Rent, induced me to set it up to be bid for in Wheat.[1]

Not meeting with any person who could give me a satisfactory acct. of the Navigation of the Cheat River (tho' they generally agreed it was difficult where it passed thro' the Laurel Hill) nor any acct. of the distance & kind of Country between that, or the Main branch of the Monongahela and the Waters of Potomack—nor of the Country between the little Kanhawa and the Waters of Monongahela tho' all agreed none of the former came near ten Miles Creek as had been confidently asserted; I gave up the intention of returning home that way—resolving after settling matters with those Persons who had seated my Lands on Millers run, to return by the way I came; or by what is commonly called the Turkey foot Road.[2]

[1] The general shortage of hard currency was evident in the bidding for GW's livestock and other effects on Simpson's place. The crier whom GW hired to conduct the sale could elicit only £3 6s. 8d. Virginia currency in cash from the crowd, but bonds and notes received may have totaled as much as £146 18s. 7¾d. Virginia currency (Cash Memoranda, DLC:GW; LEDGER B, 233).

Wheat about this time cost GW 5s. 6d. to 6s. Virginia currency a bushel in the Mount Vernon area (LEDGER B, 182). Thus, he had good reason to be pleased with the rent set for Simpson's plantation. However, the deal had one major drawback; the tenant was to be Gilbert Simpson. Simpson was reluctant to commit himself to more than a one-year lease and acquiesed to the advertised ten-year term only at GW's insistence. "I told him *explicitly*," GW later remembered, that "he must take it for the period on which it was offered, or not at all; as I did not intend to go thro' the same trouble every year by making an annual bargain for it." In consideration of Simpson's leasing the plantation, he was allowed to hire GW's slaves there, now about eight in number, at a rate that GW considered "cheap" (GW to Thomas Freeman, 16 Oct. 1785, DLC:GW). Nevertheless, by the following spring Simpson was threatening to quit his lease, "the seasons being difficult and the Rent so high" (Thomas Freeman to GW, 9 June 1785, DLC:GW). He apparently left Washington's Bottom by the end of the year (Thomas Freeman to GW, 27 July 1785, DLC:GW).

[2] Turkey Foot Road, a relatively new alternative to much of Braddock's Road, offered travelers a more direct route between Fort Cumberland and Fort Pitt than had previously been available. However, it failed to become popular, and most of it was later abandoned. The western end of Turkey Foot Road connected with Braddock's Road near present-day Mount Pleasant, Pa., about 12 miles northeast of Washington's Bottom. From that junction the road ran southeast to the Turkey Foot settlement on the Youghiogheny River (now Confluence, Pa.) and then turned more to the east, crossing the Alleghenies to Wills Creek, through the Narrows of which it passed to Fort Cumberland (WELLFORD, 16–17; VEECH, 34; see also entries for 22 Sept. and 4 Oct. 1784).

16th. Continued at Simpsons all day—in order to finish the business which was begun yesterday. Gave leases to some of my Ten[an]ts on the Land whereon I now am.[1]

[1] GW's tract at Washington's Bottom contained, besides Simpson's 600-acre plantation and the mill tract, five small farms leased to tenants whose names and length of tenure are not fully clear (Thomas Freeman to GW, 18 Dec. 1786, DLC:GW). Some of the tenants were much behind in their rent, and as there was evidently some confusion, real or feigned, about the terms under which they were leasing, GW today took the opportunity to explain his terms in person and to make new and apparently more stringent leases with them. Nevertheless, when GW's agent attempted to collect rents a few months later, the tenants denied that any were then due, claiming that they had agreed to take the new leases only on the "footing that all arrears whatever was done away" (Thomas Freeman to GW, 9 June 1785, DLC:GW).

GW vigorously refuted that argument and demanded payment; legal action was threatened and may have eventually been taken (GW to Thomas Freeman, 16 Oct. 1785, and Freeman to GW, 27 July 1785, DLC:GW).

17th. Detained here by a settled Rain the whole day—which gave me time to close my accts. with Gilbert Simpson, & put a final end to my Partnership with him.[1] Agreed this day with a Major Thomas Freeman to superintend my business over the Mountains, upon terms to be inserted in his Instructions.[2]

[1] "I do not expect," GW had written Simpson 10 July 1784, "to be compensated for my losses, nor mean to be rigid in my settlement, yet common sense, reason and justice, all require that I should have a satisfactory account rendered of my property which has been entrusted to your care, in full confidence of getting something for ten or twelve years use of it" (DLC:GW). Details of the settlement are vague. Some division of the livestock and other effects on the plantation apparently had been made before the sale, and at some time during GW's visit, Simpson gave him a Negro woman who was supposedly a slave worth £30, but who later was found to be entitled to her freedom (Thomas Freeman to GW, 18 Dec. 1786, DLC:GW). On 16 Sept., Simpson paid GW £4 11s. 8d. Virginia currency in cash and today gave him a bond for £26 13s. 6d. Pennsylvania currency, or £21 6s. 7¼d. Virginia currency, leaving about £600 Virginia currency due GW mostly on account of money spent to build the mill (LEDGER B, 87, 138). In an attempt to recover part of that sum, GW later tried to collect $339 53/90 that the Confederation government owed the partnership for flour and meal sold during the war, but seems to have had little success (GW to Clement Biddle, 27 July 1785, WRITINGS, 28:211–12; GW to Biddle, 18 May 1786, DLC:GW). The partnership account was closed with the cryptic undated note: "Settled by a payment in depreciated paper Money"; no amount was indicated, and no attempt was made to balance the figures (LEDGER B, 138).

[2] Thomas Freeman of Red Stone served as GW's western agent until the spring of 1787, when he moved to Kentucky (Freeman to GW, 18 Dec. 1787, DLC:GW; LEDGER B, 233). He may be the Thomas Freeman who served as a justice of the peace in Mercer County, Ky., from 1790 until his death there in 1808 (SHELBY, 203, 208; MERCER COUNTY, 104, 106, 107). GW gave written instructions to him on 22 Sept.

18th. Set out with Doctr. Craik for my Land on Millers run (a branch of Shurtees [Chartier's] Creek). Crossed the Monongahela at Deboirs Ferry—16 Miles from Simpsons[1]—bated at one Hamiltons about 4 Miles from it, in Washington County,[2] and lodged at a Colo. Cannons on the Waters of Shurtees Creek—a kind hospitable Man; & sensible.[3]

Most of the Land over which we passed was hilly—some of it

very rich—others thin. Between a Colo. Cooks[4] and the Ferry the Land was rich but broken. About Shurtee, & from thence to Colo. Cannon's, the soil is very luxurient and very uneven.

[1] James Devore (d. 1779) operated this ferry as early as July 1773, running it from his house on the northeast bank of the river across to the mouth of Pigeon Creek, now the site of Monongahela, Pa. It was established as a public ferry Feb. 1775 by the Virginia court for the district of West Augusta, which then claimed jurisdiction over the area, and in Oct. 1778 it was further established by act of the Virginia General Assembly (CRUMRINE [1], 531; HENING, 9:546). Joseph Parkinson, who settled at the mouth of Pigeon Creek about 1770, apparently took over the ferry after Devore's death and soon began operating it under Pennsylvania jurisdiction (VAN VOORHIS, 83–84; MULKEARN AND PUGH, 329–30). However, the name "Devore's Ferry" continued to be used by some travelers until at least 1804 (FOORD, 19).

[2] David Hamilton of Ginger Hill and John Hamilton (1754–1837), who lived nearby, were both prominent residents of the Mingo Creek area west of Devore's ferry. Both men later became Washington County judges, and both became much involved with the rebels in the Whiskey Insurrection of 1794. John Hamilton served as Washington County sheriff 1793–96 and as a United States congressman for one term 1805–7 (CONGRESSIONAL DIRECTORY, 1057; BALDWIN [2], 247).

[3] John Cannon (d. 1799), of Washington County, owned about 800 acres on Chartier's Creek, site of present-day Canonsburg, Pa., which he laid out in 1787. A justice of the Virginia courts for the district of West Augusta and for Yohogania County 1775–80, he was appointed a Washington County justice in 1785, serving until his death. His title of colonel derived from service as a sublieutenant of the Washington County militia 1781–83. Cannon acted as GW's western agent 1786–94, but proved unsatisfactory in his attention to GW's business (CRUMRINE [2], 226; WASHINGTON COUNTY SUPPLY TAX–1781, 713; GW to Thomas Smith, 23 Sept. 1789, DLC:GW).

[4] Edward Cook (1738–1808), of Fayette County, lived near the Monongahela River in the vicinity of present-day Belle Vernon, Pa. His handsome limestone mansion built 1774–76 was reputed to be at that time "the most pretentious home west of the Alleghenies" (MULKEARN AND PUGH, 242). A conservative and well-to-do Presbyterian elder, Cook owned a number of slaves (HEADS OF FAMILIES, PA., 111). In 1776 he was a member of both the Pennsylvania Provincial Congress and the state constitutional convention and during the war served as county sublieutenant and eventually county lieutenant of Westmoreland County, which embraced all of present-day Fayette County before Fayette's formation in 1783 (EGLE, 3:320).

19th. Being Sunday, and the People living on my Land, *apparently* very religious, it was thought best to postpone going among them till tomorrow[1]—but rode to a Doctr. Johnsons who had the Keeping of Colo. Crawfords (Surveying) records—but not finding him at home was disappointed in the business which carried me there.[2]

[1] These settlers were members of the Associate Presbyterian Church, commonly called the Seceders' Church, a Presbyterian sect that had broken with the main church in 1733 in a dispute over lay control, especially in the calling of ministers. Rev. Matthew Henderson organized a Seceder church in the Chartier's Creek area in 1775 and currently had charge of it and another Seceder church near present-day Buffalo, Pa. (BUCK, 120, 408; MULKEARN AND PUGH, 319, 338).

[2] Four Johnstons held property in the neighborhood of Col. John Cannon's home in 1781: John Johnston, 300 acres; William Johnston, 134 acres; William Johnston, Sr., 360 acres; and Mathew Johnston, 300 acres (WASHINGTON COUNTY SUPPLY TAX–1781, 715).

20th. Went early this Morning to view my Land, & to receive the final determination of those who live upon it. Having obtained a Pilot near the Land I went first to the plantation of Samuel McBride, who has about 5 Acres of Meadow & 30 of arable Land under good fencing– a Logged dwelling house with a punchion roof, & stable, or small barn, of the same kind–the Land rather hilly, but good, chiefly white oak. Next–

James McBride. 3 or 4 Acres of Meadow. 28–Do. of Arable Land. Pretty good fencing–Land rather broken, but good–white & black oak mixed–A dwelling House and barn (of midling size) with Puncheon roofs.

Thomas Biggart. Robt. Walker living thereon as a Tenant. No Meadow. Abt. 20 Acres of Arable Land. A dwelling House and single Barn–fences tolerable and Land good.

William Stewart. 2½ Acres of Meadow. 20 Do. of Arable Land. Only one house except a kind of building adjoining for common purposes–Good Land and Midling fences.

Matthew Hillast [Hillis]. Has within my line–abt. 7 Acres of Meadow. 3 besides, Arable–also a small double Barn.

Brice McGeechen [McGeehan]. 3 Acres of Meadow. 20 Do. arable–under good fencing. A small new Barn good.

Duncan McGeechen [McGeehan]. 2 Acres of Meadow. 38 Do. Arable Land. A good single Barn, dwelling House Spring House & several other Houses. The Plantation under good fencing.

David Reed. Claimed by the last mentioned (Duncan McGeechin). 2 Acres of Meadow. 18 Do. Arable Land. No body living on this place at present–the dwelling House and fencing in bad order.

John Reed Esquire. 4 Acres of Meadow. 38 Do. Arable Do. A small dwelling House–but Logs for a large one, a still House–good Land and fencing.

David Reed. 2 Acres of Meadow. 17 Do. arable. A good logged dwelling House with a bad roof–several other small Houses and an indifferent Barn, or Stable—bad fences; but very good Land.

William Hillas [Hillis]. 20 Acres of Arable Land. No Meadow. But one house, and that indifferent—fences not good.

John Glen. 2 or 3 Acres of Meadow within my Line—his plantation & the rest of his Land without.

James Scott. Placed on the Land by Thomas Lapsley. Has 17 acres under good fencing—only a dwelling House (which stops the door of a Cabbin built by Captn. Crawford) —white oak Land —rather thin—but good bottom *to clear* for Meadow.

Matthew Johnson. 2 Acres of Meadow. 24 Do. Arable Land. A good Logged house—Materials for a dble. Barn—very gd. Land, but indifferent fences.

James Scott. A large Plantation—about 70 Acres of Arable Land. 4 Do. of improved Meadow. Much more may be made into Meadow. The Land very good, as the fences also are. A Barn dwelling House & some other Houses.

The foregoing are all the Improvements upon this Tract which contains 2813 acres.[1]

The Land is leveller than is common to be met with in this Part of the Country, and good; the principal part of it is white oak, intermixed in many places with black oak; and is esteemed a valuable tract.

Dined at David Reeds, after which Mr. James Scot & Squire [John] Reed began to enquire whether I would part with the Land, & upon what terms; adding, that tho' they did not conceive they could be dispossed, yet to avoid contention, they would buy, if my terms were moderate. I told them I had no inclination to sell; however, after hearing a great deal of their hardships, their religious principles (which had brought them together as a society of Ceceders) and unwillingness to seperate or remove; I told them I would make them a last offer and this was—the whole tract at 25/. pr. Acre, the money to be paid at 3 annual payments with Interest; or to become Tenants upon leases of 999 years, at the annual Rent of Ten pounds pr. ct. pr. Ann. The former they had a long consultation upon, & asked if I wd. take that price at a longer credit, without Interest, and being answered in the negative they then determined to stand suit for the Land; but it having been suggested that there were among them some who were disposed to relinquish their claim, I told them I would receive their answers individually; and accordingly calling upon them as they stood

James Scott
William Stewart

Thomas Lapsley
Saml. McBride
Brice McGeechin
Thomas Biggar
David Reed
William Hillas
James McBride
Duncan McGeechin
Matthew Johnson
John Reed &
John Glen—they severally answered, that they meant to stand suit, & abide the Issue of the Law.[2]

This business being thus finished, I returned to Colo. Cannons in company with himself, Colo. Nevil,[3] Captn. Swearingen (high Sherif)[4] & a Captn. Richie,[5] who had accompanied me to the Land.

[1] Although the arable and meadow lands total only a little more than 400 acres, the settlers also claimed much uncleared land, thus disputing most, if not all, of GW's 2,813 acres. In 1781 Washington County taxed them for holdings in the Millers Run area ranging in size from 40 acres for James McBride and 70 acres for Thomas Biggert to 500 acres for David Reed and 800 acres for Duncan McGeehan. William Hillis and tenant Robert Walker had no land there then; the rest held between 200 and 350 acres each (WASHINGTON COUNTY SUPPLY TAX–1781, 713–20, 774).

Not all of the settlers' lands lay within GW's lines. Matthew Hillis's 300 acres and John Glenn's 250 acres adjoined GW's tract, overlapping it only slightly. Samuel McBride's 350 acres were in tracts of 200 and 150 acres respectively, one of which probably lay out of the disputed area. Portions of some of the other settlers' claims may likewise have been outside of GW's tract. In addition, several settlers owned lands in other parts of Washington County. William Stewart had 150 acres and Thomas Lapsley 100 acres to the east in Peters Township; Robert Walker had 250 acres to the west in Donegal Township; James McBride had 300 acres and Thomas Biggert 250 acres to the north in Robinson Township (WASHINGTON COUNTY SUPPLY TAX–1781, 715–17, 729, 758, 761–62, 768, 774).

Thomas Biggert (c.1740–1829) settled on his land in Robinson Township soon after bringing his family to America from Ireland in 1773, but Indian troubles forced his removal to Millers Run for most of the war years. Now, with his 70 acres on Millers Run leased to Robert Walker, he apparently was living again in Robinson Township, where he remained until his death (CRUMRINE [2], 901).

Biggert was typical of the Millers Run claimants in that he did not leave Washington County. The claimants were not itinerants drifting west with the frontier, but nearly all family men with strong ties to church and community. Of the 15 men named here by GW, 12 obtained warrants for additional Washington County lands between 1784 and 1789 (see WASHINGTON COUNTY WARRANTEES), and only 3 of their names do not appear in the

1790 Washington County census: Thomas Lapsley was nearby in Allegheny County, while Brice McGeehan and William Hillis are not listed in Pennsylvania (HEADS OF FAMILIES, PA., 16, 245–58). In the 1800 census only Duncan McGeehan's name is missing from the state. Lapsley was still in Allegheny County; Brice McGeehan appears in Beaver County; and William Hillis was in Washington County, where the other 11 names remain (see PA. IN 1800).

Thomas Biggert was also typical of his claimants in his relative obscurity. Only the brothers David Reed and Squire John Reed (d. 1816) achieved any real local prominence. Having moved to Millers Run from Lancaster County, Pa., in 1777, they served as officers in the frontier militia during the war: David as a captain and John as a lieutenant. Upon creation of Washington County in 1781, John Reed became one of the first justices of the county court and was again appointed a judge in 1788 (CRUMRINE [2], 859–60; PA. RANGERS, 266, 282, 310).

[2] According to a Reed family tradition, GW today replied to James Scott and the Reeds "with dignity and some warmth, asserting that they had been forewarned by his agent, and the nature of his claim fully made known; that there could be no doubt of its validity, and rising from his seat and holding a red silk handkerchief by one corner, he said, 'Gentlemen, I will have this land just as surely as I now have this handkerchief' " (CRUMRINE [2], 858–59).

The unexpected unity with which the Millers Run people stood against GW today was attributed by GW and his Pennsylvania lawyer Thomas Smith to the influence of James Scott, Jr., whom Smith viewed as "the ringleader or director of the rest" (Smith to GW, 7 Nov. 1786, DLC:GW). GW's suit apparently was considered to be somewhat of a test case; "I have . . . been told," GW wrote Edmund Randolph 13 Aug. 1785, "that the decision of this case will be interesting to numbers whose rights are disputed on similar grounds" (DLC:GW). Scott, a brother of Washington County's influential court clerk Thomas Scott, certainly must have been aware of the local political implications of the suit, as was Thomas Smith. In a letter to GW dated 9 Feb. 1785, Smith declared: "I . . . have the strong & fomented prejudices of Party to contend with, and I have some reason to believe that a good deal of art & management were used before the People were prevailed with to stand the Ejectments" (DLC:GW). Nevertheless, all of the defendants fought GW to the last in court (Smith to GW, 7 Nov. 1786, DLC:GW).

The only claimant who did not stand with the others today was Matthew Hillis (d. 1803). Most of his 300 acres lay outside of GW's tract, leaving only a small portion in dispute, apparently not enough to justify the expense of a defense against GW's suit (WASHINGTON COUNTY SUPPLY TAX–1781, 774; CRUMRINE [2], 860). In 1787 GW agreed to consider Hillis "as a preferable purchaser of that piece which runs along his line so as to include his improvements, provided it does not affect the sale of the rest" (GW to John Cannon, 13 April 1787, DLC:GW). No such sale was ever made to Hillis.

[3] Presley Neville (1756–1818), a wealthy and aristocratic young man, lived on Chartier's Creek about six miles west of Pittsburgh in a house known as Woodville. Nearby on the opposite side of the creek stood Bower Hill, home of his father, John Neville (1731–1803), who at this time was in Philadelphia serving as a member of the Pennsylvania Supreme Executive Council (PA. ARCH., COL. REC., 14:209). The Nevilles moved to Chartier's Creek from

Frederick County, Va., about 1775, but served in the Virginia line during the War of Independence, John being breveted a brigadier general and Presley a lieutenant colonel in the course of the war. A favorite of Lafayette, Presley served for a time as one of the marquis's aides-de-camp. He was captured with the Virginia troops at Charleston, S.C., in 1780, but was exchanged the following year, and served until the end of the war (BALDWIN [2], 45–46; HEITMAN [1], 308).

[4] Van Swearingen (died c.1793) was high sheriff of Washington County from Nov. 1781 to Nov. 1784. He and his brother Andrew Swearingen apparently moved to this area from Virginia in the early 1770s (CRUMRINE [2], 710–11; *D.A.R. Mag.*, 44:310). In the War of Independence he commanded an independent company in western Pennsylvania Feb. to Aug. 1776 and then served three years as a captain in the 8th Pennsylvania Regiment. Detached to Daniel Morgan's riflemen in 1777, he fought at Saratoga where he was wounded and temporarily captured (PA. ARCH., 2d ser., 10:647–49; HEITMAN [1], 390). GW considered Swearingen a superb officer for "Frontier, desultory service" (GW to Daniel Brodhead, 25 June 1779, DLC:GW). Nevertheless, he received no promotion and resigned from the army Aug. 1779.

[5] Matthew Ritchie (d. 1798), of Washington County, was a well-to-do bachelor who over a period of years acquired large landholdings in southwestern Pennsylvania. He was appointed sublieutenant for the county in 1781, was a county representative to the General Assembly 1782–84, and became a judge of the county court of common pleas in 1784. Ritchie bought all of GW's land on Millers Run 1 June 1796 for $12,000 (CRUMRINE [2], 483, 859).

21st. Accompanied by Colo. Cannon & Captn. Swearingin who attended me to Debores ferry on the Monongahela which seperates the Counties of Fayette & Washington,[1] I returned to Gilbert Simpson's in the Afternoon; after dining at one Wickermans Mill near the Monongahela.[2]

Colo. Cannon, Captn. Sweringin & Captn. Richie all promised to hunt up the Evidences which could prove my possession & improvement of the Land before any of the present Occupiers ever saw it.

[1] Devore's ferry in 1784 connected Westmoreland and Washington counties; in 1788 the northeast landing of the ferry became part of newly formed Allegheny County while the southeast landing remained part of Washington County. GW apparently did not realize that he had crossed from Fayette to Westmoreland County near Col. Edward Cook's house on 18 Sept. (BUCK, 172; ALLEGHENY, pt. 1, 120).

[2] Adam Wickerham of Washington County, a German immigrant, lived on the bank of the Monongahela near Devore's ferry. According to tradition, he avoided arrest during the Whiskey Insurrection of 1794 by feigning idiocy (VAN VOORHIS, 165–67).

22d. After giving instructions to Major Thomas Freeman respecting his conduct in my business,[1] and disposing of my Baggage which was left under the care of Mr. Gilbert Simpson—consisting of two leather & one linnen Valeses with my Marquee & horseman's Tent Tent Poles & Pins—all my bedding except Sheets (which I take home with me)—the equipage Trunk containing all that was put into it except the Silver Cups and Spoons—Canteens—two Kegs of Spirits—Horse Shoes &ca.[2] I set out for Beason Town,[3] in order to meet with & engage Mr. Thos. Smith to bring Ejectments, & to prosecute my Suit for the Land in Washington County, on which those, whose names are herein inserted, are settled.[4] Reached Beason Town about dusk about (the way I came) 18 Miles.

Note. In my equipage Trunk and the Canteens—were Madeira and Port Wine—Cherry bounce[5]—Oyl, Mustard—Vinegar and Spices of all sorts—Tea, and Sugar in the Camp Kettles (a whole loaf of white sugar broke up, about 7 lbs. weight). The Camp Kettles are under a lock, as the Canteens & Trunk also are. My fishing lines are in the Canteens.

At Beason Town I met with Captn. Hardin[6] who informed me, as I had before been informed by others, that the West fork of Monongahela communicates very nearly with the waters of the little Kanhawa—that the Portage does not exceed Nine Miles and that a very good Waggon Road may be had between—That from the Mouth of the River Cheat to that of the West Fork, is computed to be about 30 Miles, & the Navigation good—as it also is up the West fork—that the South or Main branch of the Monogahela [Tygart Valley River] has considerable impediments in the way, and were it otherwise would not answer the purpose of a communication with the North or South branch of Potomack from the westerly direction in which it runs—That the Cheat River, tho' rapid and bad, has been navigated to the Dunkard bottom about 25 Miles from its Mouth[7] and that he has understood a good way may be had from thence to the North branch, which he thinks must be about 30 Miles distant. He also adds, that from the Settlemts. on the East of the Alligany [Mountains] to Monongahela Court House[8] on the West, it is reported a very good road may be opened, and is already marked; from whence to the Navigable Water of the little Kanhawa is abt. [   ] Miles.

From this information I resolved to return home that way; & My baggage under the care of Doctr. Craik and Son, having, from Simpsons, taken the rout by the New (or Turkey foot) road as it is called (which is said to be 20 Miles near than Braddocks) with a view to make a more minute enquiry into the Navigation of the Yohiggany Waters–my Nephew and I set out about Noon, with one Colo. Philips for Cheat River;[9] after I had engaged Mr. Smith to undertake my business, & had given him such information As I was able to do.

Note, It is adjudged proper to ascertain the date of the Warrt. to Captn. Posey and the identity of his hand writing to his Bond to me; the latter so as to give it authenticity–as also the date of Lewis's return, on which my Patent Issued–because if this is antecedent to the settlement of the occupiers of my Land, it will put the matter out of all kind of dispute; as the claim of those people rests upon their possessing the Land before I had any legal Survey of it; not viewing Crawfords as authentic. 'Tis advisable also, to know whether any location of it was ever made in the Land, or Surveyors Office, and the date of such Entry. And likewise, what Ordainance it is Captn. Crawford speaks of in his Letter of the 20th. of Septr. 1776 which passed he says at the last Convention, for saving equitable claims on the Western Waters.[10]

[1] GW's written instructions to Freeman are dated 23 Sept. in his letter book (DLC:GW). One of the two main tasks he assigned Freeman was securing tenants for his lands on the Ohio and Kanawha rivers, for the Great Meadows tract, and for the mill and other still vacant lands at Washington's Bottom. As compensation Freeman would be allowed 20s. Pennsylvania currency for each tenant obtained and two dollars for every farm laid off for those tenants, together "with such reasonable expences as may be incurred thereby." Freeman's other main task was to collect rents from the western tenants and debts from the purchasers at the recent partnership sale. Bonds and notes totaling £183 13s. 3½d. Pennsylvania currency, or £146 18s. 7¾d. Virginia currency, were today put in Freeman's hands (LEDGER B, 233). His commission was to be 5 percent of all money collected. GW also authorized Freeman "to act and do (where no particular instruction is given) in the same manner as you would for yourself under like circumstances; endeavouring in all cases by fair and lawful means to promote my interest in this Country" (GW's instructions to Freeman, 23 Sept. 1784, DLC:GW). Nevertheless, GW would demand detailed and fairly frequent reports in the coming months (GW to Freeman, 11 April 1785, DLC:GW).

[2] GW obviously anticipated returning to this area at some future date, possibly as early as the next spring (Thomas Freeman to GW, 9 June 1785, DLC:GW). He could not know that he would never again come so far west.

The two kegs each contained eight gallons "of West India rum, one of them of the first quality" (GW to Thomas Freeman, 16 Oct. 1785, DLC: GW).

[3] Beeson's Town was laid out on the upper reaches of Red Stone Creek in 1776 by the Quaker settler Henry Beeson (b. 1743). When Fayette County was formed in September 1783, the town was designated the county seat under its present-day name, Uniontown (WALKINSHAW, 2:181–83). In early

A section from Reading Howell's 1792 map of Pennsylvania, showing the area traversed by Washington in 1784. From a facsimile in *The Pennsylvania*

Archives, 3d ser., appendix for vols. 1–10, n.d. (Rare Book Department, University of Virginia Library)

1784 the town, according to newly arrived Ephraim Douglass, consisted of "a court-house and school-house in one, a mill . . . four taverns, three smith-shops, five retail shops, two Tanyards, one of them only occupied, one saddler's shop, two hatter's shops, one mason, one cake woman, we had two but one of them having committed a petit larceny is upon banishment, two widows and some reputed maids. To which may be added a distillery" (DOUGLASS, 50).

[4] Thomas Smith, whom GW had known in Philadelphia before the war, had recently established a law practice in Carlisle, Pa., from whence he made regular circuits of the western courts. At Uniontown he and GW agreed on a basic strategy for prosecuting the people on Millers Run: the cases would be removed as soon as possible from the relatively hostile Washington County court to the friendlier Pennsylvania Supreme Court, members of which periodically traveled across the mountains from Philadelphia to hold sessions in the western counties. Although the cases in either court would be tried before a jury of western Pennsylvanians, the Supreme Court justices could be expected to make out a less hostile jury list and to rule much more favorably on points of law. GW's suits were tried before Supreme Court justices in Washington County 24–26 Oct. 1786. In each instance the jury returned a verdict for GW, and the settlers vacated his land soon afterwards (Thomas Smith to GW, 9 Feb. 1785, 17–26 Nov. 1785, and 7 Nov. 1786, DLC:GW).

[5] A drink "made by steeping cherries in brandy with sugar" (GREEN, 111).

[6] John Hardin (1753–1792), a miller and experienced Indian fighter, lived on George's Creek in southwestern Fayette County. Born in Fauquier County, Va., he came to Pennsylvania with his parents about the age of 12. He served as an ensign in Dunmore's War of 1774 and during the War of Independence was a lieutenant in the 8th Pennsylvania Regiment 1776–79. Like Van Swearingen, he was detached to Daniel Morgan's riflemen in 1777, fighting with them at the Battle of Saratoga where he was wounded. He resigned from the Continental Army in Dec. 1779, but in the spring of 1782 served as a captain on William Crawford's disastrous volunteer expedition against the Indians on the Upper Sandusky. Hardin moved his wife and children to Kentucky in 1786 and participated in several more Indian campaigns before his death at the hands of Indians while acting as an emissary (ROSENTHAL, 156, 308).

[7] Dunkard's Bottom, located on the east bank of the Cheat River near present-day Kingwood, W.Va., was first settled in the 1750s by members of the Church of the Brethren, a German Baptist sect whose adherents were known as Dunkers or Dunkards (DURNBAUGH, 160–62, 165–67).

[8] Final settlement of the Virginia-Pennsylvania boundary having put the first courthouse of Monongalia County, Va., into Pennsylvania, the Virginia General Assembly in May 1783 designated Col. Zackquill Morgan's home at the confluence of the Monongahela River and Decker's Creek as the temporary courthouse (HENING, 11:255–56). In late 1783 and early 1784 Col. Morgan laid off Morgantown, Va. (now W.Va.), on his property, where a permanent courthouse was built, but Morgantown was not officially established by the General Assembly until Oct. 1785 (CALLAHAN [2], 30–33, 51–52; HENING, 12:212–14).

[9] GW and Bushrod Washington were to meet the Craiks at Warner Washington's house in Frederick County, Va. (see entry for 29 Sept. 1784).

The Craiks took that part of GW's baggage which had not been left with Gilbert Simpson and which GW would not need on his journey home.

Theophilus Phillips (died c.1789), of Fayette County, lived about 2½ miles north of the mouth of the Cheat River near present-day New Geneva, Pa. He came to this area in 1767, apparently from New Jersey, accompanied by his brother-in-law James Dunlap, a Presbyterian minister. The first courthouse of Monongalia County, Va., was Phillips's converted blacksmith shop, and he was probably both clerk and one of the justices of that court. When the 1780 boundary settlement between Virginia and Pennsylvania put his property a few miles inside Pennsylvania, he seems to have had little difficulty in transferring his allegiance to the Pennsylvania government. In 1782 he appears as a lieutenant colonel in the Westmoreland County militia, and in 1783 he was one of the men directed by the Pennsylvania legislature to purchase land for the courthouse of newly formed Fayette County. He was elected to the legislature in 1789, but before he could serve he died at sea while returning from a business trip to New Orleans by way of New York (WALKINSHAW, 2:83–84, 181; MULKEARN AND PUGH, 245–46; WESTMORELAND MILITIA, 295).

[10] This information was requested today by Thomas Smith for use in the suits against the settlers on Millers Run.

GW's patent for his Millers Run land was based on a military warrant for 3,000 acres which John Posey had obtained under the Proclamation of 1763 for service in the French and Indian War and had sold to GW in 1770 (GW to John Harvie, 19 Mar. 1785, DLC:GW). The date of this warrant proved to be of little use in prosecuting the settlers, because although Posey's bond assigning the warrant to GW was dated 14 Oct. 1770, the warrant itself, for some reason unknown to GW, was dated 25 Nov. 1773, later than the Oct. 1773 date which his opponents claimed for their settlement (GW to Smith, 14 July 1785 and 28 July 1786, DLC:GW).

Also of little use was the date on which William Crawford's survey of the Millers Run land was sent by Thomas Lewis, surveyor of Augusta County, Va., to the secretary of the colony in Williamsburg for issuance of GW's patent. Crawford made his survey in 1771, but it was the spring of 1774 before he entered it with Lewis, because not until Nov. 1773 did the Virginia council exempt holders of the 1763 military warrants from the general ban on patents west of the Appalachians (Crawford to GW, 8 May 1774, DLC:GW; VA. EXEC. JLS., 6:549). The survey had to be taken to Lewis, because in 1774 the Millers Run area was considered by Virginia to be part of Augusta County.

If GW's prior right to the land could not be established by the date of entry for the survey, it might be established by the date of entry for the proposed location of the survey, provided such an entry had been made. Standard patenting procedure apparently stipulated that a precise location of the area that one intended to survey be officially recorded before proceeding to do it in order to avoid overlapping surveys by warrantees (HENING, 10:54). However, in the case of the Millers Run land no previous location was found in the records of either the county surveyor or the state land office in Richmond (GW to Smith, 28 July 1786, DLC:GW).

William Crawford's letter to GW 20 Sept. 1776 (DLC:GW) apparently refers to a resolution passed by the Virginia Convention 24 June 1776, which stated in part "that all persons who are now actually settled on any unlocated or unappropriated land in Virginia, to which there is no other claim, shall have the pre-emption, or preference, in the grants of such lands" (*Va. Gaz.*, P, 28 June 1776).

23d. Arrived at Colo. Philips abt. five oclock in the afternoon 16 Miles from Beason Town & near the Mouth of Cheat Rivr. The land thro' wch. I rid was for the most part tolerably level—in some places rich—but in general of a second quality. Crossed no water of consequence except Georges Creek.[1]

An Apology made to me from the Court of Fayette (thro' Mr. Smith) for not addressing me; as they found my Horses Saddled and myself on the move.

Finding by enquiries, that the Cheat River had been passed with Canoes thro' those parts which had been represented as impassable and that a Captn. Hanway—the Surveyor of Monongahela County lived within two or three Miles of it, Southside thereof; [2] I resolved to pass it to obtain further information, & accordingly (accompanied by Colo. Philips) set of in the Morning of the

[1] George's Creek flows west through southern Fayette County, entering the Monongahela River about five miles below the mouth of the Cheat River.

[2] Samuel Hanway (1743–1834) became surveyor of Monongalia County 3 June 1783 with the provision that his appointment would be voided should his predecessor, who was "supposed killed by the Indians," turn up alive, but he held the office for most of the rest of his life (VA. COUNCIL JLS., 3:265). Born in Chester County, Pa., he came to Charles County, Va., about 1768 and later was a merchant in Petersburg. At the beginning of the War of Independence he raised and led a unit of Amelia County minutemen and then served several months as a captain of state marines before resigning his commission in Dec. 1776 (VA. COUNCIL JLS., 1:262, 2:405, 498, 506). He apparently moved to Monongalia County about the time of his appointment as surveyor (JOHNSTON [4], 4:45).

24th. And crossed it at the Mouth, as it was thought the river was too much swelled to attempt the ford a little higher up.[1] The fork was about 2 Miles & half from Colo. Philups, & the ground betwn. very hilly tho' rich in places. The Cheat at the Mouth is about 125 yds. wide—the Monongahela near dble. that. The colour of the two Waters is very differt., that of Cheat is dark (occasioned as is conjectured by the Laurel, among which it rises; and through which it runs). The other is clear; & there appears a repugnancy in both to mix, as there is a plain line of division betwn. the two for some distance below the fork; which holds, I am told, near a mile—the Cheat keeping the right shore as it descends, & the other the left.

The Line which divides the Commonwealths of Virginia & Pensylvania crosses both these Rivers about two miles up each from the point of fork & the Land between them is high as the line runs being a ridge which seperates the two Waters—but higher up the fork a good road (it is said) may be had from one river to the other.

From the Fork to the Surveyors Office, which is at the house of one Pierpoint, is about 8 Miles along the dividing ridge.[2] At this Office I could obtain no information of any Surveys or Entries made for me by Captn. Wm. Crawford; but from an examination of his books it appeared pretty evident that the 2500 acres which he (Crawford) had surveyed for & offered to me on the little Kanhawa (adjoining the large Survey under the proclamation of 1754) he had entered for Mr. Robert Rutherford and that the other tract in the fork between the Ohio & little Kanhawa had been entered by Doctr. Briscoe & Sons.[3]

Pursuing my enquiries respecting the Navigation of the Western Waters, Captn. Hanway proposed, if I would stay all Night, to send to Monongahela C[our]t House at Morgan town, for Colo. Zachh. Morgan and others;[4] who would have it in their power to give the best accts. that were to be obtained, which, assenting to, they were sent for & came, & from them I received the following intelligence

viz.

That from the fork of Monongahela & Cheat, to the Court House at Morgan Town, is, by Water, about 11 Miles, & from thence to the West fork of the former is 18 More. From thence to the carrying place between it and a branch of the little Kanhawa, at a place called Bullstown, is about 40 Miles, by Land—more by Water and the Navigation good.[5]

The carrying place is nine Miles and an half between the navigable parts of the two Waters; and a good road between; there being only one hill in the way, and that not bad. Hence to the Mo[uth] of the [Little] Kanhawa is 50 Miles.

That from Monongahela Court House, 15 Miles along the new road which leads into Braddocks road, East of the winding ridge,[6] and McCulloch's path, to one Joseph Logston's on the North branch of Potomack[7] is about 40 Miles—that this way passes through Sandy Creek glades, and the glades of Yohiogany, and may be made good. But, if the road should go from Clarke's Town on the Western fork of Monongahela,[8] 15 Miles below the [Bulltown] carrying place to the aforesaid Logston's, it would

September 1784

lies at Leesburgh, where we Dined—The Baggage having joined we proceeded to Mr. Israel Thompsons & lodged makg. ab. 36 M.

3d.

Having business to transact with my Tenants in Berkeley; & others, who were directed to meet me at my Brother's (Colo. Charles Washington's); I left Docr. Craik and the Baggage to follow slowly and set out myself about Sun rise for that place—where after Breakfasting at Keys's ferry I arrived about 11 Oclock.—distant ab. 17 Miles.—

Colo. Warner Washington, Mr. Wormeley, Genl. Morgan, Mr. Trickett and many other Gentlemen came here to see me.—& one object of my journey being to obtain information of the nearest and best communication between the Eastern and Western waters, & to facilitate as much as in me lay the Inland Navigation of the Potomack; I conversed a good deal with Genl.

A page from Washington's 1784 diary. (Library of Congress)

cross the Tyger Valley River (the largest branch of Monongahela) above the falls therein,[9] go through the glades of Monongahela;[10] cross Cheat river at the Dunkers bottom (25 Miles from its Mouth) and thence through the Glades of Yohiogany–in all f[ro]m the [Little] Ka[naw]ha 85 Miles.

That the Cheat river where it runs through the Laurel hill is, in their opinion, so incomoded with large rock stones, rapid, and dashing water from one rock to another, as to become impassable; especially as they do not think a passage sufficient to admit a Canal can be found between the Hills & the common bed of the river–but of these matters none of them pretended to speak from actual knowledge, or observation; but from report, and partial views.[11]

That from these rapids to the Dunkers bottom, & four Miles above, the navigation is very good, after which for 8 Miles the river is very foul, & worse to pass than it is through the Laurel hill; but from thence upwards, thro' the horse Shoe bottom,[12] & many miles higher, it is again good, & fit for transportation; but (tho' useful to the Inhabitants thereof) will conduce nothing to the general plan, as it is thought no part of the Cheat River runs nearer to the navigable part of the No. branch of Potomack than the Dunkers bottom does, which they add is about 25 Miles of good road. From the Dunkers bottom to Clarkes Town they estimate 35 Miles, and say the Tyger Valley fork of the Monongahla affords good navigation above the falls which is 7 Miles only from the Mouth, & is a Cateract of 25 feet.

[1] GW used Samuel Kinkade's ferry to cross the Cheat River (*Cash Memoranda,* DLC:GW; FAYETTE COUNTY STATE TAX, 566, 630).

[2] John Pierpont (d. 1795) settled here before the War of Independence and married Ann (Nancy) Morgan, daughter of Col. Zackquill Morgan (CALLAHAN [2], 34, n.12; AMBLER, 4–10).

[3] The 2,500 acres on the Little Kanawha lay 15 to 20 miles above the mouth of that river on the south side. William Crawford in Sept. 1774 offered GW two tracts in this area, one "of about 3000 Som od acres the other about 2500," and the following March he sent surveys of those lands to Mount Vernon (Crawford to GW, 20 Sept. 1774 and 6 Mar. 1775, DLC: GW). GW had only to enter the surveys with military land warrants in the county surveyor's office, but it was not done. The coming of the War of Independence put a stop to nearly all that sort of business for GW, and he seems to have been somewhat reluctant to take those tracts anyway (GW to Thomas Lewis, 1 Feb. 1784, and William Crawford to GW, 14 Nov. 1774, DLC:GW). Robert Rutherford, GW's friend and former French and Indian War comrade (see main entry for 2 Feb. 1771), obtained six grants on the Little Kanawha totaling 1,950 acres in 1785, but there is no record of one of 2,500 acres there for him (SIMS, 497).

The tract at the fork of the Ohio and the Little Kanawha rivers (now

Parkersburg, W.Va.) was to have been equally divided between Crawford and GW. Crawford originally surveyed this land for himself, but finding that the acreage to which he was entitled as a French and Indian War veteran would not cover the whole survey, he wrote GW 12 Nov. 1773 and proposed to split the tract with him if GW would apply some of his military warrants to the uncovered part (DLC:GW). GW agreed and had two warrants ready for his section of the land. However, Crawford for some reason was unable to get a warrant for his part, and rival claims to the land were soon discovered, a fact that apparently discouraged GW from pursuing the matter vigorously (Crawford to GW, 10 Jan. 1774 and 6 Mar. 1775, GW to Thomas Lewis, 1 Feb. 1784, and GW to John Harvie, 10 Feb. 1784, DLC: GW). Although Dr. John Briscoe (1717–1788) of Berkeley County and his sons may have entered a survey for this land, it was not granted to them, for Robert Thornton had apparently staked out a prior claim to 1,350 acres at the mouth of the Little Kanawha in 1773. Ten years later Alexander Parker of Pittsburgh bought out Thornton's claim for $50 and in 1787 patented the land in two tracts, one of 950 acres and one of 400 acres (DANDRIDGE, 60, 304; W.P.A. [5], 261; SIMS, 489).

[4] Morgantown lay about four miles southwest of Pierpont's house. Zackquill (Zackwell) Morgan (c.1735–1795) was born in Berkeley County, Va.; moved as a young man to southwestern Pennsylvania where he lived until 1771; and then settled at the site of Morgantown. With the formation of Monongalia County in 1776, he became the first sheriff and one of the first justices of the new county and a few months later was appointed county lieutenant. During 1778 he was suspended from the latter position and was court-martialed for the alleged murder of a Loyalist prisoner. Although subsequently acquitted of the charge, he ceased being county lieutenant before May 1780 (*Va. Council Jls.*, 1:234, 348, 2:143, 175; CALLAHAN [2], 43; VSP, 1:348). Morgan kept a tavern in Morgantown for many years (MORGAN [2], 193–220).

Among the other men who met with GW at Pierpont's house on this date may have been Albert Gallatin (1761–1849), later Thomas Jefferson's secretary of the Treasury. Young Gallatin was in the area at this time, trying to establish a store on the Monongahela River a few miles north of the Virginia-Pennsylvania line and attempting to speculate in lands. For his reminiscences of the meeting, told to a friend in old age, see ADAMS [3], 56–58.

[5] Bulltown, located on the south bank of the Little Kanawha River in present-day Braxton County, W.Va., was established as an Indian village about 1764 by the Delaware chief, Captain Bull, and a small group of followers. The Indian inhabitants were massacred in 1772 by white settlers who mistakenly blamed them for the murder of a nearby white family (MCWHORTER, 86–88; BULLTOWN, 1–8).

[6] Winding Ridge stretches across the Maryland-Pennsylvania line between Little Meadows and the Great Crossing of the Youghiogheny, intersecting Braddock's Road a short distance northwest of the line.

[7] Joseph Logston of Washington County, Md., lived near present-day Gorman, Md. (see entry for 26 Sept. 1784). He enrolled in the Washington County militia 28 Aug. 1776 (*Md. Geneal. Bull.*, 4 [1933], 17).

[8] Clarksburg, seat of Harrison County, Va. (now W.Va.).

[9] The Tygart Valley River runs east of the West Fork River, joining it at

present-day Fairmont, W.Va., to form the Monongahela River. Valley Falls, a series of cascades, lies about 12 miles above the mouth.

[10] These glades were apparently east of the Tygart Valley River, about four miles from present-day Grafton, W.Va., in the area drained by Glade and Swamp runs.

[11] The Cheat River flows through a deep gorge in the vicinity of Cooper's Rock, about eight miles due east of Morgantown. Chestnut Ridge, which was often called Laurel Hill, is on the northeast side of the gorge.

[12] Horseshoe Bottom is on a sharp bend of the Cheat River in present-day Tucker County, W.Va. A group of Germans settled there early in 1774 but left before the end of the year to escape the threat of Indian attacks. Returning two years later, they established a settlement at St. George about two miles downstream (MAXWELL, 19–21, 34–40).

25th. Having obtained the foregoing information, and being indeed some what discouraged from the acct. given of the passage of the Cheat river through the Laurel hill and also from attempting to return by the way of the Dunkers bottom, as the path it is said is very blind, & exceedingly grown up with briers, I resolved to try the other rout, along the New road to Sandy Creek; & thence by McCullochs path to Logstons; and accordingly set of before Sunrise.

Within 3 Miles I came to the river Cheat abt. 7 Miles from its Mouth at a ferry kept by one Ice;[1] of whom making enquiry, I learnt that he himself, had passed from the Dunkers bottom both in Canoes and with rafts—that a new Canoe which I saw at his Landing had come down the day before only, (the owner of which had gone to Sandy Creek) that the first rapid was about 1½ Miles above his ferry—that it might be between 50 and 100 yards thro' it—that from this to the next, might be a Mile, of good water—That these 2 rapids were much alike, & of the same extent; that to the next rapid, which was the worst of the three, it was about 5 Miles of smooth water—That the difficulty of passing these rapids lies more in the number of large Rocks which choak the river, and occasion the water not only (there being also a greater dissent here than else where) to run swift, but meandering thro' them, renders steerage dangerous by the sudden turnings—That from his ferry to the Dunkers bottom, along the river, is about 15 Miles; and in his opinion, there is room on one side or the other of it at each of the rapids for a Canal.

This acct. being given from the Mans own observation, who seemed to have no other meaning in what he asserted than to tell the truth, tho' he, like others, who for want of competent skill in these things cou'd not distinguish between real & imaginary difficulties, left no doubt on my Mind of the practicability of opening an easy passage by Water to the Dunker bottom.[2] The river at his house may be a hundred or more yards wide, & according to his acct. (which I believe is rather large) near a hundred miles by water to Fort Pitt.

The Road from Morgan Town, or Monongahela C[our]t House, is said to be good to this ferry—distance abt. 6 Miles. The dissent of the hill to the river is rather steep & bad and the assent from it, on the North side, is steep also tho short, and may be rendered much better. From the ferry the Laurel hill [Chesnut Ridge] is assended by an easy and almost imperceptible slope to its summit, thro' dry white oak Land. Along the top of it, the road continues for some distance, but is not so good, as the Soil is richer, deeper, & more stony, which inconveniences (for good roads) also attends the dissent on the East side, tho it is regular, & in no places steep. After crossing this hill the road is very good to the ford of Sandy Creek at one James Spurgeons, abt. 15 Miles from Ice's ferry.[3]

At the crossing of this Creek McCullochs path, which owes it origen to Buffaloes, being no other than their tracks from one lick to another & consequently crooked & not well chosen, strikes off from the New road which passes great Yohiogany 15 Miles further on, and enters Braddock road at the place before mentioned [east of Winding Ridge], at the distance of 22 Miles.

From Spurgeons to one Lemons, which is a little to the right of McCullochs path, is reckoned 9 Miles, and the way not bad;[4] but from Lemons to the entrance of the Yohiogany glades which is estimated 9 Miles more thro a deep rich Soil in some places, and a very rocky one in others, with steep hills & what is called the briery Mountain to cross is intolerable[5] but these [ascents] might be eased, & a much better way found if a little pains was taken to slant them.

At the entrance of the above glades I lodged this night, with no other shelter or cover than my cloak; & was unlucky enough to have a heavy shower of Rain. Our horses were also turned loose to cator for themselves having nothing to give them. From this place my guide (Lemon) informed me that the Dunkers bottom was not more than 8 Miles from us.

It may not be amiss to observe, that Sandy Creek has a fall within a few miles of its mouth of 40 feet, & being rapid besides, affords no navigation at all.

[1] Andrew Ice obtained a patent for 400 acres on the Cheat River during this year (SIMS, 474). The ferry was about six miles northeast of Morgantown.

[2] Before GW left Pierpont's house, he asked Samuel Hanway to view the Cheat between Ice's ferry and Dunkard's Bottom. On 26 Jan. 1785 Hanway reported to GW that "I Examin'd the falls of Cheat river agreeable to your request and find that it will be Imposible to affect a naviagation up it through the Laurell Hill." The best route for a road from the North Branch of the Potomac, he concluded, would be from Logston's place to the falls of Tygart Valley River (MnHi).

[3] James Spurgen moved to the Sandy Creek Glades from the Fort Cumberland area earlier this year and in 1785 received a grant for 400 acres on Big Sandy Creek. The ford was apparently near present-day Bruceton Mills, W.Va. (MORTON [2], 1:396; SIMS, 501).

[4] George Lemon appears in the 1782 Monongalia County census as refusing to give the number of persons in his household. In 1785 he was granted 355 acres on Crab Orchard Creek in the county (HEADS OF FAMILIES, VA., 36; SIMS, 479).

[5] Briery Mountain stretches across the eastern half of present-day Preston County, W.Va., running from the Cheat River near Rowlesburg northeast toward Cranesville, in the vicinity of which GW crossed today.

26th. Having found our Horses readily (for they nevr. lost sight of our fire) we started at the dawning of day, and passing along a small path much enclosed with weeds and bushes, loaded with water from the overnights rain, & the showers which were continually falling, we had an uncomfortable travel to one Charles friends, about 10 Miles; where we could get nothing for our horses, and only boiled Corn for ourselves.[1]

In this distance, excepting two or three places which abounded in stone, & no advantage taken of the hills (which were not large) we found the ground would admit an exceeding good Waggon road with a little causeying of some parts of the Glades; the ridges between being chiefly white oak land, intermixed with grit & Stone.

Part of these glades is the property of Govr. Johnson of Maryland who has settled two or three families of Palatines upon them.[2] These glades have a pritty appearance, resembling cultivated Lands & improved Meadows at a distance; with woods here and there interspersed. Some of them are rich, with a black and lively soil—others are of a stiffer, & colder Nature. All of them feel, very early, the effect of frost. The growth of them, is a grass not much unlike what is called fancy grass, without the variegated colours of it; much intermixed in places with fern and other weeds, as also with alder & other Shrubs. The Land between these glades is chiefly white oak, on a dry stony Soil. In places there are walnut & Crab tree bottoms, which are very rich. The glades are not so level as one would imagine. In general they rise from the small water courses which run through all of them to the ridges which seperate one from another—but they are highly beneficial to the circumjacent Country from whence the Cattle are driven to pasture in the Spring & recalled at Autumn.

A Mile before I came to Friends, I crossed the Great branch of Yohiogany, which is about 25 or 30 yards over; and impassable, according to his Acct., between that [crossing] and Braddocks road [at the Great Crossing] on acct. of the rapidity of the Water, quantity of stone, & Falls therein—but these difficulties, in the eyes of a proper examiner might be found altogether imaginary; and if so, the Navigation of the Yohiogany & No. Branch of Potomack may be brought within 10 Miles, & a good Waggon road betwn.; but then, the Yohiogany lyes altogether in the State of Pensylvania, whose inclination (regardless of the interest of that part which lyes west of the Laurel hill) would be opposed to the extension of their navigation; as it would be the inevitable means of withdrawing from them the trade of all their western territory.

The little Yohiogany[3] from Braddocks road [at the Little Crossing] to the Falls [of the Youghiogheny River] below the Turkey foot, or 3 forks, may, in the opinion of Friend, who is a great Hunter, & well acquainted with all the Waters, as well as hills, having lived in that Country and followed no other occupation for nine years, be made navigable and this, were it not for the reason just assigned, being within 22 Miles of Fort Cumberland, would open a very important door to the trade of that Country.

He is also of opinion that a very good road may be had from the Dunkers bottom to the No. Branch of Potomack, at or near where McCullochs path crosses it; and that the distance will not exceed 22 Miles, to pass by his house, i.e. 10 to the No. Branch, & 12 to the Dunkers bottom—half of which (10 or 11 Miles) will go through the glades, & white oak ridges which seperate them.

There will be an intervention of two hills in this road—the back bone near the [North] Branch[4] and the Briery Mountain near the [Dunkard's] Bottom, both of which may be easily passed in the lowest parts by judicious slants, & these with some Causeys in the richest & deepest parts of the glades will enable a common team to draw twenty hundred with ease from one place to the other.

From Friends I passed by a spring (distant 3 Miles) called Archy's, from a Man of that name[5]—crossed the backbone & descended into Ryans glade.[6] Thence by Joseph Logstons, & McCulloch's ford of the No. Branch, to old Mr. Thos. Logston's (the father of Joseph).[7] The way & distances as follow—to the foot of the back bone, about 5 Miles of very good ground for a road; being partly glady, and partly White Oak ridges—across the ridge to Ryans glade one Mile and half bad, the hill being steep & in places stony—to Joseph Logston's 1½ Miles very good going—to the No. Branch at McCullochs path 2 Miles—infamous road and to Thos. Logstons 4 more, partly pretty good, & in places very bad. But it has been observed before to what fortuitous circumstances the paths of this Country owe their being, & how much the ways may be better chosen by a proper investigation of it; & the distances from place to place reduced. This appeard evident from my own observation and from young Logston, who makes hunting his chief employment; and according to his own Acct. is acquainted with every hill & rivulet between the North Branch & the Dunkers bottom.

He asserts that from Ryan's glade to the No. branch, 2 Miles below the Mouth of Stony river (wch. is about 4 below McCullochs crossing) a very good road may be traced, and the distance not more than it is from the same place to the crossing last mentioned, which is a circumstance of importance as the No. Branch above its junction with Stony river (which of the two seems to contain most water) would hardly afford water for Navigation.

He agrees precisely with Charles Friend respecting the Nature of the road between the North Branch and the Dunkers bottom; but insists upon it that the distance will not exceed 20 Miles & that Friends ought to be left two Miles to the Westward. This may acct. for their difference of opinion; the latter wanting his House to be introduced as a stage and here it may be well to observe, that however knowing these people are, their accts. are to be received with great caution—compared with each other and these again with one's own observatns.; as private views are as prevalent in this, as any other Country; and are particularly exemplified in the article of Roads; which (where they have been marked) seem calculated more to promote individual interest, than the public good.

From the reputed distances, as I have given them from place to place between Monongahela Court House and the No. branch at McCullochs ford, & description of the Country over which I travelled, it should seem that Colo. Morgan and those with whom I had the meeting at Captn. Hanways are mistaken in two points—viz. measurement, & the goodness of road—They making the distance between these places only 40 Miles and the way good, whereas by my Acct. the first is computed 55 Miles and a part of the road very bad. Both however are easily accounted for; the rout being circuitous, & beasts, instead of Men, having traced it out. Altho' I was seldom favored with a sight of the Sun but handsomely besprinkled with rain the greater part of the way it was evident to me that from Pierpoints (Captn. Hanways Quartrs.) to the crossing of Sandy Creek, I rid in a No. Et. direction–from thence for many Miles South and afterwards South Easterly.

I could obtain no good Acct. of the Navigation of the No. Branch between McCulloch's crossing and Wills's Creek (or Fort Cumberland). Indeed there were scarce any persons of whom enquiries could be made, for, from Lemon's to old Logston's there is only Friend & young Logston living on the track I came and none on it for near 20 Miles below him–but in general I could gather from them, especially from Joseph Logston, who has (he says) hunted along the water course of the river that there is no fall in it–that from Fort Cumberland to the Mouth of Savage river the water being good is frequently made use of in its present State with Canoes and from thence upwards, is only rapid in places with loose Rocks which can readily be removed.

From the Mouth of Savage River the State of Maryland (as I was informed) were opening a road to their western boundary which was to be met by another which the Inhabitants of Monongahela County (in Virginia) were extending to the same place from the Dunkers bottom through the glades of Yohiogany making in the aggregate abt. 35 Miles. This road will leave Friends according to his Acct. a little to the Eastward & will upon the whole be a *good* road but not *equal* to the *one* which may be traced from the Dunkers bottom to the No. Branch at, or below the fork of it & Stony River.[8]

At this place–viz. Mr. Thos. Logston's–I met a brother of his, an intelligent man, who informed me that some years ago he had travelled from the Mouth of Carpernters Creek (now more generally known by the name of Dunlaps) a branch of Jacksons, which is the principal prong of James River to the Mouth of Howards Creek wch. emptys into the Greenbrier a large branch of New River abe. Great Kanhawa–that each river, at the Mouths of these Creeks is large & very competent for navigation–that the distance between them does not exceed 20 Miles and not a hill in the way.[9] If this be fact, and he asserts it positively, a communication with the western Country that way, if the falls in the Great Kanhawa (thro' the gauly Mountn.)[10] Can be rendered navigable will be as ready, perhaps more direct than any other for all the Inhabitants of the Ohio & its waters below the little Kanhawa and that these Falls are not so tremendous as some have represented I am inclined to believe from several Circumstances—one of which, in my mind, is conclusive—so far at least—as that they do not amount to a Cataract, and that is that Fish ascend them—it being agreed on all hands that the large Cats and other fish of the Ohio are to be met with in great abundance in the river above them.

[1] Charles Friend, a squatter on a 5,025-acre glades tract called Small Meadows, lived about 1½ miles southwest of present-day Oakland, Md. He had previously dwelt at three other locations in the Youghiogheny valley. About 1765 he and several brothers settled near present-day Friendsville, Md. Later he moved to the Turkey Foot settlement in Pennsylvania and then to Buffalo Marsh near present-day McHenry, Md., his last stop before coming to Small Meadows. Friend remained at Small Meadows until sometime in the 1790s when he went west, possibly to Missouri (FRIEND, 62; WESTERN MD., 292, n.4).

[2] GW's friend Thomas Johnson served as Maryland's first state governor 1777–79. In 1786 two patents on or near McCullough's Path northwest of present-day Oakland, Md., were granted to Johnson: one of 2,000 acres called Thomas and Ann, which had been surveyed for Johnson 5 Mar. 1774, and another of 1,200 acres called The Promised Land, which had been surveyed for James Brooks 11 April 1774 and subsequently acquired by Johnson (GARRETT COUNTY SURVEYS AND PATENTS, 118).

[3] GW is referring to the Little Youghiogheny River (now Casselman River) that flows into the Youghiogheny at present-day Confluence, Pa. Another Little Youghiogheny flows into the Youghiogheny near the point where GW crossed it today.

[4] Backbone Mountain is a high ridge that roughly parallels the upper part of the North Branch of the Potomac, stretching from the Savage River near present-day Bloomington, Md., southwest toward the Cheat River in the vicinity of present-day Parsons, W.Va.

[5] Archey's Spring lies a short distance south of present-day Loch Lynn Heights, Md. A settler named Archey or Archer built a cabin near here, but apparently it was now abandoned (WESTERN MD., 294, n.7).

[6] Ryan's Glade was probably the area around the headwaters of Glade Run, a tributary of the North Branch of the Potomac. Later the name was applied to an election district embracing the southernmost tip of present-day Garrett County, Md.

[7] Thomas Logston lived in Hampshire County, Va. (now Grant County, W.Va.) about halfway between McCullough's crossing (near present-day Gormania, W.Va.) and the Stony River, a tributary of the North Branch of the Potomac. In 1787 he obtained three patents totaling about 500 acres on Stony River (SIMS, 206).

[8] The Virginia General Assembly in October of this year and the Maryland General Assembly in November each appropriated money "to defray

one half of the expense of examining, surveying, cutting, clearing, improving, and keeping in repair, a proposed road from the waters of Potowmack river to the river Cheat, and, if necessary, to the Monongahela" (OLD STATE ROAD, 313; VA. COUNCIL JLS., 3:444; see entry for 3 July 1786).

[9] Jackson and Cowpasture rivers meet to form the James River near present-day Clifton Forge, Va. Dunlap Creek flows generally northeast through present-day Alleghany Couny, Va., to join the Jackson River at Covington, Va. Howard Creek in present-day Greenbrier County, W.Va., flows generally southwest, passing through White Sulfur Springs, W.Va., and entering the Greenbrier River near Caldwell, W.Va. Allegheny Mountain separates the two creeks.

[10] Gauley Mountain in present-day Fayette County, W.Va., lies between the Gauley and New rivers near the point where they meet to form the Kanawha River. The Kanawha falls are about two miles downstream from that junction.

27th. I left Mr. Logston's a little after day-break. At 4 Miles thro' bad road, occasioned by Stone, I crossed the Stony River; which, as hath been before observed, appears larger than the No. Branch. At ten Miles I had by an imperceptible rise, gained the summit of the Alligany Mountain and began to desend it where it is very steep and bad to the waters of Pattersons Creek which embraces those of New Creek.[1] Along the heads of these, & crossing the Main [Patterson's] Creek & Mountain bearing the same name (on the top of which at one Snails I dined)[2] I came to Colo. Abrahm. Hites at Fort pleasant on the South Branch about 35 Miles from Logstons a little before the Suns setting.[3]

My intention, when I set out from Logstons, was to take the Road to Rumney by one Parkers;[4] but learning from my guide (Joseph Logston) when I came to the parting paths at the foot of the Alligany (abt. 12 Miles) that it was very little further to go by Fort pleasant, I resolved to take that Rout as it might be more in my power on that part of the Branch to get information of the extent of its navigation than I should be able to do at Rumney.

[1] The headwaters of New Creek and of the North Fork of Patterson's Creek nearly coincide east of Allegheny Front in present-day Grant County, W.Va. New Creek roughly parallels the main branch of Patterson's Creek, flowing northeast to join the North Branch of the Potomac at present-day Keyser, W.Va. GW probably followed the North Fork of Patterson's Creek east through New Creek Mountain at Greenland Gap.

[2] William Snale (Snall) appears on the 1782 Hampshire County census list as the head of a household consisting of two white persons and on the one for 1784 as head of a household of four whites (HEADS OF FAMILIES, VA., 25, 70). Patterson's Creek Mountain generally parallels the upper waters of Patterson's Creek, separating them from the waters of the South Branch of the Potomac which lie to the east.

[3] Fort Pleasant (also called Fort Van Meter) was built on the river near present-day Old Fields, W.Va., in 1756 as a link in the chain of forts designed to protect the Virginia frontier during the French and Indian War. Although the fort apparently had been abandoned for many years, at least part of its "cabins, palisades, and blockhouses" still stood (KOONTZ, 139–40).

Abraham Hite (1729–1790), a son of Jost Hite, settled in this part of Hampshire County (now Hardy County, W.Va.) about 1762 when he obtained two grants in the area, including one of 110 acres on the South Branch of the Potomac. In succeeding years he received four more Hampshire grants and one in Kentucky. He apparently became county lieutenant of Hampshire about 1765 and represented the county in the House of Burgesses 1769–71. He was a member of the Virginia Convention of 1776, raised a company of Hampshire rangers during the early months of the War of Independence, and later served as a commissioner for purchasing Continental Army provisions in northwestern Virginia. Hite moved to Jefferson County, Ky., about 1788 (SIMS, 196; VA. COUNCIL JLS., 1:62, 2:65–66; SALLEE, 186–88).

[4] GW traveled part of this more northerly route 10 Oct. 1770. Several Parkers lived west of Romney at this time on Mill, Patterson's and New creeks (SIMS, 217–18; HEADS OF FAMILIES, VA., 26–27, 70–71).

28th. Remained at Colo. Hite's all day to refresh myself and rest my Horses, having had a very fatieguing journey thro' the Mountains, occasioned not more from the want of accomodation & the real necessaries of life than the showers of Rain which were continually falling & wetting the bushes—the passing of which, under these circumstances was very little better than swimming of rivulets.

From Colo. Hite, Colo. Josh. Neville[1] & others, I understood that the navigation of the South Branch in its present State, is made use of from Fort pleasant to its Mouth—that the most difficult part in it, and that would not take £100 to remove the obstruction (it being only a single rift of rocks across in one place) is 2 Miles below the old Fort. That this [distance to the mouth of the river], as the road goes, is 40 Miles; by water more and that, from any thing they knew, or believe to the contrary, it might at this moment be used 50 Miles higher, if any benefits were to result from it.[2]

[1] Joseph Neville (1740–1819) of Hampshire County became a justice of the county in 1772, served as one of its burgesses 1773–75, and represented it in the Virginia Convention that met 1 Dec. 1775. A military contractor and recruiter for the state during the early part of the War of Independence, he was appointed county lieutenant for Hampshire in 1781. In the fall of 1782 he acted for Virginia in running the temporary boundary line between western Pennsylvania and western Virginia, a line that he helped to establish permanently nearly three years later (JOHNSTON [4], 5:220; VSP, 2:625, 3:283; VA. COUNCIL JLS., 2:419, 3:228, 421, 474).

[2] GW traveled part of the South Branch both above and below the site of Fort Pleasant 27 Mar.–10 April 1748 as a young surveyor for Lord Fairfax.

29th. Having appointed to join Doctr. Craik and my Baggage at Colo. Warner Washington's, but finding it required only one day more to take the rout of Mr. Thos. Lewis's (near Stanton) from whose Office I wanted some papers to enable me to prosecute my ejectments of those who had possessed themselves of my Land in the County of Washington, State of Pensylvania; [1] and that I might obtain a more distinct acct. of the Communication between Jackson's River & the green Brier; I sent my Nephew Bushrod Washington (who was of my party) to that place [Warner Washington's] to request the Doctr. to proceed [to Mount Vernon] & accompanied by Captn. Hite, son to the Colonel,[2] I set out for Rockingham in which County Mr. Lewis now lives since the division of Augusta.

Proceeding up the So. fork of the So. Branch about 24 Miles—bated our Horses, & obtained something to eat ourselves, at one Rudiborts.[3] Thence taking up a branch & following the same about 4 Miles thro' a very confined & rocky path, towards the latter part of it, we ascended a very steep point of the So. Branch Mountain, but which was not far across, to the No. fork of Shanondoah; [4] down which by a pretty good path which soon grew into a considerable road, we discended until we arrived at one Fishwaters in Brocks gap, about Eight Miles from the foot of the Mountain—12 from Rudiborts & 36 from Colonl. Hites. This gap is occasioned by the above branch of Shannondoahs running thro the Cacapehon & North Mountains for about 20 Miles and affords a good road, except being Stony & crossing the water often.[5]

[1] Thomas Lewis (1718–1790), a brother of GW's deceased friend Andrew Lewis, lived on the South Fork of the Shenandoah River about 20 miles northeast of Staunton, Va. He was surveyor and a justice of Augusta County from its formation in 1745 until 1777 when his home became part of newly created Rockingham County (WAYLAND [2], 224; AREY, 26–27, 74). Now surveyor of Rockingham, he nevertheless retained records of his tenure as Augusta County surveyor. In response to a letter of 1 Feb. 1784 from GW (DLC:GW), Lewis had assured him that he had "in Safe keeping" the warrants and assignments for both the Millers Run land and a tract on the Ohio known as "the round bottom," which GW also claimed (Lewis to GW, 24 Feb. 1784, ViMtV).

Staunton, seat of Augusta County, had been laid off by Lewis 1747–48 and had been established by the General Assembly in 1761 (HARRISON [7], 140–41).

[2] Abraham Hite, Jr. (1755–1832), enlisted in the Virginia Continental line as a second lieutenant 15 Nov. 1776. He reached the rank of captain in April 1779 and was a regimental paymaster after 1778. He was among the Virginia troops taken prisoner by the British at the fall of Charleston, S.C., 12 May 1780, but was soon paroled. Before the war Hite had explored and surveyed lands in Kentucky and after the war settled there, apparently preceding his father (HILLIER, 78, 89–96; HEITMAN [2], 292).

[3] Johann Reinhart Rohrbach (d. 1821), of Hampshire County, lived on the South Fork of the South Branch of the Potomac near the mouth of Rohrbaugh Run, about four miles north of the present-day boundary between Hardy and Pendleton counties, W.Va. He arrived in Philadelphia from the Palatinate or from Switzerland in 1749 and lived in Berks County, Pa., before moving to the South Fork about 1767. On Virginia records his name often appears as John Rorebaugh, John Roraback, or John Rohrbaugh (ROHRBAUGH, 332–39).

The South Fork (also called the Moorefield River) joins the South Branch of the Potomac near present-day Moorefield, W.Va.

[4] GW followed Rohrbaugh Run southeast to South Branch Mountain (now Shenandoah Mountain) and after crossing it, continued southeast along Overly Run, Bennett Run, or Crab Run to the North Fork of the Shenandoah River near present-day Bergton, Va.

[5] John Fitzwater, of Rockingham County, lived about two miles southeast of present-day Bergton, Va., "at a place called the Slippery Ford," where in 1771 he had bought 130 acres of land (CHALKLEY, 3:513; WAYLAND [2], 198). A captain in the Rockingham County militia during the War of Independence, he also served the county as a justice 1778–85 (GWATHMEY, 276; VA. COUNCIL JLS., 3:460).

Brocks Gap, located a short distance west of present-day Cootes Store, Va., is an opening in Little North Mountain through which the North Fork of the Shenandoah River flows into the broad level valley beyond. However, in the eighteenth century the name was also applied to the gorge above the gap, including Fitzwater's place about 11 miles upstream. This gorge is flanked on the east by Church Mountain, an extension of Big North Mountain, and on the west by Hughs Mountain.

30th. Set out early—Captn. Hite returning home and travelled 11 or 12 Miles along the River, until I had passed thro' the gap. Then bearing more westerly by one Bryan's [1]—the widow Smiths [2] and one Gilberts,[3] I arrived at Mr. Lewis's about Sundown, after riding about 40 Miles—leaving Rockingham C[our]t House to my right about 2 Miles.[4]

[1] From Brocks Gap, GW rode southwest for several miles along the base of Little North Mountain and then turned southeast to cross Linville Creek about two miles northeast of present-day Edom, Va. Several Bryans had settled in the Linville Creek area, and two of their homes stood west of the creek on the road which GW traveled today. John Bryan, who apparently settled there about 1744, built a house near the creek, while Thomas Bryan, who bought an adjoining 300 acres in 1762, had a house about a quarter of a mile farther west (WAYLAND [3], 10, 14–15, 29–30, 52).

[2] Jane Harrison Smith (1735–1796), widow of Daniel Smith (1724–1781), lived at Smithland plantation about two miles northeast of Harrisonburg, Va. The eldest daughter of Capt. Daniel Harrison, she married Smith in 1751 and subsequently gave birth to at least 12 children. Her husband was a justice of Augusta County until 1777 and of Rockingham County after that date. He served as a captain at the Battle of Point Pleasant in 1774, became county lieutenant of Rockingham in Mar. 1781, and died in the fall of that year from injuries sustained when his horse threw him during a militia review in celebration of the Yorktown victory (HARRISON [7], 200, 245, 318–19).

[3] Felix Gilbert for many years kept a store near Cub Run about five miles southeast of Harrisonburg. Although an Augusta County justice as early as 1763, he did not become a Rockingham justice when the new county was formed. In May 1778 the Rockingham County court "convicted him of speaking treasonable words" against the Patriot cause (CHALKLEY, 2:364). He apparently moved to Wilkes County, Ga., about 1786 after empowering an agent to collect the many debts owed him in Rockingham (John Preston to Francis Preston, 26 Dec. 1786, PRESTON, 47; WAYLAND [2], 219).

[4] The first permanent courthouse for Rockingham County was built at Harrisonburg 1780–81 (TERRELL, 42–43).

[October]

October 1st. Dined at Mr. Gabriel Jones's,[1] not half a mile from Mr. Lewis's, but seperated by the South fork of Shannondoah; which is between 80 and a hundred yards wide, & makes a respectable appearance altho' little short of 150 Miles from its confluence with Potomack River; and only impeded in its navigation by the rapid water & rocks which are between the old bloomery[2] and Keys's ferry; and a few other ripples; all of which might be easily removed and the navigation according to Mr. Lewis's account, extended at least 30 Miles higher than where he lives.

I had a good deal of conversation with this Gentleman on the Waters, and trade of the Western Country; and particularly with respect to the navigation of the Great Kanhawa and it's communication with James, & Roanoke Rivers.

His opinion is, that the easiest & best communication between the Eastern & Western Waters is from the North branch of Potomack to Yohiogany or Cheat River; and ultimately that the Trade between the two Countries will settle in this Channel. That altho James River has an easy & short communication from the Mouth of Carpenters or Dunlaps Creek to the Greenbriar which in distance & kind of Country is exactly as Logston described them, yet, that the passage of the New River, abe.

Gabriel Jones, "The Valley Lawyer," by Edward C. Bruce, after a painting by Gilbert Stuart. (Miss Louisa M. Crawford)

Kanhawa, thro' the gauly Mountain from every acct. he has had of it, now is, and ever will be attended with considerable difficulty, if it should not prove impracticable. The Fall he has understood, altho it may be short of a Cateract, or perpendicular tumble, runs with the velocity of a stream discending a Mountain, and is besides very Rocky & closely confined between rugged hills. He adds, that from all appearance, a considerable part of the Water with which the River above abounds, sinks at, or above this rapid or fall, as the quantity he says, from report, is greatly diminished. However, as it is not to his own observations, but report these accts. are had, the real difficulty in surmounting the obstructions here described may be much less than are apprehended; wch. supposition is well warranted by the ascention of the Fish.

Mr. Lewis is of opinion that if the obstructions in this River can be removed, that the easiest communication of all, would be by the Roanoke, as the New River and it are within 12 Miles, and an excellent Waggon road between them and no difficulty that ever he heard of, in the former, to hurt the inland Navigation of it.

[1] Gabriel Jones (1724–1806), an able but hot-tempered lawyer given to outbursts of profanity, had long been prominent in Shenandoah Valley affairs. He studied law in England and returned to Virginia in the 1740s. He was appointed king's attorney for Frederick County in 1744 and for Augusta Country in 1746, making him thereby responsible for prosecuting public suits

in much of western Virginia during the next three decades. To his contemporaries he became known as "the Valley Lawyer" (GRIGSBY, 2:16–19; BLUE COAT BOYS, 44–45; BARTON, 19–22). He also served the Shenandoah counties as a burgess at various times, representing Frederick 1748–54, Hampshire 1754–55 and 1758–61, and Augusta 1756–58 and 1769–71. It was due in part to Jones's influence and activity that GW was first elected to the House of Burgesses from Frederick County in 1758 (Jones to GW, 6 July 1758; DLC:GW; GW to Jones, 29 July 1758, PHi). Jones lived in Frederick County near present-day Kernstown, Va., from 1747 to about 1753, when he moved to Augusta County, taking up residence at the place where GW visited him today, about 2½ miles down the South Fork of the Shenandoah from present-day Port Republic. His move may have been prompted by the fact that Thomas Lewis and another neighbor, John Madison, were both married to sisters of Jones's wife, Margaret Strother Morton Jones (d. 1822). After 1777, when Jones's home passed into Rockingham County, he became prosecuting attorney for the new county, serving until 1795 (WAYLAND [4], 350–51; WAYLAND [2], 220–23, 226).

At Gabriel Jones's home today GW met Jones's son-in-law, John Harvie (1743–1807), register of the Virginia land office 1780–91 (HESTER, 4, 32). GW had corresponded frequently with Harvie earlier this year about warrants and surveys on the Ohio and on Millers Run (GW to Harvie, 10, 29 Feb., and 18 Mar. 1784 and 19 Mar. 1785, and Harvie to GW, 21 Feb., 12 and 14 April 1784, DLC:GW).

[2] Bloomery, W.Va. See entry for 9 May 1760.

2d. I set off very early from Mr. Lewis's who accompanied me to the foot of the blew ridge at Swift run gap,[1] 10 Miles, where I bated and proceeded over the Mountain. Dined at a pitiful house 14 Miles further where the roads to Fredericksburgh (by Orange C[our]t House) & that to Culpeper Court House fork.[2] Took the latter, tho in my judgment Culpeper Court House was too much upon my right for a direct Course. Lodged at a Widow Yearlys 12 Miles further where I was hospitably entertained.[3]

[1] Swift Run Gap, located about seven miles southeast of present-day Elkton, Va., long provided settlers and traders a convenient route across the Blue Ridge Mountains. The Virginia General Assembly authorized the building of a road through the gap in 1765 and approved its repair in 1772 and 1789 (HENING, 8:152, 548, 13:82–83).

[2] Traveling southeast from Swift Run Gap, GW passed through the western part of Orange County (now Greene County) and then turned northeast to cross the Rapidan River into the western part of Culpeper County (now Madison County). The Orange County Court House was at the site of the present-day county seat, Orange, Va., and the Culpeper County Court House was at the site of its present-day seat, Culpeper, Va.

[3] WIDOW YEARLYS: probably Jane Paschal Early, widow of Joseph Early (c.1740–1783) of Culpeper County, an active Baptist who served as a lieutenant in the 5th Virginia Regiment during the War of Independence. She lived with her seven children about four miles southwest of present-day

Madison, Va. According to a family tradition, GW gave a watch to one of the children during his stay (EARLY, 205–6).

3d. Left Quarters before day, and breakfasted at Culpeper Court house which was estimated 21 Miles, but by bad direction I must have travelled 25, at least.[1] Crossed Normans ford[2] 10 Miles from the Court Ho[use] and lodged at Captn. John Ashbys[3] occasioned by other bad directions, which took me out of the proper road, which ought to have been by Elk run Church[4] 3 or 4 Miles to the right.

[1] GW took his breakfast at "Kemps" (LEDGER D, 200).

[2] Norman's ford on the Rappahannock River lay between Culpeper and Fauquier counties, about two miles south of present-day Remington. Isaac Norman, for whom the ford was named, obtained a patent on the Culpeper side in 1726 and was later bought out by Robert "King" Carter, whose son Charles Carter of Cleve began public ferry service at the ford in 1736. Charles's son Landon Carter now owned the land on both shores and was planning a town to be called Carolandville for the Fauquier side. The General Assembly established the town in Oct. 1785, but it was stillborn, never existing except on paper (HARRISON [1], 500, n.37; HENING, 4:531, 10:365, 12:217).

[3] John Ashby, whom GW had visited on the Shenandoah River 12–14 Mar. 1748, bought land on Licking Run in southern Fauquier Couny 28 Nov. 1757 and moved there about 1760 (BERRY'S FERRY, 12; REESE, 11–34).

[4] Elk Run Church, located on the headwaters of Elk Run in southern Fauquier County, was one of two churches serving Hamilton Parish. A large, handsome brick building finished in 1769, it had replaced an earlier wooden structure on the same site. Nevertheless, it proved to be poorly situated for the shifting population patterns of the ensuing years, and like many Anglican churches, it was dealt a severe blow by the dissolution of the established church during the War of Independence. By 1811 the building was abandoned and falling into ruin, and it eventually disappeared almost completely (MEADE [1], 2:216–17; HARRISON [1], 296–97; GROOME [3], 257–58).

4th. Notwithstanding a good deal of rain fell in the night and the continuance of it this morning (which lasted till about 10 Oclock) I breakfasted by Candlelight, and Mounted my horse soon after day break; and having Captn. Ashby for a guide thro' the intricate part of the Road (which ought, tho' I missed it, to have been by Prince William old Court Ho[use])[1] I arrived at Colchester, 30 Miles, to Dinner; and reached home before Sun down;[2] having travelled on the same horses since the first day of September by the computed distances 680 Miles.

And tho' I was disappointed in one of the objects which induced me to undertake this journey namely to examine into the situation quality and advantages of the Land which I hold upon

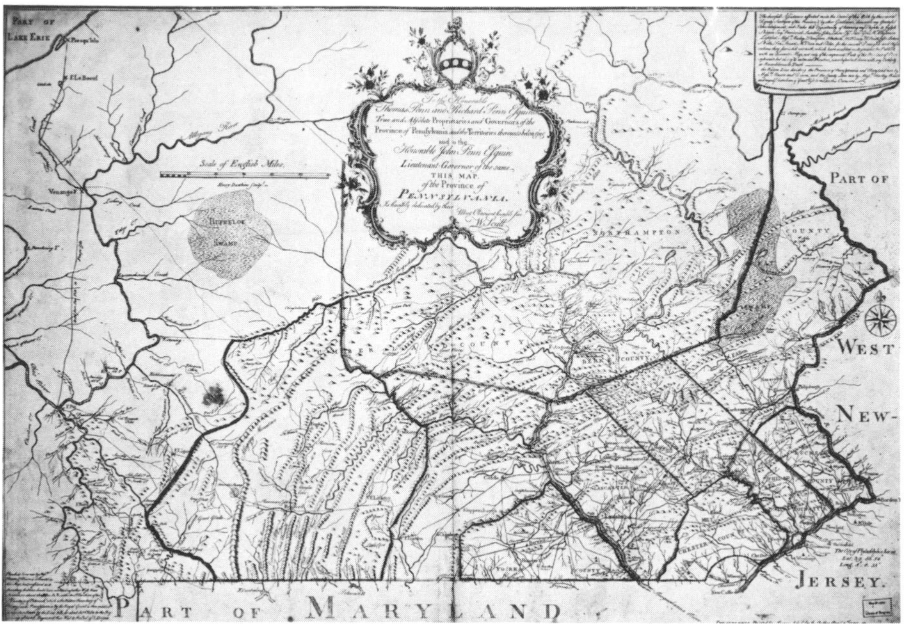

Scull's 1770 map of Pennsylvania, used by Washington. (Map Division, Library of Congress)

the Ohio and Great Kanhawa and to take measures for rescuing them from the hands of Land Jobbers & Speculators—who I had been informed regardless of my legal & equitable rights, Patents, &ca.; had enclosed them within other Surveys & were offering them for Sale at Philadelphia and in Europe. I say notwithstanding this disappointment, I am well pleased with my journey, as it has been the means of my obtaining a knowledge of facts—coming at the temper & disposition of the Western Inhabitants and making reflections thereon, which, otherwise, must have been as wild, incoher[en]t, & perhaps as foreign from the truth, as the inconsistencys of the reports which I had received even from those to whom most credit seemed due, generally were.

These reflections remain to be summed up.

The more then the Navigation of Potomack is investigated, & duely considered, the greater the advantages arising from them appear.

The South, or principal branch of Shannondoah at Mr. Lewis's is, to traverse the river, at least 150 Miles from its mouth; all of which, except the rapids between the Bloomery and Keys's ferry, now is, or very easily may be made navigable for inland Craft, and extended 30 Miles higher. The South Branch of Potomack is already navigated from its Mouth to Fort Pleasant; which, as the road goes, is 40 computed Miles; & the only difficulty in the way (and that a very trifling one) is just below the latter, where the River is hemmed in by the hills or Mountains on each side. From hence, in the opinion of Colo. Joseph Neville and others, it may, at the most trifling expense imaginable, be made navigable 50 Miles higher.

To say nothing then of the smaller Waters, [of the Potomac River], such as Pattersons Creek, Cacapehon [Cacapon River], Opeckon [Opequon Creek] &ca.; which are more or less Navigable; and of the branches on the Maryland side, these two alone (that is the South Branch & Shannondoah) would afford water transportation for all that fertile Country between the blew ridge and the Alligany Mountains; which is immense, but how trifling when viewed upon that immeasurable scale which is inviting our attention!

The Ohio River embraces this Commonwealth [Virginia] from its Northern, almost to its Southern limits. It is now, our western boundary & lyes nearly parallel to our exterior, & thickest settled Country.

Into this river French Creek, big bever Creek, Muskingham, Hockhocking, Scioto, and the two Miames (in its upper region) and many others (in the lower) pour themselves from the westward through one of the most fertile Country's of the Globe; by a long inland navigation; which, in its present state, is passable for Canoes and such other small craft as has, hitherto, been made use of for the Indian trade.

French Creek, down whh. I have myself come to Venango, from a lake near its source, is 15 Miles from Prisque Isle on lake Erie; and the Country betwn. quite level.[3] Both big bever Creek and Muskingham, communicate very nearly with Cayahoga; which runs into lake Erie; the portage with the latter (I mean Muskingham) as appears by the maps, is only one mile; and by many other accts. very little further; and so level between, that the Indians and Traders, as is affirmed, always drag their Canoes from one river to the other when they go to War—to hunt, or trade.[4] The great Miame, which runs into the Ohio, communicates with a river of the same name, as also with Sandusky, which empty themselves into lake Erie, by short and easy Portages.[5] And all of these are so many channels through which not only the produce of the New States, contemplated by Congress, but the trade of *all* the lakes, quite to that of the Wood,[6] may be conducted according to my information, and judgment—at least by one of the routs, thro' a shorter, easier, and less expensive communication than either of those which are now, or have been used with Canada, New Y[or]k or New Orleans.

That this may not appear an assertion, or even an opinion unsupported, I will examine matters impartially, and endeavor to state facts.

Detroit is a point, thro which the Trade of the Lakes Huron, & all those above it, must pass, if it centres in any State of the Union; or goes to Canada; unless it should pass by the River Outawais, which disgorge's itself into the St. Lawrence at Montreal and which necessity only can compel; as it is, from all accts., longer and of more difficult Navigation than the St. Lawrence itself.[7]

To do this, the Waters which empty into the Ohio on the East side, & which communicate nearest & best with those which run into the Atlantic, must also be delineated.

These are Monongahela and its branches, viz., Yohiogany & Cheat and the little and great Kanhawas; and Greenbrier which emptys into the latter.

The first (unfortunately for us)[8] is within the jurisdiction of Pensylvania from its mouth to the fork of Cheat indeed 2 Miles higher—as (which is more to be regreted) the Yohiogany also is, till it crosses the line of Maryland; these Rivers, I am perswaded, afford *much* the shortest routs from the Lakes to the tide water of the Atlantic but are not under our controul; being subject to a power whose interest is opposed to the extension of their navigation, as it would be the inevitable means of withdrawing from Philadelphia all the trade of that part of its western territory, which lyes beyond the Laurel hill—Though any attempt of that Government to restrain it I am equally well perswaded, w[oul]d cause a seperation of their territory; there being sensible men among them who have it in contemplation at this moment—but this by the by. The little Kanhawa, which stands next in order, & by Hutchins's table of distances (between Fort Pit and the Mouth of the River Ohio)[9] is 184½ Miles below the Monongahela, is navigable between 40 and 50 Miles up, to a place called Bulls Town. Thence there is a Portage of 9½ Miles to the West fork of Monongahela. Thence along the same to the Mouth of Cheat River, and up it to the Dunker bottom; from whence a portage may be had to the No. branch of Potomack.

Next to the little is the great Kanhawa; which by the above Table is 98½ Miles still lower down the Ohio. This is a fine Navigable river to the Falls; the practicability of opening which,

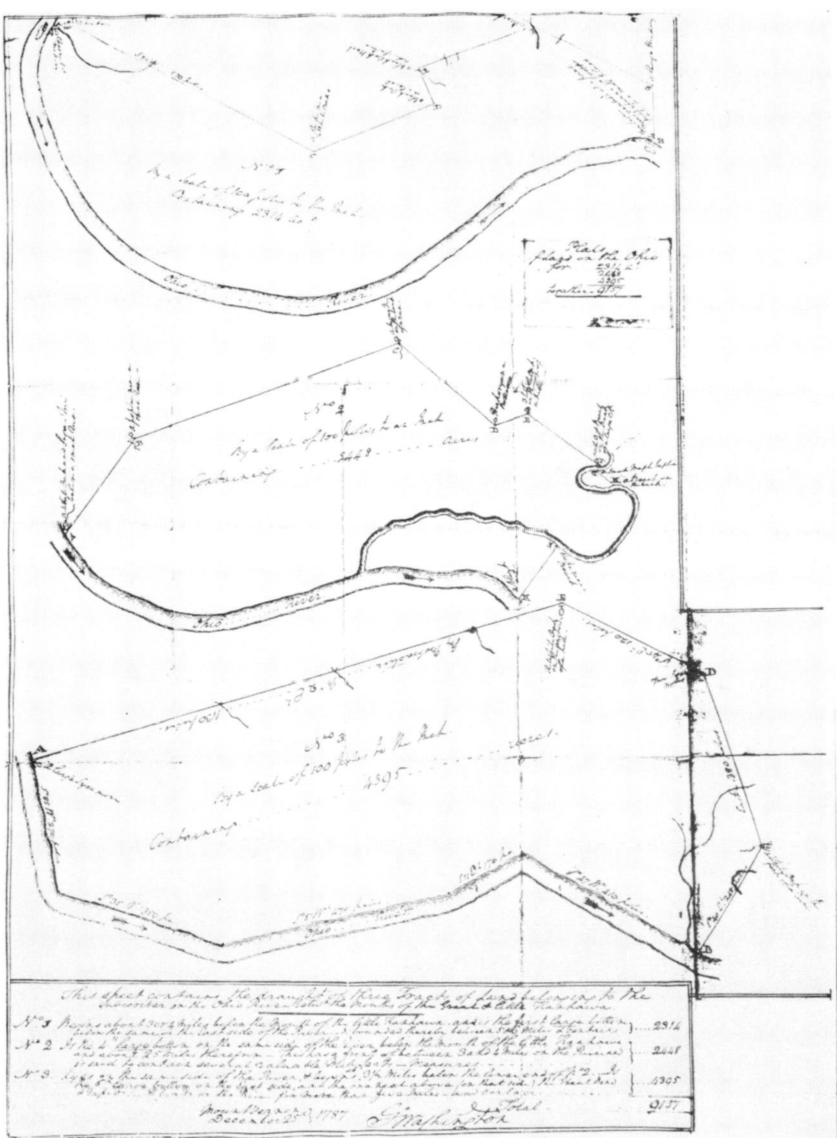

Washington's map, drawn in 1787, of three tracts of his land on the Ohio River between Great and Little Kanawha rivers. From *George Washington Atlas,* Washington, D.C., 1932. (Rare Book Department, University of Virginia Library)

seems to be little understood; but most assuredly ought to be investigated.

These then are the ways by which the produce of that Country; & the peltry & fur trade of the Lakes may be introduced into this State [Virginia]; & into Maryld.; which stands upon similar ground. There are ways, more difficult & expenceve indeed by which they can also be carried to Philadelphia—all of which, with the rout to Albany, & Montreal, and the distances by Land, and Water, from place to place, as far as can be ascertained by the best Maps now extant—by actual Surveys made since the publication of them and the information of intelligent persons—will appear as follow—from Detroit—which is a point as has been observed as unfavorable for us to compute from (being upon the North Western extremity of the United [States] territory) as any beyond Lake Erie can be:

viz.—

From Detroit to Alexandria
is

To Cayahoga River	125	Miles
Up the same to the Portage	60	
Portage to Bever C[ree]k	8	
Down Bever C[ree]k to the Ohio	85	
Up the Ohio to Fort Pitt	25	
		303
The Mouth of Yohiogany	15	
Falls of Ditto[10]	50	
Portage	1	
Three forks or Turkey foot	8	
Fort Cumberld. or Wills Creek	30	
Alexandria	200	
		304
Total		607
To Fort Pitt—as above		303
The Mouth of Cheat River	75	
Up it, to the Dunker bottom	25	
North branch of Potomack	20	
Fort Cumberland	40	
Alexandria	200	
		360
To Alexanda. by this Rout		663

From Detroit to Alexandria avoiding Pensylvania [11]

To the Mo[uth] of Cayahoga		125 Miles
The Carrying place with Muskingham river	54	
Portage	1	
The Mo[uth] of Muskingham	192	
The little Kanhawa	12	
		384
Up the same	40	
Portage to the West Bra.[12]	10	
		50
Down Monongahela to Cheat	80	
Up Cheat to the Dunker Bottm.	25	
Portage to the No. bra. Potomk.	20	
Fort Cumberland	40	
Alexandria	200	
		365
Total by this Rout		799

From Detroit to Richmond

		Miles
To the Mouth of the little Kanhawa as above		384
The Great Kanhawa by Hutchns's Table of distances	98½	
The Falls of the Kanhawa from information	90	
A portage (suppe.)	10	
The Mouth of Green brier & up in to the Portage	50	
Portage to James R[ive]r	33	
		281
Richmond		175
Total		840

Note–This rout *may be* more incorrect than either of the foregoing as I had only the Maps, and vague information for the Portages and for the distances from the Mouth of the Kanhawa to the Carrying place with Jacksons (that is James) river and the length of that River from the Carrying place to Richmond. The length of the carrying place above is also taken from the Map tho' from Information one would have called it not more than 20 Miles.

From Detroit to Philadelphia is

		Miles
To Presqu' Isle		245
Portage to Le beauf	15	
Down french Creek to Venan[go]	75	
Along the Ohio to Toby's Creek [13]	25	
		115
To the head spring of Do.	45	
By a Strait line to the nearest Water of Susque[hanna] [14]	15	
Down the same to the West branch	50	
Fort Augusta at the Fork [15]	125	
Mackees (or MacKoneys) C[ree]k [16]	12	
Up this	25	
By a strait line to Schuylkl.	15	
Reading	32	
Philadelphia	62	
		381
Total		741
By another rout–		
To Fort Pitt as before		303
Up the Ohio to Tobys C[ree]k		95
Thence to Phila. as above		381
Total		779

Note–The distances of places from the Mouth of Tobys Creek to Philada. are taken wholly from a comparitive view of Evans's and Sculls Maps.[17] The number, and length of the Portages, are not attempted to be given with greater exactness than these and for want of more competent knowledge, they are taken by a strait line between the sources of the different waters which by the Maps have the nearest communication with each other. Consequently, these Routs, if there is any truth in the Maps, must be longer than the given distances–particularly in the Portages, or Land part of the Transportation, because no road among Mountns. can be strait or waters navigable to their fountain heads.

From Detroit to Albany is

To Fort Erie, at the No. end of Lake Erie	350	
Fort Niagara–18 Miles of wch. is Land transpn.[18]	30	
		380

Oswego[19]		175
Fall of Onondaga River[20]	12	
Portage	1	
Oneida Lake–by Water[21]	40	
Length of Do. to Wood C[ree]k[22]	18	
Wood C[ree]k very small and Crooked	25	
Portage to Mohawk	1	
		97
Down it to the Portage	60	
Portage[23]	1	
Schenectady	55	
Portage to Albany[24]	15	
		131
In all		783
To the City of New York		160
Total		943

From Detroit to Montreal is

To Fort Niagara as above		380
North end of Lake Ontario	225	
Oswegatche[25]	60	
Montreal–very rapid	110	
		395
In all		775
To Quebec		180
Total		955

Admitting the preceding Statement, which as has been observed is given from the best and most authentic Maps and papers in my possession–from information and partly from observation, to be tolerably just, it would be nugatory to go about to prove that the Country within, and bordering upon the Lakes Erie, Huron, & Michigan would be more convenient when they come to be settled–or that they would embrace with avidity our Markets, if we should remove the obstructions which are at present in the way to them.

It may be said, because it has been said, & because there are some examples of it in proof, that the Country of Kentucke, about the Falls, and even much higher up the Ohio, have carried flour and other Articles to New Orleans–but from whence has it proceeded? Will any one who has ever calculated the difference between Water & Land transportation wonder at this? Especially in an infant settlement where the people are poor and weak handed and pay more regard to their ease than to loss of time, or any other circumstance?

Hitherto, the people of the Western Country having had no excitements to Industry, labour very little; the luxuriency of the Soil, with very little culture, produces provisions in abundance. These supplies the wants of the encreasing population and the Spaniards, when pressed by want have given high prices for flour. Other articles they reject: & at times (contrary I think to sound policy) shut their ports against them altogether—but let us open a good communication with the Settlemts. west of us—extend the inland Navigation as far as it can be done with convenience and shew them by this means, how easy it is to bring the produce of their Lands to our Markets, and see how astonishingly our exports will be encreased; and these States benefitted in a commercial point of view—wch. alone, is an object of such Magnitude as to claim our closest attention—but when the subject is considered in a political point of view, it appears of much greater importance.

No well informed Mind need be told, that the flanks and rear of the United territory are possessed by other powers, and formidable ones too—nor how necessary it is to apply the cement of interest to bind all parts of it together, by one indissolvable band—particularly the Middle States with the Country immediately back of them. For what ties let me ask, should we have upon those people; and how entirely unconnected shod. we be with them if the Spaniards on their right, or Great Britain on their left, instead of throwing stumbling blocks in their way as they now do, should envite their trade and seek alliances with them? What, when they get strength which will be sooner than is generally imagined (from the emigration of Foreigners who can have no predeliction for us, as well as from the removal of our own Citizens) may be the consequence of their having formed such connections and alliances, requires no uncommon foresight to predict.

The Western Settlers—from my own observation—stand as it were on a pivet—the touch of a feather would almost incline them any way. They looked down the Mississipi until the Spaniards (very impoliticly I think for themselves) threw difficulties in the way, and for no other reason that I can conceive than because they glided gently down the stream, without considering perhaps the tedeousness of the voyage back, & the time necessary to perform it in; and because they have no other means of coming to us but by a long land transportation, & unimproved roads.

A combination of circumstances make the present conjuncture more favorable than any other to fix the trade of the Western Country to our Markets. The jealous & untoward disposition of the Spaniards on one side, and the private views of some individuals, coinciding with the policy of the Court of G. Britain on the other, to retain the Posts of Oswego, Niagara, Detroit &ca. (which tho' done under the letter of the treaty is certainly an infraction of the Spirit of it, & injurious to the Union) may be improved to the greatest advantage by this State [Virginia] if she would open her Arms, & embrace the means which are necessary to establish it. The way is plain & the expence, comparitively speaking deserves not a thought, so great would be the prize. The Western Inhabitants would do their part towards accomplishing it. Weak as they now are, they would, I am perswaded, meet us half way rather than be *driven* into the arms of, or be in any wise dependent upon, foreigners; the consequence of which would be, a seperation, or a War.

The way to avoid both, happily for us, is easy, and dictated by our clearest interests. It is to open a wide door, and make a smooth way for the produce of that Country to pass to our Markets before the trade may get into another channel. This, in my judgment, would dry up the other sources; or, if any part should flow down the Mississipi, from the Falls of the Ohio, in Vessels which may be built—fitted, for Sea & sold with their cargoes the proceeds I have no manner of doubt, will return this way; & that it is better to prevent an evil than to rectify a mistake none can deny; commercial connections, of all others, are most difficult to dissolve—if we wanted proof of this look to the avidity with which we are renewing, after a *total* suspension of Eight years our corrispondence with Great Britain; So, if we [Virginians] are supine; and suffer without a struggle the Settlers of the Western Country to form commercial connections with the Spaniards, Britons, or with any of the States in the Union we shall find it a difficult matter to dissolve them altho a better communication should, thereafter, be presented to them. Time only could effect it; such is the force of habit!

Rumseys discovery of working Boats against stream by mechanical powers principally, may not only be considered as a fortunate invention for these States in general but as one of those circumstances which have combined to render the present epocha favorable above all others for securing (if we are disposed to avail ourselves of them) a large portion of the produce of the Western Settlements, and of the Fur and Peltry of the Lakes, also—the importance of which alone, if there were no political considerations in the way, is immense.

It may be said perhaps, that as the most direct routs from the Lakes to the Navigation of Potomack are through the State of Pensylvania and the inter[es]t of that State opposed to the extension of the Waters of Monongahela, that a communication cannot be had either by the Yohiogany or Cheat River; but herein I differ. An application to this purpose would, in my opinion, place the Legislature of that Commonwealth in a very delicate situation. That it would not be pleasing I can readily conceive, but that they would refuse their assent, I am by no means clear in. There is, in that State, at least 100,000 Souls West of the Laurel hill, who are groaning under the inconveniences of a long land transportation. They are wishing, indeed looking, for the extension of inland navigation; and if this can not be made easy for them to Philadelphia—at any rate it must be lengthy—they will seek a mart elsewhere; and none is so convenient as that which offers itself through Yohiogany or Cheat River. The certain consequence therefore of an attempt to restrain the extension of the navigation of these rivers (so consonant with the interest of these people) or to impose any extra duties upon the exports, or imports, to, or from another State, would be a seperation of the Western Settlers from the old & more interior government; towards which there is not wanting a disposition at this moment in the former.

[1] This Prince William County courthouse, which served the county from c.1743 to c.1760, stood near a branch of Cedar Run about three miles southwest of present-day Independent Hill, Va. The court moved to this site because the creation in 1742 of Fairfax County from northern Prince William left the county's first courthouse, which was located near the mouth of Occoquan Creek, at one edge of the county and a more central location was desired. However, with the 1759 formation of Fauquier County from western Prince William, the county's center of population was again shifted, and the court moved east to the then rapidly growing port of Dumfries, where it remained until 1822 (HARRISON [1], 314–17; W.P.A. [1], 76, 110).

[2] Dr. Craik had been at Mount Vernon with GW's baggage two days earlier and had apparently proceeded with little delay to his home in Maryland. However, before leaving Mount Vernon, he had written a brief report for GW on the transportation between the Youghiogheny and Potomac rivers. The Little Youghiogheny (now Casselman) River, he thought, would be of little use in helping to link the two main rivers, because a long difficult

navigation on it would save only a few overland miles. A total land route by Braddock's Road or Turkey Foot Road was preferable, and of the two, Craik tended to favor the latter: "It is infinitely better and above two miles shorter. Indeed I found the whole Turkey foot Road across the mountains much better & nearer than Braddocks Road, that if there were good entertainment no one could hesitate in the choice" (Craik to GW, 2 Oct. 1784, MnHi).

[3] GW traveled down French Creek from Fort Le Boeuf (now Waterford, Pa.) to Venango (now Franklin, Pa.) 16–22 Dec. 1753. Lake Le Boeuf, near which the fort stood, lay south of Presque Isle (now Erie, Pa.).

[4] The headwaters of the Cayahoga River, the Tuscarawas River (a major branch of the Muskingum River), and the Mahoning River (a major branch of the Beaver River) all lie near one another in the vicinity of present-day Akron, Ohio. The mouth of the Cayahoga is at present-day Cleveland, Ohio.

[5] The Miami River flowing into Lake Erie is now called the Maumee, a corruption of its earlier name. It is the Auglaize River, one of the Maumee's main branches, that runs close to the Great Miami River, the two rivers having headwaters near one another in the area southeast of present-day Lima, Ohio.

The Sandusky River comes within about 35 miles of the source of the Great Miami near present-day Upper Sandusky, Ohio, but it lies much closer there to the headwaters of the Scioto River, another tributary of the Ohio.

[6] The Lake of the Woods lies on the border between the United States and Canada west of the Great Lakes.

[7] The Ottawa (Outauais) River flows for most of its length along the border between the Canadian provinces of Quebec and Ontario, entering the St. Lawrence River a few miles west of Montreal.

[8] Virginians.

[9] This table is an appendix to Thomas Hutchins, *A Topographical Description of Virginia, Pennsylvania, Maryland and North Carolina* (London, 1778).

[10] The falls are at present-day Ohiopyle, Pa. GW visited them in May 1754 (GW to Joshua Fry, 23 May 1754, WRITINGS, 1:52–53; VAUGHAN, 24–25).

[11] In the manuscript an asterisk at the end of this line refers to a marginal note that states: "the mouth of Cheat River & 2 Miles up it is in Pensyla."

[12] West Fork River.

[13] The Clarion River, a branch of the Allegheny River, was known as Toby's or Stump Creek until the early part of the nineteenth century (ESPENSHADE, 146–47).

[14] The headwaters of the Clarion River (near present-day Johnsonburg, Pa.) lie several miles west of the headwaters of the Driftwood Branch of Sinnemahoning Creek. Sinnemahoning Creek enters the West Branch of the Susquehanna River near present-day Keating, Pa.

[15] Fort Augusta, built in 1756, stood near present-day Sunbury, Pa., just below the junction of the west and main branches of the Susquehanna River (FRONTIER FORTS, 1:354–58).

[16] Mahanoy Creek flows into the Susquehanna River about 12 miles below the site of Fort Augusta. The upper reaches of the creek extend east to present-day Mahanoy City, Pa., a few miles north of the headwaters of the Schuylkill River.

[17] GW was using Lewis Evans's *A General Map of the Middle British Colonies, in America* (Philadelphia, 1755) and William Scull's *Map of the Province of Pennsylvania* (Philadelphia, 1770).

Lewis Evans (c.1700–1756), a Pennsylvania surveyor, published two maps. His first one, *A Map of Pensilvania, New-Jersey, New-York, And the Three Delaware Counties,* appeared in 1749 and was a work of fairly limited scope, showing principally the Delaware, Susquehanna, Hudson, and Mohawk valleys. His 1755 map of the middle colonies, issued with a 32-page explanatory *Analysis,* was much more comprehensive, covering the area from Virginia north to Montreal and from Rhode Island west to the falls of the Ohio River. It was also more popular, being one of the first maps to show the region west of the Appalachians with much detail and accuracy. In the half century following publication of the map, it went through many editions, both authorized and unauthorized (STEVENS [5]; GIPSON). GW probably owned a copy of the first edition, for he was using the map as early as Aug. 1756 to help conduct his French and Indian War military operations (GW to Adam Stephen, 5 Aug. 1756, DLC:GW). Over the years he retained a good opinion of it. Writing to Benjamin Harrison 10 Oct. 1784, he remarked that Evans's map and *Analysis* "(considering the early period at which they were given to the public) are done with amazing exactness" (DLC:GW).

William Scull, another Pennsylvania surveyor, owned land in Northumberland County near Fort Augusta. He was sheriff of Northumberland in 1775 and later became a captain in the 11th Pennsylvania Regiment. From Jan. to Sept. 1778 he was an assistant to the geographer and surveyor general of the Continental Army. However, ill health forced him to resign from the service, and he sought a position in the newly created Pennsylvania land office (William Scull to Joseph Reed, 26 Jan. 1780, PA. ARCH., 1st ser., 8:94). Scull's map of Pennsylvania, which covered the state from Philadelphia west to Fort Pitt, was based on his own work and on that of other surveyors, including his grandfather Nicholas Scull (1687–1761), who was surveyor general of Pennsylvania from 1748 to his death (GARRISON, 277–79).

[18] These two forts were at opposite ends of the Niagara River. Fort Erie, built in 1764 and destroyed in 1779, lay in ruins at the head of the river, the southern end where it flowed out of Lake Erie. Fort Niagara, built in 1726, stood at the mouth of the river, the northern end where it entered Lake Ontario. The 18-mile portage was required to bypass Niagara Falls.

[19] Oswego, N.Y., located on Lake Ontario at the mouth of the Oswego River, had been an important Indian trading center and military post since the 1720s.

[20] Oswego Falls are at present-day Fulton, N.Y., about 12 miles above the mouth of the Oswego River. On Evans's map the Oswego River and its northern branch, the Oneida River, appear to be one river called the Onondaga.

[21] The Oneida River flows from the western end of Oneida Lake and joins downstream with the Senaca River to form the Oswego.

[22] Wood Creek, which flows into Oneida Lake from the east, runs close to the headwaters of the Mohawk River in the vicinity of present-day Rome, N.Y.

[23] This portage was around the Little Falls of the Mohawk River.

[24] The 70-foot high Cohoes Falls at the mouth of the Mohawk River made

this portage necessary in order to reach the Hudson River (SHAW, 9; W.P.A. [7], 627). Schenectady on the Mohawk is about 21 miles above the falls; Albany on the Hudson is about 11 miles below them.

[25] Oswegatchie (now Ogdensburg, N.Y.) was a military outpost on the St. Lawrence River. The British army held it until 1796 (W.P.A. [7], 533–34).

At Home at Mount Vernon

1785

January 1785

First Monday. Colo. Bassett, who brought his daughter Fanny to this place to remain on the 24th. of last Month set off on his return to the Assembly now sitting at Richmond.

I took a ride to my Plantations in the Neck, & called to see my neighbour Humphrey Peake who has been long afflicted with ill health and appears to be in the last stage of life & very near his end.

Wind Southwardly. The day very fine & pleasant.

Frances (Fanny) Bassett's mother, Anna Maria Dandridge Bassett, had died in 1777, and since then Fanny seems to have spent much time visiting various relatives. She came to Mount Vernon in Dec. 1784 to make her permanent home with her aunt and uncle.

Sunday 2d. Doctr. Craik came here to Dinner & stayed all Night.

Drizzly Morning which first turned to rain, & then to snow.

Monday 3d. Doctr. Stuart—his wife Betcy & Patcy Custis who had been here since the 27th. ulto. returned home.

Doctr. Craik visited Mr. Peake & returned to Dinner.

While we were at Dinner Colo. Blackburne & his daughter Sally came. The whole remained the Evening.

Variable & very squally weather with Snow & Sunshine alternately. Towards evening the Wind came from the No. West & blew violently. Turned very cold & froze hard.

Dr. David Stuart (1753–c.1814) had, late in 1783, married John Parke Custis's widow, Eleanor Calvert Custis. Stuart was the son of Rev. William Stuart of St. Paul's Parish, then located in Stafford County (HARDY, 493). Stuart attended the College of William and Mary and graduated from the University of Edinburgh in 1777. He practiced medicine in Alexandria, and was at this time living four miles above the city. Elizabeth Parke (Betsy) Custis (1776–1832) and Martha Parke (Patsy) Custis (1777–1854), the two eldest children of John Parke Custis, lived with their mother and stepfather. The two youngest children lived at Mount Vernon. Stuart was a member of the Virginia Assembly 1785–88 and of the Virginia ratifying convention of 1788 and was one of the first three commissioners appointed by GW for the District of Columbia. About 1792 he moved his family to his Hope Park farm and, in later life, to Ossian Hall, both in Fairfax County. In the 1780s

Stuart served as translator for the many French letters that GW received, and during the presidency, he helped to keep GW informed of public sentiments in Virginia.

Sarah (Sally) Blackburn was the daughter of Col. Thomas and Christian Scott Blackburn of Rippon Lodge.

Tuesday 4th. Colo. Blackburne went to Alexandria leaving his daughter here.

Doctr. Craik attempted to cross the river at my Ferry, but failing on acct. of the Ice returned, & stayed dinner & the evening.

Wind variable & cold.

Wednesday 5th. The Doctr. in vain attempted my ferry & being disappointed went to George Town with a view of crossing on the Ice.

Colo. Blackburn returned this Evening from Alexandria.

Wind Northwardly & cold.

Thursday 6th. Colo. Blackburn & his daughter left this after breakfast.

Wind from the Southwest, raw, cold & disagreeable.

Friday 7th. Road to my Mill, Ferry, Dogue run, & Muddy hole Plantations.

Fanny Bassett, painted by Robert Edge Pine at Mount Vernon in 1785. (Mount Vernon Ladies' Association of the Union)

Preparing my dry well, and the Well in my New Cellar for the reception of Ice.

But little wind, and that Southwardly. Day very pleasant—tho' it thawed but little.

The well in the new cellar was to prove unsatisfactory (see entry for 5 June). The dry well that GW used as an icehouse was first mentioned in 1773, when it was being repaired (LEDGER B, 140). It was located at the southeast corner of the river lawn. In 1784 GW had considered building a new icehouse but decided instead to repair and improve the old one. On 2 June he wrote Robert Morris that the snow with which he had packed his icehouse was already gone, and requested advice and a description of Morris's icehouse (DLC:GW). Morris suggested, among other things, that GW not use snow but pound ice into small pieces so it would freeze into a mass (15 June 1784, DLC:GW).

Saturday 8th. Drawing Ice from the river to my well in the Cellar—got it 3/4 full & well pounded, as it was thrown in.

Wind pretty fresh from the Southwest.

The little Snow, not exceeding 2 Inches with which the ground was covered began to disappear and the ground to soften very much. The day for the greater part was lowering & variable.

Sunday 9th. Not much wind, and that at West, & So. West.

Moderate & thawing a little. The Mercury in the Thermometer was at 32 this afternoon. Appearances of Rain.

Monday 10th. Mercury at Sun rise was at 38—at Noon the same and at Night 42.

Drizzly all day with but little wind—that westerly.

Made a finish of the Ice in my well in the Cellar and began to fill the dry well—but the Ice unexpectedly leaving the Shore was obliged to quit.

But little thawing to day, notwithstanding the wind & weather.

Tuesday 11th. Mercury at 38 in the Morning 40 at Noon & 44 at Night.

Until Noon it was foggy, with but little wind.

Afternoon it cleared, & was very pleasant. The wind pretty fresh from the So. West—which bringing the Ice to the Shore again I renewed the Work of filling my dry Well with it by assembly Carts & hands from my Plantations.

Wednesday 12th. Mercury at 42 in the Morning—40 at Noon & 38 at Night.

Morning very fine with but little Wind from the So. Wt. At 10 o'clock it shifted to the No. Wt. blew very hard & turned Cold.

Road to my Mill Swamp, where my Dogue run hands were at work & to other places in search of the sort of Trees I shall want for my walks, groves, & Wildernesses.

At the Sein Landing & between that & the point at the old Brick kiln I found about half a dozn. young Elm trees, but not very promising ones. Many thriving ash trees on high (at least dry) ground of proper size for transplanting and a great abundance of the red-bud of all sizes. In the field which I bought of Barry & Miss Wade along the drain, & prongs of it, are one or two more; but rather of large size—but in the latter (a prong of the drain in Barry's field) there are great abundance of the white thorn (now full of the red Berries in clusters). Within the Meadow fence at the Mill, & within that Inclosure next Isaac Gates's are some young Crab apple trees and young Pine trees in the old field of all sizes. And in the Branch of Hell hole betwn. the Gate & its mouth are a number of very fine young Poplars—Locusts—Sasafras and Dogwood. Some Maple Trees on high ground & 2 or 3 Shrubs (in wet ground) wch. I take to be of the Fringe tree.

About Sundown Lewis Lemart—one of my Tenants in Fauquier & Collector of the Rents arising from the Tract on which he lives came in with some money & stayed all Night.

WALKS, GROVES, & WILDERNESSES: Before the Revolution, GW designed a formal English landscape for the western front of Mount Vernon. Little work was done on it, however, until after the war. The design called for a small circular courtyard, bounded by a carriage road. Beyond this was to be a bowling green with a serpentine drive bordering both sides down to a gate at the road. On the outer edges of this serpentine drive, between the drive and the north and south gardens, were what GW called his shrubberies and wildernesses. The shrubberies extended from each side of the courtyard to a point just beyond the gardens, while the wildernesses, more thickly planted areas, stretched from the shrubberies to the road. At the north and south ends of the mansion were to be thick plantings of trees which GW called his groves.

The trees named here are *Ulmus americana,* American elm; *Fraxinus americana,* white ash; *Cercis canadensis,* redbud; *Crataegus crus-galli,* white thorn; *Malus coronaria,* American crab; *Pinus virginiana,* Virginia scrub pine; *Liriodendron tulipifera,* tulip poplar; *Robinia pseudo-acacia,* black locust; *Sassafras albidum,* sassafras; *Cornus florida,* dogwood; *Acer* sp., maple; *Chionanthus virginica,* fringe tree.

Thursday 13th. Mercury in the Thermomiter at 26 about Sunrise—30 at Noon & 32 at Night.

Morning clear & cold, the Wind being fresh from the No. West, Which, about Noon, died away and grew moderate.

Was envited, & went to the Funeral of Mr. Peake who died on Tuesday night.

Returned to Dinner, accompanied by the Revd. Doctr. Griffith. Found a Mr. Dalby (an English Gentleman) here–both of whom stayed all Night.

David Griffith (1742–1789), a native of New York, was educated for the medical profession and practiced in New York for several years before studying for the ministry. He was ordained by the bishop of London in 1770. In 1771 he became minister of Shelburne Parish in Loudoun County. During the Revolution, Griffith served as chaplain and surgeon of the 3d Virginia Regiment. In Feb. 1780 he was chosen rector of Fairfax Parish (Christ Church, Alexandria), where he remained until his death. Griffith was a deputy at the first general convention of the Episcopal church in 1785 and was chosen first bishop of Virginia in 1785. A lack of funds kept him from journeying to London for consecration, and he resigned from the post in 1789.

Philip Dalby, a merchant, in May 1785 opened a store in Alexandria on the corner of Royal and Cameron streets. He offered "a large Assortment of Goods" for cash, produce, or credit (*Va. Journal,* 12 May 1785).

Friday 14th. Mercury at 32 in the Morning 34 at Noon & 38 at Night.

The Wind tho' there was not much of it came from the So. West and continued at the same point the whole day.

Appearances of Snow in the Forenoon but clear afterwards until Sunset–when it went down in a bank.

Mr. Griffith & Mr. Dalby both went away after breakfast.

Received an Invitation to the Funeral of Mr. Thos. Kirkpatrick at 3 oclock tomorrow, but excused myself.

Yesterday, & this day also was closely employed in getting Ice into my dry well.

Thomas Kirkpatrick, of Fairfax County, was in 1782 head of a household of two whites and one black (HEADS OF FAMILIES, VA., 16). He signed the resolution forming the Virginia nonimportation association, in Williamsburg in 1770, as a merchant from Alexandria (VA. REG., 3:79). Thomas Kilpatrick, probably the same man, was a wheat purchaser and inspector of flour at Alexandria in 1775 (HARRISON [1], 417).

Saturday 15th. Mercury at 38 in the Morning–42 at Noon and the same at Night.

Wind Easterly in the Morning but before noon it shifted to the So. West & blew fresh & towards Night it veered round to the No. Wt. & blew very hard.

With the Easterly wind there was a little rain which ceased with it. Grew clear & turned cold.

Sunday 16th. Mercury at 36 in the morning–38 at Noon & night.

Wind light all day from the No. West. Weather clear & pleast.

Monday 17th. Mercury at 34 in the Morning–36 at Noon & 46 at Night.

Day fine & pleasant–wind at South.

Went to and returned from Alexandria to day.

At my return found dispatches from the assembly respecting the Potomack Navigation.

On 22 Jan. 1785 GW wrote to William Grayson, a member of the Virginia House of Delegates for Fairfax County, acknowledging receipt of "your letter, with the Books, Potomac bill and other papers" (DLC:GW). Included in the dispatches was the actual engrossed copy, "spared indulgently from the Clerks office," of "An act for opening and extending the navigation of Potowmack river" (HENING, 11:510–25), passed by the Virginia Assembly on 5 Jan. 1785; a "cover" note from the House clerk, John Beckley; several books for enrolling the subscriptions of the private capital authorized to finance the Potomac Company; and a list of "the James River rate of Tolls" for the newly authorized James River Company, authorized to open navigation on the James River above Richmond (GW to John Fitzgerald and William Hartshorne, 18 Jan. 1785, DLC:GW; HENING, 11:450–62).

Also included in today's dispatches from Grayson was a letter to GW from James Madison (1751–1836), member of the Virginia House of Delegates for Orange County (9 Jan. 1785, ICU). Madison had visited Mount Vernon just before the fall 1784 session of the Virginia General Assembly in which he shepherded the Potomac and James River navigation bills through the lower house. In his letter to GW he enclosed three resolutions regarding internal improvements passed in that session (see MADISON, 8:235).

Tuesday 18th. Mercury at 50 this Morning–55 at Noon & 58 at Night.

Wind Southwardly & fresh all day and now and then dripping of rain. In the evening the Clouds dispersed & the Sunset clear.

Sent the dispatches which came to me yesterday to Messrs. Fitzgerald and Hartshorne (managers named in the act for improving & extending the Navigation of Potomack and) who are appointed to receive Subscriptions–that they might get copies of the Act printed and act under them.

William Hartshorne, a Pennsylvania Quaker, was a merchant in Alexandria. He was elected treasurer of the Potomac Company on 17 May 1785 and served until Jan. 1800 (BACON-FOSTER, 61, 100).

The Virginia Act provided: "Whereas . . . many persons are willing to subscribe large sums of money to effect so laudable and beneficial a work; and it is just and proper that they, their heirs, and assigns, should be empowered to receive reasonable tolls forever, in satisfaction for the money advanced by them in carrying the work into execution, and the risk they run . . . it shall and may be lawful to open books in the city of Richmond, towns of Alexandria and Winchester in this state, for receiving and entering subscriptions for the said undertaking." Hartshorne and John Fitzgerald were named in the act to be the managers of the Alexandria subscription book (HENING, 11:510–11). Subscription books also were opened in Annapolis, Georgetown, and Frederick, Md.

Wednesday 19th. Mercury at 48 in the Morning—the same at Noon and at Night.

Day clear & fine. The Wind at No. West & Cool.

Employed until dinner in laying out my Serpentine road & Shrubberies adjoining.

Just as we had done dinner a Mr. Watson—late of the House of Watson & Cossoul of Nantes—and a Mr. Swift Merchant in Alexandria came in, and stayed all Night.

Elkanah Watson (1758–1842), born in Massachusetts, was apprenticed just before the Revolution to John Brown, of Providence, a merchant who became active in importing gunpowder and other supplies for the army. In 1779 Watson went to France as agent for Brown and others. He opened a mercantile business in Nantes in partnership first with Benjamin Franklin's grandnephew, Jonathan Williams, and later with a M. Cassoul (Cossoul). The business failed in 1783 and Watson returned to the United States in 1784 (HEDGES, 245–54). While he was abroad, Watson sent GW some Masonic ornaments from France (GW to Watson & Cassoul, 10 Aug. 1782, DLC:GW). Watson was greatly interested in both agriculture and canals and, in later life, founded the Berkshire (Mass.) Agricultural Society and endeavored to raise capital for building canals. He came to Mount Vernon bearing a gift for GW from Granville Sharp, the British philanthropist and founder of the colony of Sierra Leone in Africa. Sharp had entrusted to Watson two bundles of books for GW, "embracing his entire publications on emancipation and other congenial topics" (WATSON [2], 233). During his visit to Mount Vernon, Watson and GW discussed canals at great length, and particularly the Potomac Company and its plans for navigation of that river (WATSON [2], 244–45).

Jonathan Swift (d. 1824) was a merchant who had moved to Alexandria from New England sometime before 1785. In September of this year, he married Ann Roberdeau, daughter of Brig. Gen. Daniel Roberdeau. In his later years, Swift served as a consular agent for several European countries (BUCHANAN [2], 122–23).

Thursday 20th. Mercury at 40 in the Morning—42 at Noon and 45 at Night.

Wind at No. Et.—day raw—lowering—damp & disagreeable.

Mr. Watson and Mr. Swift went away after breakfast. I continued my employment of yesterday—arranging the Walk &ca.

Began to grub & clear the under growth in my Pine Grove on the margin of Hell hole.

Friday 21st. Mercury at 52 in the Morning—54 at Noon & 55 at Night.

More or less rain all night and variable wind—which, at times, blew exceedingly hard.

In the Morning the wind was at No. Et. attended with rain. Before Noon it shifted to the Southward—blowing pretty fresh. The weather then cleared.

This day a large Ship went up—on Tuesday last 4 square rigged vessels also went past wch. was the first day the Navigation opened so as to admit this since the frost commenced, on the 4th. instant.

Saturday 22d. Mercury at 45 in the Morning—the same at Noon & 44 at Night.

Clear weather—the wind being at No. West all day.

In the Evening Doctr. Craik Junr. came here & stayed all Night.

James Craik, Jr. (died c.1803), was the son of Dr. James Craik. His company, Jas. Craik & Co., did some business with GW in 1786 (LEDGER B, 212). In 1787 he dissolved his mercantile business but continued selling drugs and medicines in his store (MOORE [1], 190). There is no indication that he ever practiced medicine, although he received a medical degree from the University of Pennsylvania in 1782 and was frequently referred to as Dr. Craik, Jr. (LIPPINCOTT, 32).

Sunday 23d. Mercury at 36 in the Morning—38 at Noon & 42 at Sun setting.

Clear & quite calm all the forenoon. Towards evening the Wind sprung up from the Eastward.

Doctr. Craik left this after breakfast—attending Miss Bassett to his Fathers—to the wedding of his Sister Sally.

Sarah (Sally) Craik, daughter of Dr. James Craik, was married 25 Jan. 1785 to Dr. Daniel Jenifer, Jr. (1756–c.1809).

Monday 24th. Mercury at 41 in the morning—57 at Noon & 54 at Night.

Drizzly at intervals all day—Fresh wind from the South.

Renewed my labors on the Walks, Shrubberies &ca.—but was much interrupted by the unsettledness of the weather.

In the Night it rained pretty much.

Tuesday 25th. Mercury at 46 in the Morning 38 at Noon—and [ ] at Night.

In the Morning early it rained a little, but the wind coming out from the No. West it soon cleared—blowing hard until night when it moderated & soon ceased.

A little before Dinner a Doctor Gilpin & a Mr. Scott—two West India Gentlemen came here introduced by a letter from Mr. Rob. Morris of Philadelphia and a little after them a Mr. Blaine all of whom stayed the Evening.

Day very cold—latter part.

A third member of Dr. Gilpin and Mr. Scott's party, called Mr. Colby, "remained indisposed at Baltimore" (GW to Robert Morris, 1 Feb. 1785, DLC:GW). MR. BLAINE: may be Thomas Blane (Blaine) of Westmoreland County.

Wednesday 26th. Mercury at 29 in the Morning, 38 at Noon & 39 at Night.

But little Wind and that from the Southward—day clear & very pleasant overhead, but sloppy & disagreeable under foot, after it began to thaw—the ground having been hard froze in the Morning—which freezings & thawings it is apprehended, will be very injurious to the Winter grain.

Thursday 27th. Mercury at 32 in the Morning—the same at Noon & 37 at Sunsetting.

Wind at No. West & clear all day—air pretty sharp in the forenoon.

Made Mr. & Mrs. Lund Washington a mornings visit—from thence I went to Belvoir and viewed the ruined Buildings of that place. In doing this I passed along the side of Dogue Creek & the river to the white Ho[use] in search of Elm & other Trees for my Shrubberies &ca. Found none of the former but discovered one fringe Tree and a few Crabtrees in the first field beyond my line and in returning home (which I did to Dinner) by the way of Accatinck Creek I found several young Holly trees growing near Lawson Parkers.

In 1779 Lund Washington married his cousin Elizabeth Foote, daughter of Richard Foote of Prince William County. The couple lived at Mount Vernon until 1784 when they moved into their newly built home, Hayfield, located on the Alexandria Road five miles south of Alexandria. Lund's property consisted of about 450 acres, comprising most of the three parcels of land GW had acquired from Simon Pearson and George and John Ashford in 1761–63 and a small piece of wasteland obtained in 1771. This land was not formally deeded to Lund by GW until 25 Feb. 1785. However, there seems to have been an earlier lease on at least a part of the land, probably with GW's promise to deed the land to Lund at a later date. GW specified in the deed that the land was in repayment of £5,304 Lund had earlier paid to Thomas Hanson Marshall for land on GW's behalf (Fairfax County Deeds, Book P-1, 415–17, Vi Microfilm; see entry for 15 Feb. 1785).

RUINED BUILDINGS: Belvoir had been badly damaged by fire in 1783. GW wrote George William Fairfax of this visit to his home: "I took a ride there the other day to visit the ruins—& ruins indeed they are. The dwelling house & the two brick buildings in front, under went the ravages of the fire; The walls of which are very much injured: the other Houses are sinking under the depredation of time & inattention, & I believe are now scarcely worth repairing. In a word, the whole are, or very soon will be a heap of ruin. When I viewed them—when I considered that the happiest moments of my life had been spent there—when I could not trace a room in the house (now all rubbish) that did not bring to my mind the recollection of pleasing scenes; I was obliged to fly from them; & came home with painful sensations, & sorrowing for the contrast" (27 Feb. 1785, DLC:GW). In 1814 the remaining walls of Belvoir were leveled by shells from British ships (MUIR, 23). HOLLY: *Ilex opaca,* American holly.

Friday 28th. Mercury at 32 this Morning—42 at Noon and the same at Night.

Wind pretty fresh from the Southward, with Sun shine, and appearances of rain alternately. In the evening it lowered very much.

Road to day to my Plantations in the Neck—partly with a view to search for Trees; for which purpose I passed through the Wood and in the first drain beyond the Bars in my lower pasture, I discovered in tracing it upwards, many small & thriving plants of the Magnolio and about & within the Fence, not far distant, some young Maple Trees; & the red berry of the Swamp. I also, along the Branch within Colo. Masons field, where Mr. T. Triplett formerly lived came a cross a mere nursery of young Crabtrees of all sizes & handsome & thriving and along the same branch on the outerside of the fence I discovered several young Holly Trees. But whether from the real scarcity, or difficulty of distinguishing, I could find none of the fringe tree.

MAGNOLIO: This may be any one of several varieties indigenous to the area: *Magnolia virginiana,* or sweet bay, which in the eighteenth century was called *Magnolia glauca,* or swamp laurel; *Magnolia tripetala,* or umbrella tree, a deciduous variety; or *Magnolia acuminata,* or cucumber tree. RED BERRY OF THE SWAMP: *Ilex verticillata,* black alder or winterberry.

Saturday 29th. Mercury at 42 in the Morning and the same at Noon & Night.

Raining until about 10 Oclock when it ceased. About 12 the

Sun appeared and the day became exceedingly pleasant afterwards.

The Wind, until some time after noon came from the Southward but not very fresh. Towards the evening it inclined to the westward more—blew fresh & grew cold.

Sunday 30th. Mercury this morning at 26 at Noon 32 and at Night 28.

Wind fresh from the No. Wt. & Cold—day clear.

In the Afternoon Mr. Willm. Scott with the two Miss Blackburns came in and stayed the Night.

William Scott (c.1751–c.1787) was a son of Rev. James and Sarah Brown Scott of Dettingen Parish, Prince William County, and the uncle of the Blackburn girls. Scott lived at Strawberry Vale "near the Lower Falls of Potomack, in Fairfax County" (*Va. Journal,* 15 April 1784). There were four unmarried Blackburn girls at this time—Julia Ann (Nancy), Sarah, Catherine, and Mary Elizabeth (Polly). Sarah Blackburn was to marry Nathaniel Craufurd of Prince George's County, Md., in about two weeks and Nancy Blackburn (1768–1829) would marry GW's nephew Bushrod Washington on 13 Oct. 1785.

Monday 31st. Mercury at 22 in the Morning 28 at Noon & 29 at Night.

Wind at No. Wt. & pretty fresh in the forenoon—less of it & from the Eastward in the afternoon. Day clear until the Evening when it lowered & after dark turned very cloudy.

About one oclock Mr. Wm. Hunter of Alexa. with a Mr. Hadfield (a Manchester Mercht.) recommended by Colo. Sam Smith of Baltimore & Colo. Fitzgerald & a Mr. Dawson came in. Dined & returned to Alexandria.

William Hunter, Jr. (1731–1792), a Scottish-born merchant of Alexandria, carried on extensive trade with London and Liverpool. He was a member of GW's Masonic lodge and mayor of the city 1788–90 (BROCKETT, 95; POWELL, 237, 361).

Joseph Hadfield (1759–1851), a member of the Manchester firm of Hadfield & Co., was one of a host of British agents who came to America after the Revolution to try to collect pre-Revolutionary debts owed to their firms by American merchants (HADFIELD, v–vii).

Samuel Smith (1752–1839) served in the Continental Army 1775–79 and was commissioned lieutenant colonel of the 4th Maryland Regiment in 1777. After the war, Smith returned to his father's mercantile house in Baltimore, becoming a prosperous trader and land speculator.

Mr. Dawson was possibly George Dawson, a friend of Hadfield who had served under Banastre Tarleton during the Revolution as a captain in the King's Orange Rangers, a Loyalist company. He accompanied Hadfield on some of his travels through the colonies (SABINE, 2:504; WRIGHT, 131, 137).

February—1785

Tuesday 1st. Mercury at 29 in the Morning, 28 at Noon and 34 at Night.

Snowing, raining, or Hailing all day & Night and very disagreeable.

Wind at No. Wt. and West the whole time.

Wednesday 2d. Mercury at 28 in the Morning 32 at Noon and [ ] at Night.

The Snow this morning is about 9 Inches deep & pretty well compressed.

Wind at No. West and very cold.

Mr. Scott went away after Breakfast. Employed myself (as there could be no stirring without) in writing Letters by the Post and in Signing 83 Diplomas for the members of the Society of the Cincinnati and sent them to the care of Colo. Fitzgerald in Alexandria—to be forwarded to General Williams of Baltimore the Assistant Secretary of the Society.

The Society of the Cincinnati, founded in 1783, was open to American officers who had served for three years in the army, or were in the army at the end of the Revolution, and to French officers of the rank of colonel

Be it known that
is a Member of the Society of the Cincinnati, instituted by the Officers of the American Army, at the Period of its Dissolution, as well to commemorate the great Event which gave Independence to North America, as for the laudable Purpose of inculcating the Duty of laying down in Peace Arms assumed for public Defence, and of uniting in Acts of brotherly Affection, and Bonds of perpetual Friendship, the Members constituting the same.

In Testimony whereof I, the President of the said Society, have hereunto set my Hand at in the State of this Day of in the Year of our Lord One Thousand Seven Hundred and and in the Year of the Independence of the United States.

By order,

Secretary.

G Washington President

Blank diploma of the Society of the Cincinnati, signed by Washington. (Beinecke Rare Book and Manuscript Library, Yale University)

and above. Later, naval officers were also included. The hereditary nature of the new society in particular aroused much bitter opposition. It was usual practice for GW to sign blank diplomas and send them to the state secretaries to be completed and issued to members (HUME, xi–xvii).

Otho Holland Williams (1749–1794) was born in Prince George's County, Md., the son of Joseph and Priscilla Holland Williams. He was secretary of the Maryland chapter of the Society of the Cincinnati and the first assistant secretary general of the national society. Williams had joined the army as a lieutenant in 1775 and retired as a brigadier general in 1783. After the war, he was appointed naval officer of Baltimore and, under the new Constitution, collector of customs for the port of Baltimore, a post he retained until his death.

Thursday 3d. Mercury this morning at 22 at Noon [ ] and at Night 28.

Wind at No. West all day but it did not blow hard—clear & cold.

Mr. Benja. Dulany came here to Dinner & returned afterwards.

We concluded a bargain which has been long in agitation for the Exchange of his Land in this Neck which he & his wife have the reversion of for the tract I bought of Messrs. Adam Dow & McIver on Hunting Creek. The Exchange is simply Tract for Tract—but as he cannot put me in possession of his, Mrs. French his wife's mother having her life in it he is to pay me, during that period—or until she shall relinquish her right therein, and the full & absolute possession is vested in me—the same annual rent I now receive from Mr. Dow—viz. One hundd. and twenty pounds Virga. Curry.

Writings & conveyances to this effect to be drawn by Mr. Charles Lee—Who from both is to be furnished with the necessary Papers.

HIS LAND IN THIS NECK: a tract of 543 acres on Dogue Creek, part of the 5,000 acres granted by Lord Culpeper to Nicholas Spencer and John Washington in 1674. With the exception of a small tract still held by the heirs of Harrison Manley, GW, by this exchange, now would control the entire neck of land lying between Little Hunting Creek and Dogue Creek, which had composed the original grant. To own the whole grant had long been one of GW's ambitions, and he made every effort over a period of years to purchase the French-Dulany land. In 1782 GW had bought the 376-acre Dow tract, located on Hunting Creek and up the Long Branch of Hunting Creek, for the express purpose of trading it for the French-Dulany land. However, despite Mrs. Penelope French's earlier approval of a trade for land nearer her home, a change of heart had led to a stubborn refusal on her part to relinquish her lifetime rights to the land (Benjamin Dulany to GW, 28 Feb. 1782, and GW to Lund Washington, 21 Nov. 1782, two letters, DLC:GW; Lund Washington to GW, 20 Nov., 4 and 11 Dec. 1782 and 8 Jan. 1783, ViMtV). It was not until 1786 that the Dulanys and GW finally prevailed upon Mrs. French to sign a deed giving up her rights. Peter Dow, one of the former owners of the Hunting Creek Tract, was then living on that land (agreement between Dulany and GW, 4 Feb. 1785, PHi: Gratz Collection).

Charles Lee (1758–1815), the brother of Col. Henry (Light Horse Harry) Lee, was naval officer of the South Potomac District. In 1789 he was appointed collector of customs at Alexandria and from 1793 to 1795 was a member of the Virginia General Assembly from Fairfax County. He also practiced law in Alexandria and after the Revolution handled much of GW's legal work. In 1795 GW appointed him attorney general of the United States.

Friday 4th. Mercury at 22 in the Morng.—28 at Noon and at 32 at Night.

Calm, clear, and very pleasant over head, all day.

The Snow began to melt a little.

The two Miss Blackburns left this after breakfast, in order to return home—but it is to be feared they would meet with some difficul⟨ty⟩ at the ferry at Occoquan.

Saturday 5th. Mercury at 25 in the Morning—32 at Noon & 32 at Night.

Day lowering with appearances of Snow. In the Morning the Wind (tho' there was not much of it) was at No. West. At Noon there was scarce any and towards night that which did blow came from the No. East.

Sunday 6th. Mercury at 31 in the morning—38 at Noon and 39 at Night.

Morning lowering with appearances of Snow or rain. Abt. Noon the Sun came out—but soon disappeared and became thick & lowering. No Wind.

Doctr. Brown was sent for to Frank (waiter in the House) who had been seized in the Night, with a bleeding of the Mouth from an Orifice made by a Doctr. Dick who some days before attempted in vain to extract a broken tooth & coming about 11 Oclock stayed to Dinner & returned afterwards.

Elisha Cullen Dick (1762–1825), of Alexandria, was a Pennsylvanian who had received his medical degree from the University of Pennsylvania in 1782. He settled in Alexandria after taking his degree and soon became a popular member of Alexandria society. One of the founders of the Masonic lodge at Alexandria, he served as its master 1787–99, except for a year and a half when GW was master. He held several offices in Alexandria, including that of mayor. GW seems not to have used Dick's services again after his servant's unfortunate experience. Dick was, however, one of the doctors called in for consultation by Dr. Craik during GW's final illness.

Benjamin Tasker Dulany, by an unknown artist. (Mrs. Thomas B. Atkinson)

Dr. Elisha Cullen Dick. (Alexandria-Washington Lodge No. 22, A. F. & A. M., Alexandria, Va.)

Monday 7th. Mercury at 39 this morning—44 at Noon and 48 at Night.

Day clear, perfectly calm, Warm & pleasant. The Snow began to dissolve fast.

Tuesday 8th. Mercury at 39 in the morning—42 at Noon—46 at Night.

Morning lowering—clear at Noon, & cloudy afterwards.

Wind in the forenoon abt. So. East. Afterwards it veered more Easterly, & blew fresher. Thawed a good deal.

Finding that I should be very late in preparing my Walks & Shrubberies if I waited till the ground should be uncovered by the dissolution of the Snow—I had it removed Where necessary & began to Wheel dirt into the Ha! Haws &ca.—tho' it was it exceeding miry & bad working.

HA! HAWS, &CA: A ha-ha wall was a sunken wall which prohibited cattle from approaching the house, but left an uninterrupted view of the landscape.

Wednesday 9th. Mercury at 44 in the morning—at Noon 50 and at Night 56.

Morning lowering—but clear, calm, warm & pleast. afterwards

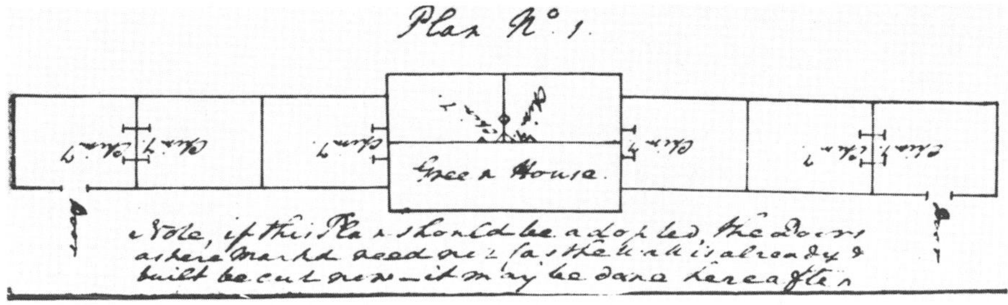

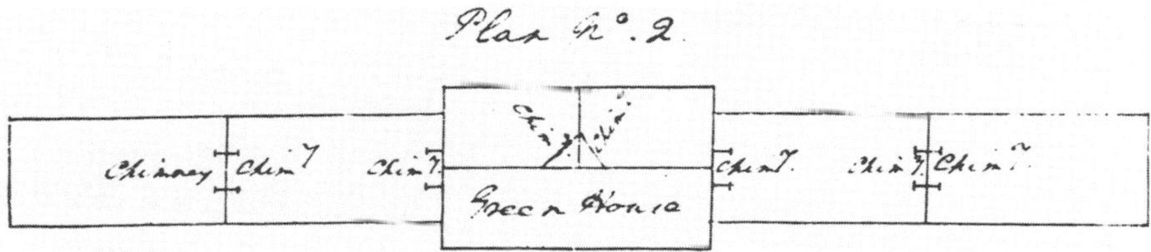

Two alternate floor plans for his greenhouse drawn by Washington. (Mount Vernon Ladies' Association of the Union)

which with the rain that fell last night had uncovered the ground in many places & was dissipating the Snow very fast.

Transplanted an English Walnut tree from the Corner near where the old School house stood to the opposite side wch. with the one that was moved in the fall were intended to answer the two remaining ones—but from their size and age I have little expectation of their living. Also moved the Apricots & Peach Trees which stood in the borders of the grass plats which from the same causes little expectation is entertained of their living. These were placed under the Wall in the North Garden on each side of the Green House and an old pair tree was movd at the same time into the lowr. Square of the South Garden from which less hopes of its living were entertained than of any of the others.

Road to where my Dogue run people were grubbing in the Mill Swamp & Meadow.

In the Afternoon Fanny Bassett returned from Doctr. Craiks accompanied by his son William.

The schoolhouse was a small building at the west end of the north garden. The greenhouse was located at the north end of the north garden, and at this time was incomplete. GW had undertaken the construction of the greenhouse soon after his return from the war. On 11 Aug. 1784 he wrote his former aide, Tench Tilghman, for the dimensions and other details of a greenhouse at Mrs. Margaret Tilghman Carroll's plantation in Maryland (RPJCB). Tilghman replied on 18 Aug., sending details and sketches (DLC:GW). Completion of the building was delayed, and not until 1787 were the roofing and flooring finished (Mount Vernon Store Book, ViMtV).

Badge of the Society of the Cincinnati.

The two wings designed as slave quarters were not finished until after 1791 (GW to Anthony Whitting, 14 Aug. 1791, ViMtV).

Thursday 10th. Mercury this Morning at 46 at Noon [ ] and at Night 52.

Day clear, calm, & pleasant until the Evening when it grew a little hazy & the Sunset in a bank. The little wind that stirred came from the Southward.

Road up to Alexandria today and dined with Colo. Fitzgerald.

Friday 11th. Mercury at 46 this Morning—51 at Noon and the same at Night.

The first part of the Morning was hazy & rather cool. Before Noon it grew clear, warm, and pleasant and towards the Evening it lowered & the Sun set in a bank.

The Wind in the Morning was Northwardly. Afterwards it got round to the Southward but there was very little of it.

Employed all day in marking the ground for the reception of my Shrubs.

In the Evening a Mr. Andrews, Jeweller in Philadelphia,

called to shew me an Eagle medal, which he had made, & was about to offer as Specimen of his Workmanship to the Members of the Society of Cincinnati in hopes of being employed by them in that way. He was accompanied by a Mr. [ ] name not known.

EAGLE MEDAL: Maj. Pierre-Charles L'Enfant, a French engineer who served in the Continental Army, designed the badges and diplomas for the Society of the Cincinnati and had them produced in France. He returned to America with a supply in time for the May 1784 meeting. The medal was a gold eagle, with an enameled medallion on its breast bearing a motto and a representation of Lucius Quintus Cincinnatus, the Roman general-farmer after which the Society was named. It was suspended from a sky-blue ribbon edged in white (HUME, xii–xiv). Andrews seems not to have been successful in making the gold eagles.

Saturday 12th. Mercury at 44 this Morning, 44 at Noon and 44 at Night.

Planted Eight young Pair Trees sent me by Doctr. Craik in the following places—viz.

2 Orange Burgamots in the No. Garden, under the back wall —3d. tree from the Green House at each end of it.

1 Burgamot at the Corner of the border in the South Garden just below the necessary.

2 St. Germains, one in each border (middle thereof) of the upper Squares by the Asparagas Bed & Artichoake Ditto upper bordr.

3 Brown Beuries in the west square in the Second flat—viz. 1 on the border (middle thereof) next the Fall or slope—the other two on the border above the walk next the old Stone Wall.

Received an Invitation to the Funeral of Willm. Ramsay Esqr. of Alexandria—the oldest Inhabitt. of the Town; & went up. Walked in a procession as a free mason—Mr. Ramsay in his life time being one & now buried with the Ceremony & honors due to one.

The ground getting uncovered, I again with my people from the Quarters, began to clean up the ground under the Pines, and along the hollow of H. Hole & its branches. This Work I renewed yesterday, & contd. it to day.

Mr. Willm. Craik called and dined in his way home.

The Sun rose clear this Morning, but it soon overcast begun to Snow & then to rain wch. continued until abt. 10 Oclock. About Noon the wind sprung up pretty fresh from the No. West & grew colder.

EIGHT YOUNG PAIR TREES: Varieties not previously mentioned are the St. Germain, a large, long pear which is picked green and allowed to ripen for winter use, and the "Brown Beuries." Many varieties were called *Beurre* or butter pears, which GW is here rendering as "Beuries."

Asparagus officinalis, asparagus, and *Cynara scolymus,* French or globe artichoke, were common garden vegetables at the Mansion House.

WILLIAM RAMSAY: GW undoubtedly means the earliest inhabitant of Alexandria.

Sunday 13th. Mercury at 34 this Morning, 38 at Noon, & the same at Night.

Wind at No. West all day but not fresh—clear & not unpleasant—ground hard froze.

Monday 14th. Mercury at 31 in the Morning—34 at Noon and 33 at Night.

Morning clear and calm—Ground hard froze. Wind afterwards, fresh from the No. West with flying Clouds which gave a rawness & chill to the air.

In company with Mrs. Washington made a visit to Colo. McCarty & family. Dined there and returned home afterwds.

Tuesday 15. Mercury at 28 this morning—at noon not observed, but at Night 36.

Morning fine, wind Southwardly, which shifted to the Eastward & grew colder. Abt. Noon it began to Snow, & continued to do so until past 3 oclock.

Went this day to ascertain the quantity of Land given to, and received from Mr. Willm. Triplett by way of exchange & to run a dividing line betwn. him & the Land I let Mr. Lund Washington—but the badness of the day prevented the execution. Thursday next I appointed to go again on this business.

GW needed a small piece of land owned by William Triplett which bordered on GW's tumbling dam and millrace. He proposed to give Triplett some small strips of land in exchange. The negotiations had gone on for years because of boundary disputes and GW's long absence during the war. Some of the land GW was leasing to Lund Washington was also involved in the dispute. On 18 May 1785 a deed was signed giving Triplett 29 acres on the northwest side of the millrace. The acreage involved was part of land GW had bought from George Ashford and Simon Pearson, and also a small strip of wasteland granted him in 1771. In return, Triplett gave GW 26 acres on the lower, or east, side of the millrace with 5s. token fee (Fairfax County Deeds, Book P-1, 432–35, Vi Microfilm).

Wednesday 16th. Mercury at 36 in the Morning—45 at Noon & 49 at Night.

Wind Southwardly & pretty fresh in the forenoon—calm afterwards and somewhat lowering.

Mountain laurel, from Washington's copy of *Curtis's Botanical Magazine,* 1796. (Mount Vernon Ladies' Association of the Union)

Transplanted along the So. side of the Wall of the No. Garden, the Ivy; which I had taken up with as much dirt about the roots of it as I could obtain.

Weather soft and thawing–the Southwardly having dissolved all the Snow that fell yesterday.

IVY: Here GW is not referring to *Hedera helix,* the classic English ivy, or even to the domestic *Parthenocissus quinquefolia,* the Virginia creeper. Rather, it is *Kalmia latifolia,* the mountain laurel. Curtis's *Botanical Magazine,* which GW had in his own library, reproduces a drawing of *K. latifolia* and describes it as vulgarly called mountain ivy. Writing some instructions to Lund Washington 19 Aug. 1776, GW explained his wishes for plantings in his groves by the mansion house (CSmH). In the south grove he wanted flowering trees such as crabapple, dogwood, and tulip poplar, interspersed with such evergreens as holly, pine, cedar, and ivy. Evidently he was attempting to produce a showy undergrowth among his flowering trees and was not calling for a climbing ivy. The flowers of GW's ivy were coming into bloom when he made his 30 May 1785 diary entry, another indication that this was mountain laurel.

Thursday 17th. Mercury at 39 in the Morng.—46 at Noon and 49, at Night.

Wind at No. West all day but not hard. Clear and cold in the Morning. More moderate about Noon & very pleasant in the Afternoon being calm.

In the morning early I went to Mr. L. Washingtons (to Breakfast) in order to finish the Work I had began on Tuesday last but after having plotted & measured the slipes which were to be given in Exchange for the Land below the Race, I found it did not agree with my former measurements & therefore left the business undetermined until I could go there again & run some lines of Harrisons Patent or compare it more carefully with my former works.

Dined with Mr. Willm. Triplett & returned home in the Afternoon—soon after which the two Doctr. Jenifers came, & stayed the Evening.

The two doctors are Dr. Walter Hanson Jenifer and Dr. Daniel Jenifer, Jr. (1756–c.1809), of Maryland, sons of Daniel and Elizabeth Hanson Jenifer (see main entry for 28 Aug. 1774).

Friday 18th. Mercury at 36 this Morning, 40 at Noon and 44 at Night.

Not much Wind. In the forenoon, the little that blew was Northwardly—in the afternoon Eastwardly.

The two Doctr. Jenifers went to Alexandria after breakfast.

Planted border of Ivy under the No. side of the So. Garden wall.

Also four Lime or Linden Trees, sent me by Govr. Clinton of New York which must have been out of the ground since the middle of Novr. without any dirt about the Roots and only a covering of Mat. These were planted in the Serpentine Roads to the door—the 3d. trees on each side next the Walls & the second trees on each side next the grass plat.

LIME OR LINDEN TREES: *Tilia americana,* linden or basswood. GW wrote to Gov. George Clinton that the seedlings had been delayed at Norfolk by the severity of the winter and that he did not expect them to live. He asked for other plants and seeds, saying he would make no apology because "I persuade myself you will have pleasure in contributing to an innocent amusement" (20 April 1785, DLC:GW).

Saturday 19th. Mercury at 40 in the Morning, 43 at Noon, and 48 at Night.

Morning lowering, but the Clouds dispelling about Noon, it became warm & pleasant afterwards. The Sun set in a bank.

Little or no wind at any time of the day.

Went to Mr. Tripletts and rectified the mistakes in running the Lines and finished the business respecting the quantities of Land given in Excha. and the partition between him and Mr. Lund Washington.

Finished planting Ivy in front of the Gardens.

My Nephew George Steptoe Washington came here to Dinnr. from the Acadamy at George Town.

George Steptoe Washington (c.1773–1808) was the second of the three sons of Samuel Washington and his fourth wife, Anne Steptoe Washington. He and his younger brother, Lawrence Augustine Washington (1775–1824), were being educated under GW's supervision and largely at his expense. Samuel Washington had left his estate badly encumbered by debts, and its proceeds were not enough to provide for his children. GW placed George and Lawrence in Rev. Stephen Bloomer Balch's academy at Georgetown in 1784, but their extravagances led him to remove them in November to the Alexandria academy. The two boys were to cause problems for GW for several years. During his presidency, GW sent them to the University of Pennsylvania, and in 1792 both went to study law with Atty. Gen. Edmund Randolph, then living in Philadelphia (DECATUR, 180, 270). The money that GW expended on behalf of the two nephews was never recovered, but by the terms of his will the debt, amounting to nearly £450, was erased.

Sunday 20th. Mercury at 43 in the Morning, 47 at Noon and 50 at Night.

Wind pretty fresh all day from the Southward. Morning lowering. About Noon great appearances of rain—but towards sunsetting the clouds dispersed and the Sun came out.

A large, but not a very distinct circle about the moon.

Monday 21st. Mercury at 42 in the Morning [ ] at Noon, and 46 at Night. Wind at No. West, and pretty fresh all day—weather clear and very pleasant.

Went to Alexandria with Mrs. Washington. Dined at Mr. Dulany's and exchanged Deeds for conveyance of Land with him & Mrs. Dulany—giving mine, which I bought of Messrs. Robt. Adam, Dow & McIvor for the reversion of what Mrs. Dulany is entitled to at the death of her Mother within the bounds of Spencer & Washington's Patent.

Fanny Bassett who went on Thursday last to the wedding of

Miss Blackburn returned–accompanied by my Nephew Bushrod Washington. George Steptoe Washington returned this morning to the Academy at George Town & in the Evening the Manager of his & Brothers Estate came here with some money for their use–Sent by my Brother Charles.

The manager of the estate of George Steptoe Washington and his brother was probably Robert Carter (LEDGER B, 229, 301).

Tuesday 22d. Mercury at 36 in the Morning, 42 at Noon and the same at Night.

Wind pretty fresh all day from the No. Wt. and Cool. Weather perfectly clear–ground hard froze. Removed two pretty large & full grown Lilacs to the No. Garden gate–one on each side, taking up as much dirt with the roots as cd. be well obtained–also a Mock Orange to the Walk leading to the No. Necessary.

I also removed from the Woods and old fields, several young Trees of the Sassafras, Dogwood, & red bud to the Shrubbery on the No. Side the grass plat.

Syringa vulgaris, lilac, and *Philadelphus coronarius,* mock orange.

Wednesday 23d. Mercury at 36 in the Morning–40 at Noon and 42 at Night.

In the Morning it was calm and clear. About 10 oclock the wind, for about an hour, blew pretty fresh and cool from the No. West. It then shifted to the Eastward–died away and grew cloudy and towards Night had all the appearances of falling weather.

Planted trees on the South Shrubbery similar to those of yesterday, in the South Shrubbery except the Lilacs for which I thought the ground too wet.

Brought down a number of young Aspan trees from one Saml. Jenkins's near the old Court House to transplant into the Serpentine Avenues to the Door. As they came late I had the roots buried until they could be transplanted in the places they are intended to grow.

In his second reference to "South Shrubbery" in this entry GW apparently should have written "North Shrubbery." ASPAN TREES: *Populus tremuloides,* aspen or quaking aspen.

Fairfax Old Court House was built in 1742 on the road leading from Hunting Creek to Key's, or Vestal's, Gap. In 1755 the county seat was moved to Alexandria and in 1800 removed to its present location southwest of the old courthouse, on the road from Alexandria to Williams', or Snickers' Gap (HARRISON [1], 321–26).

Thursday 24th. Mercury at 40 in the Morning, 44 at Noon and 42 at Night.

About two Inches of Snow fell in the Night. Before daylight, it began to rain, and continued to do so until near Sundown when it ceased, & the horizon became clear to the Westward.

Prevented by the weather from preparing my grounds or transplanting trees.

Wind Eastwardly in the forenoon & westwardly afterwds.

Friday 25. Mercury at 40 in the Morng. 42 at Noon and 38 at Night.

Wind Westwardly and cloudy all day—rather cool—although the ground was not frozen this morning.

Laid off part of the Serpentine Road on the South side the grass plat, to day. Prevented going on with it, first by the coming in of Mr. Michael Stone about 10 oclock (who went away before noon)—then by the arrival of Colo. Hooe, Mr. Chas. Alexander, & Mr. Chs. Lee before dinner and Mr. Crawford, his Bride & sister after it.

The same cause prevented my transplanting trees in my Shrubberies, & obliged me to cover the roots of many which had been dug up (particularly Dogwood, Maple, Poplar, & Mulberry) the ground not being marked for their reception.

Colo. Hooe, Mr. Chs. Alexander & Mr. Lee went away after Dinner.

Charles Lee by Cephas Thompson. (National Portrait Gallery, Smithsonian Institution, Washington, D.C.)

GW is probably referring to Michael Jenifer Stone (1747–1812), the son of David Stone and his second wife, Elizabeth Jenifer Stone, of Charles County, Md. Stone served in the Maryland House of Delegates 1781–83, as a member of the Maryland ratification convention in 1788, and in the federal House of Representatives 1789–91. He was appointed judge of the first Maryland judicial district in 1791. MR. CRAWFORD: probably Nathaniel Craufurd and his new wife, Sarah Blackburn Craufurd.

Saturday 26th. Mercury at 33 in the Morning, 38 at Noon and 37 at Night.

Wind at No. West all day and at times pretty fresh—more or less cloudy and in the evening lowering. The ground was hard froze this morning.

Finished laying out my Serpentine Roads. Dug most of the holes where the trees by the side of them are to stand and planted some of the Maple which were dug yesterday and some of the Aspan which had been brought here on Wednesday last.

Sunday 27th. Mercury at 30 in the Morning 34 at Noon and 37 at Night.

Weather clear—Wind fresh from the No. West all day.

After Breakfast Mr. Crawford, his wife & Sister went away—they crossed at my Fer⟨ry⟩ to Marlborough. Mr. Bushrod Washington also set off for his fathers passing through Maryland.

Monday 28th. Mercury at 33 in the Morning 36 at Noon and 43 at Night.

Wind No. Wt. & westerly all day & cool—ground hard froze—Flying clouds but no appearance of rain.

Planted all the Mulberry trees, Maple trees, & Black gums in my Serpentine walks and the Poplars on the right walk—the Sap of which and the Mulberry appeared to be moving. Also planted 4 trees from H. Hole the name unknown but of a brittle wood which has the smell of Mulberry.

BLACK GUMS: *Nyssa sylvatica.*

March 1785

Tuesday 1st. Mercury at 34 in the morning 38 at Noon and 42 at Night.

Wind at No. West all day, & sometimes pretty fresh; at others very moderate. In general clear with some flying clouds.

Planted the remainder of the Poplars & part of the Ash Trees —also a circle of Dogwood with a red bud in the Middle close to the old Cherry tree near the South Garden Ho[use].

Began with my two Tumblers to Cart Dung upon the Ground designed for Clover and Orchard grass.

Wednesday 2d. Mercury at 35 this Morning—40 at Noon and 39 at Night.

Wind at No. West all day, and for the most part of it pretty fresh and cold. Cloudy and towards Sunsetting much the appearance of Snow. Planted the remainder of the Ash Trees—in the Serpentine walks—the remainder of the fringe trees in the Shrubberies—all the black haws—all the large berried thorns with a small berried one in the middle of each clump—6 small berried thorns with a large one in the middle of each clump—all the swamp red berry bushes & one clump of locust trees.

Thursday 3d. Mercury at 34 in the Morng., 40 at Noon and [ ] at Night.

Morning calm, warm, and very pleasant—wind afterwards from the Southward & pretty fresh. Sun set in a bank.

Planted the remainder of the Locusts—Sassafras—small berried thorn & yellow Willow in the Shrubberies, as also the red buds—a honey locust and service tree by the South Garden House. Likewise took up the clump of Lilacs that stood at the Corner of the South Grass plat & transplanted them to the clusters in the Shrubberies & standards at the south Garden gate. The Althea trees were also planted.

Employed myself the greatest part of the day in pruning and shaping the young plantation of Trees & Shrubs.

In the Evening Mr. Story formerly an assistant to Genel. Greene & afterwards Aide de Camp to Lord Stirling came in and spent the Evening.

His yellow willow is *Salix pentandra,* now called the bay-leaved willow, and his service tree is *Amelanchier obovalis,* serviceberry or juneberry. A specimen of the English service tree, *Sorbus domestica,* was still standing in 1917 near the northwest corner of the bowling green (SARGENT [2], 12–13), perhaps surviving from the cuttings of this species which GW acquired from William Bartram in 1792. The althea, *Hibiscus syriacus,* is also called rose of Sharon.

Maj. John Story (1754–1791), of Massachusetts, served as deputy quartermaster general of the Continental Army from 1777 to 1780, having earlier held several minor posts. He later acted for a short time as aide to Maj. Gen. Lord Stirling until the general's death in 1783.

Friday 4th. Mercury at 42 in the Morning. 46 at Noon and the same at Night.

Morning thick and heavy, with appearances of rain. Before noon the Sun made some feeble efforts to shine, but was again obscured in the afternoon; & towards Night it began a mizling rain and in the Night there fell more, so as to wet the ground.

Planted two more Service trees at the North Garden wall one on each side the gate—two Catalpas (large) West of the Garden Houses—28 Crab trees and the like number of Magnolia—besides a number of little Sprouts, from 6 Inches to two feet high of the last mentioned tree. The Magnolia had good roots wch. were well enclosed with the Earth they grew in. Also compleated my Serpentine walks with Elm trees.

After breakfast Mr. Story went away and about Noon Colo. Mercer came in & spent the remaining part of the day & Night here.

Catalpa bignonioides, catalpa.

Lt. Col. John Francis Mercer (1759–1821) was the son of John Mercer of Marlborough. During the Revolution he served in the Continental Army, at one time acting as aide-de-camp to Maj. Gen. Charles Lee. He was a member of the Continental Congress 1782–85 and the Virginia House of Delegates 1782 and 1785–86. On 3 Feb. 1785 Mercer married Sophia Sprigg (1766–1812), eldest daughter of Richard Sprigg of Strawberry Hill at Annapolis. Soon after his marriage he moved to his wife's home in Annapolis, and in 1789 moved to the Sprigg family farm in Anne Arundel County. He later served in the Maryland House of Delegates, the United States House of Representatives, and as governor of Maryland.

Saturday 5th. Mercury at 45 in the Morning [ ] at Noon and 54 at Night.

Morning cloudy; but clear by 10 Oclock; the wind being at No. West tho' neither fresh nor cool. About noon the wind shifted to So. West grew quite warm & pleasant. Sun Set in A Bank.

Planted all the Holly trees to day—most of them with a good deal of dirt about the Roots—but they were very indifferent trees having stragling limbs & not well leeaved.

Colo. Mercer went away after breakfast. I rid into the Neck & to Muddy hole Plantn.

Sunday 6th. Mercury at 48 in the morning, 50 at Noon and 55 at Night.

Morning a little lowering & calm—Wind afterwards pretty fresh from the Southward—weather Mild.

Munday 7th. Mercury at 50 in the Morning, 50 at Noon and 48 at Night.

Wind Southwardly in the forenoon & until about 3 oclock when it shifted to the No. West blew pretty fresh & turned cold.

The morning lowered, and until Noon, sprinkled rain at Intervals. About 12 Oclock the Sun came out very warm & pleasant & continued so until the wind shifted which brot. up Clouds again.

Planted all my Cedars, all my Papaw, and two Honey locust Trees in my Shrubberies and two of the latter in my groves—one at each ⟨side⟩ of the House and a large Holly tree on the Point going to the Sein landing.

Began to raise the Bank of Earth & to turf it, along the Northernmost row of Trees in the Serpentine Walk in the right.

Finished Plowing the Ground adjoining the Pine Grove, designed for Clover & Orchard grass Seed.

Juniperus virginiana, red cedar, and *Asimina triloba,* papaw.

Tuesday 8th. Mercury at 43 in the Morning, 42 at Noon and 38 at Night.

In the Night there fell a good deal of rain which about Sun rise changed to hail & sleet wch. prevailed through the day and loaded the Trees with Ice with the weight of which the Evergreen in my Shrubberies were a good deal bowed.

Wind pretty fresh all day at East. The ground was covered about an Inch with the hail &ca.

Wednesday 9th. Mercury at 38 in the morning, 44 at Noon and 48 Night.

A great deal of rain fell last Night and the heaviest Sleet I ever recollect to have seen.

The bows of all the trees were incrusted by tubes of Ice, quite round, at least half an Inch think—the weight of Which was so great that my late transplantation in many instances sunk under it either by bending the bodies of the young trees—breaking the limbs—or weighing up the roots. The largest pines, in my outer circle were quite oppressed by the Ice; and bowed to the ground: whilst others were loosened at the roots and the largest Catalpa trees had some of their principal branches broken. The ground also where the holes had been dug to receive the Trees, and Where it had not been rammed, was a mere quagmire.

The ground this morning was covered nearly two inches deep with Snow—little of wch. remained at Night.

The morning was cloudy with the wind at No. West wch. soon died away and then, abt. Noon, sprung up pretty brisk from the Southwest—which a little before sun down again Shifted to the No. West and as Night approached came on to blow pretty fresh & cold.

The ground being covd. with Snow the fore part of the day, & in no condition to work the latter part I set the jobbers to pounding the plaister of Paris by hand for want of other & better convenience to do it.

GW began experimenting with plaster of paris (gypsum) as a fertilizer about this time. The plaster was pounded into a powder and spread over the ground. Although he mentions in his entry of 9 May 1785 that he can see no benefit from its use on the circle in his courtyard, the results were evidently satisfactory in other instances, for he continued to use it on grass and some crops for the rest of his life.

Thursday 10th. Mercury at 34 in the Morning, 38 at Noon and 32 at Night.

Wind fresh from the No. Wt. all day and cold. Ground hard froze in the morning and but little thawed through the day.

Sent my Waggon with the Posts for the Oval in my Court Yard to be turned by a Mr. Ellis at the Snuff Mill on Pohick & to proceed from thence to Occoquan for the Scion of the Hemlock to plant in my Shrubberies.

Continued with my jobbers to pound the Plaister of Paris as the Earth was too hard frozen to be dealt with.

Went to return the visits of Colo. Mason and others in his Neighbourhood. Called first at Mr. Lawrence Washington's, who being from home, I proceeded to Colo. Masons, where I dined & lodged.

MR. ELLIS: GW means William Allison, who, in partnership with Col. George Mason's son Thomson Mason, operated a snuff mill or factory in Fairfax County. The mill was on Pohick Creek above Gunston Hall, on land owned by George Mason of Pohick (MASON [2], 2:777–79, 874).

SCION OF THE HEMLOCK: In grafting today, a scion is considered to be that portion of the plant to be grafted to the main stock. Here and elsewhere GW uses the term to mean young seedlings. The hemlock is *Tsuga canadensis.*

Lawrence Washington (1740–1799), Lund's brother, had moved from the Chotank area during the Revolution and settled at Belmont, the old Catesby Cocke home near the mouth of Occoquan Creek in Fairfax County.

Friday 11th. Mercury at 30 in the Morning, 34 at Noon and 41 at Night.

Left Colo. Masons about 12 oclock. Dined with Mr. Martin Cockburn, & came home in the afternoon.

Planted the Hemlock Scions which were brought home yesterday, 28 in Number in the Shrubbs—2 poplar trees wch. had been omitted (by an oversight) in my Serpentine Walks before; and 13 Weeping and 13 Yellow Willow trees alternately along the Post & rail fence from the Kitchen to the South ha-haw & from the Servants Hall to the Smith's Shop.

Brought 9 Scions of the Portugal Peach from Mr. Cockburn with me.

The weeping willow is ordinarily *Salix babylonica,* but GW often interchanges the words "weeping" and "yellow." Here he may be referring to *S. alba vitellina,* an introduced species. SERVANTS HALL: The new dependency adjoining the mansion on the north was used for white servants. The blacksmith shop lay a short distance north of the servants' hall.

The Portugal peach is a large clingstone. In sending a few pits to George Mason, Thomas Jefferson said the Portugal required more care than common peaches but, when carefully cultivated, was the finest he had ever tasted (BETTS [2], 91).

Saturday 12th. Mercury at 34 in the morning, 38 at Noon & 44 at Night.

Day clear and pleasant until about 5 oclock, when it began to lower, and the Sun set in a bank.

Wind Southerly all day. After dark it shifted to the No. Et. blew pretty fresh and grew colder.

Went to Abingden to see Mr. John Lewis who lay sick there. Returned in the Afternoon and brot. Betcy Custis home with me.

Planted two Hemlock trees in a line with the East end of my Kitchen, & Servants Hall; & 10 feet from the corner of the Post & rail fence at each.

Had a Bushel of the Plaister of Paris (which my people had been pounding) sifted & Weighed—which, in this State, amounted to 82 lbs.

Laid the borders of the gravel walk to the No. Necessary—from the circle in the Court yard.

Abingdon, the home of Jacky Custis's widow, Nelly, and her second husband, David Stuart, was situated on the Potomac River just north of Four Mile Run. Jacky and Nelly Custis, who had lived at the Custis White House on Pamunkey River after their marriage, had both wanted to return to the Mount Vernon–Mount Airy neighborhood. In 1778 Jacky bought this house and about 900 acres of land from Robert Alexander, agreeing to pay him £12 per acre, the principal and compound interest to be paid in 24 years. GW was horrified at this latest example of his stepson's fecklessness and reminded him that "£12,000 at compound Interest, [amounts] to upwards of

£48,000 in twenty four Years. . . . No Virginia estate . . . can stand simple Interest; how then can they bear compound Interest"? (GW to John Parke Custis, 3 Aug. 1778, DLC:GW). The Stuarts lived at Abingdon until about 1792 (STETSON [1], 24–27; STETSON [2], 78–79).

Sunday 13th. Mercury at 42 this Morning, 46 at Noon and 48 at Night.

Wind very fresh from the So. West, and great appearances of Rain in the forenoon. About Noon the wind ceased, and the Sun came out—after which it again clouded—the wind shifted to the No. Et. and it set in for a serious rain about 5 oclock which was unlucky on acct. of an open Boat load of Flour from my Mill, bound to Alexandria for Mr. Hartshorne and wch. I was obliged to detain at my Fish house under as good cover as I could provide for it.

Munday 14th. Mercury at 48 in the Morning, 46 at Noon and 48 at Night.

A great deal of rain fell in the Night, which never ceased until after 8 oclock.

My Boat with the flour went off about day break but whether the flour received any damage or not I cannot tell.

The wind remained at No. East until 9 oclock when it died away and sprung up pretty fresh from the No. West when the Sun came out. It did not turn cold notwithstanding the point from whh. the wind blew and the freshness of it.

Planted the 9 young peach Trees which I brought from Mr. Cockburns in the No. Garden—viz.—4 on the South border of the second walk (two on each side of the middle walk) —2 in the border of the Walk leading from the Espalier hedge towards the other cross walk and 3 under the South wall of the Garden; that is two on the right as we enter the gate & one on the left. The other Peachtree to answer it on that side & the two on the West Walk, parralel to the Walnut trees were taken from the nursery in the Garden.

Drove Stakes to support the largest of the evergreens in my Shrubberies—the wind shaking & giving too much disturbance to the roots of them especially when the ground is soft.

Tuesday 15th. Mercury at 36 in the morning—38 at Noon and 40 at Night.

Ground hard frozen in the Morning—Wind brisk (and cold) all day from the No. West; which made the borders to my Walk, progress slowly.

Laid out a walk for the wilderness, intended on the No. of the Serpentine road on the right.

Began to open Vistos throw the Pine grove on the Banks of H. Hole.

Visited my Plantations at the Ferry, Muddy hole, & Dogue run.

Wednesday 16th. Mercury at 26 in the morng.—27 at Noon and 33 at Night.

Ground very hard froze & air Sharp from the No. West all day which prevented any movement of Earth.

About 1 Oclock a Mr. Alexander Donald came here introduced by a letter from Govr. Henry.

Alexander Donald was a Richmond merchant who often acted for Robert Morris in business matters. He had been for many years an intimate friend of Thomas Jefferson (JEFFERSON [1], 12:132, 347). GW did business with Donald over a period of several years, probably on behalf of the Custis estate. For a brief time after 1789, Donald was in London as a partner in the firm of Donald & Burton, which failed in 1793 (HAMILTON [2], 15:619, n.3).

Thursday 17th. Mercury at 24 in the Morning—32 at Noon and 30 at Night.

Ground hard froze—the Creeks quite fast with Ice & the river covered with it to the channel.

Wind Southerly all day, but not very fresh. The day, until after the middle of the afternoon, was very clear—it then began to lower, & at Sunset looked very much like rain.

No earth could be moved until the afternoon; and even then, it not being in good order, it was not attempted.

Laid out a walk for the Wilderness intended on the South of the Serpentine road on the left.

After breakfast Mr. Donald went away and to dinner Colo. Andrew Lewis (son of Genl. Andw. Lewis) and a Mr. Neiley, came—afterwch. they crossed into Maryland.

Trimmed the Weeping and Yellow trees which were transplanted on the 10th. & put 80 cuttings of the former into a nursery.

Col. Andrew Lewis (1759–1844) was a son of Brig. Gen. Andrew Lewis (1720–1781), the hero of Point Pleasant. Lewis at this time resided on the south side of the Roanoke River in Botetourt County (MCALLISTER, 183; KEGLEY, 566). MR. NEILEY: possibly one of the several sons of Capt. James Neely, who lived near Col. Andrew Lewis (KEGLEY, 566–67).

Friday 18th. Mercury at 38 in the Morning—42 at Noon and 44 at Night.

Wind Southerly all day—very lowering in the forenoon. Soon after 12 Oclock there began a light mixture of Snow & rain, which continued through the day; encreasing as it advanced.

I went to my Dogue run Plantation to make choice of the size, & to direct the taking up of Pine trees, for my two wildernesses. Brought 3 waggon load of them home, and planted every other hole round the Walks in them. Began with that on the right, which was planted before the wet fell, & better planted; that is with more pains the other (on the left) being hurried more and the ground wet and sticky.

Also planted 20 Pine trees in the lines of Trees by the sides of the Serpentine roads to the House.

Received from Mr. Josh. Parke of Norfolk a box containing young trees of the live oak and 10 Acorns which I presume is from the same sort of Trees.

A good deal of rain fell in the Night.

MR. JOSH. PARKE: Col. Josiah Parker (1751–1810), of Macclesfield, Isle of Wight County, had been a member of the committee of safety and the Virginia conventions of 1775 and an officer in the American army. After resigning as colonel of the 5th Virginia Regiment on 1 April 1778, Parker became commander of all Virginia militia south of the James River until the end of the war. In 1780 and 1781 he was a member of the House of Delegates and from 1783 to 1789 was naval officer and collector at Portsmouth. He served in the United States Congress 1789–1801.

Quercus virginiana, live oak, is an evergreen ranging along the east coast of the United States from Virginia to Florida.

Saturday 19th. Mercury at 40 in the Morning—42 at Noon and 43 at Night.

Wind at No. Et. all day; and more or less rain mixed in sml. degree with Snow; which with what fell in the Night made the ground so wet that I could plant no trees to day. Many of those planted yesterday yielded to the Wind & Wet, and required propping.

Received a Swan, 4 Wild Geese, & two Barrels of Holly Berries (in Sand) from my Brother John and a Barrel of the early Corn from New York.

The early corn from New York had been sent by Gov. George Clinton, who called it "small white Indian corn." On 5 Mar. 1785 he told GW that if it thrived in Virginia he ought to obtain new seed every three years. It was probably a flint variety, as were most northern corns of that period (DLC:GW).

Sunday 20th. Mercury at 39 in the Morning—42 at Noon and 40 at Night.

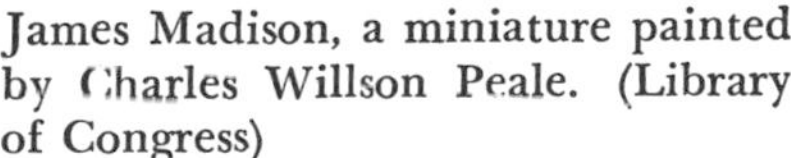
James Madison, a miniature painted by Charles Willson Peale. (Library of Congress)

Thomas Stone, painted by John Beale Bordley. (State House, Annapolis, Maryland, Maryland Commission on Artistic Property)

Morning lowering. About Noon the Sun came out and the Weather looked promising but in the afternoon it clouded & threatned, and sometime after dark began a mixture of Snow and rain.

Wind was at East, and So. East all day—sometimes pretty fresh but for the most part of it moderate.

Major Jenefir came here to dinner and my carriage went to Gunston Hall to take Colo. Mason to a meeting of Comrs. at Alexandria for settling the Jurisdiction of Chesapeak Bay & the rivers Potomack & Pocomoke between the States of Virginia & Maryland—The Commissioners on the Part of Virginia being Colo. Mason—The Attorney General—Mr. Madison & Mr. Henderson—on that of Maryland, Major Jenifer Thoms. Johnson, Thos. Stone & Saml. Chase Esqrs.

Conflicting claims of colonial Virginia and Maryland over the control of the Potomac River and the Chesapeake Bay were put to rest only temporarily during the Revolution. In 1784 Virginia authorized the four commissioners here named to confer with agents of Maryland for the purpose of settling those questions. The Virginians were also authorized to consult with the Maryland commissioners on how to gain the cooperation of Pennsylvania in developing a water and land route from the Potomac Valley to the Ohio Valley, wherein the Potomac River water route would be developed by the

Potomac Company recently authorized by Maryland and Virginia. GW hoped that the project "may be of great political, as well as commercial advantages . . . as it may tie the Settlers of the western Territory to the Atlantic States by interest, which is the only knot that will hold" (GW to Benjamin Lincoln, 5 Feb. 1785, DLC:GW).

ATTORNEY GENERAL: Edmund Randolph (1753–1813) was at this time attorney general of Virginia and a delegate to the Continental Congress. He was the son of John Randolph, the attorney general of the colony who had fled with Governor Dunmore at the outbreak of the Revolution. Randolph served as an aide to GW, 1775–76, and was a member of the Virginia Convention of 1776.

James Madison, of Montpelier, Orange County, sponsored the resolutions establishing the Virginia commission. Thomas Stone (1743–1787), one of the six sons of David and Elizabeth Jenifer Stone of Poynton Manor, Charles County, Md., studied law in Annapolis under Thomas Johnson, who appears here. He married Margaret Brown (d. 1787), one of nine daughters of Dr. Gustavus Richard Brown (1689–1762) of Rich Hill, Charles County, Md. His home, Habre-de-Venture, was near Port Tobacco in Charles County, Md. Stone, one of the signers of the Declaration of Independence for Maryland, was now serving his second term in the senate of that state. Samuel Chase (1741–1811), a lawyer, merchant, and speculator, now of Annapolis, had been a Maryland leader in the Revolution, and as a member of both Continental Congresses, he had been a strong supporter of GW throughout the war. GW later appointed Chase to the United States Supreme Court where, although impeached during Jefferson's presidency, he served until his death.

The Virginia commissioners had not been notified that this first meeting was to be held in Alexandria this week, and only George Mason and Alexander Henderson, who both lived nearby, were present on the day appointed (see FREEMAN, 6:30; MASON [2], 2:812–23; MADISON, 8:89–90, 206–7, 337–39).

Monday 21st. Mercury at 40 in the Morning [ ] at Noon and 46 at Night.

Very little wind all day but foggy and moist which carried away the Snow & hail that fell in the Night rather better than an Inch thick.

Staked up the largest of my Trees in the avenues and Wilderness and Shrubberies to day, which from the softness of the ground & impression made on them by the Wind were leaning.

Bought 150 Bushels of clean & good Oats from an Eastern shore man at 2/4 pr. Bushel.

Major Jenifer left this for Alexandria after Dinner.

Tuesday 22d. Mercury at 45 in the Morning, 52 at Noon and 51 at Night.

Mizling Morning and very little Wind. About 8 Oclock it

sprung up at No. West, & encreasing, blew hard all the remaining part of the day from that point & West.

Mrs. Grayson sent me 8 Yew & 4 Aspan trees & Colo. Mason some Cherry Grafts. Planted the intermediate holes round the Walk in the Wilderness on the right and filled the spaces between with young Pines.

Went to Alexandria—dined & returned in the Evening.

Eleanor Smallwood Grayson was the wife of GW's friend and former aide, Col. William Grayson. GW had written William Grayson, asking him to send him scions of the aspen and shoots of the yew or hemlock growing along Quantico Creek near Dumfries, which Grayson had offered during an earlier conversation. "Plantations of this kind are now become my amusement & I should be glad to know where I could obtain a supply of such sorts of trees as would diversify the scene" (22 Jan. 1785, DLC:GW). Grayson replied from New York that he had procured some aspen trees from Landon Carter's plantation on Bull Run and that Mrs. Grayson promised to send them to Mount Vernon along with any of the yew scions she could procure (10 Mar. 1785, DLC:GW).

If GW went to Alexandria today to check on the progress of the Potomac commissioners, he discovered they had already "waited some Days" for the two absent Virginia commissioners (George Mason to James Madison, 9 Aug. 1785, MASON [2], 2:826).

Wednesday 23d. Mercury at 40 in the Morning—40 at Noon and 40 at Night.

Wind fresh and cool all day from the No. West. Very clear.

Finished Planting the Pine trees in the wilderness on the left and planted 4 of the live Oak Trees (which I had received from Norfolk) in the Shrubberies on the right and left on the grass plat in front of the House. Staked most of the Pines that had been planted.

Thursday 24th. Mercury at 40 in the Morning—45 at Noon and 45 at Night.

Wind Southerly. The Sun, tho' it rose clear had a Watery look and soon became obscured. The Weather very lowering. About 4 Oclock it began to Snow (fine Snow) & continued to do so with a small mixture of rain until I went to bed.

Finding the Trees round the Walks in my wildernesses rather too thin I doubled them by putting (other Pine) trees between each.

Laid off the Walks in my Groves, at each end of the House.

Sent my Carriage to Alexandria for Colo. Mason according to appointment—who came in about dusk.

The "appointment" was probably an agreement made on 22 Mar. that if the two absent Virginia commissioners did not appear in another day, the remaining commissioners would accept GW's hospitality at Mount Vernon to proceed with their conference. GW and Mason had this evening and the following morning to review prospects for the meeting.

Friday 25th. Mercury at 42 in the Morning–45 at Noon and 45 at Night.

A thick fog, or mist, all day; with little or no wind.

Planted some of the largest Pine trees on the Circular bank which is intended to inclose the Court yard, Shrubberies &ca. and Staked most of those wch. had been planted in the two Wildernesses.

About One O'clock Major Jenifer, Mr. Stone, Mr. Chase, & Mr. Alexr. Henderson arrived here.

In his letter of 9 Aug. 1785 to James Madison, George Mason reported that the Potomac conference had "adjourn'd to Mount-Vernon . . . at the particular Invitation of the General" (MASON [2], 2:827).

Saturday 26th. Mercury at 42 in the Morning–45 at Noon and 44 at Night.

Morning clear, but a watery Sun, which was soon obscured by clouds; the whole day was lowering; towards Sundown it began to Snow, which continued until it became two Inches deep.

The Wind was at No. East all day & was raw & chilling.

My jobbers spent the greater part of this day in placing stakes for the Support of the young Pine trees. Mr. G. Mason Jr. & Dr. Brown came, dined, & returned.

Sunday 27th. Mercury at 42 in the Morning [ ] at Noon and 52 at Night.

All the Pines, & other evergreen Trees which were not well staked, being heavily loaded with Snow, yeilded to the weight, and where the ground was very soft (which was the case in many places) quite laid to the ground.

Wind Southerly all day but not much of it. Morning cloudy & more or less so all day.

The Snow which was not more than two Inches deep, soon disappeared.

Mr. Waltr. Stone dined here and went away afterwards. Mr. Henderson also went to Colchester after dinner to return in the morning.

Walter Stone may be either Walter Stone (died c.1791), son of David and Elizabeth Jenifer Stone, or Walter Hanson Stone (1765–1792), son of Samuel and Anna Hanson Mitchell Stone.

Monday 28th. Mercury at 44 in the Morning–52 at Noon and 56 at Night.

Wind Southerly all day and clear weather.

Mr. Henderson returned to the Meeting of the Commissioners abt. 10 Oclock and Mr. Chase went away after dinner.

The commissioners' final agreement and official letters all were dated Mount Vernon, 28 Mar. 1785, and historians have since referred to this meeting as the Mount Vernon Conference (see MASON [2], 2:812–22; FREEMAN, 6:30).

Tuesday 29th. Mercury at 52 in the Morning [ ] at Noon and 54 at Night.

The Sun rose with a watery appearance tho' the hemisphere was clear–which however soon clouded & towards evening began to rain.

Wind at No. East all day but not very fresh until dark.

Major Jenifer, Mr. Stone and Mr. Henderson went away before breakfast & Colo. Mason (in my carriage) after it by the return of which he sent me some young Shoots of the Persian Jessamine & Guilder Rose.

Transplanted in the groves at the ends of the House the following young trees. Viz.–9 live oak–11 Yew or Hemlock–10 Aspan–4 Magnolia–2 Elm–2 Papaw–2 Lilacs–3 Fringe–1 Swamp berry & 1 H ⟨ ⟩

Doctr. Stuart came in the afternoon.

Syringa persica, Persian jasmine, and *Viburnum opulus roseum,* guelder rose or snowball.

Wednesday 30th. Mercury at 58 in the Morning–62 at Noon and [ ] at Night.

A good deal of rain fell in the Night–showers all day with thunder; & alternate Squals and calm.

Doctr. Stuart went away after breakfast & carried the three Children Betcy, Nelly, & Washington Custis with him to Abingdon.

Arthur Lee Esqr. came to Dinner.

Eleanor Parke (Nelly) Custis (1779–1852) and George Washington Parke Custis (1781–1857), usually called Washington, were the two youngest children of David Stuart's wife Nelly and her first husband, John Parke Custis. Little Nelly had been brought to Mount Vernon soon after her birth for her mother was too ill to take care of her. Washington, too, had lived with his grandparents most of his life. Although there seem to have been no legal documents drawn up, GW spoke of these two youngest children as "adopted" by him and Mrs. Washington (GW to Lawrence Lewis, 20 Sept. 1799, DLC:GW).

The "Virginian Scarlet Honey-suckle," or trumpet honeysuckle, from *Catalogus Plantarum,* London, 1730. (Beinecke Rare Book and Manuscript Library, Yale University)

Arthur Lee, who served in the Virginia House of Delegates 1781–83 and the Continental Congress 1781–84, was one of the commissioners who concluded treaties with the Indians in Oct. 1784 and Jan. 1785, and was at this time awaiting the action of the Congress on his nomination to the Board of Treasury.

Thursday 31st. Mercury at 52 in the Morning—56 at Noon and 60 at Night.

Wind very hard all day from west—weather clear.

Mr. Lee went away after Breakfast and in the Afternoon Mr. Thos. Hanson & two of his Sisters arrived and Nelly Hanson came in.

Planted the Scarlet or French honey suckle (as my Gardner calls it, & which he says blows all the Summer) at each Column of my covered ways—as also against the circular walls between the Store house &ca. and the two new necessaries.

Also planted the Gilder rose & Persian Jessamine opposite thereto on the Walks leading up to these necessaries—4 of the first and Six of the latter on each walk.

Capt. Thomas Hawkins Hanson, son of Samuel Hanson of Green Hill, had served in the 3d Maryland Battalion of the Flying Camp in 1776. He was married to Rebecca Dulany Addison, widow of Thomas Addison (d. 1774), and lived at the old Addison farm, Oxon Hill, across the Potomac River from Alexandria. He was probably a partner in the Alexandria firm of his brother, Samuel Hanson of Samuel. Hanson had several sisters including Sarah Hawkins, Anna, and Chloe. Nelly Hanson may have been a niece or cousin.

Lonicera sempervirens, trumpet honeysuckle. MY GARDNER: Philip Bateman (Bottiman), GW's gardener, had been at Mount Vernon as early as 1773 (GW's tithable list for 1773, DLC:GW). In 1783 Lund Washington had written GW: "As to Bateman (the old gardener) I have no expectation of his ever seeking another home. Indulge him but in getg. Drunk now and then, and he will be Happy. He is the best Kitchen gardener to be met with" (Lund Washington to GW, 1 Oct. 1783, ViMtV). Philip Bater, gardener, who appears in the ledgers from 1786 through 1789, is probably the same man.

April—1785

[1.] Mercury at 50 in the Morning—54 at Noon and 58 at Night.

Wind variable—from So. West to No. Wt.—pretty fresh, and towards Evening more cool; then being at No. West.

Mr. Hanson went away after breakfast.

Grafted 12 Duke, 12 May Duke and 12 black May heart

Cherries & 12 Burgamy Pears. The Cherries were chiefly on Stocks wch. had been taken up a considerable time, & the roots covered with Earth. These Cherries and pears are planted on the left of the Area leading from the Gate to the Green House in the following manner–next the cross walk are the Duke Cherries–then the May Duke–then the black May Heart and lastly the Burgamy Pears. A Peg is driven between each sort–the last being nearest the back Wall.

Again began to right my Trees & ram round them.

Rid to my Ferry and Muddy hole Plantations.

Saturday 2d. Mercury at 50 in the Morning–46 at Noon and 42 at Night.

Wind at No. Et. & pretty fresh until the afternoon, when it got to the No. West & turned cold.

About day breaking it began to Snow, & continued to do so until the ground was covered with it about an inch deep, after which there fell a mixture of Snow & rain till about ten oclock when it turned to constant rain the remainder of the day; accompanied by pretty sharp thunder.

Sunday 3d. Mercury at 38 in the Morning–42 at Noon and 44 at Night.

Wind very fresh all day from So. Wt. & West, and unpleasant.

After Dinner Mr. George Lewis & his wife & Mr. Chas. Carter and his wife and Child came here having been detained on the Road by the Weather.

George Lewis (1757–1821) was a son of Fielding and Betty Washington Lewis. At the beginning of the Revolution, he had been captain of an independent troop of cavalry which acted as part of GW's personal bodyguard. In 1777 this troop was incorporated into the newly established 3d Continental Dragoons. Lewis was married during the Revolution to Catherine Daingerfield (1764–1820), daughter of Col. William and Mary Willis Daingerfield of Coventry, Spotsylvania County. They lived for a time near Berryville in what was then Frederick County, but by 1785 seem to have been living in Fredericksburg. In 1796 they moved to Marmion in King George County.

Charles Carter (1765–1829), son of Edward and Sarah Champe Carter of Blenheim, was married in 1781 to GW's niece, Betty Lewis (1765–1830), daughter of Fielding and Betty Washington Lewis. The Carters lived for a time in Culpeper County, and Charles was often designated as "of Culpeper." They later moved to Frederick County and then to Pittsylvania. At this time Betty and Charles Carter had two children.

Monday 4th. Mercury at 40 in the Morning– [ ] at Noon and 46 at Night.

Wind fresh indeed hard at No. W. all day, with flying Clouds.

Grafted Six of the May white heart Cherry growing in my walk and Six of the small cherry opposite, or transplanted stocks, which were placed by the Area in front of the Green Ho[use] left hand approaching it, and in a line with the young Mulberry Cuttgs.—the first sort standing next the cross Walk, with a stake between them and the second sort. And my Gardener to shew his cunning, grafted ten Pairs from the Tree transplanted from the grass plat Feby. 9 (as will appear from this Diary) on Plumb Scions, & removed them to the Area above mentioned and along side the 12 Cherries wch. I grafted & planted as above.

Went to Alexandria to attend the Funeral of Mrs. Ramsay who died (after a lingering illness) on Friday last and to present Colo. Hooe with Major Jenifer's order, & to obtain a draft, consequent thereof on New York towards payment of my debt to Governor Clinton—but his indisposition prevented my doing business with him. Dined at Mr. Muirs & after the funerl. obsoques were ended returned home.

GRAFTED . . . ON PLUMB SCIONS: No gardener today is "cunning" enough to make pears grow on plum stocks. GW does not say whether or not the grafts were successful.

Ann McCarty Ramsay, daughter of Dennis and Sarah Ball McCarty, was the widow of William Ramsay, whose funeral GW attended 13 Feb. Mrs. Ramsay's son Dennis Ramsay wrote on 7 April 1785 to his absent brother Dr. William Ramsay, Jr., to say their mother had been buried "on Monday Evening attended by a very respectable number of the Inhabitants and Strangers in this place [Alexandria], the Revd Mr Griffith preached a Sermon on the unhappy event" (DSI: Ramsay Papers).

DEBT TO GOVERNOR CLINTON: GW had been forced to borrow money from Gov. George Clinton of New York to make his purchase of the land from Adam, Dow & McIver (see entry for 3 Feb. 1785). For further information see George Clinton's bond with GW, 1 Dec. 1782, NjP; GW to Clinton, 18 Dec. 1782, GW to Robert Morris, 8 Jan. 1783, DLC:GW.

Tuesday 5th. Mercury at 44 in the Morning— 50 at Noon and 53 at Night.

Wind very brisk all day from the No. West, & cool for the Season.

Mr. Carter and Mr. Geo. Lewis went to Abingdon after breakfast.

Wednesday 6th. Mercury at 47 in the Morning—[ ] at Noon and [ ] at Night.

Clear, calm & pleasant in the Morning. Wind afterward springing up from the Eastward, it began to lower and before Night had much the appearance of rain.

Sowed the semicircle North of the front gate with Holly berries sent me by my Brother John—three drills of them—the middle one of Berries which had been got about Christmas and put in Sand—the other two of Berries which had been got earlier in the year, gently dried, & packed in Shavings.

Planted in a Nursery in my Vineyard 17 Live Oaks sent me by Colo. Parker of Norfolk 13 of one, and 7 of another kind of what I suppose to be the wild Honeysuckle, they being in different Bundles, and he having been written to for the wild Honey Suckle.

Sent my Shad Sein and Hands to the Ferry to commen⟨ce⟩ Fishing for Mssrs. Douglas & Smith who had engaged to take all the Shad & Herring I can catch in the Season—the first at 15/. a hundred, and the other at 4/. a thousand.

A Mr. Vidler, to whom I had written (an Undertaker at Annapolis) came here and opened the cases wch. contained my Marble chimney piece—but for want of Workmen could not undertake to finish my New room.

Mr. Carter, & Mr. Geo. Lewis returned here this afternoon.

Lonicera periclymenum, wild honeysuckle. NURSERY IN MY VINEYARD: This was one of several experimental or nursery areas GW had on his Mount Vernon farms. The vineyard was behind the stables, south of the mansion house. DOUGLAS & SMITH: Smith & Douglass of Alexandria, also bought the shad and herring for the 1786 season, paying GW a slightly increased rate (LEDGER B, 225). The firm partnership was dissolved late in 1786 (*Va. Journal,* 26 Oct. 1786).

There was an Edward Vidler living in Annapolis in 1785 (*Va. Journal,* 25 Aug. 1785). AN UNDERTAKER: a contractor or subcontractor.

MY MARBLE CHIMNEY PIECE: Samuel Vaughan, a London merchant in the colonial trade, had enthusiastically supported the colonies during the Revolution, and had immigrated with his family to Philadelphia in 1783. He was a great admirer of GW and wrote to him in 1784 offering to send a marble chimney piece for his New Room at Mount Vernon (8 April 1784, DLC:GW). The chimney piece, packed in ten cases, arrived in Alexandria in Feb. 1785 aboard Capt. W. Haskell's brig *May.* GW wrote Vaughan's son Benjamin that "by the number of cases . . . I greatly fear it is too elegant & costly for my room, & republican stile of living" (GW to Benjamin Vaughan, 5 Feb. 1785, DLC:GW; *Va. Journal,* 3 Feb. 1785).

NEW ROOM: the large room at the north end of the mansion, now called the Banquet Hall, but always referred to by GW as the New Room. Construction on this room had been begun during the Revolution by Going Lanphier under Lund Washington's supervision (see main entry for 25 April 1774), but Lanphier had left before the interior of the room was completed. After his return to Mount Vernon GW was anxious to have work resumed on the unfinished structure.

Thursday 7th. Mercury at 48 in the Morng.–[ ] at Noon and 52 at Night.

Wind at East & fresh all day; Morning heavy, with great appearances of rain which began to fall about One clock moderately, but encreasing, it came on by Night to rain hard and in the Night much fell.

This day I had Assembled a number of Plows to prepare, if possible, the enclosure by my Barn & the Pine groves for sowing my Grass Seeds; but I had not plowed one half of it before the Rain obliged me to desist.

Sowed the South Semicercle–rather half of it, for the lower part was too wet, with Holly berries in the same manner I did the No. one with this difference, that the middle drill was sowed with the berries which had been dried & were packed in Shavings & the outr. drills of the othr. sort.

Colo. Willm. Fitzhugh of Maryland, & a Mr. Clare came here to Dinner; as did Nelly & Washn. Custis.

Col. William Fitzhugh (1721–1798) was the son of George Fitzhugh (died c.1722), of Stafford County. He represented Stafford in the House of Burgesses 1748–58. Shortly after his second marriage, to Ann Frisby Rousby of Maryland in 1755, Fitzhugh moved to Rousby Hall in Calvert County, Md. He was a member of the Maryland Council 1769–74 and commissary general of the state from 1773 until the Revolution. Fitzhugh served with GW's half brother Lawrence in the Cartagena campaign and his close friendship with GW dated back to the French and Indian War. Mr. Clare may have been a relative or a retainer of Fitzhugh's, for the colonel was infirm and blind at this time, and would have needed a traveling companion to care for him.

Friday 8th. Mercury at 47 in the Morning–[ ] at Noon and 52 at Night.

Morning clear, wind fresh from the No. West, which rather decreased wth. the Sun's altitude and in its decline, became nearly calm.

The ground being too wet to stir where it had been before plowed or worked, I was unable to touch that which I had been preparing for grass; and therefore began to hoe that wch. lyes between the New circular ditches, & the Wild rose hedges; on which I propose to make experiments of the quantity of the Plaister of Paris which is most proper to manure an acre of Land & to sow the same in grass seed.

Colo. Fitzhugh & Mr. Clair went away after breakfast. I rid to the Sein Landing at the Ferry.

Scattered 2½ bushels of the Powdered plaister of Paris on little more than half of the circle in my Court yard—next the Servants Hall (on the poor part of the ground) ; the Mould having been taken off that to raise the other side, which was the lowest.

WILD ROSE HEDGES: *Rosa eglanteria,* sweetbrier or eglantine. The sweetbrier is not a wild rose in the sense of being a native species but can grow into a disheveled planting if not trimmed.

Saturday 9th. Mercury at 47 this morning—52 at Noon and 50 at Night.

Morning calm & clear. Abt. Nine Oclock the wind sprung up at No. West, with flying Clouds and abt. Noon shifted to the So. West, & looked showery; but only a few drops of rain fell.

Laid of a piece of my Wheat field, containing 2 A[cres] 3 R[ods] 22 P[erches] At Muddy hole, & part of the adjoining field, containing 4 A[cres] 0 R[ods] 8 P[erches] for Grass seeds. The first I propose to sow Orchard grass seed on, & to roll it in. The other having been spread pretty thick with Dung from the Farm yard, I set the Plows to breaking it up & to prepare it for the reception of the Seed.

From hence I rid to my Dogue run Plantation and thence to the fishing Landing at the Ferry.

Mr. Geo. Lewis, his Wife and Sister (Mrs. Carter) went up to Abingdon to see their Brother Mr. John Lewis; & returned in the Evening. The two Miss Hansons crossed the river in order to return—but their Carriage not having arrived—came back again.

Continued Hooeing the grd. between my Circles by the outer gate, as noted on friday.

Dactylis glomerata, orchard grass.

Sunday 10th. Mercury at 46 in the Morning—52 at Noon and 60 at Night.

Clear all day—Morning calm; about 8 Oclock the Wind sprung up pretty fresh from the South West; which before ten got to No. West, & continued to blow hard.

Just as we had dined the two Doctr. Jenifers and Mr. Willm. Craik came in. The eldest of the Jenifers after getting his Dinner went away, to visit Mr. Wagener.

ELDEST OF THE JENIFERS: Walter Hanson Jenifer.

Monday 11th. Mercury at 52 in the Morning—68 at Noon and the same at Night.

Clear all day, with appearances of dry settled weather.

Calm in the Morning, but pretty brisk Southerly wind the remainder of the day.

As the ground had dryed a good deal I set the plows (tho' it was not in such order as I could wish) to work in the field they were driven from by the rain on Thursday last and the Hooes also in the piece adjoining.

Rid to Muddy hole & Neck Plantations.

After breakfast Mr. Carter, Wife & Child—Mr. Lewis & his wife, Mr. Craik & the youngest Doctr. Jenifer went away. Soon after which a Mr. Duchi a french Gentleman recommended by the Marquis de la Fayette to me, came in.

YOUNGEST DOCTR. JENIFER: Dr. Daniel Jenifer, Jr. (1756–c.1809).

Gaspard Joseph Amand Ducher was a Parisian lawyer who came to America to study the commercial laws of the states. In a shipwreck on the Long Island coast he lost a large part of his personal fortune and suffered badly from exposure (NUSSBAUM, 14). Lafayette's letter of introduction asked GW's advice and patronage for him (14 Sept. 1784, PEL). GW replied that there was nothing he could do to help Ducher, since he was a foreigner and spoke no English. Many states, he added, demanded a period of residence and study as a prerequisite to practice in the courts. His suggestion was that Ducher's friends procure him a consular post (GW to Lafayette, 12 April 1785, owned by Mr. Sol Feinstone, Washington Crossing, Pa.). On 1 Sept. 1785 Ducher was appointed vice-consul ad interim at Portsmouth, N.H., and in 1787 he was transferred to Wilmington, N.C. His extensive reports and writings were influential in forming French commercial policies, including the Navigation Act of 21 Sept. 1793 (NUSSBAUM, 14–17, 34–36; NASATIR AND MONELL, 560).

Tuesday 12th. Mercury at 50 in the Morning, 58 at Noon and 66 at Night.

Clear all day; Wind until late in the afternoon, pretty fresh from No. West- Sunset red with appearances of dry Weather.

Plowing, rolling, and Harrowing my ground for grass seeds.

Sowed on the inner side of the Post & rail fences running from the Kitchen to the South Haw, ha! & from the Servts. Hall to the North Haw ha! three rows of Holly berries 6 Inches a part—the middle one of the berries wch. were preserved in Shavings. The first row is 9 Inches from the outer edge of the Posts.

Mr. Duchi went away after breakfast.

Wednesday 13th. Mercury at 56 in the Morning—62 at Noon and 61 at Night.

Wind variable. In the morning it was Eastwardly. About 10 Oclock it came from the Southward and after Noon fresh from the No. West. Clear all day.

Received from Colo. Henry Lee of Westmoreland 12 Horse Chesnut Trees (small) and an equal number of cuttings of the Tree Box. They appeared to have been sometime out of the ground being very dry. Planted 4 of the Chesnuts in my Serpentine Walks and 4 of the Box in my shrubberies—two on each side—the rest in the Vineyard.

Sowed the Guinea grass seed sent me by [ ] in the ground I had been preparing in the Hop inclosure—4 Rows and a piece next the fence. At the beginning & end of each Row drove in a peg—Rows 18 Inches a part.

Planted & Sowed in boxes placed in front of the Green House the following things—Box No. 1 partition No. 1 Six buck eye nuts, brought with me from the Mouth of Cheat River; they were much dried & shrivelled—but had been steeped 24 hours in water—Same Box partn. No. 2, Six acorns, which I brought with me from the South Branch. These grew on a tree resembling the box Oak, but the cup which contained the Acorn, almost inclosed it; & was covered with a soft bur. Same Box partn. No. 3 Eight Nuts from a tree called the Kentucke Coffee tree; these had been steeped 48 hours. Box No. 2 partn. No. 1 Ten acrons sent me by Colo. Josiah Parker with the first live Oak Trees; and which I take to be the Acorn of that Tree. Same box, Partn. No. 2, Six Acrons from the same Gentleman wch. came in a Paper accompanying the second parcel of Trees, & a small Keg of Acorns—which I also suppose to be those of the live Oak. Box No. 6 a Scarlet triangular berry the cover of which opens in 3 parts and looks well upon the Shrub. Box 7 Berry of a Shrub, brot. from the western waters with me. Box 8 a Seed brot. from the same place. Box 9 Seed of a cluster of red Berrys which looks pretty and if I recollect right grows on a Vine. Rid to Muddy hole Plantation and the fishing Landing at the Ferry between breakfast & Dinner.

Henry (Light Horse Harry) Lee was now master of Stratford Hall, having married in 1782 Matilda Lee, elder daughter of Philip Ludwell Lee (1727–1775).

The horse chestnut tree is *Aesculus hippocastanum.*

Guinea grass, or *Panicum maximum,* is a coarse perennial, reaching ten feet in height. It does not endure frost and it is unlikely that GW succeeded in growing it. The species was brought from the coast of Guinea to Jamaica and at one time was second only to sugarcane as a Jamaican crop. It is now commonly grown in the South.

The common Ohio buckeye is *Aesculus glabra;* those planted by GW this day were nuts that he had brought from the Cheat River, an affluent of the Monongahela, in 1784. Botanist Charles S. Sargent once thought that this planting was *A. octandra* var. *virginica,* sweet buckeye, and called it the only tree known to have been discovered and first planted by GW. Sargent later decided that the trees in question could not be of that variety. Today no specimen of the Ohio buckeye is growing at Mount Vernon and the lone remaining specimen of *A. octandra* has been shown by trunk borings to have been growing no earlier than the 1840s.

BOX OAK: *Quercus stellata,* post oak. Jefferson had not heard of this species in 1803 (BETTS [2], 288).

His "Kentucke Coffee tree" is still the Kentucky coffee tree, *Gymnocladus dioica.*

SCARLETT TRIANGULAR BERRY: *Euonymus americana,* strawberry bush, the fruit or seed pods of which have a triangular appearance, and the seeds of which have a red skin.

Thursday 14th. Mercury at 48 in the Morning–50 at Noon and 58 at Night.

Winds variable–in the Morning Easterly–then, Southerly–then Calm. Afterwards pretty fresh at So. West–Sometimes with appearances of rain–but generally clear.

Sowed the ground at Muddy hole, which had been twice plowed–once harrowed & gone over with the Hoes to break the clods.

Began to Sow the field at the House, but my Seedsman (Dolls Will) by sowing it much thicker than I intended, put 60 pints, or pounds of Clover Seed, on abt. [ ] Acres of Ground. Leaving a space of about 6 feet, I sowed half a bushel of Orchard grass Seed & five pints (or lbs.) of clover Mixed, in a breadth through the Field.

On the ground at Muddy hole I sowed 40 lbs. of clover seed. It was in tolerable good tilth considering the Season, but ought to have been in better. The field at the House had been three times Plowed–twice Rolled, & twice harrowed; upon the last of which the Seed was Sowed & was in better order than I ever expected to get it, from the unfavorable weather which we have had during the winter and Spring.

Sowed 5 rows and a small piece of the bird grass seed (sent me by Mr. Sprig of Annapolis) by the side of the Guinea grass, leaving 3 feet between the kinds; & the rows 18 Inches apart, as in the other.

At the end of the piece of a row of the Guinea grass & to the next stake I planted the everlasting Pea–one at every Six Inches.

And by the side of the bird grass but 3 feet from it, are planted two rows and a piece of the Acorn of the live Oak 6 Inches apart in the rows, & the rows 18 Inches asunder. The piece of a row I planted with the Spanish Nut.

Rid to Muddy hole Plantation with Miss Bassett.

DOLLS WILL: GW had several slaves named Doll and Will. This is probably the dower slave Will, who was made overseer of Muddy Hole farm later in the year (see entries for 19 Dec. 1785 and 18 Feb. 1786). He was probably the son of Doll, a dower slave at the River plantation.

BIRD GRASS: *Poa trivialis,* rough-stalked meadow grass.

MR. SPRIG OF ANNAPOLIS: Richard Sprigg of Strawberry Hill, near Annapolis. He also sent GW grass seed in 1786 and corresponded with him at various times concerning farm matters. Sprigg's home was famous for its gardens and orchards (GW to Richard Sprigg, 28 June 1786, DLC:GW).

EVERLASTING PEA: *Lathyrus latifolius,* perennial or everlasting pea. It is considered an ornamental today but GW may have been trying to develop it as a field crop, as it was recommended for large yields of hay and pasture grass.

SPANISH NUT: *Castanea sativa,* Spanish or Eurasian chestnut; the foreign variety best known in GW's day, with a nut nearly as large as that of the horse chestnut (DOWNING, 262). GW had bad luck with this variety; at first the crop seemed promising but later the burs began to fall prematurely, as he advised Samuel Powel in a letter 23 Sept. 1788 (PHi: Gratz Collection).

Friday 15th. Mercury at 48 in the Morning–[ ] at Noon and 52 at Night.

Rid to my Muddy hole Plantation and thence to the Fishing Landing at the Ferry.

Sowed the 2 A[cres] 3 R[ods] 22 P[erches] which I had laid of (on Saturday last) in my Wheat field at Muddy hole, with 3 Bushels of Orchard grass Seed, and 6 bushels of the Plaister of Paris, in powder; which I ordered to be rolled in.

Harrowed with a bush, the clover seed which was sowed at that place yesterday and ordered it to be rolled also.

Leaving a space of Six feet between the breadth which was sowed yesterday with Clover & orchard grass, I sowed 4½ Pecks of the orchard grass Seed unmixed; & had the whole of both days sowing, harrowed with a brush harrow.

Next the Planting of the acorns of the live Oak, I planted (two feet from them, & six Inches a part in the Row) a row of the Shellbark hickory Nutt, from New York.

Winds variable to day & fresh, first from East with appearances of rain–then from No. West until the Afternoon, then at East again & very raw and cold.

Mr. Delasier & Mr. Dulany; Doctr. Craik, his wife, & three Daughters came here to Dinner. The two first went away after it, & in the Evening Colo. Allison & Miss Harrison (Daughter of Judge Harrison) came here.

This day was very unfavorable for sowing my Seeds—but the advanced Season, and fear of rain which might retard the operation I did not incline to Postpone it—but to render the disadvantage as small as possible instead of Sowing up and down the Land I sowed all one way.

SHELL-BARK HICKORY NUTT: *Carya ovata,* shellbark hickory. MR. DELASIER: a member of the Delozier family of Maryland, possibly Daniel Delozier (d. 1813), who was deputy collector of customs at Baltimore c.1786–93. In 1793 he was appointed surveyor for the district of Baltimore and inspector of the revenue for the port of Baltimore (EXECUTIVE JOURNAL, 1:143; Delozier to GW, 8 Aug. 1793, DLC:GW).

The three daughters of Dr. James and Mariamne Ewell Craik were Sarah, who was married to Dr. Daniel Jenifer, and Mariamne and Nancy, still unmarried.

Col. Allison is probably Lt. Col. John Allison, an Alexandria merchant. He had served with a Virginia state regiment throughout most of the Revolution. Robert Hanson Harrison had two daughters, Sarah and Dorothy. Their mother was a daughter of George Johnston of Belvale.

Saturday 16th. Mercury at 44 in the Morning—50 at Noon and 54 at Night.

A great Hoar frost and Ice at least the 1/8 of an Inch thick. What injury this may have done to the fruit & vegetation, will soon be seen. The Buds of every kind of tree & Shrub are swelling. The tender leaves of many had unfolded. The Apricot blossoms were putting forth. The Peaches, & Cherries were upon the point of doing the same. The leaves of the Apple tree were coming out. Those of the weeping willow & Lilac had been out many days, and were the first to show themselves. The Sasafras was ready to open. The red bud had begun to open but not to make any show. The Dogwood had swelled into buttons. The Service tree was showing its leaf and the Maple had been full in bloom ten days or a fortnight. Of this tree I observed great difference in the colour of the blossoms; some being of a deep scarlet, bordering upon Crimson—others of a pale red, approaching yellow.

Rid to Muddy hole and discovered that the Wheat ground which had been sowed with Orchard grass Seed had received *little* or *no* benefit from the rolling it had obtaind being two hard & dry, & two much baked for the roller to make a proper impression. The Corn hills yielded but little to its weight, and the interstices scarcely being touched. It is to be feared therefore that the Seed (especially if rain shd. not come soon) will be all lost. The Clover field seems to be well broke by the Roller at the place.

Sowed one Bushel & three Pecks of the Albany, or field Pea in the inclosure behind the Garden, called the Vineyard. This ground had been Hooed in the winter–lately plowed; cross plowed; & Harrowed and the Pease harrowed in.

Cross harrowed with a bush the field of Grass which had been Sowed the two preceeding days at the Home House and began to Roll it abt. 2 Oclock for the third time.

Planted some Filberts given me by my Sister Lewis, in the row in which the Everlasting Pea was planted on Thursday; and stuck a stake where they finished. These were planted Six Inches a part in the row. After Breakfast Doctr. Craik went up to Alexandria & returned in the Afternoon. Mrs. Charles Stuart, Nelly Stuart, & Betsey Custis came to Dinner & stayed all Night. After Dinner Colo. Allison and Miss Harrison returned to Alexa.

FILBERTS: *Corylus americana,* hazelnut or filbert, which GW also calls cob nuts.

SISTER LEWIS: that is, his sister Betty Lewis.

MRS. CHARLES STUART: In June 1780 Eleanor Custis Stuart's sister, Elizabeth Calvert, had married Dr. Charles Steuart of Annapolis.

Sunday 17th. Mercury at 48 in the Morning–[ ] at Noon and 60 at Night.

Wind fresh all day from the So. West but more moderate in the Afternoon.

Doctr. Craik and his family went to Colo. McCartys after Breakfast and to Dinner came Mr. Chas. Steward & Mr. George Digges–Doctr. Walter Jenifer and his wife Mr. Wilson Mr. Hunter & a Mr. Lymebarie–all of Whom, with the two Mrs. Stuarts & Betcy Custis went away after dinner. Fanny Bassett went up with Mrs. Doctr. Stuart.

Mr. Wilson is probably William Wilson (died c.1823) of Alexandria. William and his brother James (1767–1805) emigrated from Scotland c.1777 and were partners in a Glasgow-based mercantile and shipping business, James Wilson & Sons (NORFLEET [1], 222; Alexandria City Hustings Court Deed Book C, 215–19, Vi Microfilm). Wilson was involved in the settlement of the complicated Colvill estate which had burdened GW for so many years.

MR. LYMEBARIE: Adam Lymburner (c.1745–1836), a Scottish merchant who had settled in Quebec in 1776. In 1791 he was appointed to the executive council of Lower Canada but never served. He was on a tour of the United States during the spring of 1785 (WRIGHT, 19–20, 50).

Monday 18th. Mercury at 60 in the Morning–64 at Noon and 66 at Night.

Wind Southerly with great appearances of rain until the afternoon when there was a red sky and clear horizon towards the sun setting.

Rid to Alexandria to the Election of Delegates for this County and dined at Colo. Fitzgeralds. Colo. Syme & Doctr. Steuart were chosen & for whom I gave my suffrages.

Had the Roots, shrubs (which had been grubbed) & Tussics of broom Straw in the point of New ground below the field I had been sowing in clover & Orchard grass, next the Hop inclosure raked of & burnt. I then sowed it up to stakes which run a cross the ground at a double Chesnut Tree with Barley and Orchard grass Seed. On the East side I sprinkled two Bushels of the plaister of Paris (powdered) and harrowed it in along with the Barley—after which the grass Seed was Sowed & harrowed with a Bush harrow. I intended to have sprinkled the same quantity of Plaister, on the West side, but Night coming on I could only get the Barley sowed & harrowed in with the Iron harrow, and the Grass seed with the Bush. The Plaister was postponed until the Morning. I intended this as an experiment (the ground being poor, & equal in quality) —first to try the effect of the Plaister & next whether spreading it on the Surface, or burying it with the Seed was most efficatious. The slipe adjoining the Fence of the hop ground was also sowed in Barley & Orchard grass Seed this day. This had been well spread with Stable & farm Yard Dung upon the Hooeing it had received previous to the Plowings.

COL. SYME: Charles Simms (1755–1819), son of Alexander Simms of Cecil County, Md., was lieutenant colonel of the 6th Virginia Regiment during the Revolution. Shortly before the end of the war he moved from his home near Pittsburgh to Alexandria, where he practiced law. He served in the House of Delegates from West Augusta in 1776 and in 1785–86, 1792, and 1796 he served as delegate from Fairfax County. In later years Simms was collector of the port of Alexandria and mayor of the city. He was also at this time a member of the Potomac Company.

Tuesday 19th. Mercury at 60 in the Morning—55 at Noon and 50 at Night.

Wind at East all the forenoon and fresh, with constant rain. About Noon it got more to the Northward, and turned colder. Ceased raining for a while but began again after a small intermission, & continued until Night.

Took the advantage of the intermission, & sprinkled the 2 Bushels of Plaister which was left undone last Night.

Wednesday 20th. Mercury at 44 this Morning. 44 at Noon and 42 at Night.

Morning clear and tolerably pleasant; but before eight Oclock the Wind coming hard from the No. West it clouded—grew cold and was very disagreeable, all day.

No working of ground but sent my Roller to Muddy hole to Roll the orchard grass Seed wch. had been sowed in the 2 A[cres] 3 R[ods] 22 P[erches] of Wheat, friday last, and which from the hardness of the Earth received no benefit from the former rolling.

Thursday 21st. Mercury at 40 in the Morning [ ] at Noon and 58 at Night.

Ground hard crusted with frost this morning (no hoar frost)—Ice the 1/8 of an Inch thick—day clear—Wind pretty fresh from the No. West in the Morning.

My Seedsman (foolishly) renewed his Sowing of the Barley this Morning; the ground being too wet to plough or harrow it. He sowed all the Seed he had, & left 5 or 6 rod unfinished for want of Seed. Did not sow grass seed—nor attempt to harrow the Barley in.

Rid to the Fishing Landing—No fish caught—thence through the ferry Wheat field, to Muddy hole. Found the Roller had passed once over the grass Seed. Ordered it over a second time, crosswise.

Found what is called the spice bush (a fragrant Aromatic shrub) in bloom. Perceived this to be the case on Monday also as I returned from Alexandria, & supposed it had been blown 2 or 3 days. It is a small greenish yellow flower growing round the twigs, & branches, and will look well in a shrubbery. The Sassafras not yet full out, nor the red bud. Dogwood blossom still inclosed in the button.

After an early dinner, I went up in my Barge to Abingdon, in order to bring Mr. John Lewis (who had lain there sick for more than two months) down. Took my Instruments, with intent to Survey the Land I hold by purchase on 4 Mile run of Geo. & Jas. Mercer Esqrs.

Called at Alexandria & staid an hour or two.

SPICE BUSH: *Benzoin aestivale,* also known in the southern United States as Roman laurel.

The boundaries of the two patents on Four Mile Run had been in dispute since 1774 when GW wrote James Mercer that he intended to run the lines of the two tracts himself (26 Dec. 1774, WRITINGS, 3:252–55). However, before he could do so, the war intervened (see STETSON [1] for discussion of these disputed boundaries).

Friday 22d. Mercury at 50 in the morning—56 at Noon and 63 at Night.

Took an early breakfast at Abingdon; & accompanied by Doctr. Stewart & Lund Washington, and having sent for Mr. Moses Ball (who attended); I went to a Corner of the above Land, within about 3 poles of the Run (4 Miles run) a white Oak, 18 Inches in diameter, on the side of a hill abt. 150 yards below the Ruins of an old Mill, & 100 below a small Branch which comes in on the No. Et. side and after having run one course & part of another, My Servant William (one of the Chain Carriers) fell, and broke the pan of his knee wch. put a stop to my Surveying; & with much difficulty I was able to get him to Abingdon, being obliged to get a sled to carry him on, as he could neither Walk, stand, or ride; At Mr. Adam's Mill I took Lund Washingtons horse & came home. After my return I had the grd. which was sowed yesterday Morning with Barley harrowed.

Perceived the Service tree to be full in bloom. It bears a white flour in clusters but on single stems, and is a tolerable handsome tree in bloom.

Sowed the remainder of the circle which (on acct. of wet) was left unfinished on the Seventh instant. Put both kind of the Holly Berries together mixing them well.

Moses Ball (1717–1792) received a grant from Lord Fairfax of 91 acres lying on the south side of Four Mile Run in Fairfax County near Alexandria, the land adjoining GW's on the west. He seems to have been one of the earliest patentees to clear land and live in the Four Mile Run area, and probably built a house there in 1755. GW undoubtedly requested Ball's presence as much because of his long familiarity with the area as for his personal interest in the boundaries; Ball had earlier made lengthy depositions during several boundary disputes over these and surrounding lands (see STETSON [1]).

RUINS OF AN OLD MILL: probably on the land of Moses Ball.

MY SERVANT WILLIAM: The accident to his servant put an end to the surveying of this land for another year (see entries for 4 and 5 May 1786). William (also called Billy or Will) Lee broke the other kneepan in 1788 and was a cripple for the rest of his life. GW greatly indulged Will in his later years because he was an old and faithful servant. "This is enough for the President to gratify him in any reasonable wish" (Tobias Lear to Clement Biddle, 3 May 1789, DLC:GW). In his will, GW gave William his freedom but allowed him, if he preferred, to remain at Mount Vernon in his present situation. In either case, he was to have an annuity of $30 for the rest of his life.

MR. ADAM'S MILL: GW is probably referring to a mill at the ford over Four Mile Run, where the road from the ford over Hunting Creek passed on its way north to the ferry crossing at Georgetown. This mill is listed on a 1789 map as "Adam's" (COLLES, 182), and in earlier years was called Chubb's Mill (STETSON [1], 97–98). It was probably the mill operated by Robert Adam, the Alexandria merchant.

Saturday 23d. Mercury at 60 in the Morning—68 at Noon and 71 at Night.

Wind fresh all day from the South West & weather clear and warm. Vegetation much quickened.

Sowed all the Orchard grass Seed I had remaining of my first Stock on part of the ground which was sowed on thursday with Barley. Rolled it. Sent to Alexandria for another parcel which had just arrived for me from Philadelphia, and brought it home [ ] Bushels.

Sowed three Rows of the Holly Berries next the row of shell bark Hickory Nutt; leaving 2 feet space between the Nutts and the Berries, & 18 Inches betwn. the rows of Berries—sticking a stake down at both ends of each row.

Rid to the Fishing Landing at the Ferry, and all over my Wheat field there. Found the Wheat in general good—in places greatly destroyed by the Winters frost, but some of it, by fibres wch. had retained a little footing in the ground, beginning to vegetate feebly. Whether it can recover so much as to produce Wheat remains to be tried. From here rid to my Plantation on Dogue run, & examined that Wheat, & perceived that it had sustained greater injury than that at the Ferry had done—being in places *entirely* destroyed & the ground generally, not so well covered.

No appearances of any of the Clover, or Orchard grass seed of the first sowing (now the 9th. day) coming up—which affords cause to apprehend defect in them—especially the first.

The Sassafras buds had perfectly displayed but the numerous flowers within had not opened. The Dogwood buttons were just beginning to open as the Redwood (or bud) blossom for though they had appeared several days the blossoms had not expanded. The Peach Trees were now full in bloom and the apples, Pears, and Cherries pretty full of young leaf.

Mr. John Lewis & his Brother Lawrence came down from Abingdon in my Barge before Dinner.

PARCEL . . . FROM PHILADELPHIA: a parcel of grass seed sent by Clement Biddle (GW to Biddle, 16 May 1785, NNC), who had probably procured it from Elias Boudinot. In a letter of 31 Jan. 1785, GW thanked Boudinot for grass seed the latter had promised to send through Biddle but protested against Boudinot's depriving himself of the seed (owned by Adm. Lewis L. Strauss, Brandy Station, Va.).

John Lewis's illness (see entry of 12 Mar.) must have been severe, for he would remain at Mount Vernon recuperating for almost two more months before he returned home (see entry for 15 June 1785). Lawrence Lewis (1767–1839) was the son of Fielding Lewis and his second wife, Betty Washington Lewis. He was half brother to John Lewis.

Sunday 24th. Mercury at 64 in the Morning—68 at Noon and 71 at Night.

Calm and clear all day—at least till the afternoon when there was a little breeze & variable.

Upon a close examination I perceived the clover seed was coming up—but could discover no appearance of the Orchard, Guinea, or Bird grass Seed rising.

An Express arrived with the Acct. of the Deaths of Mrs. Dandridge & Mr. B. Dandridge, the Mother and Brother of Mrs. Washington.

Mrs. Frances Jones Dandridge was Martha Washington's mother and Col. Bartholomew Dandridge her last surviving brother. Colonel Dandridge had charge of the tangled affairs of John Parke Custis's estate.

Monday 25th. Mercury at 64 in the Morning—66 at Noon and 72 at Night.

Perfectly calm all the forenoon, & very little wind in the Afternoon. Clear & very warm—all nature seemed alive. Cherries, Plumbs, Pears & Apples bloomed forth and the forest trees in general were displaying their foliage.

Got the ground, on the North side of the gate—between the outer ditch & the Sweet brier hedge in a proper state of preparation to receive grass seed; and for making a compleat experimt. of the Plaister of Paris as a manure. Accordingly, I divided it into equal sections; by a line from the Center of the old gate, between the New Garden Houses, stretched to the outer ditch at which they were 18½ feet apart and 16 apart at the outer edge of the Holly berries by the Sweet brier hedge. Each of these Sections contained 655 square feet. On the 1st. that is the one next the road I sprinkled 5 pints of the Plaister in powder—on the 2d. 4 pints—on the 3d. 3 pints—on the 4th. 2 pts. on the 5th. one pint and on the 6th. none. On the 7th. 8th. 9th. 10th. & 11th. 5, 4, 3, 2 & 1 pints again; and on the 12th. nothing and on the 13th. 14th. 15th. 16 & 17th.—5, 4, 3, 2 & 1 in the same manner as before. On these three grand divisions (as they may be called) I sowed Orchard Grass Seed. But before I did this, I harrowed the first grand division with a heavy Iron toothed harrow—The 2d. grand division was gone over with a Bush harrow (without the Iron harrow) –and the third grand division was only rolled without either of the above harrowings. The whole of this ground was, in quality, as nearly alike as ground cou'd well be and this experiment, if the grass seed comes up well, will show first what quantity is most proper for an acre (the above being, as nearly as may be, in the proportion of 1, 2, 3, 4, & 5 Bushels to the acre) and secondly, whether burying the Powder of Paris deep (as a heavy harrow will do it) –shallow–or spreading it on the Surface only, is best.

Adjoining to this, on a piece of grass ground, as nearly alike in quality as may be, I staked off 5 square rod side by side and on the 1st. Beginning at the fence I sprinkled 2 gills of the powdered Stone–on the next 4 gills–on the 3d. 6 gills–on the 4th. 8 Gills and on the 5th. 10 gills–which as nearly as may be is (also) at the rate of 1, 2, 3, 4, & 5 Bushels to the acre. On this piece of circular ground I sowed about 8 quarts of the orchard grass Seed which was Nothing like so clean as the first parcel I received.

I also finished Sowing all the ground behind the Barn, and adjoining the Pine groves, with the Orchard grass Seed which took about [ ] Pecks.

Tuesday 26th. Mercury at 69 in the Morning–71 at Noon and 76 at Night.

Quite calm, clear, and very warm all day.

The ground on the South side of the Road (between the Ditches) being prepared I sprinkled the same quantity of Powdered stone on it–sowed the same quantity of Seed (orchard Grass) on it and Managed it in all respects as I did that on the North side opposite yesterday–beginng. with the greatest quantity of powdered Stone next the road, & decreasing it Southerly, as I did Northerly yesterday. The 2 circles took 1½ Bushels of the Stone.

The Barley and Pease were seen coming up–the first very generally–the latter just making its appearance.

Doctr. Stuart came here to Breakfast, & returned after Dinner. Doctr. Griffith came to the latter, & stayed all night.

The blossom of the Red bud was just beginning to display. The Dogwood blossom tho' out make no figure yet: being small and not very white. The flower of the Sassafras was fully out and looked well. An intermixture of this and red bud I conceive would look very pretty–the latter crowned with the former or vice versa.

Wednesday 27th. Mercury at 74 in the Morning—76 at noon and 78 at Night.

Marked out a new place for my front gate & serpentine Post & rail fences from it to the Outer Ditch.

Sowed in drills, 18 Inches a part, & 3 feet from the Holly berries in the inclosure by the Hop Patch 10 rows of the small berried thorn.

Rid to Muddy hole. Upon my return, found General & Mrs. Moylan here.

Stephen Moylan (1737–1811), an Irish-born Philadelphia merchant, was appointed muster-master general of the Continental Army in Aug. 1775, secretary to GW in Mar. 1776, and quartermaster general in June 1776. From 1777 to 1783 Moylan served as colonel of the 4th Continental Dragoons. GW appointed him commissioner of loans for Pennsylvania in 1793. Moylan was married to Mary Ricketts Van Horn, of Phil's Hill, N.J.

Thursday 28th. Mercury at 72 in the Morning—75 at Noon and [ ] at Night.

Clear & warm—Wind from the So. Wt. & in the Evening pretty fresh.

To Dinner Mr. Pine a pretty eminent Portrait, & Historian

Elizabeth Parke Custis and George Washington Parke Custis, two of Mrs. Washington's grandchildren, were painted by Robert Edge Pine during his visit to Mount Vernon. (Washington and Lee University, Washington-Custis-Lee Collection)

Martha Washington's granddaughters, Eleanor Parke Custis and Martha Parke Custis, painted by Pine. (Mount Vernon Ladies' Association of the Union)

Painter arrived in order to take my picture from the life & to place it in the Historical pieces he was about to draw. This Gentleman stands in good estimation as a Painter in England, comes recommended to me from Colo. Fairfax–Mr. Morris Govr. Dickenson–Mr. Hopkinson & others. Colo. Hooe, Mr. Hibert, & a Captn. [ ] also came here to Dinner & returned after it.

Robert Edge Pine (1730–1788), an English portrait painter well known for his historical works, was in the United States to complete a series of paintings of the Revolution. During his stay at Mount Vernon, Pine also painted portraits of Martha Washington, her four grandchildren, and her niece Fanny Bassett. George William Fairfax's letter of introduction was dated 23 Aug. 1784 (DLC:GW). Robert Morris's letter, dated 15 April 1785, informed GW that Pine wanted to take Martha Washington's portrait, as well as GW's (DLC:GW). John Dickinson of Pennsylvania had moved to Delaware during the Revolution, where he became president of the executive council in 1781. After the war, he returned to Pennsylvania where he was elected president of the executive council. Francis Hopkinson (1737–1791) of New Jersey had been an active pamphleteer during the Revolution. A member of the Continental Congress in 1776, he was chairman of the Continental Navy Board 1776–78, treasurer of loans 1778–81, and judge of the admiralty court in Pennsylvania 1779–89.

MR. HIBERT: probably Mr. Huiberts, of the firm of Leertouwer, Huiman &

Huiberts of Alexandria. The firm had a store for a short time in Hooe & Harrison's house on Water Street, where it sold goods from Holland (*Va. Journal,* 29 April 1784 and 26 May 1785).

Friday 29th. Mercury at 74 in the Morning—74 at Noon and 76 at Night.

Dull day and not much wind; Weather not very warm.

Leaving Genl. Moylan & Lady, and Mr. Pine at Mt. Vernon, I set off for the appointed meeting of the Dismal Swamp Company at Richmond. Dined at Dumfries, & lodged at My sister Lewis's (after visiting my Mother) in Fredericksburgh.

Showers in the Afternoon to the Eastward of where I was.

The affairs of the Dismal Swamp Company were in abeyance during the years of the Revolution. GW wrote Hugh Williamson of North Carolina on 31 Mar. 1784 that he was "unaquainted with the opinions, & know as little of the Affairs & present management of the Swamp Company, in Virginia, (tho' a Member of it) as you do, perhaps less, as I have received nothing from thence nor have heard any thing of my interest therein, for more than nine years" (DLC:GW). On 10 April 1785 GW wrote Dr. John Walker: "I have requested a meeting of the Proprietors of the Dismal Swamp in Richmond on Monday the 2d. day of May next, at which time and place I should be glad to see you as it is indispensably necessary to put the affairs of the Company under some better management. I hope every member will bring with him such papers as he is possessed of respecting this business" (WRITINGS, 28:127; see also BROWN [3]; NORFLEET [2], 114–17; PARKER, 1–2, 8–11).

Saturday 30th. Mercury (by Mrs. W's acct.) in the Morning at 68—at Noon 69 and at Night 62.

Wind Northerly all day, & towards Night cold.

Dined at General Spotswoods, and lodged at Mr. Jno. Baylors (New Market).

Alexander Spotswood (1751–1818), son of John and Mary Dandridge Spotswood and grandson of the governor, lived at New Post, his home on the Rappahannock River in Spotsylvania County. He was married to Elizabeth Washington (1750–1814), eldest daughter of GW's half brother Augustine. Spotswood served in the 2d Virginia Regiment from Feb. 1776 until his resignation with the rank of colonel in Oct. 1777. In Mar. 1781 the Virginia legislature appointed him brigadier general and empowered him to raise two legions for the defense of the state. Spotswood shared GW's interest in scientific agriculture, and the two men often exchanged letters on this subject.

John Baylor (1750–1808), the brother of GW's former aide-de-camp George Baylor, lived at Newmarket, his farm in Caroline County. George Baylor had died in Barbados in Nov. 1784 as the result of old war wounds. It is possible that GW had received word only recently of his former aide's death, and stopped at John Baylor's to extend condolences.

May

Sunday–First. Mercury 51 in the Morning–52 at Noon and 60 at Night.

Day cool, Wind at No. West & clear all the forenoon, with flying clouds afterwards.

Took a late breakfast at Hanover C[our]t House. Went from *thence* to Mr. Peter Lyon's where I intended to dine, but neither he nor Mrs. Lyon being at home, I proceeded to, & arrived at Richmond about 5 oclock in the afternn.

Supped & lodged at the Governor's.

Peter Lyons (d. 1801) was an Irish-born Virginia lawyer. In 1763 he was attorney for Rev. James Maury in the "Parson's Cause." In 1779 Lyons was made judge of the General Court; in 1789 he became a member of the Virginia Court of Appeals and in 1803 became its president (LYONS, 184–85). Lyons's second wife, whom he married in 1773, was Judith Bassett of Williamsburg, an aunt of Mrs. Washington's niece, Fanny Bassett (*Va. Gaz.*, P&D, 30 Dec. 1773; MASON [1], 295).

Patrick Henry (1736–1799) served his fourth and fifth terms as governor of Virginia from Nov. 1784 to Nov. 1786. The governor's residence in Richmond impressed a visitor in 1782 as being "very plain but spacious," and was later described as "a very plain wooden building of two stories, with only two moderate sized rooms on the first floor" (CHASTELLUX, 2:428; MORDECAI, 73; see DUMBAULD, 220–27). Governor Henry also kept a farm, Salisbury, in Chesterfield County about 12 miles west of the capital, to which his family often retired during the summer (MEADE [3], 302, 507).

Monday–2d. Mercury at 54 in the Morning–56 at Noon and 56 at Night. Received and accepted an invitation to dine with the Sons of Saint Taminy, at Mr. Andersons Tavern, and accordingly did so at 3 Oclock.

About Noon, having Assembled a sufficient number of the Proprietors of the Swamp, we proceeded to business in the Senate Chamber; & continued thereon till dinner, when we adjourned till nine Oclock next day.

Raw & cold Easterly Wind the whole day. Towards evening it turned very cloudy & very like Rain & became quite cold.

The Sons of St. Tammany, a democratic society opposing aristocracy and privilege, was named for a seventeenth-century Delaware chief supposed to have befriended the whites. The first society was formed in 1772 in Philadelphia, as the Sons of King Tammany, a Loyalist group, but shortly afterwards, as political attitudes changed, the name was changed to the Sons of St. Tammany. After the Revolution, the number of societies in various cities greatly increased. The first of May was normally the day celebrated in St.

		Shares
G: Washington		1
Secretary Nelson		1
Fieldg Lewis decd		1
Colo. Tucker – Do		1
Mr. Farley – Do		1
Messrs. Meads	2	1
Mr Bacon		1
Docr. Walker / Mr Hornsby	2	1
Messrs. Nathl. & Wm. Nelson	2	1
Mr. Anderson & Mr Jameson	2	1
Mr. Jno. Page	1	½
	9	10½

List in Washington's handwriting of shareholders in the Dismal Swamp. (George Washington Masonic National Memorial Association)

Tammany's honor, but in 1785 the first of May fell on Sunday, thus postponing the celebration by a day.

Anderson's tavern was commonly used for civic meetings until it burned in 1787. It may have been opened by Robert Anderson (d. 1784), who operated a tavern in Williamsburg in the 1770s (MARSHALL [2], 1:140; GIBBS, 145–47).

PROCEEDED TO BUSINESS: At this meeting of the proprietors of the Dismal Swamp Company, there was a discussion of proposals for procuring a large number of laborers from Holland or Germany and for obtaining a large foreign loan to aid in the work of draining the swamp (GW to Jean de Neufville, 8 Sept. 1785, GW to John Page, 3 Oct. 1785, DLC:GW; NORFLEET [2], 115; see also editorial note for 15 Oct. 1763).

Tuesday 3d. Mercury 54 in the Morning–54 at Noon and 58 at Night.

Raining more or less all day, with the wind fresh at East.

Met according to adjournment & finished the business by 3 oclock. Dined at the Governors.

Wednesday 4th. Mercury at 56 in the Morning 59 at Noon and 64 at Night.

Raining until 7 O'clock, when the wind getting to the Westward, the Clouds broke, & the weather cleared & was tolerably pleast.

After doing a little business, & calling upon Judge Mercer and the Attorney General, I left Richmond about 11 Oclock. Dined at one Winslow's abt. 8 Miles from the City, & lodged at Clarkes Tavern 10 Miles above Hanover Court House.

JUDGE MERCER: James Mercer of Fredericksburg was a judge of the General Court 1779–89. He later served on the Virginia Court of Appeals from 1789 until his death in 1793.

Winslow's was located near the Henrico-Hanover County line. This tavern, recorded by GW in his accounts as "Winsters" (LEDGER B, 203), may have been the "Winstons' Ordinary" that was in existence in that area in 1751 (VSP, 1:244). CLARKES: The tavern located ten miles up the stage road from Hanover Court House was owned during the Revolution by James Head Lynch, of Caroline County, and appears in a 1789 map as the tavern of "Head Lynch." Clarke may have been the tavern keeper in 1785 (CAMPBELL [1], 413; COLLES, 189; and see 25 April 1786).

Thursday 5th. Mercury at 58 in the Morning–60 at Noon and the same at Night.

Wind Southerly in the forenoon & clear, but Showery afterwards where I was, between Fredericksburgh & Dumfries.

Breakfasted at the Bowling Green. Dined with my Sister Lewis in Fredericksburgh. Spent half an hour with my Mother and lodged at Stafford C[our]t House (at one Taylors Tavern).

Friday 6th. Mercury at 62 in the Morning–60 at Noon and 64 at Night. Dark foggy Morning, with little wind, but great appearances of rain all the forenoon–after noon clear & pleasant.

Breakfasted at Dumfries, & dined at home; where I found Mrs. Moylan (Genl. Moylan having gone on some business towards Fredericksburgh) Mr. Pine, Mr. Jno. Lewis & his Brother Lawrence–all of whom I had left at Mt. Vernon–and where I found everybody and thing well except little Washington Custis who had had two or three fits of the Ague & fever.

Saturday 7th. Mercury at 60 in the Morning–60 at Noon and 62 at Night.

Day clear, and tolerably pleasant till the Afternoon, when it turned cold. The Wind being at No. W. all day.

Upon enquiry, found that William Skilling, a hired man has done no work in my absence; nor since the 21st. Ulto.; occasined by a fever, and violent Cough wch. there is reason to apprehend may prove fatal to him.

Most of my transplanted trees have a sickly look. The small Pines in the Wildernesses are entirely dead. The larger ones in the walks, for the most part, appear to be alive (as yet). Almost the whole of the Holly are dead. Many of the Ivy, wch. before looked healthy & well seem to be declining. Few of the Crab Tree had put forth leaves. Not a single Ash tree has unfolded its buds whether owing to the trees decline, or any other cause, I know not; as those in their native places are all in leaf (tho' late putting out) and *some* of all the other kinds have displayed their leaves, it is somewhat singular that not *one* of these should yet have discovered signs of life. The lime trees, which had some appearance of Budding when I went away, are now withering and the Horse-chestnut & Tree box from Colo. Harry Lee's discover little signs of shooting. The Hemlock is almost entirely dead, & bereft of their leaves and so are the live Oak. In short half the Trees in the Shrubberies, & many in the Walks, are dead & declin[in]g.

The Barley & Pease seem to have come on well—but the clover has not advanced much. The first Sowed Orchard grass Seeds are making their appearance but none of the Second are yet to be seen. Nor can I discover anything yet of the Guinea, or bird grass seeds coming up; or any of the Acorns or Nutts which were planted by the side of them any more than I can of those things which were put in boxes—the seeds of the Crab apple are up and the woodbine (or Honey suckle) which I cut & set out, appears to be about half alive.

I cannot discover that the grass ground on which the Powdered plaister of Paris was strewed, in different quantities, is benefitted in the smallest degree by it—nor the circle in the Court yard.

William Skilling, a laborer, worked for GW as early as 1767 (LEDGER A, 249). Articles of agreement on 25 Feb. 1775 between Skilling and GW provided for Skilling to take GW's servants and Negroes to his Ohio lands, there to work with them on whatever was necessary (DLC:GW). There is no further word of Skilling until 1784, when GW offered him £30 per year and two pairs of shoes to work again at Mount Vernon. "It may be to ditch, to Garden, to level & remove Earth, to work alone, or with several others, & in the last case, to keep them closely employ'd as well as yourself" (GW to Skilling, 22 July 1784, DLC:GW). Skilling replied that he would come in mid-November if his health permitted (28 July 1784, DLC:GW). The last entry in GW's ledger for Skilling is for 17 July 1785, when GW paid "Negro Moll on Accot. of Willm. Skilling" £1 10s. (LEDGER B, 203). Perhaps GW was correct in apprehending that his hired man's illness might prove fatal.

Sunday 8th. Mercury at 56 in the Morning—61 at Noon and [ ] at Night.

Cool all day; Wind at No. West with flying Clouds.

Monday 9th. Mercury at 60 in the Morning—[ ] at Noon and 70 at Night.

Clear & warm—But little Wind & that Southerly.

Rid to my Muddy hole & Dogue run Plantations and from the latter to the fishing Landing at the Ferry.

Perceived the Orchard grass seeds which had been sown on the Wheat at Muddy hole were coming up tolerably well—but could not discover that the Wheat had derived any benefit from the Plaister of Paris which had been sprinkled thereon—or from the rolling.

Mathew Baldridge who had been engaged for me by Mr. John Rumney, as a Joiner, and sent over in his Brig the Caesar, Captn. Atkinson, and who arrived here yesterday, set in to work today.

The blossom of the Crab tree is unfolding, & shedding its fragrant perfume. That of the black Haw, had been out some days; and is an ornamental flower being in large clusters, tho' individually small upon single foot stems. They are white with a yellowish cast. The flower of the small berry thorn is also good looking—the tree being full of blossoms, which is not much unlike the blossom of the apple tree, but quite white.

On 3 July 1784 GW wrote John Rumney, Jr., who was going to England, to say that he, "being in want of a House Joiner & Bricklayer . . . would thank Mr. Rumney for enquiring into the terms upon which such workmen could be engaged for two or three years . . . Bed, board & tools to be found by the Employer, cloaths by the Employed." GW added that "rather than encounter delay [he] would be obliged to Mr. Rumney for entering into proper articles of agreement on his [GW's] behalf with them, & for sending them out by the Vessel to this port" (DLC:GW). The articles of agreement with Mathew Baldridge, a joiner, were signed for three years (bill from Peter How Younger, 8 Jan. 1785, DLC:GW). GW paid Baldridge £25 sterling for the first two years and £31 10s. for the third year (LEDGER B, 249). He seems to have left Mount Vernon after this three-year period.

John Rumney, Jr. (1746–1808), was a partner in the English mercantile firm of Robinson, Sanderson & Rumney, which had a store in Alexandria in the 1780s and early 1790s. In addition to his request for a joiner and a bricklayer, GW asked Rumney to make inquiries regarding flagstones for the piazza at Mount Vernon (GW to Rumney, 3 July 1784, DLC:GW). Rumney's search for a bricklayer was unsuccessful, but he did contract for the flagstones to be delivered to GW. Later, Rumney moved to Geneva, N.Y., where he lived until his death (BROCKETT, 107–8). Rumney may have been a brother of Dr. William Rumney.

The brig *Cesar,* Capt. J. Atkinson, had stopped at the Mount Vernon wharf on its way to Alexandria, where it arrived by 12 May. The brig brought European goods for sale by Robinson, Sanderson & Rumney (*Va. Journal,* 12 May, 26 May 1785).

Tuesday 10th. Mercury at 62 in the Morning–[ ] at Noon and 60 at Night. Wind pretty fresh all day from So. East–raw, cold, & not much unlike rain.

Quitted fishing at the ferry landing, as I had done at the House landing on Saturday last.

Began to weed a yard for Brick making at home.

Rid into the Neck. Found my Wheat there tolerably promising.

General Moylan returned before dinner. Doctr. Jenifer & his wife came here to dinner & stayed all Night. A Mr. Stephens from the red stone Settlement came in the afternoon & remained all Night.

Mr. Stephens is possibly Dennis Stephens, who had built the mill on GW's Pennsylvania land.

Wednesday 11th. Mercury at 57 in the Morning–56 at Noon and 59 at Night. Raining more or less all day moderately. Wind at No. Et. & pretty fresh.

Thursday 12th. Mercury at 59 in the Morning–66 at Noon and 68 at Night. Foggy Morning–Wind at So. Wt. About noon the Clouds dispersed and afterwards became clear, warm, & pleasant.

Added some more Filberts to those planted on the 16th. of last Mo[nth] in the 5th. row of the Guinea grass seeds, below the Everlasting Pease and at the end of these, & below the 3d. Stake, I planted some Cobb Nuts (given me by my Sister Lewis) at the distance of Six Inches a part.

Yesterday (tho' it escaped Notice at the time) I sowed in drills (three) on the South side the gate, adjoining the Orchard grass Seeds and upon the bank of the old ditch which I had levelled a few Seeds of a grass given me by Colo. Archibald Cary–who had it from Colo. Wm. Peachy who speaks of it in high terms. This I did just before the rain set in.

Friday 13th. Mercury at 65 in the Morning–67 at Noon and 68 at Night. Growing Weather–day clear and pleasant. Wind fresh from the Southward.

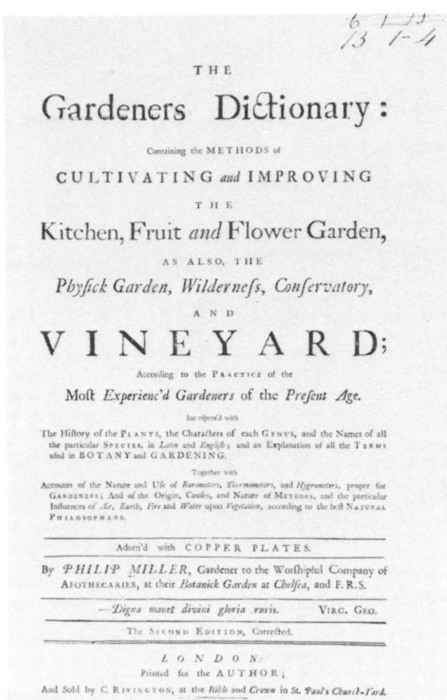
THE

Gardeners Dictionary:

Containing the METHODS of

CULTIVATING and IMPROVING

THE

Kitchen, Fruit *and* Flower Garden,

AS ALSO, THE

Physick Garden, Wilderness, Conservatory,

AND

VINEYARD;

According to the PRACTICE of the

Most *Experienc'd Gardeners* of the *Present Age.*

Interspers'd with

The History of the PLANTS, the Characters of each GENUS, and the Names of all the particular SPECIES, in *Latin* and *English*; and an Explanation of all the TERMS used in BOTANY and GARDENING.

Together with

Accounts of the Nature and Use of *Barometers, Thermometers,* and *Hygrometers,* proper for GARDENERS; And of the Origin, Causes, and Nature of METEORS, and the particular Influences of *Air, Earth, Fire* and *Water* upon *Vegetation,* according to the best NATURAL PHILOSOPHERS.

Adorn'd with COPPER PLATES.

By *PHILIP MILLER,* Gardener to the Worshipful Company of APOTHECARIES, at their *Botanick Garden* at *Chelsea,* and F.R.S.

——*Digna manet divini gloria ruris.* VIRG. GEO.

The SECOND EDITION, Corrected.

LONDON:

Printed for the AUTHOR;

And Sold by C. RIVINGTON, at the *Bible* and *Crown* in St. *Paul's Church-Yard.*

M.DCC.XXXIII.

Washington owned an abridgment of this eighteenth-century book on gardening. (Beinecke Rare Book and Manuscript Library, Yale University)

Began to set my turned Posts in the Circle in the C[our]t yard.

The Guilder roses in my Garden had just got into bloom—but as the Trees had been transplanted this spring I presume they were backened by it, for I observed some in the Gardens at Fredericksburgh (but these were in a sandy Soil) as forward eight days ago as mine are now.

Saturday 14th. Mercury at 65 in the Morning—69 at Noon and 68 at Night. Rid to My Plantations at the Ferry—Dogue run, & Muddy hole. Found the Wheat had grown a good deal since the last rain & warm weather.

The wood honey suckle wch. has been in bloom about 8 days is an agreeable looking flower and deserves a place in my Shrubberies.

My Nephew, George Augustine Washington arrived here from Charles Town after having been to Burmuda & the West Indies in pursuit of health which he had but imperfectly recovered.

George Augustine Washington sailed from Alexandria to the West Indies in the spring of 1784 in an effort to recover his health. He had suffered for some time from what may have been tuberculosis. GW gave him 100 guineas to cover his expenses (LEDGER B, 197). After visits to several of the islands, George went to South Carolina and spent the winter in Charleston and at

Sandy Hill, the nearby farm of his distant cousin, Col. William Washington (1752–1810). GW sometimes refers to George, who served as an aide to Lafayette during the Revolution, as Major Washington.

Sunday 15th. Mercury at 59 in the morning–63 at Noon and 65 at Night. General Cadwallader came here yesterday.

Today Colo. Fitzgerald–Mr. Murray,–Mr. Porter–Mr. Munser Mr. Darby & the Revd. Mr. Prince came here to dinner, & went away after it.

In the Afternoon Doctr. Stuart Mrs. Stuart & Miss Stuart came and stayed all Night.

Wind at So. East all day, with some appearances of Rain.

John Cadwalader served as a brigadier general of the Pennsylvania militia during the Revolution. In 1778 his admiration for GW led him to challenge Maj. Gen. Thomas Conway and seriously wound him in a duel, after Conway had made disparaging remarks about GW. In 1785 Cadwalader was living at his country seat in Kent County, Md., and was a member of the Maryland legislature.

Mr. Murray is probably John Murray, an Alexandria merchant. Murray's store was at this time located on Fairfax Street, nearly opposite the courthouse, but shortly afterwards moved to the corner of Prince and Water streets (*Va. Journal,* 4 Nov. 1784 and 13 April 1786).

Thomas Porter (d. 1800) was a partner in the Alexandria firm of Porter & Ingraham which operated a store near the corner of Fairfax and King streets at this time (*Va. Journal,* 23 Dec. 1784). Porter was recommended to GW by Benjamin Lincoln (GW to Lincoln, 5 Feb. 1785, DLC:GW) and seems to have become a close friend of George A. Washington.

MR. MUNSER: William Mounsher, "an intimate friend and confident" of Thomas Porter (Porter to Benjamin Lincoln, Jr., 19 July 1787, MHi: Benjamin Lincoln Papers), advertised a store, counting room, and cellar for rent on King Street in Alexandria (*Va. Journal,* 5 April 1787). A few months later he gave notice of his intended return to Europe (*Va. Journal,* 17 May 1787), but continued to visit Mount Vernon for another year. GW had difficulty with Mounsher's name and spelled it various ways (Monshur, Munsher).

MR. DARBY: probably a son of Elias Hasket Derby, a wealthy merchant and shipowner of Salem, Mass. Rev. Mr. Prince is probably John Prince (1751–1836), minister of the First Church in Salem. Derby and Prince were traveling together with a letter of introduction from William Grayson (Grayson to GW, 5 May 1785, DLC:GW).

Miss Stuart is undoubtedly Dr. David Stuart's sister Ann, who was living at Abingdon with her brother and sister-in-law at this time (TORBERT, 49). She later became the second wife of William Mason, son of Col. George Mason of Gunston Hall.

Monday 16th. Mercury at 63 in the Morning–66 at Noon, and 68 at Night. General Moylan, Mrs. Moylan, Doctr. Stuart, Wife & Sister, went away after Breakfast.

Mr. Mazzai came here to breakfast and went away afterwds.

Philip Mazzei (1730–1816), born in Italy, had been a wine merchant in London for 18 years before coming to Virginia in 1773. He purchased an estate named Colle, adjoining Thomas Jefferson's Monticello in Albemarle County, where he carried on agricultural experiments. In 1774 GW subscribed for one share at £50 sterling to Mazzei's scheme to form a company "for the Purpose of raising and making Wine, [olive] Oil, agruminous Plants and Silk" (JEFFERSON [1], 1:156–58). The project came to a halt during the Revolution, and in June 1779 Gov. Patrick Henry sent Mazzei to France to borrow money for the state. He returned in 1783 but sailed for Europe again in June 1785, shortly after his visit to Mount Vernon. In 1788 Mazzei published his history of America, *Recherches historiques et politiques sur les États-Unis de l'Amérique septentrionale* (Paris, 1788), based in part on notes Jefferson gave him.

Tuesday 17th. Mercury at 60 in the Morning–62 at Noon and 62 at Night.

General Cadwallader went away after Breakfast, and I went to Alexandria to the appointed meeting of the Subscribers to the Potomack Navigation. Upon comparing, & examining the Books of the different Managers, it was found, including the Subscriptions in behalf of the two States, & the 50 Shares which the Assembly of Virginia had directed to be Subscribed for me, (& which I then declared I would only hold in trust for the State) that their were 403 Shares Subscribed, which being more than sufficient to constitute the Company under the Act–the Subscribers proceeded to the choice of a President & 4 Directors; the first of which fell upon me. The votes for the other four fell upon Governors Johnson & Lee of Maryland and Colonels Fitzgerald & Gilpin of this State.

Dined at Lomaxs and returned in the Afternoon.

The law authorizing the creation of the Potomac Company provided for the subscription of 500 shares at 444 and 4/9 dollars (£100 sterling) each, and stipulated that if at least half the shares were not subscribed by the end of the meeting set for this day the company could not be organized (HENING, 11:512). The state governments of Virginia and Maryland each subscribed for 50 shares. In addition, the Virginia Assembly had voted 50 shares (plus 100 shares of James River navigation company stock) to GW as thanks from the state for his services in the Revolution.

Holding firm to his determination to accept no gifts or remuneration for his Revolutionary War services, GW agreed, as here stated, only to hold the shares in trust for the public benefit. By his will GW devised the Potomac Company shares to a national university, to be established in the District of Columbia (these shares depreciated and became worthless), and the James River shares to Liberty Hall Academy, Rockbridge County, Va., which later became Washington and Lee University (DIARIES, 2:376 n.4; FREEMAN, 6:28–30).

Thomas Sim Lee (1745–1819), son of Thomas Lee (d. 1749) and Christian (Catherine) Sim Lee and grandson of Philip Lee, founder of the Maryland Lees, served as governor of Maryland, 1779–82 and 1792–94, and as a Maryland delegate to the Continental Congress 1783–84. He married Mary Digges (1745–1805), daughter of Ignatius Digges of Melwood, and settled in Frederick County, Md., at Needwood, located about 12 miles west and south of Frederick Town. He had acquired the estate during the Revolution (LEE [5], 306–11; W.P.A. [2], 347).

George Gilpin (1740–1813) was born in Cecil County, Md., and settled in Alexandria before the Revolution. A wheat merchant, Gilpin was inspector of flour in Alexandria in Mar. 1775 (MERCHANTS, 246). During the Revolution he was a colonel of Fairfax County militia and a member of the committee of safety. He was one of the most active members of the Potomac Company and in July 1785 went to Seneca Falls to procure workmen (NUTE, 713, n.1). He also for many years served as a vestryman for Fairfax Parish (POWELL, 203–4, 162–63).

John Lomax's tavern, on the southwest corner of Princess and Water (now Lee) streets, was the site of today's meeting (*Va. Journal*, 21 April 1785).

Wednesday 18th. Mercury at 60 in the Morning—68 at Noon and 72 at Night.

Wind Southerly in the forenoon and Westerly afterwards.

The forepart of the day was very warm. In the Evening it turned much Cooler.

Finished Planting Corn at Muddy hole.

Rid to Alexandria to enter myself security for Doctr. Stuarts administration of Mr. Custis's Estate. At the same time exchanged Deeds in Court with Mr. Willm. Triplett for the Lands we had swapped.

The Locust blossom is beginning to display.

EXCHANGED DEEDS IN COURT: see 15 Feb. 1785.

Thursday 19th. Mercury at 66 in the Morning—63 at Noon and 66 at Night.

Mr. Pine left this (on his return to Philadelphia) in my Phaeton, which was to carry him to Annapolis.

Sent My Overseer & Barge to Popes Creek for the Baggage of Geo. Auge. Washington, and such Articles as he had brot. from the West Indies & South Carolina for my use—as also some Wild Geese which Mr. Wm. Washington had procured for me.

Wind at East all the day; until towards Sun down, when it turned quite calm.

The forenoon was a little dripping but not much rain fell.

MY OVERSEER: In the fall of 1784, GW hired John Fairfax (c.1764–1843) as his overseer for the Mansion House farm and grounds at a wage of £30 for the year, and when the contract was renegotiated in the fall of 1785 Fairfax obtained a raise to £40 (LEDGER B, 209). John was distantly related to the Fairfaxes of Belvoir through his great-grandfather, John Fairfax, a Roman Catholic who emigrated from Yorkshire to Charles County, Md., in the early eighteenth century. In 1785 the head of the Maryland Fairfaxes was William Fairfax, Sr. (d. 1793), who moved from Charles County in 1789 to settle near Occoquan, Prince William County. By his two wives he had six daughters and four sons, one of whom was John (CARTMELL, 244, 247–48).

WILD GEESE: GW must have written his nephew, William Augustine Washington, to be on the lookout for some wild geese for his Mount Vernon estate. Washington wrote GW shortly after this that he had "been industrious in inquiring for some *Wild Geese* & Swans for you, at length I have procured these Geese, which I now send you. . . . I shall indeavour to procure you some *Swans* this Winter" (William Augustine Washington to GW, 1 June 1785, CSmH).

Friday 20th. Mercury at 61 in the Morning—68 at Noon and 72 at Night.

Brisk Southerly Wind until Noon when it became calm till the Evening—then the Wind sprung up again from the same point. Day warm and clear.

Rid to my Mill, and to Morris's.

Planted in boxes No. 10 & 11 in the garden, adjoining to the other boxes 48 seeds of the Mahogany tree brot. by Mr. G. A. Washington from the West Indies.

A Mr. Noah Webster came here in the Afternoon & stayed all Night. As did one Richd. Boulton a House joiner and Undertaker recommended to me by Colo. Wm. Fitzhugh of Maryld.

Noah Webster, attributed to James Sharples. (Independence National Historical Park Collection)

Upon enquiry, found that my overseer at the ferry had begun to plant Corn on the 12th. and Morris at Dogue run on the 18th.

MAHOGANY TREE: *Swietenia mahogani.*

Noah Webster (1758–1843), of Massachusetts, had a short time before this published his *Grammatical Institute of the English Language.* The failure of Congress to enact copyright laws had led him to spend several years traveling through the states in an effort to encourage local legislation. During this year he had also published *Sketches of American Policy,* a plea for a strong federal government. He probably brought a copy to GW during this visit or during a return visit in November, for in December he wrote GW from Alexandria, asking to borrow his pamphlet long enough to have excerpts printed in the newspaper (16 Dec. 1785, PHi: Gratz Collection).

Richard Boulton of Charles County, Md., signed an agreement with GW on 21 May 1785 in which he agreed to finish the New Room "in a plain and elegant manner; either of Stucco, Wainscot, or partly of both." He was also, among other things, to make repairs to the roof of the mansion, wainscot the new piazza which had gone up under Lund Washington's supervision, and "do the necessary work of a Green House" (DLC:GW). In employing a joiner to finish the New Room, GW was contradicting his earlier assertion to Samuel Vaughan on 14 Jan. 1784 (DLC:GW): "I found my new room, towards the completion of which you kindly offered your house-joiner, so far advanced in the wooden part of it, the Doors, Windows, & floors being done, as to render it unnecessary to remove your workman with his Tools (the distance being great) to finish the other parts; especially as I incline to do it in stucco, (which, if I understood you right, is the present taste in England)." Despite his contract with GW, Boulton reneged on his promise to come to Mount Vernon, and so the finishing work on the New Room was delayed for another year (Boulton to GW, 4 June 1785, GW to Boulton, 24 June 1785, GW to William Fitzhugh, 14 July 1785, DLC:GW).

MY OVERSEER AT THE FERRY: Hezekiah Fairfax, overseer at the Ferry plantation for several years, was a son of William Fairfax (d. 1793), of Maryland and Occoquan, by his first wife, and thus a half brother to John Fairfax, GW's Home House overseer. Hezekiah married Margaret Calvert and lived in Prince William County.

Saturday 21st. Mercury at 67 in the Morning—72 at Noon and 68 at Night.

Calm all the forepart of the day, and warm. The wind came out from the Southward afterwds.; and a thunder shower of no long continuance Succeeded; thence it turned cool, the wind getting to the Westward.

My Phaeton which had been with Mr. Pine to Annapolis returned about 3 Oclock to day; as did my Barge which had been sent to Popes Creek on thursday last. The latter brought the Plants of the large Magnolio of South Carolina—Some scions of the live Oak, & a few young Trees of the Civil, or sower oranges in a box, all of which seem to be in a thriving State. As also sundry kinds of Seed which Mr. G. Washington had provided for me in his travels & the Palmeto royal which Mr. Blake of So. Carolina had sent me accompanied by some of the Plants.

Agreed with one Richd. Boulton a House joiner & undertaker, to do my New Room, & other Work—who is to be here in abt. 3 Weeks with his Tools.

Mr. Webster went away after breakfast and in the Afternoon Captn. Kalender came & stayed all Night.

THE LARGE MAGNOLIO: *Magnolia grandiflora*. CIVIL, OR SOWER ORANGE: *Citrus aurantium*, the Seville or sour orange. PALMETO ROYAL: *Sabal palmetto*, palmetto, or *S. umbraculifera*, palmetto royal; some botanists say they are the same species. For the entry on other seeds and plants brought to GW by George Augustine Washington, see 13 June 1785. William Blake, of Charleston, S.C., wrote on 20 Mar. 1785, informing GW that he was sending him the plants and seeds he requested (DLC:GW). CAPTN. KALENDER: Eleazer Callender of Fredericksburg had been a captain in the Virginia State Navy during the Revolution. He had come to Mount Vernon to visit his friend George Augustine Washington (Callender to George A. Washington, 19 May 1785, ViMtV).

Sunday 22d. Mercury at 66 in the Morning 68 at Noon and 64 at Night.

Wind Easterly all day, and at times fresh. About 9 'Oclock it began to rain & continued to do so, more or less all day.

In the Afternoon Doctr. Stuart & Mrs. Stuart arrived here.

Monday 23d. Mercury at 62 in the Morning—70 at Noon and 72 at Night.

Calm, cloudy, & warm all day; at times, when the sun came out it was hot. Veg[it]ation rapid by the warmth & moisture of the weather.

Set out the Palmeto Royal in my garden—in number [ ] Plants and put the box in which the Magnolio, live oak & Sower Oranges were in the Area in front of the Green House.

Doctr. Stuart went away after Dinner. Mrs. Stuart & the Girls remained.

Tuesday 24th. Mercury at 69 in the Morning—68 at Noon and 68 at Night.

Much rain fell in the Night (& continued Showery at intervals all day) with thundr. & Lightng.

Wind very high in the Morning, and at times through the day from the Southward.

Bought 15,114 feet of Inch Pine Plank a 10/. pr. Ct.

Laid a Margin of grass between the pavement, & the Post & rail fence from the Servants Hall, to the cross fence.

Doctr. Brown came here on a Visit to Richmond (a boy) who had hurt his Shoulder. Dined and returned afterwards.

Richmond, a dower slave, was about nine years old. He was the son of Lame Alice, a seamstress at the Home House (see entry for 18 Feb. 1786).

Wednesday 25th. Mercury at 64 in the Morning–67 at Noon and 70 at Night.

Wind pretty fresh all day from the Southward. Clear, and pleasant–very conducive to Vegetation.

The blossom of the transplanted fringe tree was beginning to display. The locust blossom full out.

Expected General Roberdeau and some Methodist Clergymen to dinner but they did not come. Had Peas for the [first] time in the season at Dinner.

Daniel Roberdeau (1727–1795), once a Philadelphia merchant dealing largely in the West Indies trade, served as a brigadier general of Pennsylvania militia during the early years of the Revolution and later served in the Continental Congress. He had moved his family to Alexandria some time before 1780, when he became a member of a fire company in that town (MOORE [1], 152).

Thursday 26th. Mercury at 65 in the Morning–68 at Noon and 67 at Night.

Wind Southerly and warm in the forenoon and till about 5 O'clock afternoon when Clouds to the westward arose attended With high wind from the No. West Which continued an hour or two & changed the temparature of the air remarkably.

Rid to Muddy hole and the Neck Plantations.

Upon my return found Mr. Magowan, and a Doctr. Coke & a Mr. Asbury here–the two last Methodest Preachers recommended by Genl. Roberdeau–the same who were expected yesterday.

Mrs. Stuart and Betcy & Patcy Custis accompanied by Fanny Basset set out for Abingdon after Breakfast and my Nephew G. A. Washington did the same for Richmond.

After Dinner Mr. Coke & Mr. Asbury went away.

Thomas Coke (1747–1814) and Francis Asbury (1745–1816) were sent to America by John Wesley as missionaries to superintend the Methodist movement in this country. Asbury came shortly before the Revolution and Coke in 1784. They were at Mount Vernon to ask GW to sign an antislavery petition which was to be presented to the Virginia legislature. Coke later wrote that GW informed them that "he was of our sentiments, and had signified his thoughts on the subject to most of the great men of the State: that he did not see it proper to sign the petition, but if the Assembly took it into consideration, would signify his sentiments to the Assembly by a letter" (VICKERS, 98).

Friday 27th. Mercury at 60 in the Morning—62 at Noon and 62 at Night.

Wind at No. Wt. all day with flying clouds and little sprinklings of rain. Cold and disagreeable.

Mr. Magowan went away after breakfast.

Saturday 28th. Mercury at 58 in the Morning—58 at Noon and 60 at Night.

Wind at No. West all day, & pretty fresh scattered Clouds and disagreeably cool.

Sunday 29th. Mercury at 58 in the Morning—62 at Noon and 64 at Night. But little wind all day and much pleasanter than it had been for several days—being also clear.

The Honble. Mr. Sitgreave a Delegate to Congress from the State of North Carolina, Mr. Tillotson & Mr. Edward Livingston came to Dinner and stayed all Night.

John Sitgreaves (1757–1802) served in the Continental Congress 1784–85 and was later appointed a district judge for North Carolina. He was on his way home to North Carolina and carried with him a copy of the Northwest Ordinance of 1785, adopted by the Congress on 20 May, providing for the surveying, subdividing, and disposal of public lands.

Thomas Tillotson (1750–1832), who served in the Maryland militia during the Revolution, in 1780 was appointed physician and surgeon general of the Northern Department. He married Edward Livingston's sister, Margaret, in 1779 and was now practicing medicine in New York.

Edward Livingston (1764–1836), son of Robert R. Livingston (1718–1775), of New York, was a young lawyer. He was later to represent both New York (1795–1801) and Louisiana (1823–31) in Congress and become mayor of New York City (1801–3), secretary of state (1831–33), and minister to France (1833–35).

Monday 30th. Mercury at 62 in the Morning—[ ] at Noon and 69 at Night.

But little Wind, and that Southwardly—warm—& pretty clear.

The Gentlemen who came here to Dinner yesterday went away after Breakfast.

I went to Alexandria to meet the Directors of the Potomack Co. Dined at Colo. Fitzgerald and returned in the Evening—after the Directors had agreed to meet at Mount Vernon tomorrow at 10 Oclock.

The flower of the Ivy is just getting pretty fully into Bloom & the trees which I transplanted from the Blind Pocoson & to which I could find no name were putting forth their blossoms—white, in small Clusters.

Tuesday 31st. Mercury at 66 in the Morning—66 at Noon and 66 at Night.

Govrs. Lee & Johnson, Colo. Fitzgerald & Colo. Gilpin came here according to appointment.

Fanny Bassett returned. Raining more or less all day—in the Evening & Night much fell.

The directors of the Potomac Company agreed at this meeting to divide the clearing of the Potomac into two areas of responsibility, one above and one below Harpers Ferry. For each of these two areas 50 men under an assistant manager would be hired, and both groups would be under a general manager to be chosen at the next meeting of the directors, set for 1 July in Alexandria (*Va. Journal,* 9 June 1785). In this way, GW wrote to the marquis de Lafayette, work could begin "in those parts which require least skill; leaving the more difficult 'till an Engineer of abilities & practical knowledge can be obtained" (25 July 1785, DLC:GW).

June 1785

Wednesday 1st. Mercury at 64 in the Morning—68 at Noon and 72 at Night.

But little Wind and that from the Southward—day clear, warm & growing.

Govrs. Johnson & Lee, and the other Gentlemen with a Son of the first went away after Breakfast.

In the Afternoon Mr. Mathew Whiting, Mr. Wm. Booth, & a Doctr. Graham [came] here & stayed all Night.

Gov. Thomas Johnson had three sons: Thomas Jennings, James, and Joshua.

Matthew Whiting (d. 1810), formerly of Gloucester County, had moved to Snow Hill on Bull Run in Prince William County by about 1770. In 1782 he paid a tax on 4 whites and 73 slaves in Prince William. Whiting had been married to Warner Washington's sister Hannah, and had by her an only son, Matthew, who was lost at sea during the Revolution (FOTHERGILL, 135; Whiting to GW, 10 Aug. 1786, DLC:GW; W.P.A. [1], 179–80).

Dr. Graham is probably either William Graham (1751–1821), son of John Graham of Dumfries and a surgeon's mate in the 2nd Virginia Regiment during the Revolution, or George Graham, a member of the committee of safety and a surgeon in the Prince William County militia during the Revolution (BLANTON, 404; W.P.A. [1], 31, 33).

Thursday 2d. Mercury at 69 in the Morning—73 at Noon and 77 at Night.

Wind, what there was of it, came from the Westward. Day very warm, & the forepart of it clear—the latter part cloudy with appearances of Rain but none fell.

Friday 3d. Mercury at 72 in the Morning—75 at Noon and 78 at Night.

Rid to my Plantations at the Ferry—Dogue Run and Muddy hole Mr. Whiting, Mr. Booth, and Doctr. Graham having first set out for Maryland, immediately after breakfast.

Very little Wind in the forenoon but Warm when the Sun was out. Afternoon Raining, with the Wind pretty violent from the So. West.

Saturday 4th. Mercury at 72 in the Morning—80 at Night [Noon] and 80 at Night.

Not much Wind, and that Southerly—very warm.

In the afternoon a thunder Gust above & below this but little rain fell here.

In the Afternoon the celebrated Mrs. Macauly Graham & Mr. Graham her Husband, Colo. Fitzgerald & Mr. Lux of Baltimore arrived here.

Catherine Sawbridge Macaulay Graham (1731–1791), a prominent English author, wrote the much-lauded *History of England from the Accession of James I to That of the Brunswick Line,* published in London, in eight volumes, 1763–83. Richard Henry Lee's letter of introduction to GW indicated that her only reason for going as far south as Virginia was to see GW (Lee to GW, 3 May 1785, DLC:GW). GW thanked Lee for the introduction to Mrs. Macaulay Graham, "whose principles are so much, & so justly admired by the friends of liberty and of Mankind. It gives me pleasure to find that her sentiments respecting the inadequacy of the powers of Congress . . . coincide with my own" (GW to Lee, 22 June 1785, PPAmP: Lee Papers). Mrs. Macaulay Graham's first husband, George Macaulay, had died in 1766 and her remarriage in 1778 to the 21-year-old William Graham, 34 years her junior, had caused her much criticism and ridicule.

Mr. Lux is probably Darby Lux, Jr. (d. 1795), a Baltimore merchant dealing mainly in the Barbados trade.

Sunday 5th. Mercury at 72 in the Morng.—80 at Noon and 80 at Night.

Opened the Well in my Cellar in which I had laid up a store

of Ice, but there was not the smallest particle remaining. I then opened the other repository (called the dry Well) in which I found a large Store.

Colo. Fitzgerald went away after Breakfast.

My Nephew Geo. Auge. Washington returned in the afternoon.

Wind Southwardly, but not much of it, warm & clear.

Monday 6th. Mercury at 76 in the Morning–79 at Noon and 78 at Night.

Wind at East all day but not very fresh–Clouds & Sunshine alternately.

Mr. Herbert (Willm.) came here to dinner & returned after it.

Mr. Lux rid to Alexandria after Breakfast.

Tuesday 7th. Mercury at 70 in the Morng. 68 at Noon and 67 at Night.

Wind at East and Cloudy all day, with fine Rain at times.

Mr. Dulany, Mr. Saml. Hanson, and Mr. Roberdeau (Son to Genl. Roberdeau) as also Doctr. Stuart came here to Dinner. The three first went away after it–the latter stayed all Night.

Mr. Lux returned in the evening.

Mr. Roberdeau is Isaac Roberdeau (1763–1829), oldest child of Daniel Roberdeau; Daniel's only other son was an infant at this time. Although some sources claim Isaac was at school in England until 1787 (BUCHANAN [2], 104), he had certainly returned by the spring of 1786, for in April of that year he was one of three men put in charge of the engine for the Sun Fire Company, in Alexandria (MOORE [1], 50). Isaac became a well-known engineer, working with Pierre L'Enfant in laying out the city of Washington.

Wednesday 8th. Mercury at 65 in the Morning–65 at Noon and [ ] at Night.

A great deal of rain fell last Night and much fine rain this day. Wind at East all day and at times pretty fresh.

Placed my Military records in to the Hands of Mrs. Macauly Graham for her perusal & amusemt. (these indeed were placed there yesterday).

Doctr. Stuart returned home after Breakfast.

MILITARY RECORDS: In 1783 GW ordered "six strong hair Trunks, well clasped and with good Locks" in which to transport his military papers (GW to Daniel Parker, 18 June 1783, DLC:GW). On 9 Nov. of that year the papers were packed, loaded on wagons, and under military escort sent to Virginia. One bundle, containing GW's accounts as commander in chief, was left with the superintendent of finance at Philadelphia. The remaining manuscripts went to Mount Vernon. These were to form the nucleus of the Washington Papers at the Library of Congress (WASHINGTON PAPERS INDEX, vi).

Thursday 9th. Mercury at 62 in the Morning—62 at Noon and 65 at Night.

Tolerably clear in the Morning, but more or less cloudy all day afterwards. Not much Wind and that Southwesterly.

Captn. Brooke dined here. I rid to my Mill and to the Dogue run & Muddy hole plantations.

CAPTN. BROOKE: probably Walter Brooke (d. 1798), a son of Thomas Brooke (1706–1748) and Sarah Mason Brooke of Charles County, Md. During the Revolution, Brooke served as captain of the sloop *Liberty* in the Virginia navy and in 1777 was made a commodore. He was now living in Fairfax County, probably in the vicinity of Mount Vernon (HEADS OF FAMILIES, VA., 86).

Friday 10th. Mercury at 67 in the Morning—71 at Noon and [ ] at Night. But little wind in the forenoon. In the afternoon it was at Et. with a pretty heavy shower of rain about 5 Oclock.

In the Afternoon Mr. Whiting Doctr. Graham and a Mr. Wyat came here.

In the Morning Mr. Lux set out on his return home.

MR. WYAT: perhaps Dr. William E. Wyatt (1762–1802) of Prince William County, who was married in 1781 to Mary Graham (b. 1753), daughter of John Graham of Dumfries (STANARD [3], 3:178).

Saturday 11th. Mercury at 71 in the Morning—75 at Noon and [ ] at Night.

After Breakfast Mr. Whiting, Doctr. Graham, & Mr. Wyatt went away and my Brother Charles Washington, Colo. Robt. H. Harrison of Maryland & Mr. Ballendine & his Sister Fanny came to Dinner.

In the Evening Colo. Jno. Mercer his wife & Miss Sprig came—All of whom stayed the Night.

Showers around us, but none fell here. The Morning was quite calm. In the Afternoon a small Southerly Breeze and very warm.

Thomas William Ballendine (died c.1797), of Prince William County, and Frances Ballendine were children of John and Frances Ewell Ballendine. Thomas attended the College of William and Mary about 1779–80 and was a member of the Phi Beta Kappa Society (TYLER [1], 224–26, 232–36).

Miss Sprigg was one of Mrs. Mercer's sisters from Strawberry Hill at Annapolis.

Sunday 12th. Mercury at 76 in the Morning—76 at Noon and [ ] at Night.

Very little Wind in the forenoon, in the Afternoon there was more, & variable with Clouds & thunder but no rain.

Captn. Conway and his Wife, Colo. Hooe & De Neufville, Colo. Henley Mr. Sanderson & Mr. George Digges dined here—all of whom went away [after] dinner except Mr. Digges.

Whilst we were at dinner, a Mr. Aldge & a Mr. Patterson came in recommended by Genl. Greene & Mr. Benjn. Harrison Junr.

Mr. Ballendine left this in the forenoon.

Capt. Richard Conway was married to Mary West Conway (died c.1805), daughter of Col. John West (d. 1777).

Leonard de Neufville was the son of Jean de Neufville (1729–1796), formerly of Amsterdam. Jean de Neufville had been a good friend and commercial agent to the United States in Holland during the Revolution. His firm, Jean de Neufville en Zoon, refitted John Paul Jones's squadron in 1779, tried to raise money for a loan for the United States, and in 1778 negotiated with William Lee an unauthorized and abortive treaty between the United States and the Netherlands. The Neufville firm by 1783 was going bankrupt, and Jean de Neufville and his son Leonard came to America and settled at Albany. On 22 April 1785 Leonard de Neufville wrote to Congress requesting payment of debts due Jean de Neufville en Zoon for its services in the Revolution, but was refused. After Jean de Neufville's death, Congress authorized the payment of $3,000 to de Neufville's widow and his son and daughter. The account of the United States with Jean de Neufville en Zoon was finally settled in 1851 (BIOGRAFISCH WOORDENBOEK, 8:1211–14; WHARTON, 3:379–80, 597, 817–18, 855–57; ADAMS [1], 2:444–45; 6 *Stat.* 29 [2 Mar. 1797]; 9 *Stat.* 814 [3 Mar. 1851]).

David Henley (1748–1823) was a partner in the Boston firm of Otis & Henley, "Agents for the purpose of supplying clothing (or materials for it) for the Army" during the Revolution (GW to Henley, 5 Sept. 1785, DLC: GW). He had also served as colonel of one of the 16 Additional Regiments of the Continental Army. About this time, Henley was made a commissioner for settling the claims of Virginia on account of the western territory ceded to the United States. Robert Sanderson was a partner in the firm of Robinson, Sanderson & Rumney of Whitehaven, Eng. The firm's Alexandria store was located on Fairfax Street.

Monday 13th. Mercury at 74 in the Morning—76 at Noon and 80 at Night.

But little wind in the Morning. At times afterwards it blew pretty fresh from the Westward, but was nevertheless very Warm.

Colo. Mercer, Lady & Sister went away after breakfast. My Brother, Mr. John Lewis and G. A. Washington dined at Mr. Lund Washingtons & returned in the Evening.

Sowed the following Nuts, & Seeds, in the inclosure I had prepared for a Nursery—viz.

In the first Section—beginning by the walk next the Ho[use]

Frontispiece of *Catalogus Plantarum,* a catalogue of plants. (Beinecke Rare Book and Manuscript Library, Yale University)

I built for a hospital (since used for Spinning)—the first row contains 17 Nuts of the Sand Box tree. Next to these are 2 rows containing 85 of the Palmetto Nut, or acorn. Next, 2 rows 87 Physic Nut; Next 3 rows of the Seed of the Pride of China. Next 9 rows containing 635 Acorns of the live oak (wch. seemed bad). Next (which compleated the section) 3 rows of a species of the Acacia (or Acasee) used in the West Indias for incircling their Gardens.

In the next section to this, (immediately back of the Salt House) the first row, and parallel thereto—is the same as the last—that is Acacia. The next is the flower fence, also used as an inclosure to Gardens. Next to this are two rows of the Bird pepper—then one row of the Cayan pepper. Then 2 rows of the Seed of the Privy. The remainder of this Section was compleated with Guinea Grass—which, as all the others, were planted and Sowed in Drills 12 Inches a part.

Colo. Harrison left this by Sunrise today.

All the planting done this day was apparently with materials brought to GW by George Augustine Washington. In addition to the plants already identified, they include:

Hura crepitans, sandbox tree, a native of the West Indies and South America, reaching a height of 100 feet.

Jatropha curcas, Barbados nut or physic nut, a small tropical tree cultivated for its purgative oil.

Melia azedarach, chinaberry, Indian lilac, or pride of China, widely planted in the South from the Atlantic to western Texas.

Acacia sp., acacia. There are about 450 species, but as GW says it was used in the West Indies to encircle gardens it is possibly *A. cavenia,* a shrub with a stout spine good for hedges, found in tropical America. Most acacias are native to Australia.

Poinciana pulcherrima, Barbados flower fence or Barbados pride.

Capsicum frutescens, bird pepper.

C. frutescens longum, cayenne pepper.

Ligustrum vulgare, common privet.

GW had written to George Augustine Washington on 6 Jan. 1785 that he would be glad to receive trees not native to his area "which would be ornamental in a grove or forest, and would stand our climate" (owned by H. Bart Cox, Washington, D.C.). His nephew replied that he would do his best, with the assistance of Col. William Washington and that of an unnamed botanist and gardener who lived in the vicinity (25 Feb. 1785, ViMtV).

Tuesday 14. Mercury at 78 in the Morning—80 at Noon And 80 at Night.

Calm in the Morning and very little wind at any time in the day. In the Morning there was rumbling thunder at a distance and Clouds indicative of rain as there also was in the Afternoon but none of it reached us.

About 7 Oclock Mr. Graham & Mrs. Macauly Graham left this on their return to New York. I accompanied them to Mr. Digges's to which place I had her Carriage & horses put over. Mr. Digges escorted her to Bladensburgh.

Sowed on each side of the Great Gate in front of the Ho[use] (between the Serpentine railing and the Orchard grass plats, & Ditches) Seeds of the Palmetto royal in Drills 15 Inches a part.

Wednesday 15th. Mercury at 78 in the Morning—80 at Noon and 84 at Night.

Mr. John Lewis after a stay of almost 8 Weeks took his departure, very well recovered. My brother Charles also left this on his return home.

Rid to my Plantations at Muddy hole, Ferry, and Dogue run. Also to the Mill.

Mr. Bushrod Washington came here before dinner.

Thursday 16th. Mercury at 80 in the Morning—84 at Noon And 86 at Night.

Light wind from the Southward all day. Weather very warm. Some appearances of rain in the afternoon, but none fell here.

Friday 17th. Mercury at 80 in the Morning—84 at Noon and 83 at Night. Between 4 & 5 Oclock it was at 85.

Westerly Wind in the forenoon & So. Wt. afterwards with rumbling thunder at a distance & some appearances of rain—but none fell near this.

Cut down the Weeds in the ground which had been sowed with Clover & Orchard Grass Seeds in the Inclosure adjoining H[ome] H[ouse]—as also those in the orchard Grass in the South Circle by the Gate, which had got high where the ground was strong & was about to Seed.

The Catalpa Trees were pretty generally displaying their Blossoms; & Chesnut also.

Mr. Geo. A. Washington went up to Alexandria to Dinner & returned in the Afternoon.

Saturday 18th. Mercury at 80 in the Morning—81 at Noon and 82 at Night.

Wind Westwardly in the forenoon, & Southwardly afterwards.

In the Afternoon my Brother John came hither from Alexandria, having gone to that place by Water.

Sunday 19th. Mercury at 78 in the Morning—80 at Noon And 82 at Night.

Very little wind all day, & none in the Afternoon.

Mr. Montgomery came here to dinner & went away afterwards.

Monday 20th. Mercury at 79 in the Morning—84 at Noon and 86 at Night.

Clear with very little wind, Sultry in the Afternoon.

My Brother John went up to Alexandria after an early Breakfast.

Began to pull the seeds of the Blew, or English grass, and cut the top from the Walnut tree wch. I transplanted in the Spring, as it seemed to be declining; the leaves which had put out falling off by degrees.

The Weather being hot and dry I commenced the Watering of the Guinea grass Seeds wch. were sowed on the 13th. Instt. & perceiving the physic Nut & the Seeds of the Flower fence & Acacia to be coming up, I watered these also.

Tuesday 21st. Mercury at 82 in the Morning—86 at Noon And 88 at Night.

Little or no Wind but extremely Sultry.

Mr. Ballendine came here abt. 5 Oclock in the Afternoon and my Brother returned from Alexandria abt. 8 Oclock.

Wednesday 22d. Mercury at 82 in the Morning—84 at Noon and 80 at Night.

Calm, and very warm in the forenoon. About one Oclock it began to cloud, and to thunder. Soon after which the clouds parted, and powerful rains went above, and below us. Very little more than laid the dust fell here, but we had a pretty high Wind from the Westward.

After Breakfast Mr. & Miss Ballendine and Mr. Bushrod Washington went away. And just as we had done dinner Colo. Bassett & his two Sons, Burwell & John, arrived.

The little rain which fell prevented my continuing to pull the Seeds of the blew or English grass altho there was not a sufficiency to wet the Earth.

Burwell Bassett was a member of the Virginia Senate, where he served from 1777 until his death in 1793. Burwell Bassett, Jr. (1764–1841), eldest surviving son of Burwell Bassett, enjoyed a long career in the Virginia House of Delegates (1787–89, 1819–21), the Virginia Senate (c.1794–1805), and the United States House of Representatives (1805–13, 1821–29). He resided at Eltham, which he inherited at his father's death in 1793. John Bassett (1766–1826), a lawyer, lived in Hanover County. In 1786 he married Elizabeth Carter Browne, daughter of William Burnet and Judith Walker Browne of Elsing Green, King William County.

Thursday 23d. Mercury at 78 in the Morning—80 at Noon and 78 at Night. Morning lowering with appearances of rain. About 10 Oclock the clouds dispersed and it turned very warm. A little after noon a cloud arose in the So. West quarter and thundered and about 3 Oclock we had a fine shower wch. gave sufficient refreshment to vegetation.

Very little Wind in the forenoon—Eastwardly afterwards.

A Mr. Brisco, introduced by a letter from Colo. R. H. Harrison came here to offer himself to me as a Secretary.

Cut the grass in my Court yard and began to do the like in the river front of the House.

Mr. Brisco after dining went away. I took 8 or 10 days to give him a definitive answer in. My Brothr. Jno. returned home.

MR. BRISCO: Harrison introduced William Briscoe as a close relative of his wife (Harrison to GW, 20 June 1785, DLC:GW). He may have been a son of Harrison's sister-in-law, Mary Hanson Briscoe and her husband, John Briscoe. Briscoe was not hired for the job. For further information on GW's search for a secretary, see 2 July 1785.

Friday 24th. Mercury at 77 in the Morning—72 at Noon and 72 at Night.

A good deal of rain fell at and before day break—continued cloudy all day with the Wind at East.

Finished cutting all the grass within the inclosures on both Sides the House.

Saturday 25th. Mercury at 72 in the Morning—72 at Noon and 77 at Night.

Clear and but little wind during the whole day.

Making, with the jobbers about the House, the Hay which had been cut the preceeding days—got it into Shocks.

My Nephew, George Steptoe Washington came here in the Afternoon.

Sunday 26th. Mercury at 74 in the Morning—76 at Noon and 77 at Night.

Southerly wind and clear. Major Edwards and a Mr. Philips came here before Dinner. Mr. Charles Lee also came to Dinner. The whole stayed all Night.

Evan Edwards of Pennsylvania served throughout the Revolution in various Pennsylvania regiments. In 1777 he acted as aide-de-camp to Maj. Gen. Charles Lee. After the Revolution, Edwards moved to Charleston, S.C. He was probably on his way north from there at this time to visit his family in Pennsylvania or to inspect land in Berkeley County which had been willed to him by General Lee (LEE [6], 4:31). Charles Lee (1758–1815), who came to dinner at Mount Vernon today, was no relation to the general.

Charles Philips bore an introduction from Jacob Read of South Carolina. He was "a Gentleman of very ample fortune in the West Indies and is now on his return to Europe after visiting his Estates." Philips, a native of Yorktown, was educated in Europe and spent most of his life there (Jacob Read to GW, 8 May 1785, DLC:GW).

Monday 27th. Mercury at 77 in the Morning—79 at Noon and 77 at Night. A little rain in the Morning—with Clouds and appearances of it in the Afternoon, but none fell here. In the Morning there was but little wind. The Clouds which appeared in the Afternoon produced a good deal of wind from the West & No. West wch. changed the Air & made it much Cooler.

Mr. Lee went away before Breakfast.

Tuesday 28th. Mercury at 69 in the Morning—72 at Noon and 72 at Night. Clear & pleasant, wind what their was of it, westerly.

Finished my Hay at and about the House & got it into large Cocks or small stacks on the grd. where cut.

Doctr. Stuart, Mr. Booth and a Mr. Hawkins came here to dinner, the first of whom went away after it. In the Afternoon my Brother Charles came.

Col. Josias Hawkins (c.1735–1789) of Charles County, Md., commanded a battalion of militia during the Revolution. He and William Booth, who appear together at Mount Vernon, probably were engaged in a business transaction of some sort, for a few months later GW wrote Hawkins at Booth's request, defending Booth's character "from the injurious aspersions, which he says have been cast at it" (GW to Josias Hawkins, 27 Feb. 1786, DLC: GW).

Wednesday 29th. Mercury at 69 in the Morning—74 at Noon And 76 at Night.

Clear & pleasant all day except being warm. Wind Westerly.

Messrs. Philips and Edwards, and Mr. Booth & Mr. Hawkins left this after Breakfast. Colo. Bassett his two Sons, Fanny Bassett, and Nelly & Washington Custis, followed soon after for Abingdon.

Mr. George Lee & Doctr. Craik came here to breakfast and after Dinner returned.

Discovered the Cayan pepper Which was sowed on the 13th. to be coming up.

George Lee is probably the son of Philip Lee of Maryland and younger half brother of Squire Richard Lee of Blenheim.

Thursday 30th. Mercury at 72 in the Morning—76 at Noon and [ ] at Night.

Clear & warm, with little Wind at any time of the day.

My Brother Charles left this after breakfast and G. Auge. Washington went up to Abingdon.

Rid to my Hay field at the Meadow—from thence to my Dogue run and Muddy hole Plantations and dined with only Mrs. Washington which I believe is the first instance of it since my retirement from public life.

[July]

July 1st. Mercury at 74 in the Morning—78 at Noon and 80 at Night.

Clear with but little Wind and warm.

Went to Alexandria to a meeting of the Board of Directors, who by Advertisement were to attend this day for the purpose of agreeing with a Manager and two Assistants to conduct the

Undertaking of the Potomack Navigation—but no person applying with proper Credentials the Board gave the applicants until thursday the 14th. to provide these & for others to offer.

Returned in the Evening accompanied by Colo. Bassett & Colo. Spait, a Member of Congress for the State of No. Carolina. Fanny Bassett, her Brothers—G. Washington & Betcy & Washington Custis came down to Dinner.

ADVERTISEMENT: The advertisement agreed to at the directors' first meeting (see 31 May 1785) was printed in newspapers in Alexandria (*Va. Journal,* 9 June 1785), in Baltimore (*Md. Journal,* 10, 14, 17, 24 June 1785), and in Philadelphia (*Pa. Packet,* 22 June 1785). The company also printed handbills to be distributed about the Potomac Valley (GW to James Rumsey, 2 July 1785, DLC:GW).

COLO. SPAIT: Richard Dobbs Spaight (1758–1804), later a member of the Constitutional Convention and governor of North Carolina.

Saturday 2d. Mercury at 76 in the Morning—80 at Noon and 84 at Night.

A little wind from the Westward in the forepart of the day & from the Southward in the Afternoon.

Doctr. Stuart, Wife & Sister, and Patcy & Nelly Custis came here to Dinner—As did Mr. McCrae & a Mr. Shaw whom Mr. Montgomerie recommended to me as a Clerk or Secretary.

All of these stayed the Night.

Robert McCrea (c.1765–c.1840), a native of Scotland, became a partner in the Alexandria firm of McCrea & Mease (POWELL, 310–11).

GW had asked various friends to be on the lookout for someone to live at Mount Vernon and help him with the voluminous correspondence and bookkeeping which made increasing demands on his time. Thomas Montgomerie recommended William Shaw, newly arrived in the United States from Canada. Although Montgomerie knew Shaw only slightly, he knew his family, and the young man came with strong recommendations from Montgomerie's friends (Montgomerie to GW, 21 June 1785, DLC:GW). GW wrote Montgomerie on 25 June that besides writing letters and keeping books, Shaw would be required to "methodize my papers (which from hasty removals into the interior country [during the Revolution], are in great disorder); ride, at my expence, to do such business as I may have in different parts of this, or the other States . . . ; & occasionally to devote a *small* portion of time to inetiate two little children (a Girl of six, & a boy of four years of age, descendants of the decd. Mr. Custis who live with me . . .) in the first rudiments of Education" (DLC:GW). Shaw would not agree to a definite term of service and demanded the large sum of £50 sterling per year, in addition to bed, board, and washing (Shaw to GW, 4 July 1785, DLC:GW). GW agreed to these terms, and Shaw returned to Mount Vernon to begin his services on 26 July. He stayed only 13 months, leaving GW's service in Aug. 1786. GW was doubtless happy to see the last of Shaw, for the young man obviously spent too much time away from his duties. The diaries for the last months of 1785 and 1786 abound with the general's unhappy references to Shaw's absences from Mount Vernon.

Sunday 3d. Mercury at 79 in the Morning—80 at Noon and [ ] at Night. A little wind from the Westward till towards Noon; then Calm until near 5 Oclock when there was a squall from the No. Wt. with appearances of rain but little or none fell here.

Mr. McCrae and Mr. Shaw left this after Breakfast, & Doctr. Stewart, his wife, Sister & Betcy & Patcy Custis after dinner. In the Evening Mrs. and Miss Blackburn came here.

Monday 4th. Mercury at 76 in the Morng.—80 at Noon and 82 at Night.

Tolerably pleasant in the forenoon, the Wind being No[rth]-wardly, but warm afterwards.

Rid to my Ferry Dogue run & Neck Plantations—at all of

Charles Willson Peale's portrait of business partners Gouverneur Morris and Robert Morris. (Pennsylvania Academy of the Fine Arts)

which my Wheat Harvests had begun. That in the Neck had commenced on thursday last.

Tuesday 5th. Mercury at 79 in the Morning—84 at Noon and 82 at Night. Very warm in the forepart of the day altho the wind was Northerly. About One Oclock a cloud arose in the So. W.; and an hour or two after, we had a fine Shower of rain for about 10 or 15 minutes, preceeded by a squall of wind from the same quarter, wch. cooled the Air & made the Afternoon pleasant.

After dinner Mr. Govournr. Morris and Mr. Wm. Craik came in.

Gouverneur Morris (1752–1816), formerly a member of the Continental Congress from New York and a longtime supporter of GW, was from 1781–85 assistant to Robert Morris, superintendent of finance. Gouverneur Morris was involved in several business deals with Robert Morris and had come to Virginia in Jan. 1785 to attend to Robert Morris's tobacco shipments and to try to collect a debt from Carter Braxton of Virginia. The Braxton lawsuit was finally settled at the end of June and Morris was on his way from Williamsburg back to Philadelphia at this time (MINTZ, 165–67, 170–71).

Wednesday 6th. Mercury at 80 in the Morning 84 at Noon and 84 at Night.

Clear and warm, with but little Wind & that variable.

Mrs. Blackburn and her daughter went away before breakfast.

General Lincoln & his Son; Mr. Porter, & a Doctr. Milne came to Dinner & returned afterwards.

Received from Genl. Lincoln 3 young trees of the Spruce Pine and two of the Fir or Hemlock in half Barrels which seemed to be healthy & vegitating.

Also received from Doctr. Craik by his Son a parcel of Chinese Seeds similar to those presented to me by Mr. Porter on the 2d Instt.

Benjamin Lincoln of Massachusetts and his son, Benjamin Lincoln, Jr. (d. 1788), were probably in Virginia on business. Their firm, Lincoln & Sons, conducted business with William Lyles & Co. and Porter & Ingraham, both of Alexandria. Thomas Porter, who appears here with them, was a close friend of both the Lincolns.

Thursday 7th. Mercury at 78 in the Morng.—82 at Noon and 86 at Night. Very little Wind at any time in the day, & that from the So. West. In the afternoon there were Clouds and appearances of Rain but very little fell here.

Rid to my Harvest fields at the Ferry—Dogue run and the Neck between Breakfast & Dinner.

Mr. Govournr. Morris went away before Breakfast as did Mr. Craik. Colo. Bassett & Mr. Geo. Washington accompanied the former as far as Alexandria. Mr. Arthur Lee came to Dinner, to which Colo. Bassett & G. W. returned.

In the afternoon a Mr. Turner, Steward to Colo. Richd. Corbin, came here with a letter from Mr. Thos. Corbin enclosing one from Colo. Geo. Fairfax respecting the said Thomas.

Richard Corbin (c.1714–1790), for many years a member of the royal governor's council and receiver general of Virginia, had, despite Loyalist sentiments, lived quietly in retirement at his home in King and Queen County during the Revolution. His son Thomas Corbin had served in the British army and had just returned to America. The letter from George William Fairfax concerned aspersions on Thomas Corbin's character by his brother, Richard Corbin, and attempted to enroll GW's support for Thomas. On 8 July, GW wrote to Thomas Corbin assuring him that he would be happy to see him at Mount Vernon. For correspondence on this subject, see George William Fairfax to GW, 19 Mar. 1785 and 23 Jan. 1786, GW to Fairfax and GW to Thomas Corbin, 8 July 1785, DLC:GW.

Friday 8th. Mercury at 81 in the Morning–82 at Noon and 85 at Night.

Exceedingly warm with little or no Wind day clear.

Colo. Bassett & Mr. Arthr. Lee went away after Breakfast & Mr. Turner before it. Mr. Burwell and Mr. John Bassett dined at Mr. Lund Washington's & returned in the Evening.

Perceived the Guinea grass Seed to be coming up.

Sowed one half the Chinese Seed given me by Mr. Porter and Doctr. Craik, in three rows in the Section next the Quarter (in my Botanical garden) beginning in that part next the garden Wall, and at the end next the Middle Walk.

First Row

Between the 1st. & 2d. pegs 1 Muc qua fa–betwn. the 2d. & 3d. Do., 1 Pung ton lean fa

3 & 4th.	1 Ting lit fa.
4 & 5.	1 Iso pung fa.
5 & 6.	1 Ci chou la fa.
6 & 7.	2 In che fa.
7th. & 8th.	Cum hung fa. 4 Seeds.
8 & 9.	2 Hung co fa.
9 & 10.	5 Be yack fa.
10 & 11.	7 Hou sun fa.
11 & 12.	sung sang fa yung
12 & 13.	Pu young fa.
13–14.	Mou Tan fa.

14 & 15.	Cum Coak fa.
15 & 16.	Pung Ki Cuun.
16 & 17.	Cin yet cou.
17 & 18.	Se me fa.
18 & 19.	Pain ba fa.
19 & 20.	Ou si fa.
20 & 21.	Tu me fa.
21 & 22.	All san fa.
22 & 23.	Young san con fa.
23 & 24.	Hon Con fa.
24 & 25.	Hoak sing fa.
25 & 26.	Isit Ye Muy fa.

Second Row

1st. & 2d.	Tits swe fa.
2 & 3.	An lee pung fa.
3 & 4.	Se Lou fa.
4 & 5.	Lung ci fa.
5 & 6.	Tiahung seen fa.
6 & 7.	Lam Coax fa.
7 & 8.	Iny hung fa.
8 & 9.	Jien pien cou fa.
9 & 10.	Pung qui fa.
10 & 11.	Ling si qui.
11 & 12.	Yuck soy hung seen fa.
12 & 13.	Yuck sou cou fa.
13 & 14.	Sing si qui fa.
14 & 15.	Bea an Ceu.
15 & 16.	Brey hung fa.
16 & 17.	Si fu he Tons.
17 & 18.	No name.

Third Row

1st. & 2.	Cum seen fa.
2 & 3.	Top pu young.
3 & 4.	No name—like a 2d. bla. bead.
4 & 5.	Ditto—like but largr. than cabbage seed.
5 & 6.	Ditto—larger & redder than clover Seed.

N.B. The above are the Chinese names which were accompanied by characters or hierogliphics. A concise description of the Seeds are annexed to their names on the Paper that enrolls them.

Although a few of GW's Chinese seeds have been identified in recent years, the matter is academic because only a few of them sprouted and none grew to maturity (see entry for 13 Aug. 1785).

Saturday 9th. Mercury at 80 in the Morng.—82 at Noon and 82 at Night.

Morning very warm, with but little Wind, which coming from the Eastward in the Evening & blowing brisk cooled the Air and made it pleasant.

Burwell & John Bassett and G. A. Washington set out after Breakfast for the Sweet Springs in Bottetourt County.

I rid to my Harvest fields at the Ferry and at Dogue run and over my Cornfields at each of those places and at Muddy hole. Found the first not good—the 2d. very indifferent and the third—viz. that at Muddy hole as good as could be expected from the Land.

A Mr. Arnold Henry Dohrman, a Gentleman of Lisbon recommended by Govr. Henry to me as a Man of fortune & one who had been exceedingly attentive and kind to the American prisoners in captivity came here, dined, and continued his journey afterwards to New York with letters of Introduction from me to the Presidt. of Congress, and to Messrs. Wilson Grayson and Chase Members of it, from me.

Arnold Henry Dohrman (1749–1813), a Portuguese merchant, aided American seamen captured during the Revolution by the English and set down penniless on the Portuguese coast. He not only gave them money and weapons but also helped them to reach home. In 1780 Congress made him United States agent in Portugal, with no pay but with his expenses to be paid by Congress. In 1785 he came to the United States to try to collect for the disbursements he had made. Dohrman left Mount Vernon with letters from GW to Richard Henry Lee (president of Congress), James Wilson of Pennsylvania, William Grayson of Virginia, and Samuel Chase of Maryland. In 1787 Congress finally awarded Dohrman $5,806 72/90 with interest from the time of the expenditure and a salary of $1,600 per annum, computed from the period "at which his expenditures commenced to the present day." Also he was granted one entire township in the Northwest Territory. He and his family settled in Steubenville, Ohio, in 1809 (JCC, 33:587–88; Dohrman to James Madison, 4 Mar. 1809, DLC: Madison Papers).

Sunday 10th. Mercury at 76 in the Morng.—78 at Noon and 78 at Night.

Morning calm—but the Wind fresh afterwards from the Eastward. Cool and pleasant.

At home all day alone.

Monday 11th. Mercury at 75 in the Morning 80 at Noon and 79 at Night.

Wind at So. West in the Morning, fresh & Cloudy. About Noon it began to thunder, & at 3 Oclock to Rain; and continued Showery at Intervals till near sun down—one of which was very hard, accompanied by heavy wind from the No. West or more Northerly.

Rid to my Harvest fields in the Neck, Dogue Run, & Ferry Plann. Perceived the Sand box trees (the Nuts of which I sowed on the 13th. of June) to be coming up.

Tuesday 12th. Mercury at 72 in the Morning—76 at Noon and 76 at Night.

Wind pretty fresh from the Westward, or No. West in the Morning, & cool & pleasant with clouds—but clear warm & still afterwards.

Rid to my Wheat fields in the Neck, Dogue run and ferry Plantations. Found great damage done in the former by yesterdays Wind, and Rain, having beat down, and entangled the Straw so as to render it difficult to cut and of consequence much left on the ground.

The Revd. Mr. Allison & Miss Ramsay dined here and returned to Alexandria afterwards.

The Brick Wall, from the No. Garden House was begun on the 8th. instt. tho' no minute was taken of it at the time.

Patrick Allison (1740–1802) was pastor of the First Presbyterian Church in Baltimore from 1763 until his death. He may have been a brother of Robert Allison, an Alexandria merchant who was married to William Ramsay's daughter Ann. The Miss Ramsay who appears at Mount Vernon with Patrick Allison is either Sarah or Amelia Ramsey, William Ramsey's two unmarried daughters.

Wednesday 13th. Mercury at 72 in the Morning—76 at Noon and 78 at Night.

Morning calm & clear. Afternoon clear with the Wind from the Southward but not very fresh.

Transplanted the Spruce & Fir (or Hemlock) from the Boxes in which they were sent to me by General Lincoln to the Walks by the Garden Gates. The Spare one (Spruce) I placed in my Nursery, or Botanical Garden.

Thursday 14th. Mercury at 72 in the Morng.—77 at Noon and 79 at Night.

Ferdinando Fairfax, third son of Bryan Fairfax, painted in later life. (Virginia Historical Society)

Day clear—with a little Wind from the Southward.

Went through my Harvest field at Muddy hole to Alexandria, to a Meeting of the Directors of the Potomack Company. Agreed with Mr. James Rumsey to undertake the Management of our works and a Mr. Stuart from Baltimore as an Assistant. Gave them directions—passed some Accts.—paid my quota of the demand for these purposes to Mr. Hartshorne the Treasurer—Made Mrs. Dalby a visit and came home in the evening.

Found Mr. Bryan Fairfax & his son Ferdinando here at my return who had come down before dinner.

GW had written Rumsey on 2 July, saying that he "took the liberty of mentioning your name to the Directors" and urged Rumsey to apply for the position of manager (DLC:GW). MR. STUART: Richardson Stewart. GW recorded the "quota" he paid today for five shares at £5 sterling per share as £33 6s. 8d. Virginia currency (LEDGER B, 203; BACON-FOSTER, 62–63).

Mrs. Mary Rose Dalby (c.1762–1790), a young Englishwoman, was the wife of Philip Dalby (WRIGHT, 189–91; WMQ, 1st ser., 10:106).

Friday 15th. Mercury at 74 in the Morng.—78 at Noon and 76 at Night. Lowering Morning with the Wind at So. West, and pretty fresh. A black cloud, with high wind, and a little rain about 3 Oclock.

Observed the Seeds of the Palmetto Royal which I had sowed on each side of the Gate in Front of the House were coming up.

Mr. Fairfax and his Son Ferdinando left this after breakfast.

Saturday 16th. Mercury at 74 in the Morning—76 at Noon and 80 at Night. Day clear & warm, with but little Wind and that Southerly.

Rid to my Wheat fields at Muddy hole and in the Neck; the first would be finished harvesting this day, the next not till Monday. Finished cutting the Wheat at Dogue run on Tuesday, and at the ferry on Wednesday last.

Sunday 17th. Mercury at 74 in the Morning—76 at Noon and 76 at Night.

Clear forenoon with the Wind pretty brisk from the Southwest—which continued all day with appearances of rain in the Afternoon but little or none fell here.

Fanny Bassett and Nelly Custis went to Church at Alexandria. Dined at Mr. Ramsays & returned in the Evening.

Mr. Ridout and Son called here between breakfast and Dinner but would not stay 'till the latter.

John and Mary Ogle Ridout had two sons, Samuel Ridout (c.1765–1840), who was now studying law in Annapolis after several years abroad, and Horatio (EDGAR, 250, 268–69, 279–80; HAMMOND, 67).

Monday 18th. Mercury at 72 in the Morning—74 at Noon and 74 at Night.

Wind Westerly in the Morning with Clouds, and appearances of rain. In the Afternoon it got to the Southwest & cleared.

Finished my Wheat Harvest in the Neck and began to cut Grass at Morris's.

Tuesday 19th. Thermomiter at 70 in the Morng.—74 at Noon and 76 at Night.

Very little Wind through the day, and in general clear.

Rid to the Plantation in the Neck—to Muddy hole, and to Dogue run at the last of which they were cutting grass and at the first just begin[nin]g.

Wednesday 20th. Thermomiter at 72 in the Morng.—75 at Noon and 76 at Night.

Wind Easterly and moderate in the Morning, but by 10 Oclock it shifted to the So. West and blew up two Showers of Rain each of which continued about 10 Minutes. In the Afternoon there were other slight Showers but altogether made but little. Fresh Southwester all the Afternoon.

Rid to the Ferry & the Plantation there.

Thursday 21st. Thermometer at 76 in the Morng.—79 at Noon and 80 at Night.

Cloudy morning, but clear Afternoon with a brisk Southerly Wind all day and warm.

Mr. Thompson, a Presbaterian Minister (introduced by Mr. Robt. Adam) came here, dined and Stayed all Night.

Friday 22d. Thermometer at 80 in the Morning—84 at Noon and 82 at night.

Southerly Wind and very warm all day with Clouds and appearances of Rain but a few drops only fell here.

Rid to the Ferry—Dogue run and Muddy hole Plantations.

Mr. Lund Washington & his Wife dined here.

And Mr. Thompson went away after Breakfast.

The leaves of the locust Trees this year, as the last, began to fade, & many of them dye. The Black Gum Trees which I had transplanted to my avenues or Serpentine Walks, & which put out leaf and looked well at first, are all dead; so are the Poplars, and most of the Mulberrys. The Crab apple trees also, which were transplanted into the Shrubberies & the Papaws are also dead, as also the Sassafras in a great degree. The Pines wholly & several of the Cedars. As also the Hemlock almost entirely. The live Oak which I thought was dead is putting out shoots from the bottom and have appearances of doing well.

Saturday 23d. Mercury at 79 in the Morning—78 at Noon and 80 at Night.

Wind Westwardly in the forenoon, but quite calm afterwards; afternoon cool. Rid to Muddy hole and River Plantations.

Finished my Hay Harvest in the Neck.

Perceived a few Plants of the Pride of China (the Seed of which were Sowed on the 13th. of June) to be coming up.

And also the Jien pien Cou fa—between the 8 & 9 pegs and the Seeds without name (only one) between the 4 & 5 pegs—the 1st. in the Second, & the other in the 3d. Row of the Chinese Sowing. These tho unnoticed at the time have been up several days.

Sunday 24th. Thermometer at 72 in the Morng.—74 at Noon and 72 at Night.

Wind Westerly all the forenoon; calm afterwards & cool.

Monday 25th. Thermometer at 72 in the Morning—76 at Night [noon] and 76 at Night.

Rid to my Plantations at the Ferry–Dogue run and in the Neck.

Southerly Wind, and warm in the Afternoon.

Tuesday 26th. Thermometer at 75 in the Morning–74 at Noon and 74 at Night.

Lowering day, with little drippings of Rain (not enough to lay the dust) through the day. Wind pretty brisk from the Southward.

With Mrs. Washington, Miss Bassett and the two Children I dined at Mr. Lund Washington's.

On my return, found Mr. Will Shaw (whom I had engaged to live with me as a Book keeper, Secretary, &ca.) here.

Wednesday 27th. Thermometer at 74 in the Morng.–80 at Noon and 80 at Night.

Morning a little lowering–forenoon perfectly calm & the wind at South afterwards. A Cloud rising about 5 Oclock afforded a pretty Shower for about 10 or 15 Minutes.

Finished cutting my Meadows at Dogue run but the Rain prevented my getting it secured either in Cocks or otherwise.

Also cut my Field Pea's the Seed of which came from Albany.

Mrs. Fendal, Miss Lee (eldest daughter of the Presidt. of Congress) Miss Nancy Lee, Grand daughter of Richd. Lee Esqr. of Maryland–Mr. Chas. Lee & Mr. Lawe. Washington, Lund Washington & their wives and Mr. Lawe. Washington, Son of Lawrence & Mr. Thos. Washington Son to Robert all dined here and went away in the Afternoon.

Mrs. Fendall was Philip Richard Fendall's second wife, Elizabeth Steptoe Lee Fendall (died c.1789), widow of Philip Ludwell Lee of Stratford. The Fendalls were married about 1780 and lived at Stratford Hall until the marriage of Mrs. Fendall's elder daughter, Matilda Lee, to Henry (Light Horse Harry) Lee in 1782. Philip Fendall and his wife then moved to Alexandria, leaving Henry and Matilda in possession of Stratford. The eldest daughter of Richard Henry Lee, president of Congress, was Mary Lee (b. 1764). In 1792 she became the second wife of GW's nephew, William Augustine Washington. Ann (Nancy) Lee was the daughter of Philip Thomas Lee (d. 1778) and granddaughter of Squire Richard Lee of Maryland.

MR. LAWE. WASHINGTON: either Lawrence Washington (1728–c.1809) of Chotank or Lund's brother Lawrence (1740–1799) of Belmont. The wife of Lawrence Washington of Chotank was Elizabeth Dade Washington. Lawrence of Belmont's wife, Catherine Foote Washington, was the sister of Lund Washington's wife Elizabeth Foote Washington. LAWE. WASHINGTON SON OF LAWRENCE: The younger Lawrence Washington who appears here, often called Lawrence Washington, Jr. (d. 1809), was the son of Lawrence Washington of Chotank. Young Washington had killed a man in a duel in 1783 and the following year found it expedient to leave King George County for a time to allow public opinion to cool (MASON [2], 2:763–65).

Thomas Washington (1758–1807) was the son of Lund Washington's oldest brother Robert. Thomas served in Grayson's Additional Continental Regiment 1777–78 and in Lee's Legion 1778 until the end of the war. He married his cousin Sarah (Sally) Washington Harper, daughter of John Washington of Leedstown and widow of Robert Harper of Alexandria.

Thursday 28th. Thermometer at 77 in the Morng.—81 at Noon and 84 at Night. Southerly wind in the forenoon. Calm afterwards until about 5 Oclock & very warm—Southerly from thence through the Night.

Finished my Harvest at Dogue run, which compleated the business of Haymaking for this year.

Friday 29th. Thermometer at 78 in the Morng.—80 at Noon and 78 at Night. A Squall of Wind and a little fine Rain came on about 6 oclock in the Morning; both of which were soon over: but the former continued pretty fresh from No. West until the Evening, when it became Calm.

Cut the Weeds, wild grass &ca. which had intermixed with the Clover that I sowed at the home house and at Muddy hole—this being the second time I cut that at home the cutting being about a week before Harvest.

Rid to my Plantations in the Neck Muddy hole, Dogue Run & Ferry—at all of which they had got their Wheat in except at the Neck Plantn.

Saturday 30th. Thermometer at 70 in the Morng.—72 at Noon and 75 at Night.

Clear with but little Wind at any time of the day.

Put shades over the Spruce & Hemlock pines, brought me by Genl. Lincoln, which seemed to be declining fast.

Mr. Shaw went this Afternoon to Dumfries.

Sunday 31st. Thermometer at 70 in the Morng.—78 at Noon and 78 at Night.

Calm & clear all day.

August 1785

Monday 1st. Mercury at 74 in the Morning—[ ] at Noon and 78 at Night.

But little wind, weather clear & day very warm.

Left home at 6 Oclock P. M. and after escorting Fanny Bassett to Alexandria I proceeded to Doctr. Stuarts where I breakfasted; and from thence went to George Town to the Annual Meeting of the Potomack Company appointed to be held at that place.

About Noon, a sufficient number of sharers having assembled to constitute a meeting, we proceeded to business—Mr. Danl. Carroll in the Chair—when the President & directors of the Company made a report of their transactions since their appointment, which was received & approved of.

The Board of Directors then sat, and after coming to some resolutions respecting rations to be allowed the Workmen—the mode of payment—manner of keeping an acct. of their work &ca. &ca. and to a determination of proceeding first to the Senneca Falls and next to those at the Mouth of Shannondoah for the purpose of investigation & to direct the operations thereat adjourned Sine Die.

Dined at Shuters Tavern, and lodged at Mr. Oneals.

SHUTERS TAVERN: In 1783 John Suter (d. 1794) opened a tavern in Georgetown, Md., on the east side of Water Street (now Wisconsin Ave.) several doors south of Bridge (now M) Street. During the 1780s this tavern was commonly used for meetings of the Potomac Company and the commissioners of Georgetown. Suter later moved his business around the corner and opened the Fountain Inn on the south side of Bridge Street near the eastern edge of the original town (see HOLMES; ECKER). Bernard O'Neill, who became a commissioner of Georgetown in 1782, was a member of the Potomac Company (ECKER, 10; BACON-FOSTER, 59).

Tuesday 2d. Thermometer at 76 in the Morng.—78 at Noon and [ ] at Night.

Weather clear and Warm with but little wind.

Left George Town about 10 Oclock, in Company with all the Directors except Govr. Lee who went to Mellwood to visit Mr. Igns. Digges (his father in Law) who lay at the point of death and being accompanied by Colo. James Johnson (Brother to Govr. Johnson) and Messrs. Beall, Johns & others who took with them a cold Collation with Spirits wine &ca. We dined at Mr. Bealls Mill 14 Miles from George Town and proceeded—that is the Directors and Colo. Johnson—to a Mr. Goldsboroughs, a decent Farmers House at the head of the Senneca falls—about 6 Miles and 20 from George Town.

Col. James Johnson (b. 1736) lived in Frederick County, Md., and helped to manage several furnaces and forges owned by the Johnson family both there and in Loudoun County, Va. He served during the Revolution as colonel of a battalion of infantry in the Flying Camp (DELAPLAINE, 13–14; WILLIAMS [2], 1062).

Thomas Beall, son of George Beall, signed his name "Thomas Beall of George" to distinguish himself from other contemporary Thomas Bealls. A commissioner for Georgetown and a local landholder, Beall was a member of the Potomac Company (ECKER, 10; BACON-FOSTER, 59). Mr. Johns was probably Thomas Johns, a merchant of Georgetown, who had been a member of the pre-Revolution Potomac navigation project (*Va. Gaz.*, D&H, 7 Jan. 1775; HEADS OF FAMILIES, MD., 86).

The 1790 federal census of Montgomery County, Md., shows no Goldsboroughs, but does list the household of Jonathan Goldsberry, with three adult males, one female, and seven slaves (HEADS OF FAMILIES, MD., 87).

Wednesday 3d. Wind at No. West & tolerably pleasant with appearances of Rain, without any falling.

Having provided Canoes and being joined by Mr. Rumsay the principal Manager, & Mr. Stewart an Assistant to him, in carrying on the Works, we proceeded to examine the falls; and beginning at the head of them went through the whole by water, and continued from the foot of them to the Great fall. After which, returning back to a Spring on the Maryland Side between the

"The Great Falls of the Potomac" painted by George Beck, c. 1796. The painting was owned by Washington and still hangs at Mount Vernon. (Mount Vernon Ladies' Association of the Union)

Seneca & Great Falls, we partook (about 5 O'clock) of another cold Collation which a Colo. Orme, a Mr. Turner & others of the Neighbourhood, had provided and returned back by the way of Mr. Bealls Mill to our old Quarters at Mr. Goldsboroughs. The distance as estimated 8 Miles.

The Water through these Falls is of sufficient depth for good Navigation; and as formidable as I had conceived them to be; but by no means impracticable. The principal difficulties lye in rocks which occasion a crooked passage. These once removed, renders the passage safe without the aid of Locks & may be effected for the Sum mentioned in Mr. Jno. Ballendine's estimate (the largest extant) but in a different manner than that proposed by him. It appearing to me, and was so, unanimously determined by the Board of Directors, that a channel through the bed of the river in a strait direction, and as much in the course of the currant as may be, without a grt. increase of labour & expence, would be preferable to that through the Gut which was the choice of Mr. Ballendine for a Canal with Locks–the last of which we thought unnecessary, & the first more expensive in the first instance, besides being liable to many inconveniences which the other is not, as it would, probably be frequently choaked with drift wood–Ice–and other rubbish which would be thrown therein through the several inlets already made by the rapidity of the currts. in freshes and others which probably would be made thereby; whereas a navigation through the bed of the river when once made will, in all probability, remain forever, as the currt. here will rather clear, than contribute to choak, the passage. It is true, no track path can be had in a navigation thus ordered, nor does there appear a necessity for it. Tracking, constitutes a large part of Mr. Ballendines estimate–The want of which, in the rapid parts of the river, (if Mr. Rumseys plan for working Boats against stream by the force of Mechanical powers should fail) may be supplied by chains buoyed up to haul by which would be equally easy, more certain, and less dangerous than setting up with Poles–whilst track paths, it is apprehended can not be made to stand, and may endanger the Banks if the Wood is stripped from them, which is their present security against washing.

The distance between the Seneca & Great Falls, is about 5 Miles; and except in one place within 3/4 of a Mile of the latter, the navigation now is, or easily may be made, very good; and at this place, the obstruction arises from the shallowness of the Water. Boats may go almost to the Spout with safety. To the place where the water passes when the river is full it is quite easy & safe to descend to, being in a Cove of still Water.

Col. Archibald Orme (1730–1812), of the Rock Creek neighborhood in Montgomery County, Md., was an active surveyor in the area. Mr. Turner may be Samuel Turner, who was living in that neighborhood in 1790, or Hezekiah Turner (1739–c.1812), of Fauquier County, Va., who was active after the Revolution as a surveyor of lands in the upper Potomac Valley (HEADS OF FAMILIES, MD., 88; MACKENZIE [1], 2:564; SCHARF [3], 1:744; BLUM, 426).

TRACK PATH: The problem GW is discussing is that of aiding boats to ascend the Seneca Falls (actually rapids). The track path was a towing path used to tow the boats through the rapid part of the river. GW disliked the cost of constructing and maintaining canals and locks and accepted the necessity of cutting a canal only when locks were clearly necessary, as at the Great Falls (GW to Edmund Randolph, 16 Sept. 1785, DLC:GW). THE SPOUT: The point in a river where the banks formed a narrow channel, thus creating rapids, was called a spout. In his tour this week GW passes through three such sections of the Potomac, referring to each as "the Spout." For the sake of clarity, each spout will be referred to by the name of the rapids or falls associated with it. This one is the Great Falls Spout, described in 1760 by Andrew Burnaby: "the channel of the river is contracted by hills; and is . . . narrow. . . . It is clogged moreover with innumerable rocks; so that the water for a mile or two flows with accelerated velocity" (BURNABY, 68–69).

Thursday 4th. In order to be more certain of the advantages and disadvantages of the Navigation proposed by Mr. Ballendine, through the Gut; we took a more particular view of it—walking down one side & returning on the other and were more fully convinced of the impropriety of its adoption first because it would be more expensive in the first instance and secondly because it would be subject to the ravages of freshes &ca. as already mentioned, without any superiority over the one proposed through the bed of the River unless a track path should be preferable to hauling up by a Chain with buoy's.

Engaged nine labourers with whom to *commence* the Work.

Thermometer [ ] in the Morng.—76 at Noon and 78 at Night.

Friday 5th. Thermometer at 74 in the Morning—76 at Noon and 76 at Night.

After Breakfast, and after directing Mr. Rumsey when he had marked the way and set the labourers to Work to meet us at Harpers ferry on the Evening of the Morrow at Harpers Ferry (at the conflux of the Shannondoah with the Potomack) myself and the Directors set out for the same place by way of Frederick Town (Maryland). Dined at a Dutch mans 2 Miles above the

Thomas Johnson and his family, painted by Charles Willson Peale. (C. Burr Artz Library, Frederick County Public Libraries, Frederick, Maryland)

Mo[uth] of Monocasy & reached the former about 5 'Oclock. Drank Tea–supped–and lodged at Govr. Johnsons.

In the Evening the Bells rang, & Guns were fired; & a Committee waited upon me by order of the Gentlemen of the Town to request that I wd. stay next day and partake of a public dinner which the Town were desirous of giving me. But as arrangements had been made, and the time for examining the Shannondoah Falls, previous to the day fixed for receiving labourers into pay, was short I found it most expedient to decline the honor.

Robert Harper (d. 1782), of Philadelphia, settled at the confluence of the Shenandoah and Potomac rivers in Virginia before 1747, and there developed a ferry which crossed the Potomac to Maryland just above the mouth of the Shenandoah. By 1785 Harper's home had become a nucleus for a small village, variously called Shenandoah Falls and Harpers Ferry (BUSHONG, 17–21). In 1795 GW, as president, chose Harpers Ferry as a site for a federal arsenal and armory.

Frederick Town was laid out and settled in the 1740s on land owned by

View of Harpers Ferry, engraved by J. W. Steel after a drawing by T. Doughty. (Library of Congress)

the Dulany family of Maryland. Lying on a major crossroads in the heart of the Monocacy River Valley, it became the seat of Frederick County, Md., when that county was formed in 1748. Its population was for many years heavily German, mostly immigrants from German communities in Pennsylvania whom the English colonists commonly referred to as "Dutch" (LAND, 180, 252). The "Dutch mans" may have been the inn located on the road between the Potomac River and Frederick Town, which in 1780 was being kept by Leonhard Heil (MERENESS, 591).

Saturday 6th. Thermometer 76 in the Morning—88 at Noon and 82 at Night.

Breakfasted in Frederick Town, at Govr. Johnsons, and dined at Harpers ferry. Took a view of the River, from the Banks, as we road up the bottom from Pains falls to the ferry, as well as it could be done on Horse back. Sent a Canoe in a Waggon from the Ferry to Keeptriest Furnace in ordr. to descend the Falls therin tomorrow.

In my ride from George Town to this place, I made the following observations. That the Land about the first, is not only hilly, & a good deal mixed with flint stone, but is of an indifferent quality 'till we left the great Road, (3 Miles from G. Town) which leads to the former. The quality of the Land then improves, and seems well adapted to the culture of small grain but continues broken and by No means in a state of high cultivation. It is also better timbered and of a sameness to the Seneca Falls. That about the Maryland Sugar Lands (1400 Acres of which belong to George Plater Esqr.) which is five Miles above Seneca It is remarkably fine, & very level. From thence to Monocasy about 12 Miles further they are less levl. and of much inferior quality. That from Monocasy to Frederick Town (distant 12 or 13 Miles) nothing can well exceed them for fertility of Soil–convenient levelness and luxurient growth of Timber. The Farms seem to be under good cultivation, which is somewhat Surprizing, as the possessors of them (on a Mannor belonging to Chs. Carroll Esqr. of Carrolton who holds in one Tract, 12 or 14,000 Acres) are Tenants at will–paying for the low grounds on Potomack & Monocasy 5/. Maryland Curry. pr. acre & for the high land 4/. for all the land within the boundaries of their respective Tenements. That from Frederick Town to the Kittoctan Mountain (about 7 Miles) the Land is *nearly* similar but not quite so luxurient to the eye. And from that Mountain to the river estimated 10 Miles it is more hilly & of a second quality but strong & very productive especially of small grain. That the remaining 3 Miles to the Ferry is river bottom and of course good.

Frederick Town stands on a branch of Monocasy, and lyes rather low. The Country about it is beautiful & seems to be in high Cultivation. It is said to contain about [ ] Houses; for the most part of wood; but there are many of Brick and Stone, & some good ones. The number of Inhabitants are computed to be [ ] Souls. There are Churches, a Court House–Work House & other public buildings. The Mechanics are numerous, in proportion to the aggregate; and the Spirit of Industry seems to pervade the place–tho' Trade, it is said, has slackened.

Johnson's house in Frederick Town was on Market Street; his country estate was about four miles northeast of the town (SCHARF [3], 1:487).

The Keep Triste iron furnace was located on the right (Virginia) bank of the Potomac near the mouth of Elk's Run, about two miles above the confluence of the Potomac with the Shenandoah River. This area is now in Jefferson County, W.Va.

GW left the Great Road to Frederick Town to follow the river road along the Potomac. The Sugar Lands were named for the stands of sugar maple trees found in the Broad Run area in the western part of Montgomery County, Md., which also extended across the Potomac into the Sugar Land Run neighborhood of Virginia.

George Plater (1735–1792), of Sotterly, on the Patuxent River in St. Mary's County, Md., practiced law in Maryland and took a leading role in the Revolution, representing Maryland in the Second Continental Congress (1778–80). In 1776 Plater participated in a joint Virginia-Maryland commission for safer navigation of the Potomac River.

Carrollton, a tract of land of over 10,000 acres in the fork of the Potomac and Monocacy rivers in Frederick County, Md., was given to Charles Carroll (1737–1832) by his father Charles Carroll (1702–1782) when the younger Charles returned to America in 1765 following his schooling in Europe. The younger Charles Carroll added "of Carrollton" to his name to distinguish himself from three other Charles Carrolls then living, although he never maintained a home at Carrollton. His regular residence was on the great plantation Doughoregan Manor in Anne Arundel (after 1851 in Howard) County, Md., about 16 miles west of Baltimore and 30 miles east of Carrollton. In 1821 Carroll divided Carrollton among a dozen members of his family, while retaining a life interest in the rentals from his tenants there (W.P.A. [2], 331; Charles Carroll to Charles Carroll [of Carrollton], 10 April 1764, *Md. Hist. Mag.*, 12:167; ROWLAND [1], 1:68–69, 180–81, 196, 2:49, 409).

GW's party apparently followed the old road from Frederick Town to the gap in South Mountain made by the Potomac River. KITTOCTAN: now Catoctin Mountain, which runs almost due south through Frederick County Md., into Loudoun County, Va., and is cut by the Potomac at Point of Rocks, Md.

Sunday 7th. Thermometer at 76 in the Morning—74 at Noon and 76 at Night.

About Sunrising, the Directors & myself rid up to Keeptrieste, where Canoes were provided, in which we crossed to the Maryland side of the river and examined a Gut, or swash through which it is supposed the Navigation must be conducted. This Swash is shallow at the entrance, but having sufficient fall, may easily (by removing some of the rocks) admit any quantity of water required. From the entrance to the foot, may be about 300 yards in a semicircular direction with many loose, & some fixed rocks to remove. Having examined this passage, I returned to the head of the Falls, and in one of the Canoes with two skilful hands descended them with the common Currt. in its Natural bed—which I found greatly incommoded with rocks, shallows and a crooked Channel which left no doubt of the propriety of preferring a passage through the Swash.

From the foot of the Swash the Water is pretty good for 3 or 400 yards further, when there is another fall of it, or rapid with an uneven bottom which occasions a considerable ripple at Top—but as their is sufficient depth, & the channel Middling straight, the difficulty here in descending is not great but to return without the aids spoke of at the Seneca falls may be labourious. From hence the Water is good to the head of the Island just above the ferry by which it is shoal on the Virginia side with some rocks and tho' deeper on the Maryland side is worse on acct. of the

Rocks which are more numerous. The distance from the head of the Falls to the Ferry may be about a Mile & half.

Here we breakfasted; after which we set out to explore the Falls below; & having but one Canoe, Colo. Gilpin, Mr. Rumsay (who joined us according to appointment last Night) and Myself, embarked in it, with intention to pass thro' what is called the Spout (less than half a mile below the ferry) but when we came to it, the Company on the shore on acct. of the smallness, and low sides of the Vessel, dissuaded us from the attempt, least the roughness of the Water, occasioned by the rocky bottom, should fill, & involve us in danger. To avoid the danger therefore we passed through a narrow channel on the left, near the Maryland Shore and continued in the Canoe to the lower end of Pains falls distant, according to estimation 3 Miles. These falls may be described as follow.

From the Ferry, for about 3 hundred yards, or more, the Water is deep with rocks here and there, near the surface, then a ripple; the Water betwn. which, and the Spout, as before. The Spout takes its name from the rapidity of the Water, and its dashings, occasioned by a gradual, but pretty considerable fall, over a rocky bottom which makes an uneven surface & considerable swell. The Water however, is of sufficient depth through it, but the Channel not being perfectly straight; skilful hands are necessary to navigate and conduct Vessels through this rapid. From hence, their is pretty smooth & even Water with loose stone, & some rocks, for the best part of a Mile; to a ridge of rocks which cross the river with Intervals; thro' which the Water passes in crooked directions. But the passage which seemed most likely to answer our purpose of Navigation was on the Maryland side being freest from rocks but Shallow. From hence to what are called Pains falls the Water is tolerably smooth, with Rocks here and there. These are best passed on the Maryland side. They are pretty Swift—shallow—and foul at bottom but the difficulties may be removed. From the bottom of these Falls, leaving an Island on the right, & the Maryland Shore on the left the easy & good Navigation below is entered.

At the foot of these falls the Directors & myself (Govr. Lee having joined us the Evening before) held a meeting—At which it was determined, as we conceived the Navigation could be made through these (commonly called the Shannondoah) Falls without the aid of Locks, and by opening them would give eclat to the undertaking and great ease to the upper Inhabitants as Water transportation would be immediately had to the Great Falls from Fort Cumberland to employ the upper hands in this work instead of removing the obstructions above, and gave Mr. Rumsey directions to do so accordingly—with general Instructions for his Governmt.

Govr. Lee, on Acct. of the death of his Father in Law, Mr. Igs. Digges, & consequent circumstances; left us at this place with a view of carrying his Lady next day to Mellwood. The rest of us returned to the Tavern at Harpers Ferry.

THE FALLS: Shenandoah Falls, running about two miles down the Potomac from Elk's Run to the mouth of the Shenandoah River. HIS GOVERNMT.: In these instructions Rumsey was directed to hire as many workers as necessary to open the Shenandoah and Seneca Falls (BACON-FOSTER, 64).

Monday 8th. Thermometer at 68 this Morning—70 at Noon and 70 at Night.

This being the day appointed for labourers to engage in the work we waited to see the issue until Evening, when Mr. Johnson & his Brother Colo. Johnson took leave of us.

Many Gentlemen of the Neighbourhood visited us here today—among whom Mr. Wormeley Senr., my Brother Charles—Colo. Morgan, Captn. Shepherd and Colo. Shepherd his Brother of Wheeling on the Ohio were of the number.

A few hands offered and were employed.

Col. William Morgan (d. 1788), of Shepherdstown, Berkeley County (now in W.Va.), was a founding justice when that county was organized in 1772 (NORRIS [1], 220–21; DANDRIDGE, 336; James Rumsey to William Hartshorne, 24 Oct. 1785, ViU). Abraham Shepherd (1754–1822), a captain in Stephenson's Maryland and Virgina Rifle Company, was captured at Fort Washington during the New York campaign (1776) and was later exchanged and returned home due to illness. The Shepherd brothers were sons of Thomas Shepherd, founder of Shepherdstown (DANDRIDGE, 346; HEITMAN [2], 493).

Tuesday 9th. Thermometer at 68 in the Morning—72 at Noon and 74 at Night.

Having provided a light & convenient Boat—hired two hands to work her and laid in some Stores, Colonels Fitzgerald & Gilpin, and myself embarked in it, leaving Mr. Rumsey to engage more hds. & to set those he had to work about 6 Oclock P.M.

In this Boat we passed through the Spout, and all the other Falls and rapids, and breakfasted at a Captn. Smiths on the Maryland side; to which place our horses had been sent the Evening before—after which and dining on our prog at Knowlands Ferry (about 15 Miles from Harpers) we lodged at the House of a

Mr. Tayler, about three Miles above the Mouth of Goose Creek and about 10 M. below Knowlands.

CAPTN. SMITHS: probably the home of Capt. John Smith, near the Smith's ferry mentioned by GW on 10 Aug. (HEADS OF FAMILIES, MD., 63). PROG: food, victuals, provender; especially provisions for a journey. KNOWLANDS FERRY: Noland's Ferry crossed the Potomac downstream of Noland's Island from Loudoun County, Va., to the mouth of Tuscarora Creek in Montgomery County, Md. The ferry was established before 1757 by Philip Noland (Knowland) and in 1785 was owned by Philip's son Thomas (HARRISON [1], 503–4). MR. TAYLER: possibly Thomas Taylor who lived in the vicinity of Harrison's Island. Taylor appears in the Montgomery County, Md., census of 1790 and his will, probated in Loudoun County in 1797, shows him as owning land in both Virginia and Maryland (HEADS OF FAMILIES, MD., 67; KING [6], 73).

Wednesday 10th. Thermometer at 72 in the Morning—74 at Noon and 80 at Night.

Before Sun rise we embarked and about Nine Oclock arrived at the head of the Seneca Falls and breakfasted with our old Landlord Mr. Goldsborough to which place our horses had proceeded the Over Night from Captn. Smiths.

The Nature of the river, from the foot of Pains falls to which a description has already been given, is—From that place to Smiths ferry, on the No. of the Island already noticed (about 2 Miles) the Water, generally, is pretty smooth, with round Stones of different sizes at the bottom and in places shallow. From hence to Luckets ferry at the Mouth of the Maryland Kittoctan (about 5 Miles further) the Water is Smooth and of sufficient depth in one part or other of the river for Boats, except at one ripple near to, and just above Luckets ferry which is occasioned principally by a fish dam. From & between this, & the Virginia Kittoctan where the river passes through the Mountain of that name is what are called Hooks falls which are no otherwise difficult than from the Shallowness of the Water & crookedness of the Channel —both of which it is presumed, may be much improved. From these Falls to Knowlands ferry, which is about 4 Miles and Six from Luckets the Navigation leaving Trammels Islands on the Left & Peach Island on the right is easy & pleasant, with only Shoal Water in one or two places which may be deepnėd without much expence. From hence to the Seneca Falls, the Navigation is in no part difficult. In one or two places, particularly above tht upper Island now, or formerly, belonging to the Hites the water is rather Shoal, but may readily be deepned (as the bottom is of round Stone) if a better passage cannot be had on the No.

side of the Island. The Fish pots, of which there are many in the River, serve to clog the Navigation, & to render the passage more difficult upon the whole.

Between the Shannondoah falls, and those of Seneca, there are many valuable Islands—but those of Lee, McCarty, Hites, & Trammels, may greatly claim the preference; the River Bottoms have also a rich & luxurient appearance & in some places look to be wide.

After Breakfasting, and spending sometime with the labourers at their different works, of blowing, removing stone, getting Coal wood &ca.—we left the Seneca Falls about 2 Oclock A.M. & crossing the River about half a mile below them and a little above Captn. Trammels we got into the great Road from Leesburgh to Alexandria and about half after Nine O'clock in the Evening I reached home after an absence from it of 10 days.

Smith's ferry, in Frederick County, Md., crossed the Potomac just below the mouth of Dutchman Creek in Loudoun County, Va. Near the ferry landing on the Maryland shore was founded in 1787 the town of Berlin, later renamed Brunswick (W.P.A. [2], 348–49).

LUCKETS FERRY: The Luckett family of that part of Frederick County in the 1780s was headed by William Luckett (FREDERICK, 55, 69; HEADS OF FAMILIES, MD., 66). TRAMMELS ISLANDS: John Trammell (d. 1794), of Frederick County, Md., owned several islands by Point of Rocks, the largest of which is now called Conoy. Lee's Island was possibly that island once owned by Thomas Lee, father of Gov. Thomas Sim Lee (LEE [5], 156). It may be the Lee's Island at the mouth of Broad Run, Loudoun County, which was later renamed Seldon's Island (SCHEEL, 5).

Thursday 11th. Thermometer 77 in the Morning—84 at Noon and 84 at Night.

The Drought, the effects of which were visible when I left home, had, by this (no rain having fallen in my absence) greatly affected vegetation. The grass was quite burnt & crisp under foot—Gardens parched and the young Trees in my Shrubberies, notwithstanding they had been watered (as it is said) according to my direction were much on the decline. In a word nature had put on a melancholy look—everything seeming to droop.

Friday 12th. Thermometer at 76 in the Morning—82 at Noon and 83 at Night.

Very little wind, but some appearances of rain in the West but none fell.

Mrs. Fendall and Miss [   ] second Daughter of the President of Congress dined here and returned home after it.

The second daughter of Richard Henry Lee, president of Congress, was Hannah Lee (1766–c.1801), who was married in 1787 to GW's nephew, Corbin Washington. GW usually followed the custom of referring to the eldest daughter of a family only by her family name (i.e., Miss Lee) and to her younger sisters by their given names (Miss Hannah Lee). Thus, since he could not remember the girl's given name, he left a blank in the manuscript.

Saturday 13th. Thermometer at 80 in the Morng.–84 at Noon and 86 at Night.

Rid to my Muddy hole and Neck Plantations, and beheld Corn in a melancholy situation, fired in most places to the Ear with little appearance of yielding if rain should soon come & a certainty of making nothing if it did not. Attempts had been made at both these Plantations to sow Wheat, but stirring the ground in the parched condition it was in, had so affected the Corn as to cause well grounded apprehensions that it would die if not restored by seasonable & sufficient Rains. This put a stop to further Seeding which is almost as bad as the injury done by it to the Corn as latter sowing in old Corn ground seldom produces. At the first mentioned place about 30 Bushels had been sowed–at the latter less.

The two kinds of Chinese Seeds which had appeared before I left home were destroyed either by the drought or insects. That between the 8th. & 9th. stakes in the 2d. row was entirely eradicated–indeed some kind of fly, or bug, had begun to prey up on the leaves before I left home. The other was broke of near the ground & cannot I fear recover.

In the Evening late, Doctr. Craik arrived, on a Visit to John Alton (my Overseer in the Neck) who has been ill, & confined to his bed for near 3 Weeks.

Sunday 14th. Thermometer at 79 in the Morning–82 at Noon and [ ] at Night.

Morning calm & clear. Abt. Noon the wind came out from the Westward and in the afternoon there were appearances of rain No. Wt. & Southward of us with rumbling thunder at a distance but the clouds vanished without shedding any of their Watry particles.

Doctr. Craik left this after Breakfast.

Monday 15th. Thermometer at 78 in the Morning–82 at Noon and [ ] at Night.

Wind Westerly in the Morning wch. died away about Noon–when clouds in the Southwest indicated Rain but none fell.

Rid to my Plantations at the Ferry, Dogue run and Muddy hole. Found the two first were suffering as I had described the other two on Saturday and that both had discontinued sowing of Wheat after putting about 30 Bushels at each place in the ground.

My Overseer at the Ferry (Fairfax) ascribes the wretched condition of his Corn to the bug which has proved so destructive to both Wheat and Corn on James River and elsewhere equally with the drought & shewed me hundreds of them & their young under the blades at the lower joints of the Stock. The Corn is effected by their sucking the juices which occasions a gradual decline of the whole plant. He also shewed me a piece of course grass that was quite killed by them, by the same kind of operation.

Mrs. Washington and Fanny Bassett went to Abingdon to day on a visit to Mrs. Stuart who had been sick of a fever and head Ach for 15 or 16 days. The former returned, the latter stayed.

In the Evening my Brother John came in.

From the Accts. given me by my Overseers the yield of my Wheat stacks is very indifferent.

THE BUG WHICH HAS PROVED SO DESTRUCTIVE: probably the chinch bug, *Blissus leucopterus.* GW also had trouble with this pest in 1786 (see entries for 22, 24, and 25 July 1786).

Tuesday 16th. Thermometer at 79 in the Morning–86 at Noon and 86 at Night.

Foggy & close morning with but little wind all day.

Accompanied my Brother to Alexandria and meeting Mr. & Mrs. Fendal & Miss [Nancy] Lee who proposed to dine here I made but little stay in Town. My Brother not being able to complete his business did not return 'till the Evening. Mr. Fendall, Mrs. Fendall &ca. stayed all Night.

Wednesday 17th. Thermometer at 78 in the Morning–84 at Noon and 86 at Night.

Cloudy & damp Morning, with the Wind at South. In the Afternoon Clouds gathered all round us with thunder & lightning and a good deal of rain appeared to fall upon Patuxent and above us on this river but not enough fell here to wet a handkerchief.

Mr. [and] Mrs. Fendall and Miss Nancy went away before breakfast and my Brother John directly after it.

Doctr. Craik came here to Dinner on a visit to John Alton and stayed all Night.

Thursday 18th. Thermometer at 81 in the Morning—86 at Noon and 88 at Night. About 4 Oclock the Mercury was at 90.

The fore part of the day was quite calm, and the whole of it intensely hot. About Noon it began to cloud & sprinkle rain which went off again. At 4 another cloud arose, out of which we had a pretty shower for about 15 or 20 Minutes, but not sufficient to wet the ground more than an Inch where it had been fresh worked. On Patuxent there was the appearance of abundant rain.

Doctr. Craik set off after brakfast to return home—but a Messenger recalled him to Jno. Alton where he remained all day & Night.

Mrs. Washington & Nelly Custis visited Mrs. Stuart, and returned in the Evening with Fanny Bassett.

Began with James and Tom to work on my Park fencing.

Cut down the two Cherry trees in the Court yard.

JAMES AND TOM: two of GW's slave carpenters. Tom is called Tom Nokes in the 1786 list of slaves (see main entry for 18 Feb. 1786).

PARK FENCING: GW was laying out an English-style deer park or paddock in the area between the mansion house and the Potomac River. He planned to stock it with English and native species and received deer from several friends, including Benjamin Ogle of Maryland, Andrew Lewis, and William Fitzhugh of Chatham (GW to George W. Fairfax, 25 June 1786, MoSW; GW to Lewis, 1 Feb. 1788, GW to Fitzhugh, 11 Nov. 1785, DLC:GW). In his long absence from Mount Vernon during the presidency, the fences surrounding the park fell into disrepair and the deer escaped to roam over much of the farm, doing considerable damage to the gardens and shrubberies. In spite of this, GW would not permit them to be hunted and killed, either by his own dependents or by neighbors (GW to the Messrs. Chichester, 25 April 1799, DLC:GW). He wrote a neighbor in 1792 that he had given up all his own foxhounds because they frightened the deer (GW to Richard Chichester, 8 Aug. 1792, DLC:GW).

Friday 19th. Mercury at 79 in the Morning—82 at Noon and 82 at Night.

Morning lowering, and very like for rain, but about noon it cleared after a very slight sprinkling, not enough to wet a man in his shirt.

Doctr. Craik returned from John Alton's, took breakfast, & proceeded home.

Encouraged by the little rain which had fallen, and the hope that more would fall I sowed about half an Acre of Turnips at home, and some at Dogue run Plantation.

Saturday 20th. Mercury at 78 in the Morning—82 at Noon and 82 at Night.

Clear, with the wind at East the greater part of the day but not very fresh. Mr. Shaw went to Dumf[rie]s.

Rid to all my plantations, and visited John Alton, who still lay ill, and in great danger.

At Muddy hole, there appeared to have fallen more rain than at any other of my Plantations. At this place my Overseer had recommenced sowing of Wheat, & was continuing it. In the Neck they had done the same, but finding the ground only superficially wet, they had discontinued it. Neither at the Ferry nor dogue run had they attempted to sow any, tho at the latter there had been a good shower, but by no means a sufficiency of Rain.

Sunday 21st. Mercury at 78 in the Morning–82 at Noon and 82 at Night.

Calm & foggy Morning with but little Wind all day, and no appearances of rain.

Monday 22d. Mercury at 78 in the Morning–77 at Noon and 77 at Night.

Very cloudy morning with the Wind at So. West. About 8 Oclock it began to rain moderately and with intervals continued to do so through the day, and Night–but as the rain was fine, & not const[an]t the ground was not penetrated deep by it especially where it was before hard.

Tuesday 23d. Mercury at 76 in the Morning–74 at Noon and 75 at Night.

Morning lowering, with drops of rain now and then, but none fell to wet the ground. Wind for the most part of the day Easterly.

Doctr. Craik came here before Dinner. Visited John Alton in the Evening and returned and stayed all Night.

Mr. Shaw returned home in the Afternoon.

With the Guinea grass Seed I had on hand, I began to make good the missing spaces of what was sowed in my small or Botanical Garden on the 13th. of June last but did not finish half of it.

The botanical garden was a plot of ground between the spinning house and the flower garden. It was used for experimenting with seeds and fertilizers.

Wednesday 24th. Mercury at 76 in the Morning–75 at Noon and 74 at Night.

Weather clear and but little wind and that variable.

Doctr. Craik went away after Breakfast.

Sowed some more of the Guinea Grass seed today in the manner of yesterday.

Measured round the ground which I intend to inclose for a Paddock, and find it to be abt. 1600 yards.

Receiv'd Seven hounds sent me from France by the Marqs. de la Fayette, by way of New York viz. 3 dogs and four Bitches.

My Boat went to Alexandria and brought home 100 Bushels of Salt, a hogshead of common rum, and a Cask of Nails 20d.

GW had requested Lafayette to send him some French hounds. Lafayette wrote GW that "French Hounds are not now very easily got because the King Makes use of english dogs, as Being more swift than those of Normandy. I However Have got seven from a Normand Gentleman Called *Monsieur le Comte doilliamson*. The Handsomest Bitch Among them was a favourite with his lady who Makes a present of Her to You" (13 May 1785, PEL). The dogs were accompanied from France to New York by young John Quincy Adams and were shipped from New York to Mount Vernon in Capt. S. Packard's sloop *Dove* (Lafayette to GW, 16 April 1785, PEL; William Grayson to GW, 5 Sept. 1785, DLC:GW; *Va. Journal,* 1 Sept. 1785).

Thursday 25th. Mercury at 74 in the Morning–80 at Noon and 78 at Night.

Wind Southwardly in the forenoon, but not much of it. About Noon a Cloud arose in the West & promised rain but none fell here, but the Wind shifting to the Westward it blew hard for a few minutes & the cloud went above us.

Finished sowing the Spaces of the Guinea Grass in the little Garden.

Friday 26th. Mercury at 72 in the Morng.–[ ] at Noon and 76 at Night.

Clear with but little wind at any time of the day.

A Mr. Mar⟨t⟩el (or some such name) a Frenchman came in and dined, and just before dinner Mr. Arthur Lee, and Mr. P. Fendall got here; all of whom went away after it was over. In the Afternoon–Doctr. Marshall and his Sister, and Miss Hanson crossed the River, drank Tea, and returned.

Received 63 Bushels of Stone Lime from Loudoun for which I paid 2/6 pr. Bushl. & allowed 18/ for the difference of coming to this place instead of going to Alexandria.

My Boat brot. home another 100 Bushels of Salt from Alexandria and two Casks of 30d. Nails containing upwards of 13 M. The Cask of 20d. Nails which were brot. home on Wednesday, being returned.

Dr. Thomas Marshall (c.1757–1829), son of Thomas Hanson Marshall of Marshall Hall, Charles County, Md., had lost his eyesight during his service as a surgeon in the Revolution. His sister, Mary Marshall (1767–1789), married Philip Stuart in 1787 (GERALD, 173–75).

Saturday 27th. Mercury at 74 in the Morning–80 at Noon and 80 at Night.

Morning clear with the wind pretty fresh from the Southward. About 10 Oclock it clouded up, and rained a little; then cleared; but about 5 Oclock, a very black and heavy cloud arose in the Southwest, out of which (about Six oclock) proceedd for a few minutes very heavy wind, & a powerful Shower, the last of which continued about 12 or 15 Minutes. This being succeeded by lighter Showers, wch. with intervals continuing thro the Night afforded abundance of rain.

Before this came up (and during the slight shower in the Morning) I planted in a small piece of ground which I had prepared in the inclosure below the Stable (vineyard) about 1000 grains of the Cape of Good Hope Wheat (which was given to me by Colo. Spaight) in Rows 2 feet a part, and 5 inches distant in the Rows.

Fanny Bassett crossed the River immediately after dinner, on a visit to Miss Hanson.

CAPE OF GOOD HOPE WHEAT: GW tried this variety for three years in succession without much luck. It never produced a full grain, and one year succumbed to frost.

Sunday 28th. Mercury at 74 in the Morng.–76 at Noon and 76 at Night.

Wind Southerly; with clouds, slight Showers, and Sunshine by intervals all day.

In the Afternoon Doctr. Craik came here–on a visit to Jno. Alton.

Monday 29th. Mercury at 74 in the Morning–74 at Noon and 73 at Night.

Wind Southerly, with Showers in the Morning, and Clouds all day, with appearances of Rain but none fell after noon.

Doctr. Craik after visiting John Alton before breakfast, went after it to see Lund Washingtons child who had been siezed with fits & the family alarmed by it.

Lund and Elizabeth Foote Washington had at least two daughters who died in infancy.

Tuesday 30th. Mercury at 72 in the Morning—72 at Noon and 74 at Night.

But little Wind and that westerly—clear and pleasant.

Rid to my Plantations at the Ferry—Dogue run and Muddy hole. Found the Corn a good deal improved in its looks, and that it had put forth many young Shoots but it is to be apprehended that the tassel in a great deal of it had got too dry for the farina to impregnate the grain.

The Wheat which had been Sowed before the late rains fell was up, and coming up, very well.

I observed that Corn, whh. had been planted under the Persimon trees in the fields looked as thriving and well as that which was not shaded—the same thing I had observed before (formerly) with respect to Wheat under these sort of trees and also of grass which proves them to be a valuable tree in Inclosures.

Mrs. Washington visited the Sick Child of Mr. L. Washington, and returned to dinner.

Finished gravelling the right hand Walk leading to the front gate from the Court yard.

Wednesday 31st. Mercury at 70 in the Morning—72 at Noon and 72 at Night.

Westerly wind and Clouds all day. Rid the Plantations in the Neck, & at Muddy hole. Found the Corn at the first as mentioned yesterday at the other places.

Mrs. Washington rid to see the Sick Child of Mr. Lund Washington from whence Doctr. Craik came here to Breakfast—after which he visited John Alton, and then returned to Maryland.

The Cape of Good hope Wheat which I sowed on Saturday, was perceived to be coming up to day.

And the Bird pepper which was sowed in the Botanical garden on the 13th. of June was just making its appearance and thick.

Mr. Shaw went to Alexandria immediately after breakfast and did not return to day.

This day I told Doctr. Craik that I would contribute One hundred Dollars pr. Ann., as long as it was necessary, towards the Education of His Son Geo. Washington either in this Country or in Scotland.

SICK CHILD: manuscript reads "silk child."

George Washington Craik (1774–1808) was one of several children whose education GW helped to finance. Young Craik probably studied law; he practiced for a short time in Alexandria but was appointed a private secretary to GW in 1796. In 1799 he became a lieutenant of light dragoons and served until 1800 (CRAIK [2], 135–37).

September

Thursday first. Mercury at 70 in the Morng.—69 at Noon and 68 at Night.

Cloudy Morning—with the Wind at East. Between 9 & 10 Oclock it began to drip slow rain, in which I planted the remainder of the Wheat from the Cape of Good Hope leaving 230 grains to replant the missing seeds, & some that had been washed up by the late rains; the whole number of grains given me by Colo. Spaight amounting to 2476; which in measure, might be about half a Gill.

Below the Wheat, and in a continuation of the rows, nearly to the bottom of the Inclosure, I sowed the Guinea grass Seed which I reserved from my sowing on the 13th. of last June in my Botanical Garden.

Mr. Shaw came home about Noon.

In the Afternoon—about 4 Oclock the wind got more to the Northward—nearly No. Et. and began a close (tho not hard) & constant rain.

Friday 2d. Mercury at 64 in the Morning—64 at Noon and 65 at Night.

Wind at No. Et. and pretty fresh all day, with misling Rain wch. sometimes became stronger.

Saturday 3d. Mercury at 65 in the Morning—66 at Noon and 66 at Night.

Much such a day as yesterday until the Evening when the Sun made a feeble effort to appear and the clouds began to thin and disperse.

In the Evening James Madison Esqr. came in.

Sunday 4th. Mercury at 66 in the Morning—68 at Noon and 68 at Night. Foggy, or Misling morning, and Cloudy most part of the day, with but little Wind.

Monday 5th. Mercury at 68 in the Morning—70 at Noon and 72 at Night.

Day clear & pleasant with very little wind. About 2 Oclock, Fanny Bassett and Mr. [ ] Craik third Son of the Doctr. came here; the last of whom went away after dinner.

Mr. Madison left this after Breakfast.

Began to spade up the Lawn in front of the Court yard. And also began to prepare the Scaffolds for Cieling the Piazza.

The third son of Dr. Craik was probably Adam Craik. He later married Mrs. Sarah Harrison Jordan, a daughter of GW's friend and former aide, Robert Hanson Harrison. In the 1790 census Adam Craik was listed as head of a household in Charles County, Md.

LAWN IN FRONT OF THE COURT YARD: The lawn on the west front of the house was to be made into a bowling green.

Tuesday 6th. Thermometer at 67 in the Morning–70 at Noon and 73 at Night.

Wind at No. West, and fresh all day, yet warm in the Sun.

Fanny Bassett went to Mr. Lund Washington's and stayed all Night. I rid to my Plantations at the Ferry, Dogue run and Muddy hole and returned about 12 Oclock.

A Mr. Tayler, Clerk to the Secretary for Foreign Affairs came here whilst we were at Dinner, sent by Mr. Jay, by order of Congress, to take Copies of the report of the Commissioners who had been sent in by me to New York, to take an Acct. of the Slaves whch had been sent from that place (previous to the evacuation) by the British.

George Taylor, Jr., in 1785 was appointed clerk to the secretary for foreign affairs, John Jay. Commissioners for embarkation had been appointed by GW in 1783 to go to New York to superintend the embarkation of the British troops and to try to enforce article seven of the provisional treaty of peace of Nov. 1782, which forbade British troops to carry off any American property, notably runaway slaves. There was, however, little the commissioners could do to enforce the provision, and so they withdrew. The report GW refers to is probably that of 30 May 1783, written by Egbert Benson and William Stephens Smith, two of the commissioners (DLC:GW). On 23 June of that year GW sent a letter to Congress, enclosing copies of his entire correspondence with the commissioners (DLC:GW).

Wednesday 7th. Mercury at 67 in the Morning–68 at Noon and 70 at Night.

Clear day with the Wind fresh & Cool from the No[th]ward in the forenoon but still & warm in the Afternoon.

Fanny Bassett returned before Dinner, and Doctr. Craik came to it & went away afterwards to visit John Alton, and his Children at Mr. Chichesters from thence.

About Noon brought two Negro men from the River Plantation to assist in spading up the ground in front of the Court yard and Cornelius being Sick Tom Davis went to assist them.

Bought 28,430 good Cyprus Shingles.

At Night, a Man of the name of Purdie, came to offer himself to me as a Housekeeper, or Household Steward. He had some testimonials respecting his character—but being intoxicated, and in other respects appearing in an unfavorable light I informed him that he would not answer my purposes, but that he might stay all night.

Cornelius was undoubtedly the Irishman, Cornelius McDermott Roe, who signed an agreement with GW on 1 Aug. 1786 for one year as a "Stone Mason, Bricklayer, and (when not employed in either of these) in other jobs which he may be set about." McDermott Roe was to receive £32 in addition to board, washing, and lodging "as he has been usually accustomed to in the family; and will give him the same allowance of spirits with which he has been served" (DLC:GW). This portion of the agreement indicates that McDermott Roe had already been employed at Mount Vernon under an earlier arrangement, and he appears several times in the diaries before the Aug. 1786 agreement. Tom Davis, a dower slave, worked primarily as a bricklayer and stonemason. He also occasionally did painting and carpentry.

GW had advertised for a *"House Keeper, or Household Steward,* who is competent to the charge of a large family, and attending on a good deal of company" (*Va. Journal,* 18 Aug. 1785). Because of the increasing number of visitors at Mount Vernon since the Revolution, GW felt it necessary to hire someone to help run the household.

Thursday 8th. Thermometer at 64 in the Morning—68 at Noon and 68 at Night.

Calm clear and pleasant. Rid to my Plantations at Muddy hole and in the Neck. Found that at the first they had begun to sow Rye yesterday (as they had also done at the Ferry Plantation) and at the latter to day.

Doctr. Craik came here to Breakfast & crossed the river afterwards. Purdie went away.

Friday 9th. Thermometer at 66 in the Morning—72 at Noon and 72 at Night.

Clear and rather warm, with but little Wind.

Rid up to Alexandria with Mrs. Washington, who wanted to get some cloathing for little Washington Custis; and for the purpose of seeing Colos. Fitzgerald & Colo. Gilpin on the business of the Potomack Company. Returned home to Dinner.

GW and the directors, after discussing reports of unruly Potomac Company workers at the Shenandoah Falls, agreed to inquire into the purchasing of indentured servants and the hiring of slaves (see PICKELL, 77; GW to Thomas Johnson and Thomas Sim Lee, 10 Sept. 1785, DLC:GW).

Saturday 10th. Thermometer at 68 in the morning—70 at Noon and 72 at Night.

Calm and warm, with some appearances of rain which vanished in the evening.

Rid with Fanny Bassett, Mr. Taylor and Mr. Shaw to meet a Party from Alexandria at Johnsons Spring (on my Land where Clifton formerly lived) where we dined on a cold dinner brought from Town by water and spent the Afternoon agreeably—returning home by Sun down or a little after it.

From the Scarcity of Apples generally this year and the depredations which were committing every Night upon the few I have, I found it necessary (tho much too early) to gather & put them up for Winter use. Finishd the Cieling of the Piaza.

Johnston's (Johnson's) Spring was on Clifton's Neck (now GW's River Farm) near the ferry-house, which served travelers using Clifton's (Johnston's) ferry to cross over into Maryland. This locality across from Broad Creek and Piscataway in Maryland was a favorite with eighteenth-century duelists (SNOWDEN, 34, 37).

Sunday 11th. Thermometer at 69 in the Morning—74 at Noon and 74 at Night.

Wind fresh at No. West all day & clear—warm notwithstanding.

Mr. Potts, and Doctors Mortimer and Craik Junr. dined here and returned to Alexandria in the Evening.

Mr. Shaw and Mr. Tayler went to Alexandria after breakfast in my barge & did not return until after midnight.

John Potts, Jr. (1760–1809), a Pennsylvanian, in partnership with William Herbert operated an import store on the corner of Fairfax and Queen streets in Alexandria. The partnership was dissolved in 1787 (*Va. Journal,* 19 May 1784 and 4 Oct. 1787). Potts was a subscriber to the Potomac Company and for several years was secretary of the company.

Dr. Charles Mortimer, Jr., advertised in 1784 that he was setting up a practice in Alexandria. He claimed to be "bred to the practice of Physic, Surgery, and Midwifery, both in America and Europe" (*Va. Journal,* 9 Dec. 1784). Mortimer was probably a son or nephew of Dr. Charles Mortimer of Fredericksburg, Mrs. Mary Washington's personal physician.

Monday 12th. Thermometer at 66 in the Morng.—68 at Noon and 71 at Night.

Wind pretty fresh at No. West in the forenoon, but calm afterwds. and perfectly clear.

Rid to my Ferry—Dogue run—& Muddy hole plantations.

A Mr. Cawood, Sheriff of Charles County in Maryland, came here in the forenoon with an acct. of Taxes of the Land I hold in that County & in Nangemy Neck. Promised to get Doctr. Craik to enquire into the matter & to lodge money with him to pay it.

Benjamin Cawood, Jr., was the sheriff of Charles County, Md. GW later stated that "this was the first application ever made to me, for the same" and noted that he intended to ask Lund Washington whether he had had any earlier demands for the taxes (GW Memoranda, 30 Mar. 1787, DLC: GW). This was the land GW had acquired from Daniel Jenifer Adams (see main entry for 22 Jan. 1775), and consisted of "Josias's help, 109 acres; Wades Addition, 33½; Adam's Retirement, 100; Ditto Outlet, 50 and Williams's folly 260" (LEDGER B, 99).

Tuesday 13th. Thermometer at 68 in the Morning–72 at Noon and 74 at Night.

Calm morning, but a brisk Southerly wind all day afterwards and clear.

Began to level the ground which had been spaded up in the lawn fronting the House, having turned it up as far as to where the old cross wall of the former Gardens stood.

Colo. Willm. Fitzhugh of Maryland & his Son William and Doctor Marshall came here to Dinner and stayed all Night.

William Fitzhugh, Jr. (c.1760–1839), was a son of Col. William Fitzhugh (1721–1798) by his second wife, Ann Frisby Rousby Fitzhugh. He served as an officer in the 3d Continental Dragoons during the Revolution. After the war he moved to Hagerstown, Md., where he remained until about 1800, when he moved his family to Livingston County, N.Y. Col. William Fitzhugh had written GW on 25 July that he had to attend a land sale in Virginia on 20 Sept. and intended stopping at Mount Vernon (DLC:GW). Before leaving Mount Vernon, he paid GW £10 for the use of the treasurer of the Potomac Company (LEDGER B, 204). He also collected £46 17s. 9½d. from GW for some surplus building materials he sent GW earlier (Fitzhugh to GW, 13 May and 25 July 1785, DLC:GW; LEDGER B, 204).

Wednesday 14th. Thermometer at 72 in the Morning–76 at Noon and [ ] at Night.

Wind still at So. and pretty fresh in the Morning with Clouds and some Appearances of rain in the forenoon but more in the Afternoon as there was distt. thunder and a good deal of Lightning.

Colo. Fitzhugh & Son and Doctr. Marshall went away after Breakfast, and Docter Craik came to Dinner, and stayed all Night.

Thursday 15th. Mercury at 72 in the Morning–74 at Noon and 73 at Night.

Brisk Southerly wind all the forenoon, and cloudy– in the Afternoon the wind was more moderate & clear.

Doctr. L'Moyer came in before Dinner.

Jean Pierre Le Mayeur (Lamayner, L'Moyer), a French dentist who came to New York during the Revolution, went to GW's headquarters in 1783 to do some work on his teeth (GW to Le Mayeur, 16 July 1783, GW to William Stephens Smith, 15 May and 18 June 1783, Smith to GW, 20 May 1783, DLC:GW). Le Mayeur visited Mount Vernon in the summer of 1784 and evidently became a favorite with little George Washington Parke Custis. He played games with the child and in August sent him a new red toy horse "just big Enough for the little house which master George and myself built on the side of the hill" (Le Mayeur to GW, 14 Aug. 1784, DLC:GW). After this visit to Mount Vernon, Le Mayeur went to Richmond where he advertised that he performed "operations on the teeth, hitherto performed in Europe, such as transplanting, &c., &c., &c." Le Mayeur also offered a payment of three guineas for good front teeth from anyone but slaves (*Va. Mag.*, 10 [1902–3], 325).

Friday 16th. Thermometer at 69 in the Morning—70 at Noon and 75 at Night.

Calm and clear in the forenoon—Southerly wind afterwards with clouds and appearances of rain but none fell here.

Mr. Hiebert came here to dinner and returned to Alexandria afterwards.

Sent my Chariot at the request of Mrs. Stuart with Betcy & Patcy Custis to Mr. Calverts. Nelly & Washington Custis went with them to return with the Carriage.

MR. HIEBERT: probably Mr. Huiberts (see entry for 28 April 1785).

Saturday 17th. Thermometer at 72 in the Morning—71 at Noon and 70 at Night.

At or before Sunrising it began to rain moderately—after which it continued by hard Showers with intervals until between One & two in the Afternoon accompanied with sharp lightning and loud thunder.

The rain coming on moderately, induced me to Sow the Ground which I had levelled of the Lawn whilst it was raining—but the heavy showers wch. fell afterwards washed and floated it into heaps.

In the Afternoon when the rain had ceased, I made an experiment of transplanting Turnips to see if the method would succeed in practice. In a part of the Turnip Inclosure, where the Seed had been sowed the 19th. of last Mo[nth], I pulled up all that growed on a square of about ten feet—cut the Taproot of a sufficient Number of Plants and transplanted them thereon at the distance of a foot each way, from one another.

Sunday 18th. Thermometer at 66 in the Morng.—67 at Noon and 69 at Night.

Clear, and the Wind fresh from No. West all day.

Colo. Henley, Mr. Porter, Mr. Hunter and Doctr. & Colo. Ramsay came here, dined and returned in the afternoon.

Dr. William Ramsay, Jr., and Col. Dennis Ramsay were the two sons of William and Ann McCarty Ramsay of Alexandria, whose funerals GW attended earlier this year. Doctor William, whose education at the College of New Jersey at Princeton was financed by GW, served as a naval surgeon in the Revolution, making at least one voyage on the *George Washington,* a privateer out of Alexandria (*Va. Mag.,* 17:175–78). He then returned to Alexandria to practice medicine. William's younger brother Dennis (1756–1810), whose colonelcy was apparently in the militia, began his business career in Alexandria with the firm of Jenifer & Hooe.

Monday 19th. Thermometer at 68 in the Morning 70 at Noon and 70 at Night.

Clear, calm, and serene all day.

Rid to the Plantations at the Ferry, Dogue run, and Muddy hole. Took my French Hounds with me for the purpose of Airing them & giving them a knowledge of the grounds round about this place.

Upon my return, found a Mr. John Defray here—a Dane from Copenhagen, who had been cast away on the coast of No. Carolina.

Doctr. La Moyer left this for Alexandria in my Carriage after Breakfast.

Tuesday 20th. Thermometer at 68 in the Morning—68 at Noon and 68 at Night.

Wind Easterly. Morning & whole day lowering. About Sunsetting it began to rain slow and moderately & continued to do so through the Night.

About Noon, agreeably to an appointment I set off for the Seneca Falls. Dined at Colo. Gilpins and proceeded afterwards with him to Mr. Bryan Fairfaxs where we lodged.

Wednesday 21st. Thermometer at 68 in the Morning—68 at Noon and 68 at N.

The rain continuing without intermission until 10 or 11 Oclock, and no appearances of fair weather until Noon, we did not leave Mr. Fairfax's 'till a little after it and then meeting much difficulty in procuring a vessel, did not get to the works at the Seneca fall until the labourers had quit them. We then went to our old quarters at Mr. Goldsboroughs were lodged. Mr. Fairfax accompanied us. The Wind for the greater part of the day (though there was not much of it) was at No. West.

Thursday 22d. Thermometer at 66 in the Morning—62 at Noon and 62 at Nig[ht].

The Wind having shifted to the Eastward in the Night it commenced a fine raining again, and did not altogether cease until Noon. However about 10 Oclock we left Mr. Goldsboroughs, & in a boat passed down the Seneca falls to the place where the work men were blowing Rocks, but the Water having raised, and the river being muddy, I could form no accurate judgment of the progress which had been made. To me it seemed, as if we had advanced but little—owing to the fewness, and sickliness of the hands which it appeared ought to be encreased and their Wages raised in order to obtain them.

After viewing the works we crossed to the Virginia side and proceeded to the Great Falls where by appointment we were to have met Colo. Fitzgerald and Vessells to take us by Water to the little Falls in order to review the river between the two. The latter we found, but not the first, & parting with Mr. Fairfax here, and sending our Horses by Land to Mr. Hipkins's at the Falls Warehouse we did, after having examined the ground along wch. it is proposed to open the Canal, and which nature seems clearly to have marked out, embarked about 3 Oclock; Colo. Gilpin myself & one hand in one Canoe, and two other people in another Canoe, and proceeded down the river to the place where it is proposed to let the water again into a Canal to avoid the little Falls.

The place for the Canal at the Great Falls as I have just observed is most evidently marked along a glade which runs quite from the still water above the spout, or Cataract, to the river 3/4 or a Mile below it & from appearance will not be deep to dig; but at the upper and lower end, is a good deal incommoded with rocks. The glade itself seems tolerably free from them but how the bottom may turn out when the Soil is taken of I know not. More than probably it will be found Stony.

At the Mouth of the branch wch. issues from this glade locks I think may be well secured by the point of a hill & Rocks just above it. Here we embarked in smooth water, that is not very rapid; and in a quarter of a mile passed a short rapid not difficult—a Mile further another rapid rather worse but not very bad and afterwards two more the last of which in its present state is the worst but none of them very bad. In many parts the River is tolerably smooth—the current by no means rapid, and upon the whole easier than I had conceived. In places it is tole[r]ably wide and not deeper than I had supposed. Between the two Falls, there are several smal Islands, most of them rocky but one tolerably large & to appearance of good Land.

The place at which it is proposed to take the Canal out, above the little falls, seems favourably formed for it by an Island which may be abt. half a mile above the Falls & the Land through which it must pass on the Maryland Side level but Stoney all the way to the mouth or near it of the Canal begun by Mr. Ballendine if it is carried on a slope. If on the other h[an]d it is to go on a level the Hill side adjoining does not appear unfavourable.

Lodged this Night at Mr. Hipkens's at the Falls warehouse where we arrived at Dark tho' we were only 2 hours & an half from the place of embarkation at the Great Falls to the debarking above the little Falls. The little falls, if a Rock or two was removed might be passed without any hazard—more especially if some of the Rocks which lye deep & which occasion a dashing surface could be removed.

MR. HIPKINS'S: Lewis Hipkins (died c.1794), of Fairfax County, lived near the Virginia tobacco warehouse at the Little Falls which had been authorized in 1742 (HEADS OF FAMILIES, VA., 17, 86; HARRISON [1], 149; HENING, 5:143). The island with "good Land" may have been Sycamore Island. The island about "half a mile above the Falls" was probably High Island, just off the Maryland shore. Shortly before the Revolution, John Ballendine had begun cutting a canal around the Little Falls on the Maryland side on a piece of land that he named Amsterdam (BACON-FOSTER, 26–28; TAGGART, 177). A canal "on a slope," carrying a downstream current just as in the river, would make locks unnecessary.

Friday 23d. After taking an Early breakfast at Mr. Hipkins's I set out & reached home about 11 Oclock.

Thermometer at 62 in the Morning—62 at Noon and 62 at Night.

Morning cloudy, and afternoon raining. Wind at No. Et.

About One Oclock My Nepw. G. A. Washington & the two Mr. Bassetts arrived.

Found the late rains had brought up the Seeds of the pride of China, and several more of the Palmetto.

Saturday 24th. Thermometer at 62 in the morning—62 at Noon and 62 at Night.

Wind at No. & No. Et. all day & tempestuous with allmost a constant rain.

Sunday 25th. Thermometer at 64 in the Morng.—66 at Noon and 69 at Night.

Clear & serene with the Wind & pretty fresh about Midday. Morning & Evening calm.

Doctr. La Moyer & Doctr. Craik came here to Dinner. The latter went away afterwards. The other stayed all Night.

Monday 26th. Thermometer at 63 in the Morning—62 at Noon and 60 at Night.

Clear day, and calm Morning but brisk wind afterwards from the No. West.

Went up to Alexandria to meet Colonels Gilpin & Fitzgerald on business of the Potomack Compa. Doctr. La Moyer, Mr. B. Bassett and G. A. Washington accompanied me the first of whom remained there. Dined at the New Tavern, kept by Mr. Lyle.

Brought home Mr. Thomas McCarty, with whom I had agreed to serve me in the capicity of a Ho[use] keeper—or Household Steward at Thirty pounds pr. Ann.

GW and the directors of the Potomac Company ordered that 60 indentured servants be purchased in Philadelphia or Baltimore (PICKELL, 78). NEW TAVERN: Capt. Henry Lyles (d. 1786) of Maryland had recently opened the commodious, three-story Alexandria Inn and Coffeehouse on the corner of Fairfax and Cameron streets. Lyles, who had served in the 3rd Maryland Regiment during the Revolution, also had a store on Fairfax Street near King Street (*Va. Journal,* 12 May and 29 Sept. 1785 and 18 May 1786).

Thomas McCarty was probably not related to GW's close neighbor, Daniel McCarty. He worked for only a year at Mount Vernon and proved unsatisfactory as a steward (see 12 Aug. 1786).

Tuesday 27th. Thermometer at 57 in the Morng. 59 at Noon and 62 at Night.

Wind fresh from the No. West with flying Clouds, and Cold.

Doctr. Craik who came here last Night, returned this Morning to Maryland.

Wednesday 28th. Thermometer at 58 in the Morng. 60 at Noon and 62 at Night.

Morning lowering, with appearances of rain but Evening clear, wind still to the No[rth]ward.

Doctr. Jenifer and his wife came here to Dinner, and went away after it, to Colo. McCartys.

Mr. Tayler having finished the business which brought him here, I sent him up to Alexandria to take a passage in the Stage, for New York.

Thursday 29th. Thermometer at 60 in the Morning–65 at Noon and 66 at Night.

Day clear, and not much wind, especially in the Afternoon.

Mr. Sanders, an Undertaker in Alexandria, came down between breakfast & Dinner to advise a proper mode of Shingling–putting Copper in the Gutters between the Pediments & Dormants, and the Roof and to conduct the Water along the Eves to Spouts & promised to be down again on Tuesday next to see the work properly begun.

MR. SANDERS: John Saunders, a joiner and carpenter in Alexandria, seems to have been originally from Philadelphia. He later served as a member of the Alexandria City Council (Fairfax County Deed Book M-1, 15, 41–46; Alexandria City Hustings Court Deed Book, D, 74–81, 330–41). DORMANTS: dormers.

Friday 30th. Thermometer at 60 in the Morng. 68 at Noon and 70 at Night.

Day clear, wind pretty brisk from the Southward–till the Evening when it veered more to the Eastward.

Mr. Hunter, and the right Honble. Fred. von Walden, Captn. in the Swedish Navy–introduced by Mr. Richd. Soderstroin came here to Dinner, and returned to Alexandria afterwards. In the Evening a Mr. Tarte–introduced by letter from a John Lowry of Back river came in to request my Sentiments respecting some Entrys they, in Partnership, had made in the Great Dismal Swamp, which I gave unreservedly, that they had no right to.

One of the Hound Bitches wch. was sent to me from France brought forth 15 puppies this day; 7 of which (the rest being as many as I thought she could rear) I had drowned.

Run round the ground which I designed for a Paddock for Deer & find it contains 18 A[cres] 3 R[ods] 20 P[erches].

Began again to Smooth the Face of the Lawn, or Bolling Green on the West front of my House–what I had done before the Rains, proving abortive.

Capt. Frederick von Walden on 28 July laid before Congress a plan of coinage of "copper to the amount of 100,000 £ Stg." No action had yet been taken on his plan, and he may have been at Mount Vernon to try to enlist GW's support for the scheme (LMCC, 8:171, 210–11; JCC, 29:587).

RICHD. SODERSTROIN: Richard Söderström, the new Swedish consul at Boston, had been recently embroiled in a controversy with Congress because he had presented his credentials to the governor of Massachusetts before presenting them to Congress. Söderström's act was soon recognized, not as a sign of disrespect, but as an innocent blunder (see LMCC, 8:33, 51–52; JCC, 28:360–61, n.2, 393–94; State of Söderström's Case, n.d., MHi: Knox Papers). Söderström's letter of introduction was dated 12 Sept. 1785 (DLC:GW).

John Lowry was probably the son of John Lowry (died c.1766) and Mary Lowry of Elizabeth City County. Back River runs through Elizabeth City County and empties into the Chesapeake Bay, midway between James and York rivers. Several members of the Tarte (Tart) family lived in Elizabeth City County–Norfolk County area.

October

Saturday first. Thermometer at 66 in the Morning–70 at Noon and 72 at Night.

Southerly Wind and clear.

Began to raise a Scaffold for Shingling the Front side of my House, next the Court yard.

Rid to my River, Muddy hole, and Dogue run Plantations.

Doctr. Stuart came in whilst we were at Dinner & stayed all Night.

Sunday 2d. Thermometer at 70 in the Morning–76 at Noon and [ ] at Night.

Weather warm. Forenoon clear, Afternoon lowering.

Went with Fanny Bassett, Burwell Bassett, Doctr. Stuart, G. A. Washington, Mr. Shaw & Nelly Custis to Pohick Church; to hear a Mr. Thompson preach, who returned home with us to Dinner, where I found the Revd. Mr. Jones, formerly a Chaplin in one of the Pensylvania Regiments.

After we were in Bed (about Eleven Oclock in the Evening) Mr. Houdon, sent from Paris by Doctr. Franklin and Mr. Jefferson to take my Bust, in behalf of the State of Virginia, with three young men assistants, introduced by a Mr. Perin a French Gentleman of Alexandria, arrived here by water from the latter place.

James Thomson (1739–1812), the minister of Leeds Parish, Fauquier County, 1769–1812, was a Scotsman who had emigrated to Virginia as a tutor in 1767. He went to England in 1769 to take holy orders and returned to Fauquier County where he preached at the four churches in Leeds Parish (MEADE [1], 2:218–19). David Jones (1736–1820), minister of the Great Valley Baptist Church, Chester County, Pa., had been a chaplain in the 3rd and 4th Pennsylvania regiments during the Revolution.

Virginia in 1784 adopted a resolution commissioning a statute of GW; and Thomas Jefferson and Benjamin Franklin, then ministers to the Court of France, agreed to locate and engage an outstanding sculptor for the commission. Jean Antoine Houdon (1741–1828) agreed to make the statue but insisted that he come to America to make a life mask of GW and then return to France to complete the work. Jefferson's agreement with Houdon provided for a salary of 1,000 guineas plus expenses to America and the purchase of an insurance policy on the sculptor's life during the journey. Although the fee was much less than Houdon had asked, he was eager to make

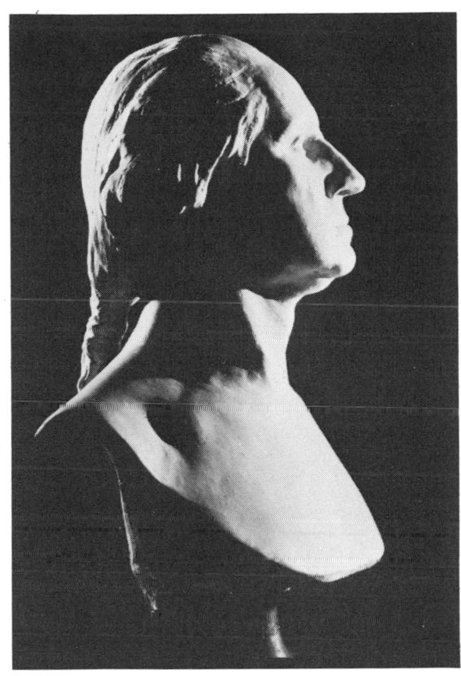

Houdon's bust of Washington. (Mount Vernon Ladies' Association of the Union)

a statue of GW and agreed to the terms, leaving such clients as Catherine the Great of Russia to await his return to Europe (JEFFERSON [1], 7:566–67, 8:282–84, 279–80).

Joseph Marie Perrin, a merchant in Alexandria, had a store on Royal Street next to John Wise's tavern and opposite the courthouse. By Aug. 1786 the business was operated under the name of Perrin & Brothers (*Va. Journal,* 21 April 1785 and 17 Aug. 1786). Perrin came to Mount Vernon as an interpreter for Houdon's party.

Monday 3d. Thermometer at 70 in the Morning—68 at Noon and 66 at Night.

Wind at So. West, weather variable until Noon when it became more cloudy & dripping. Towards evening it began to Rain and the Night was wet.

The two reverend Gentlemen who dined and lodged here, went away after breakfast.

Tuesday 4th. Thermometer at 63 in the Morning—62 at Noon and 66 at Night.

Wind at So. West, veering more Westerly. Morning wet, and till Noon dripping; Clear afterwards, and wind fresh.

Wednesday 5. Thermometer at 60 in the Morng. [ ] at Noon and 68 at Night.

Brisk wind from the Southward all day. Weather clear.

Stripped the Shingles of the South side of the Pediment of the West front of the House, in expectation of Mr. Sanders's coming to direct the Shingling of it, but he never appeared.

Colo. Ramsay introducing a Mr. McComb, & a Mr. Lowry; dined here, & went away afterwards.

Mr. Perin went from this after Breakfast.

MR. MCCOMB: GW may mean James McKenna, formerly a partner of William Lowry in the firm of Lowry & McKenna. McKenna continued to carry on a retail business in Alexandria for a number of years (SPROUSE [2], 27; *Va. Journal,* 23 June 1785).

Mr. Lowry is William Lowry, an importer of English goods who had a store in 1784 on Fairfax Street, at the corner of Queen Street in Alexandria (*Va. Journal,* 16 Sept. and 21 Oct. 1784). Lowry, an Englishman, had by 1787 moved his wife and seven children to Alexandria (VAUGHAN, 58).

Thursday 6th. Thermometer at 65 in the Morning–65 at Noon and 66 at Night.

Flying clouds and a Rainbow in the Morning with but little wind; drippings of rain, more or less all day.

Mr. Burwell Bassett, and Mr. Shaw set out after Breakfast for Dumfries.

The appearances of the day, and the impracticability of giving, on acct. of the clammyness of the Earth, an even face to any more of my lawn, until the grd. should get dryer, of which there is no immediate prospect, I sowed what was levelled & smoothed of it, with English grass Seeds; and as soon as the top was so dry, as not to stick to the Roller, I rolled & cross rolled it; first with a light wooden roller; and then with a heavy wooden roller; with a view of compressing the Ground–smoothing the Surfice of it & to bury the Seeds.

Mr. Sanders not coming according to expectation I began with my own people to shingle that part of the Roof of the House wch. was stripped yesterday, & to copper the Gutters &ca.

Friday 7th. Thermometer at 62 in the Morning–64 at Noon and [ ] at Night.

Wind Southwardly all day and weather clear, warm, & pleasant.

Sat to day, as I had done yesterday, for Mr. Houdon to form my Bust.

Mrs. Jenifer, wife of Doctr. Walter Jenifer, dined here, and returned afterwards; and Doctr. Craik came here in the afternoon, and stayed all Night.

Mr. Shaw and Mr. Bassett returned from Dumfries about Noon

& Doctr. Brown came in the afternoon to visit a sick Servant of the Mr. Bassetts, & returned.

Finished trenching my Lawn, the spading of which had recd. several interruptions by odd Jobs intervening. The ground getting a little drier I began again to level & smooth it.

Plowed up a Cowpen in order to sow the ground with Orchard Grass Seeds.

PLOWED UP A COWPEN: This cow pen, containing about a quarter of an acre, was on the west front of the house, on ground intended for the bowling green (GW's "Notes and Observations," 1785–86, DLC:GW).

Saturday 8th. Thermometer at 63 in the Morning—66 at Noon and 68 at Night.

But little wind—weather clear, and exceedingly pleasant.

Sowed the ground which was plowed yesterday, and which might amount to about a quarter of an Acre, with near half a Bushel of the Orchard Grass Seeds; which was neither very clean nor I fear not very good.

Also sowed with English Grass Seeds, as much more of the Lawn as I could get levelled & smoothed and rolled it in the same manner as that on thursday last was done.

Sunday 9th. Thermometer at 64 in the Morng. 70 at Noon and 70 at Night.

Morning and Evening lowering. Midday tolerably clear, warm & pleasant.

Accompanied by Mr. Houdon and the two Mr. Bassetts, attended the Funeral of Mrs. Manley at the Plantation of Mr. Willm. Triplett, and returned to Dinner.

Sarah Harrison Manley (d. 1785), a sister of George Harrison of Fairfax, had been married first to John Triplett and second to John Manley. William Triplett, at whose home the funeral took place, was probably a relative of her first husband, and was, moreover, the executor of the estate of her son, Harrison Manley.

Monday 10th. Thermometer at 68 in the Morng. 70 at Noon and 74 at Night.

Thunder about day. Morning threatning but clear & pleasant afterwards.

A Mr. Jno. Lowe, on his way to Bishop Seabury for Ordination, called & dined here. Could not give him more than a general certificate, founded on information, respecting his character; having no acquaintance with him, nor any desire to open a Corrispondence with the *new* ordained Bishop.

Observed the process for preparing the Plaister of Paris, & mixing of it—according to Mr. Houdon. The Oven being made hotter than it is usually heated for Bread, the Plaister which had been previously broken into lumps—that which was hard, to about the size of a pullets egg; and that which was soft, and could be broken with the hands, larger; was put in about Noon, and remained until Night; when, upon examination, it was further continued until the Morning without any renewal of the heat in the Oven, which was close stopped. Having been sufficiently calcined by this operation, it was pulverized (in an Iron Mortar) & sifted for use through a fine lawn sieve, & kept from wet.

When used, it is put into a Bason, or other Vessel with water; sifted through the fingers, 'till the Water is made as thick as Loblolly or very thick cream. As soon as the plaister is thus put into the Water, it is beat with an Iron spoon (almost flat) until it is well Mixed, and must be immediately applied to the purpose for which it is intended with a Brush, or whatever else best answers, as it begins to turn hard in four or five minutes, and in Seven or ten cannot be used, & is fit for no purpose afterwards as it will not bear wetting a second time. For this reason no more must be mixed at a time than can be used within the space just mentioned.

The brush (common painters) must be put into water as soon as it is used, and the plaister well squeezed out, or this also becomes very hard. In this case to clean it, it must be beaten 'till the plaister is reduced to a powder, & then washed.

John Lowe (1750–1798), a minor Scottish poet, was born in the Galloway district of Scotland and educated at the University of Edinburgh. He came to Virginia in 1772 and became a tutor in the family of John Augustine Washington. He later ran an academy in Fredericksburg attended by Fielding Lewis's children. After his ordination at St. George's Church, Hempstead, Long Island, he became minister at Hanover Parish in King George County, Va.

Samuel Seabury (1729–1796) was the first bishop of the Episcopal church in America. He had been an outspoken and active Tory before and during the Revolution, and his choice by the Episcopal clergy of Connecticut as their candidate for consecration caused much controversy among the American churchmen and laity. The fact that he was consecrated in Scotland rather than in England made some question the validity of his office, and he was a controversial figure until his death.

PLAISTER OF PARIS: Houdon used the plaster of paris to make a life mask of GW, from which he made two busts. One of these he took back to France with him, along with the mask; the other remained at Mount Vernon.

Tuesday 11th. Thermometer at 68 in the Morning–70 at Noon and 71 at Night.

A Very heavy fog until near 10 Oclock, with very little wind, from the Eastward. From thence till five P. M. it was tolerably clear; when it clouded again, & looked like rain.

Sowed more English grass Seed on All the ground that had been levelled, & Smoothed on the Lawn.

Began the foundation of the House at the Southwest Corner of the South Garden.

Mr. Dulany, Mr. Sanderson and Mr. Potts dined here and returned afterwards to Alexanda.

After dark it began to rain and continued to do so fast, more or less, all Night–which appeared to have washed all the Seeds (at least all the Chaff with its contents) which had been just sowed from the ground, and carried it to the lowest parts of it.

Wednesday 12th. Thermometer at 66 in the Morning–64 at Noon and 62 at Night.

The Rain which fell last Night had made the ground so Wet that I could neither level or in any manner work it. I was obliged therefore to employ the labourers thereon in other Jobs.

Mr. Livingston (son of Peter Van brugh Livingston of New York) came to Dinner, & stayed all Night. And in the Evening Mr. Madison arrived.

Wind at No. Et. and thick weather all day; and fine Rain with intervals.

Peter Van Brugh Livingston (1710–1792), of New York, was the brother-in-law of William Alexander, Lord Stirling, and had been his partner in a mercantile business. In 1775 Livingston had been presiding officer of the New York provincial congress but resigned shortly afterwards because of ill health. Livingston's two sons were Philip Peter Livingston (b. 1740) and Peter Van Brugh Livingston (b. 1753).

Thursday 13th. Thermometer at 62 in the Morning–62 at Noon and 62 at Night.

Wind at No. Et. all day, and raining more or less–sometimes hard.

Mr. Livingston, notwithstanding the Rain, returned to Alexandria after dinner. A Suspension of all out doors work.

Friday 14th. Thermometer at 62 in the Morning–65 at Noon and 66 at Night.

Lowering most of the day, but no wind.

Mr. Madison went away after Breakfast. My Chariot which went up for, brought down Miss Sally Ramsay & Miss Kitty Washington, to be Bridesmaids tomorrow at the wedding of Miss Bassett.

Mr. George Washington, & Mr. Burwell Bassett went to the Clerks Office & thence to Colo. Masons for a license, & returned to Dinner; having accomplished their business.

The ground being too wet, I employed the labourers who had been levelling the Lawn, in cleaning & weeding the Shrubberies.

FOR A LICENSE: In order to obtain a marriage license for the wedding of his underage daughter, Fanny, to George Augustine Washington, Col. Burwell Bassett had to give his consent personally before the clerk of the court or in writing with two witnesses. His eldest son, Burwell, was probably taking this written permission with him to Alexandria at this time. The clerk then issued the license, certified that bond was given, and certified "the consent of the father, or guardian, and the manner thereof, to the first justice sworn in commission of the peace, or in his absence to the next justice sworn in that county, who is hereby authorised and required to sign and direct the same" (HENING, 6:81–85). George Mason, who was a Fairfax justice by 1749 (SPROUSE [1], 16), was probably the oldest justice in point of service, and had therefore to sign the license.

Saturday 15th. Thermometer at 66 in the Morng. 68 at Noon and 68 at Night.

A Heavy lowering morning with the wind at South. Clear afternoon and fine Evening.

The Reverend Mr. Grayson, and Doctr. Griffith; Lund Washington, his wife, & Miss Stuart came to Dinner—All of whom remained the Evening except L. W.

After the Candles were lighted George Auge. Washington and Frances Bassett were married by Mr. Grayson.

The ground continuing too wet to level, the labourers worked in the Shrubberies.

Put two thousand of the Common Chestnuts into a box with dry Sand—a layer of each & two hundred of the Spanish Chesnut in like manner to plant out in the Spring. These were put into Sand in a day or two after they were taken from the Trees.

Spence Grayson (1734–1798) was a son of Benjamin Grayson of Prince William County and a brother of William Grayson. He lived at Belle Air, two miles from Occoquan River, and had been for a number of years minister of Cameron Parish, Loudoun County. At this time Grayson was serving as minister of Dettingen Parish, Prince William County, which included two churches, one near Dumfries and the other near Broad Run and Slater Run. During the Revolution, Spence Grayson served as chaplain of Grayson's Additional Continental Regiment, commanded by his brother William.

David Griffith was probably at Mount Vernon to deliver to GW some Cape of Good Hope wheat, which Samuel Powel of Philadelphia had sent (GW to Powel, 2 Nov. 1785, DLC:GW).

Miss Stuart is probably David Stuart's sister Nancy.

Although he was still concerned about George Augustine's health (see 14 May 1785), GW wrote Fanny's father on 23 May 1785, "It has ever been a maxim with me thro' life, neither to promote, nor to prevent a matrimonial connexion, unless there should be something indispensably requiring interference in the latter . . . & therefore, neither directly nor indirectly have I ever said a syllable to Fanny or George upon the subject of their intended connexion; but as their attachment to each other seems to have been early formed, warm & lasting, it bids fair to be happy: if therefore you have no objection, I think the sooner it is consummated the better." He added that he and Mrs. Washington wished the young couple to live at Mount Vernon (GW to Burwell Bassett, DLC:GW).

Sunday 16th. Thermometer at 66 in the Morng. 68 at Noon and 72 at Night.

Morning thick and lowering, with appearances of rain, which vanished about Noon; after which it was clear and very pleasant —wind continuing at South.

Mr. Grayson went away very early in the Morning, & Mr. Griffith, Mrs. Lund Washington and Miss Stuart after Dinner.

Monday 17th. Thermometer at 68 in the Morning–[ ] at Noon and [ ] at Night.

Foggy & lowering morning, with but little wind. Clear afterwards, and Wind at No. West & cool.

Set out to meet the Directors of the Potomack Navigation at George Town. Where, having all assembled, we proceeded towards the Great Falls, and dispersing for the convenience of obtaining Quarters, Govr. Johnson and I went to Mr. Bryan Fairfax–Govr. Lee, Colo. Fitzgerald, Mr. Potts the Secretary, Mr. Rumsay the Manager, & Mr. Stuart the Assistant, went to a Mr. Wheelers near the G. Falls. Colo. Gilpin–I should have said before–had proceeded on to prepare the way for levelling &ca. at that place, in the morning.

Mr. Wheeler's may have been the home of Samuel Wheeler, who in 1791 was living between Difficult Bridge and Old Courthouse Run in Fairfax County (SPROUSE [2], 35).

Tuesday 18th. Thermometer at [ ] in the Morning–[ ] at Noon and [ ] at Night.

After an early breakfast at Mr. Fairfax's, Govr. Johnson & I set out for the Falls (accompanied by Mr. Fairfax) where we met the other Directors and Colo. Gilpin in the operation of levelling the ground for the proposed cut or Canal from the place where it is proposed to take the Water out, to the other where it will be let into the river again. In the highest of which, and for near 70 rod, it is between five & Seven feet higher than the Surface of the water at the head. After which it descends, & for at least 300 yards at the lower end, rapidly. This Cut, upon the whole, does not appear to be attended with more difficulty than was apprehended, for tho' the ground is higher than was expected—it appears from some experiments of sticking a spiked stake down in those parts, that there is two or 3 feet of soft earth at Top, & the lower end of the Canal well calculated to receive locks to advantage; as also to dam the water, to throw it back into the Canal, & thereby reduce the digging—wch. may also be done at the head by loose Stones being thrown into the River to a Rocky Island. The length of the Cut, from the work of to day, is found to be about 2400 yards—a little more or less—upon exact measurement.

Took a view of the River from the Spout, or Cateract to the proposed entrance of the Canal below, to see if I could discover (as some supposed there was) the advantage of a Canal on the Maryland side in preference to one on this, but saw no likely appearances of it. About 400 yds. below the Cateract, there is a Cove into which emptys a small part of the river, thro deep & steep rocks on both sides which is a good defence to it, and some little distance below this again, is another Cove, but how a Canal was to be brought thither, I could not (having the river between) discover. However, at, & below both, is rapid water—one little, if any, inferior to the Spout at Shanondoah.

Having taken a rough level of the proposed cut, formed general ideas for the Canal—determined to go on with it this winter, as soon as our operations on the water, on acct. of the Season must cease—& come to some resolutions respecting the hireg. of Negros, we broke up, after dark & I returned to Mr. Fairfax's.

The lock canal around the Great Falls became the major project of the Potomac Company. Completed in 1802 with five locks, it was the most ambitious civil engineering project in America in the eighteenth century (see BROWN [2]).

Wednesday 19th. Thermometer at [ ] in the Morng. [ ] at Noon and [ ] at Night.

Wind which had been at No. Wt. yesterday, & clear, had now shifted to the So. Et. and lowered till Night, when it began to

A crayon drawing of Washington's nephew, William Augustine Washington, by Saint-Mémin. (Mrs. Richard Washington)

rain; which it did more or less through the Night, the wind blowing fresh.

Immediately after breakfast I set out for my return home—at which I arrived a little after Noon. And found my Brother Jno., his Wife; Daughter Milly, & Sons Bushrod & Corbin, & the wife of the first—Mr. Willm. Washington & his wife & 4 Children & Colo. Blackburn—to whom was added in the Evening Mr. Willm. Craik.

Mr. Houdon having finished the business which brot. him hither, went up on Monday with his People, work, and impliments in my Barge, to Alexandria, to take a Passage in the Stage for Philadelphia the next Morning.

Sowed (after making good the vacancies of the former) about a pint of the Cape of Good hope Wheat, sent me by Mr. Powell of Philadelphia, in 14 rows alongside of the other in the enclosure behind the Stables.

Also—sowed about a table Spoonful of the Buffaloe or Kentucke Clover sent me by Doctr. Stuart alongside of the Guinea grass at the foot of the above Wheat & continuance of the rows thereof.

THE WIFE OF THE FIRST: Bushrod Washington was married on 13 Oct. to Julia Ann (Nancy) Blackburn (1768–1829), daughter of Col. Thomas Blackburn, of Rippon Lodge.

GW's nephew, William Augustine Washington, and his wife, Jane, usually called Jenny, were now living at Blenheim in Westmoreland County. This house was only a short distance inland from Wakefield, their former residence, which had burned in 1780. Shortly after this visit, the Washingtons moved again, to Haywood, across Bridges Creek from Wakefield. Their four children living at this time were Hannah Bushrod Washington (c.1778–c.1801), Augustine Washington (c.1780–1797), Ann Aylett Washington (1783–1804), and Bushrod Washington, Jr. (1785–1830).

MR. POWELL OF PHILADELPHIA: Samuel Powel (1739–1793) held several political offices in Philadelphia and was for many years mayor of the city. He strongly supported the Revolution and had subscribed £5,000 for the support of the Continental Army. Powel was a member of the American Philosophical Society, a founder of the University of Pennsylvania, a manager of the Pennsylvania Hospital, and president of the newly founded Philadelphia Society for Promoting Agriculture. Powel and his wife, Elizabeth Willing Powel, became intimate friends of the Washingtons during GW's presidential years.

BUFFALOE OR KENTUCKE CLOVER: *Trifolium stoloniferum,* a native perennial found in open woodlands and prairies from West Virginia to South Dakota.

Thursday 20th. Thermometer at 67 in the Morng. 66 at Noon and 65 at Night.

Wind fresh at South East and weather threatning, with Showers of rain (some pretty heavy) through the day.

George Washington & his wife, Bushrod Washington, his wife Sister & Brother, the two Mr. Bassetts, Mr. Craik and Mr. Shaw, notwithstanding the weather set out for the races at Alexandria, and were disappointed of seeing them, as they were put off. They did not return.

Friday 21st. Thermometer at 57 in the Morning—55 at Noon and 53 at Night.

Flying Clouds and cold, with appearances of Snow; wind being at No. West.

My Brother, Mr. Willm. Washington and his wife went up with me to this days races at Alexandria. We dined at Colo. Ramsays & returned in the Evening with the Company who went from here the day before, Except Mr. Wm. Washington, the two Mr. Bassetts and Mr. Shaw.

There were two races in Alexandria on this day. In the morning, the Alexandria Jockey Club Purse of 100 guineas was won by Capt. Edward Snickers's horse Careless. The afternoon race, for a purse of 50 guineas, also sponsored by the Jockey Club, was won by "Mr. Hammersley's bay Colt Spry" (*Va. Journal,* 27 Oct. 1785).

Saturday 22d. Thermometer at 52 in the Morning—52 at Noon and 52 at Night.

Wind at No. West and fresh; & Cold with appearances of unsettled weather.

Went up again to day, with my Brother, and the rest of the Gentlemen to the Race, & dined at Mr. Herberts. All returned, except Mr. Jno. Bassett, who got hurt on the race field, and Mr. Shaw. Mr. Willm. Scott came here in the Evening, from Alexandria.

The race today, for the Alexandria Town Purse of 50 guineas, was won by Gen. Alexander Spotswood's horse Cumberland (*Va. Journal,* 27 Oct. 1785).

Sunday 23d. Thermometer at 50 in the Morng. 56 at Noon and 59 at Night.

Fine & pleasant all day, with the Wind at South. No frost as was expected.

My Brother, his wife Daughter and Son; Mr. Willm. Washington his wife & 4 Children; Mr. Bushrod Washington & wife; and Mr. Scott all went away after Breakfast. Mr. Jno. Bassett & Mr. Shaw came home in the forenoon and Mr. Fitzhugh of Chatham, Genl. Spotswood, Mr. McCarty of Pope Creek, and a Colo. Middleton of South Carolina came here to dinner, & went away afterwards.

Perceived the Orchard Grass Seeds which I sowed on the 8th. Instt. in the same Inclosure of the Turneps, to be coming up thick & well.

William Fitzhugh (1741–1809), of Chatham in Stafford County, was the son of Lucy Carter and Henry Fitzhugh (1706–1742) of Eagle's Nest. He had been a member of the House of Burgesses 1772–75, the Virginia conventions of 1775 and 1776, and the Continental Congress 1779–80. He served in the House of Delegates 1776–77, 1780–81, and 1787–88 and in the Senate 1781–85. Fitzhugh was one of the foremost enthusiasts in Virginia of breeding and racing horses.

MR. MCCARTY OF POPE CREEK: The second son of Speaker Daniel McCarty, named Daniel McCarty (d. 1744), remained at the original family home, Longwood, at Pope's Creek, Westmoreland County. He was a neighbor of the Augustine Washington family during their years at their Pope's Creek home, and Augustine and Daniel named each other as executors in their wills. This Daniel had one son, also named Daniel (d. 1795), of Pope's Creek, who appears here. A contemporary of GW's, he is often confused with his first cousin and GW's close neighbor, Colonel Daniel McCarty of Mount Air in Fairfax County.

Arthur Middleton (1742–1787), of Middleton Place near Charleston, had been in the South Carolina militia during the Revolution. He served in the South Carolina assembly, was a member of the council of safety, and in 1776 had been on the committee which prepared the South Carolina constitution. Middleton served in the Continental Congress for several terms.

Monday 24th. Thermometer at 56 in the Morning—58 at Noon and 58 at Night.

Variable, & squally with a little rain. Wind at South in the Morning, and Westwardly afterwards.

The two Mr. Bassetts (Burwell and John) left this after breakfast, to return home.

In the Afternoon Doctr. Craik came in, and stayed all Night.

I rid to my Plantations at the Ferry, Dogue run, and Muddy hole—found the Orchard grass Seeds which had been sowed at Dogue run come up very well—as the Timothy also had—and that my Corn fields, now that the Fodder was taken off, looked miserably bad—the wheat on the other hand very good.

Tuesday 25th. Thermometer at 54 in the Morng. 58 at Noon and 56 at Night.

Forenoon clear and serene, and pleasant; but the Afternoon Windy & cold, with flying clouds. Wind about West.

Doctr. Craik went away before Breakfast—he intended to [go to] Alexa. but was to call upon John Alton.

Rid to my Plantation in the Neck. Found my Corn & Wheat

The honey locust, from *Catalogus Plantarum*. (Beinecke Rare Book and Manuscript Library, Yale University)

there similar with those at the other plantations as described yesterday.

Finding the Seeds of the Honey locust had come nearly, or quite to a state of maturity although the thick part of the pod still retained its green colour I had them gathered, lest when ripe they should be gathered by others, to eat.

Wednesday 26th. Thermometer at 50 in the Morng. 56 at Noon and 56 at Night.

"The Imported and very Docile ASS," from *American Farmer,* 16 March 1821. (Sterling Memorial Library, Yale University)

A large white frost this morning. Wind brisk and cold from the No. West all the day, after 9 O'clock.

Took the cover off my dry Well, to see if I could not fix it better for the purpose of an Ice House, by Arching the Top, and planking the sides.

Having received by the last Northern Mail advice of the arrival at Boston, of one of the Jack Asses presented to me by His Catholic Majesty, I sent my Overseer John Fairfax, to conduct him, and his Keeper, a Spaniard, home safe; addressing him to Lieutt. Governor Cushing, from whom I received the information.

Sent to Morris (Overseer of my Dogue run Plantation) a Bushel of clover seed (reserving Six pounds) to sow as fast as he could get the ground which is intended for the reception of it, in order.

Yesterday I transplanted a Cornation Cherry tree, and Apricot tree, which were within the Lawn before the door into the North Garden—little expecting that either will live—the first being 33 Inches in circumference and the latter 21 inches and a good deal decayed.

Finished the Shingling on the West front of the House.

GW had decided not to build a new icehouse but to remodel the old one extensively along lines suggested in Robert Morris's letter of 15 June 1784 (DLC:GW). The rebuilt icehouse had an inner well within the first, which was lined with wood for better insulation. Over the well was an arch, covered with soil and sodded. There was a tunnel in the face of the hill through which the ice could be carried from the river (MVAR, 1939, 30–31).

ONE OF THE JACK ASSES: Knowing that Spain produced excellent jackasses, GW made some inquiries about how he might obtain one for breeding purposes. Upon learning of this, Charles III, king of Spain, sent word that two Spanish jacks were being shipped to him as a gift (Thomas Jefferson to GW, 10 Dec. 1784, DLC:GW). Early in October, GW was notified by Lt. Gov. Thomas Cushing, of Massachusetts, that one of the jacks had arrived at Beverly in the care of Pedro Tellez, and that another animal was expected soon (Cushing to GW, 7 Oct. 1785, GW to Francisco Rendon, 19 Dec. 1785, DLC:GW). GW dispatched John Fairfax to Boston with instructions to escort the Spaniard and the two jacks (26 Oct. 1785, DLC:GW). It later developed that the second jack had died at sea (GW to Tench Tilghman, 30 Nov. 1785, DLC:GW). Setting out from Boston on 10 Nov., Fairfax and Tellez reached Mount Vernon on 5 Dec. (Cushing to GW, 16 Nov. 1785, DLC:GW; see entry for 5 Dec. 1785). It soon appeared that while the jack itself was a gift, GW was expected to pay all charges except Tellez's wages (GW to Cushing, 26 Oct. 1785, GW to William Hartshorne, 20 Feb. 1786, DLC:GW). The jack, to be named Royal Gift, seemed a disappointment at first. GW wrote Lafayette 10 May 1786 that although the animal was handsome, "his late royal master, 'tho past his grand climacteric, cannot be less moved by female allurements than he is" (DLC:GW). "I have my hopes that when he becomes a little better acquainted with republican enjoyments, he will amend his manners & fall into our custom of doing business; if the case should be otherwise, I shall have no disinclination to present his Catholic Majesty with as valuable a present as I received from him" (GW to William Fitzhugh, 15 May 1786, DLC:GW). Subsequent letters indicate that Royal Gift did amend his manners. GW wrote to Richard Sprigg: "It is, I believe, beyond a doubt that your Jenny is with foal by my Spaniard" (1 April 1787, owned by Mr. Sol Feinstone, Washington Crossing, Pa.).

Thursday 27th. Thermometer at 50 in the Morng. 56 at Noon and 58 at Night.

A remarkably great white frost and the ground a little frozen.

Wind Southerly all day, after it rose in the Morning, but not very fresh. Forenoon clear but the afternoon, especially towards the Suns setting, a little hazy & lowering.

Mr. Battaile Muse came here before dinner but would not stay to it. After finishing some business with me respecting my Tenants and my agreeing to allow him Six pr. Ct. for Collecting my Rents, he went up to Alexandria.

Purchased 1000 Bushels of Wheat of him, to be delivered as fast as he could have it brot. down, at my Mill—for which I am to give Six Shillings in March next or when he comes here in April.

Began to put up my Hogs at the different Plantations, to fatten for Porke.

Battaile Muse (1751–1803), son of Col. George Muse of Caroline County, had settled in Berkeley County. Muse, who in 1784 was the agent for George William Fairfax's Virginia properties, was hired by GW as the rental agent for his tenant lands in Frederick, Fauquier, Berkeley, and Loudoun counties.

Friday 28th. Thermometer at 54 in the Morning—60 at Noon and 62 at Night.

Wind Southerly; clear and pleasant all day.

Finished levelling and Sowing the lawn in front of the Ho[use] intended for a Bolling Green—as far as the Garden Houses.

Also began to sow clover seed at Dogue run plantation.

Saturday 29th. Thermometer at 59 in the Morning 64 at Noon and 65 at Night.

Morning clear, calm, and very pleasant. About Noon it began to lower a little, and continued to do so all the Afternoon.

Rid to the Plantations at the Ferry and Dogue run—at the last of which finished Sowing the Clover Seed which I sent there the 26th.; With this I mixed 9 Bushels of the pounded Plaister of Paris; and Sowed the whole on about 4¼ acres of Ground (on the Side of the run along the old Mill race) as near as I could judge from stepping it.

Sunk the inner well in the Dry well now fitting up for an Ice house, about 8 feet untill I came to a pure sand.

Mrs. Stuart & Child Nancy, & Miss Allan, came here this Evening.

CHILD NANCY: Ann (Nancy) Calvert Stuart, born in Aug. 1784, was the eldest child of David and Eleanor Calvert Custis Stuart and the first of many half brothers and sisters to the four Custis children.

Sarah Allen lived at the Calvert home, Mount Airy. She seems to have been a close friend of Eleanor Stuart's and often helped her with the education of the Custis and Stuart children.

Sunday 30th. Thermometer at 64 in the Morning—63 at Noon and 60 at Night.

Thunder and lightning about day Break and Raining more or less all day, attended in the forenoon with very high Wind from the Westward.

Mr. Shaw went up to Alexandria after Breakfast, & stayed all Night.

Monday 31st. Thermometer at 52 in the Morng. 54 at Noon and 56 at Night.

A raw and moist air, with a westerly wind & lowering Sun.

Mr. Shaw returned to Breakfast, & Mrs. Stuart, Miss Allan &ca. went away after it.

A Captn. Fullerton came here to Dinner on business of the State Society of the Cincinnati of Pensylvania; for whom I signed 250 Diplomas as President. Went away after.

Sent half a Bushel of Clean Timothy Seed to Morris—to sow at Doeg run Plantation.

Richard Fullerton (d. 1792) served throughout most of the Revolution, first as a volunteer and then as an officer in the 3d and 1st Pennsylvania regiments. He was breveted captain in 1783. As assistant secretary of the Pennsylvania Society of the Cincinnati, he was at Mount Vernon to obtain GW's signature on a supply of blank diplomas for the state society.

November

Tuesday first. Thermometer at 50 in the Morning—56 at Noon and 56 at Night.

A White frost and damp kind of a Morning, with but little Wind. Rather hazy all day, & towards evening lowering.

Rid to my Plantations at Dogue run and Muddy hole—at the former preparing, & Sowing Ground with Timothy seed.

Mrs. Fendall, Mrs. Lee & Miss Flora Lee, daughters of the former with Doctr. Skinner, came here to Dinner. And stayed all Night.

A Mr. Sacket from Tygers Valley on the Monongahela, and another person came here before Dinner and shewed me some propositions they had to make to Congress for a large territory of Country West of the Ohio, which I discouraged them from offering, as I was sure they never would be acceded to by that body.

Mrs. Lee was Matilda Lee, the wife of Henry (Light Horse Harry) Lee. Flora Lee, Matilda's sister, was the younger daughter of Elizabeth Steptoe Lee Fendall and her first husband, Philip Ludwell Lee. In 1788 Flora married her cousin Ludwell Lee (1760–1836).

Alexander Skinner (1743–1788) served as head of the military hospital at Suffolk in 1776. He later served as surgeon of the 1st Virginia Regiment and of Lee's Legion.

MR. SACKET: possibly Nathaniel Sackett of New York who had, during the Revolution, supplied GW with intelligence from behind the British lines. He laid before Congress on 22 Aug. 1785 a plan for making a "new state intended for the relief of all our distressed and neglected citizens." For this purpose, Sackett wanted a grant of western lands bounded by the Ohio, Scioto, and Muskingum rivers and Lake Erie. Congress did not act on the memorial, and so Sackett again presented the plan with 340 supporting signatures on 28 Dec. Nothing ever came of the scheme (Sackett to GW, 23 May 1789, DNA: PCC, Item 78; Sackett to GW, 7 April 1777, GW to Sackett, 8 April 1777, NNcbgGW; BOND [2], 273; JCC, 29:650, n.3, 788, n.1, 909). GW's designation "from Tygers Valley" may have meant that Sackett had just come from a visit to Tygart Valley River.

Wednesday 2d. Thermometer at 58 in the Morng. 58 at Noon and [ ] at Night.

A Very thick, damp Morning, & heavy Fog until about 9 Oclock, when it began to Rain; & continued to do so until Noon, when it thinned, and looked as if it would be fair, but soon recommenced raining, which lasted until near night.

Perceived the Wheat from the Cape, which had been sent to me by Mr. Powell of Philada., & which I sowed on the 19th. of last Month had come up very well.

The Guinea Grass in my Botanical Garden was as much injured by the frosts which we have had, and the colour of the blade as much changed, as those of Indian Corn would have been from the same cause.

Could perceive none of the Guinea grass up which I sowed in the Inclosure behind the Stable (old Vineyard) – the 1st. day of Sepr.

Thursday 3d. Thermometer at 54 in the Morning – 60 at Noon and 58 at Night.

Morning clear, Calm, and very pleasant; but the wind springing up about 10 Oclock in the No. West, & blowing pretty fresh, it turned cool towards Evening.

Borrowed a Scow from Colo. Gilpin, with which to raise Mud

from the Bed of the river or Creek, to try the efficacy of it as a Manure, and sent it to the river Plantation for that purpose. Went over there myself to mark off a piece of ground to spread it on, after it should get mellowed by the frosts of the Winter.

Mrs. Fendal, Mrs. & Miss Lee & Doctr. Skinner went away, breakfasting first.

Took up 11 Pines of a large size & planted them in the green brier hedge & circle at the extremity of the Lawn within the Gate.

Friday 4th. Thermometer at 52 in the Morng. [ ] at Noon and 60 at Night.

Lowering, and the wind very brisk from the So. West in the Morning; but clear, calm, warm, and very pleasant afterwards.

A plan of one of John Fitch's early steamboats appeared in this December 1786 issue of *Columbian Magazine,* which Washington had in his library. (Boston Athenaeum)

Raised the heavy frame in my [Ice] House to day and planted 16 Pines in the avenues on my Serpentine Walks.

Rid to my Dogue run Plantation, where they were still preparing ground for, & sowing of, Timothy seed. Went from thence to Mr. Lund Washington's on a visit to Mr. Robt. Washington who was gone up to Alexandria. Returned home by the way of Muddy hole.

In the Evening a Mr. Jno. Fitch came in, to propose a draft & Model of a Machine for promoting Navigation, by means of a Steam.

John Fitch (1743–1798), of Bucks County, Pa., had been experimenting with a steam-driven boat for the navigation of rivers. He applied to the Continental Congress for financial assistance in Aug. 1785 and to the American Philosophical Society in September, but without success. He was at this time on his way to Richmond to try, again unsuccessfully, to procure assistance from the state legislature. On his way south, Fitch had stopped at former governor Thomas Johnson's in Frederick Town, Md., where he first heard of James Rumsey's boat. Concerned about the possibility that Rumsey too was experimenting with steam power, Fitch had, at Johnson's suggestion, stopped to ask GW whether Rumsey was experimenting with steam. According to Fitch, GW evaded a direct answer and gave him no encouragement (WESTCOTT, 127–47).

Saturday 5th. Thermometer at 60 in the Morng. 64 at Noon and 65 at Night.

Morning a little lowering with the wind pretty brisk from the Southward until about Noon when it became Calm & clear.

Went over the Creek to see how my people went on in raising mud from the bed of the Creek—their progress but slow.

Mr. Robert Washington of Chotanck—Mr. Lund Washington & Mr. Lawrence Washington dined here, as did Colo. Gilpin and Mr. Noah Webster. The 4 first went away afterwards—the last stayed all Night. In the afternoon a Mr. Lee came here to sollicit Charity for his Mother who represented herself as having nine Children—a bad husband and no support. He also stayed the Evening.

Noah Webster, in his effort to get the state to enact a copyright law, had come to request letters of introduction from GW to the governor of Virginia and to the speakers of both the Virginia Senate and House of Delegates. Webster wrote GW, on 16 Dec. 1785, to inform him that the legislature had passed such an act. He also offered to come to Mount Vernon to act, without pay, as tutor for the Custis children, provided he would be given access to GW's papers (PHi: Gratz Collection). GW refused this offer, as he needed someone who could also act as secretary (GW to Webster, 18 Dec. 1785, NN: Washington Collection).

Sunday 6th. Thermometer at 64 in the Morning—68 at Noon and 68 at Night.

Clear, Calm, and remarkably pleasant all day. Sun set in a bank.

Mr. Webster and Mr. Lee went away after breakfast.

Mr. Geo. Washington & wife went to Church at Alexandria—as did Mr. Shaw. The two first returned to dinner. The other not 'till some time in the Night—after the family were in bed.

Although it was omitted in the occurrences of Yesterday, I tried 2 quarts of the pulverized plaister of Paris; one of them burned, the other unburnt; upon two sections of the Circle in front of the House—from the Dial Post to the Center post, opposite to the pavemt. leading to the Gate by the Quarter. The section nearest the House was sprinkled with the burned Plaister. These sections are only from one Post to another in the circle, and do not contain more than about 145 square ft. A quart therefore on each is at the rate of 8 Bushels to the Acre. This was the poorest part of the Circle.

Monday 7th. Thermometer at 66 in the Morng. 69 at Noon and 69 at Night.

Clear, calm, and remarkably pleasant all day, but rather too warm for the Season.

Mrs. Peake and Miss Eagland dined here and returned in the Eveng.

Employed since I first began to supply the dead Trees in the Serpentine Walks which I compleated this day except with the lime (or Linden) and horse chesnut, neither of wch. I have or could easily get at. The numbers replanted are as follow—of Pine 19—of Elm 2—of Poplar 18—of the black Gum 17—of the Aspan 2—of the Mulberry 5—Ash 2—and of the Maple none.

MISS EAGLAND: probably Mrs. Peake's niece, Frances Edelen. GW constantly misspelled her name, calling her Eaglin, Eldredge, England, and Evelin.

Tuesday 8th. Thermometer at 60 in the Morning—66 at Noon and 66 at Night.

A very heavy fog (with little or no wind) until near Noon—when it dispelled; became clear, warm & pleasant.

Rid to Dogue run & Muddy hole Plantations—the first preparing Ground, & sowing Timothy Seed.

Began to replace the dead trees in my shrubberies.

Doctr. Craik first, and a Captn. Lewis Littlepage afterwards, came here to Dinner; the first went away after it—the other stayed all Night. This Captn. Littlepage has been Aid de Camp to the Duke de Crillon—was at the Sieges of Fort St. Phillip (on the Island of Minorca) and Gibralter; and is an extraordinary character.

In the Evening Doctr. Griffith came, & stayed all Night.

Lewis Littlepage (1762–1802), of Hanover County, served briefly in John Jay's legation in Spain in 1780 and as a volunteer with the Spanish army in the sieges of Port Mahón (Fort St. Philip) 1781–82 and Gibraltar 1782–83. He had received an invitation from the king of Poland to accept a position at his court, and had been given a year's leave of absence to arrange his affairs in America. In Richmond, Littlepage received from Gov. Patrick

Henry a letter of introduction to GW and also a draft for £300 on the state of Virginia, to be conveyed to the sculptor Houdon as a partial payment for his statue of GW. Littlepage stopped at Mount Vernon on his way to New York. After he arrived in New York a long-standing feud with John Jay almost sent him to jail, and he used the money belonging to the state of Virginia to extricate himself from his difficulties. This done, he sailed for France and by 1786 was serving as chamberlain and envoy in the service of Stanislas II Augustus, king of Poland.

Louis de Berton des Balbes de Quiers, duc de Crillon-Mahón (1717–1796), was a Frenchman in the service of Spain. In 1782 he had captured Fort St. Philip, the fortification for Port Mahón on Minorca, and then commanded an unsuccessful Franco-Spanish siege of Gibraltar.

Wednesday 9th. Thermometer at 64 in the Morning—66 at Noon and 66 at Night.

A red, & watery Sun in the Morning, which about Noon was obscured, slow rain afterwds. Wind Southerly all day; and at Night appeared to be getting to the Westward.

Mr. Griffith went away after Breakfast and Captn. Littlepage after Dinner.

Having put in the heavy frame into my Ice House I began this day to Seal it with Boards, and to ram straw between these boards and the wall. All imaginable pains was taken to prevent the Straw from getting wet, or even damp, but the Moisture in the air is very unfavourable.

Thursday 10th. Thermometer at 59 in the Morning—[ ] at Noon and [ ] at Night.

There having fallen so much rain in the Night as to convince me that the Straw which I had placed between the Cieling & the Wall of my Ice House, must have got wet, and being in some doubt before of the propriety of the measure, lest it should get damp, heat, & rot; I had it all taken out, leaving the Space between unfilled with any thing.

Went up to Alexandria to meet the Directors of the Potomack Company. Dined at Mr. Fendalls (who was from home) and returned in the Evening with Mrs. Washington. Mr. George Washington & his wife who accompanied us remaining to a Ball.

Planted 8 of the Hemlock Pine which were brought from Neabsco in my Shrubberies—More still wanting to make up the deficiencies.

Friday 11th. Thermometer at 56 in the Morng. 54 at Noon and 55 at Night.

Wind at No. Et. and fresh all day. Very cloudy and sometimes dripping. At Night it began to fall a little more seriously, but in no great qty.

Sent my Carriage up for & brought George Washington & his wife down after dinner.

Saturday 12. Thermometer at 54 in the Morng. 58 at Noon and 60 at Night.

Wind a little west of the No. and pretty fresh all the forenoon; and cloudy. Afternoon clear, still, & very pleasant.

Received 215 Apple trees (red striek) from Major Jenifer; wh[ic]h I sent to the river plantation in the Neck, to be planted. At the same time, and from the same place, received two New Town & 2 Golden Pippin trees–Two of the Bury, & two St. Germain Pear Trees and 2 duke Cherry Trees.

Rid to my Plantations at the Ferry–Dogue run and Muddy hole; at the second of which they were yet preparing ground, & sowing grass-seeds–at the last gathering Corn.

Covered my exotic plants in that section of my Botanical Garden between the Salt House & the House next the Circle; & began to cover the Guinea grass, which two days before I had cut of near the Crown–but did not finish it.

Sunday 13th. Thermometer at 59 in the Morning–65 at Noon –65 at Night.

Clear all day. Morning calm & very pleasant; but Windy afterwards from the No. West.

Mr. Saml. Hanson and his wife, Mr. Thos. Hanson and their two sisters, & Mrs. Dulany wife to Waltr. Dulany, lately from England came to Dinner, & stayed all Night.

Samuel Hanson of Samuel was married to Mary Key (Kay) Hanson, of New Jersey, and was a merchant in Alexandria at this time. GW's ledger entries between 1784 and 1786 include several business transactions with the "Messrs. Hansons" (LEDGER B, 180, 207). Maj. Walter Dulany, Jr., brother-in-law of Thomas Hawkins Hanson, served in the Maryland Loyalist Regiment during the Revolution. In 1785 he returned to Maryland from England with his new wife, Elizabeth Brice Dulany, widow of his uncle, Lloyd Dulany.

Monday 14th. Thermometer at 58 in the Morning–64 at Noon and 62 at Night.

Calm, clear, & pleasant Morning. Wind pretty brisk afterwards from the No. Wt., but fine notwithstanding.

The Company who came to dinr. yesterday, & lodged here last Night went away after breakfast—upon which I went to my Neck Plantation in the Neck with intention to take a descriptive list of my Horses, Cattle, Sheep, Working Tools &ca., but the fore-noon being far spent I could only do it of the Horses & Tools.

Began to Plant the Apple Trees which were brought from Major Jenifers on Saturday.

Finished covering the Guinea grass in my Botanical Garden except 6 rows of it which I left uncovered—and uncut—to try the effect of the Winters frosts & snows upon it.

In the Evening Mr. Willm. Craik returned from his trip over the Alligane Mountains having effected no business for his father or me, being disappointed of seeing those with whom he had it to transact.

NO BUSINESS FOR HIS FATHER OR ME: GW had given young Craik a letter to be delivered to Maj. Thomas Freeman of Red Stone, now Brownsville, Pa., detailing what Freeman was to do regarding the lands in Pennsylvania under lease to Gilbert Simpson (16 Oct. 1785, DLC:GW). Simpson was dissatisfied with his lease and had been threatening to leave the tenement (see entries for 15 and 17 Sept. 1784).

Tuesday 15. Thermometer at 54 in the Morning—56 at Noon and 60 at Noon [night].

Wind Southerly and pretty fresh. Weather somewhat hazy and Smoaky.

Went to my Neck Plantation and compleated the Acct. of my Stock there—except that of the Hogs—which stand thus.

Horses

A grey dray Stallion			1
Buck a Sorrel	16 yr. old	Working Horses	
Gilbert a black	17 Do.		
Randolph a Grey	7 Do.		
Doctr. a Grey	7 Do.		
Prentice a Bay	10 Do.		
Jolly a Black	9 Do.		
Dick a White	12 Do.		
Grunt a Bay	9 Do.		
Pompey a Bay	14 Do.		
Diamond White	9 Do.		
Possum—Grey	10 Do.		
Jack—Black	10 Do.		12

Kit . . a black Mare . .	5 yrs.	Workg. Mares		
Fly . . Dark brown . .				
Patience				
Betty White Stockgs.	9 Do.			
Punch grey flea bittn.				
Jenny light grey	9 Do.			
Brown	11 Do.			
Fanny . . . Black	9 Do.			
Oversrs. . . . Black			. .	9
A brown Horse	5	unbroke Hors.		
Bright Bay . . . . . rising	3			
Black . . . . Do.	3			
Brown Mealy Cod. . . . Do.	3			
Black . . . . Do.	3			
Black . . Small . . Do.	3			
Ditto . . . . Do.	2			
Iron Grey . . . . . . Do.	2			
Black bald face	2		. .	9
A Grey spring Colt	. . .	. . .	. .	1
Dark bay	9	unbroke Mares		
Sorrel	5			
Brown	6			
Black . . . . rising	3			
Dark brown	3			
Grey	3			
Black . . . . rising	2		. .	7
Black Spring Colt	. . .	. . .	. .	1
In all	. . .	. . .	. .	40

Cattle

Bulls y[oun]g		3
Working Oxen		7
Fatting Steers in Corn field		5
Cows		41
Heifers . . . 6 yrs. old . .	6	
3 yrs. old . .	15	
2 yrs. old . .	11	
1 yr. old . .	7	
Spring . . Cow calves . .	19	58
Steers—full grown	18	
4 yrs. old . .	2	
3 yrs. old . .	4	
2 yrs. old . .	7	

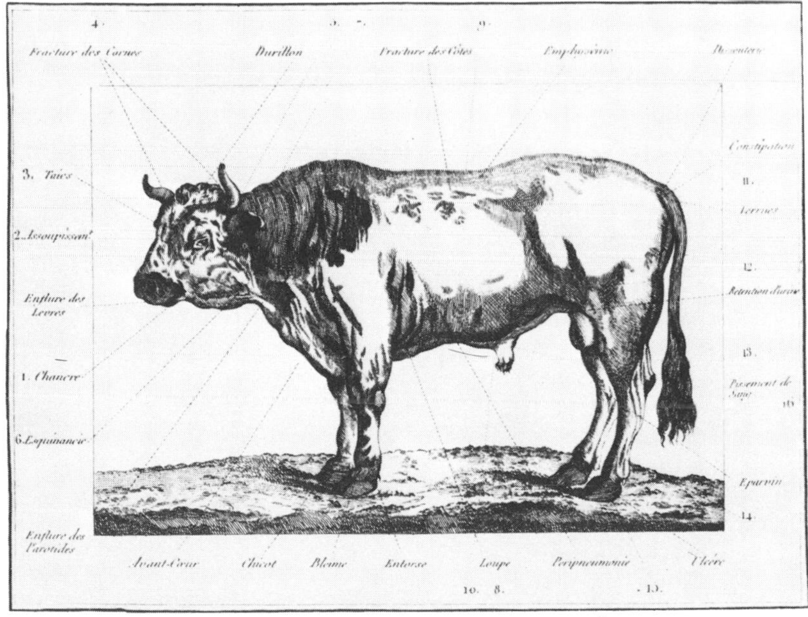

Plates depicting a ram and a bull, from *La Nouvelle Maison rustique,* Paris, 1798. (Mount Vernon Ladies' Association of the Union)

1 yr. old	3	
Spring . . Bull calves	11	45
		159
Cows brot. to the Home for Milk & to go back		8
Total Cattle		167
Sheep		
Rams		7
Ewes		92
Weathers		12
Ditto in Corn field		16
		127
Weathers brot. to Ho[me] Ho[use]		42
Total		169
Tools & Implemts.		
A Waggon Saddle and Gier for 4 Horses		1
An Oxe Cart—good	1	
Ditto not good	1	2
Oxe Chains		2
Bolts for Tongues		2
Yokes, Rings &ca.		
Bar shear Plows		9
Two pr. Iron traces to each		18
Old Bridles for ditto		18
NB. These Traces serve the Waggon		
Hilling Hoes helved	20	
unhelved pretty gd.	3	
indifferent	2	
At the Smiths Shop	2	27
Mattocks but indifft.	6	
Ditto said to have come to the Home Ho[use]	7	13
Grubbing Hoes indifft.		3
Axes	7	
Ditto at Smiths Shop	1	
Ditto old Iron	1	9
Iron Wedges—pairs		3
Open Iron wire Sieve	1	
Sand Sieve	1	2
Note these to be sent to the Home Ho[use]		
Harvest Rakes . . . 5 only gd.		13
Pitch forks		1
Half Bushels . . . new	1	

Various types of garden implements, from "Agriculture" in Diderot's *Encyclopédie,* Paris, 1780. (Mount Vernon Ladies' Association of the Union)

Old Do.	1	2
Plantation Gun		1

Wednesday 16th. Thermometer at 58 in the Morng. 66 at Noon and [ ] at Night.

A large circle round the Moon last night—a red & angry looking sky at the Suns rising and a brisk Southerly Wind all day with rain in the Evening and Night.

Finished the Arch over my Ice House to day.

Went early in the Morning to take an acct. of My Stocks &ca. at Dogue run & Muddy hole Planns.

At the first

Horses

		Height	Age		
Dabster	a grey	14¼	8	Workers	
Buck	Bay	14	6		2
Nancy	Bay	14	old	Workg. Mares	
From Camp	Ditto	14¼			
Fly	Ditto	13	8		
Brandy	Ditto	13½			
Fancy	Black	13	old		
——	Sorrel	13	old		
——	Ditto	13			
Bonny	Bay		very old		8
Englh. Hunter	Brown	15	old	Old M.	
Grey Mare bot. at Bristol			Do.		
Dray	Black	Camp	Do.		3
Bay	likely in foal	14	6	Unbroke Mares	
Bay Roan—white face		14	5		
Sorrel		14½			
Black—Snip on the nose		13			
Iron grey—dark		14	3		
Black—from Hunter			2		
Black Star & Snip likely			2		
Bay—white face			1		
Black—long star			1		
Bay near hind foot wh[ite]			1		
Bay small Star			1		
Bay (blood) near hind f[oot] W[hit]e			1		
Bay—star & snip			1		13

A Grey . snip	14	3	Unbroke Horses	
*Bay Roan wh. face		1		
*Sorrel . Snip		1		
*Dark Grey		1		
Grey Colt frm. Bristl. M[are]		Sp[rin]g		
*It is not certain whether these are horses or Mares not having distinguished them on the Spot at the time				5
In all				31

Cattle

Working Oxen			7
Fatting Steers in Meadow			2
Cows			15
Heifers	4 yrs. old	5	
	3 yrs. old	3	
	2 yrs. old	6	
	1 yr. old	2	
	Spring Calves	6	22
Steers	full grown	7	
	3 years old	1	
	2 yrs. old	2	
	1 yr. old	7	
	Spring Calves	5	22
Bulls			1
	Total		69

Sheep

Rams		7
Ewes		32
Weathers	7	
Ditto in Meadow fattg.	7	14
Total		53
Old Cows in the Meadw.		2

N.B. The Tools not being got up no Acct. was taken of them at this time.

Muddy hole Plantation

Horses

	height	age		
Jockey . a black	13½	14	W.H.	
Diamond . Ditto	14	10		2

Rankin	14	10	Workg. Mares	
Fly . . a Grey	14¼	2	Workg. Mares	
Jenny . Brown	13¼	8	Workg. Mares	
Finwick . Dun Sorrel	13½	7	Workg. Mares	
Fancy . Grey	13¼	9	Workg. Mares	5
White	13	7	unbroke Mares	
Bay . small Star &ca.	13	5	unbroke Mares	
Bay . long blaze	13	5	unbroke Mares	
Bay . very small Star	13	5	unbroke Mares	
Dark Bay sml. star & snp.	13		unbroke Mares	
Dark Brown Simpson	13½	3	unbroke Mares	
Bay . midlg. likely		1	unbroke Mares	
Bay . small Star		Spring	unbroke Mares	
Black . sml. star		Spring	unbroke Mares	9
Brown Bay . crookd blaze . 13 hands high		5 yrs. old	unbroke Hors.	
Grey . unlikely		2	unbroke Hors.	
Bay . sml. star . unlikely			unbroke Hors.	
Grey . natural pacer		spg.	unbroke Hors.	4
Total				20

Cattle

Working Oxen			4
Cows			10
Heifers	1 yr. old		1
Cow Calves	this spring		1
Steers	full grown	8	
	2 years old	2	
	1 year old	1	11
Male Calves			4
Total			31

Sheep

Rams	5
Ewes	39
Lambs	11
Total	50

Tools & Implements

A good oxe Cart—2 Oxe yokes & Iron Rings—Compleat	1

Oxe Chain	1
Bar shear plows	3
Iron Traces . pairs	6
Haims, Collars, Bridles &ca. Compt.	
2 spare Colters	2
Mattoxs	5
Axes—includg. 1 at the Home Ho[use]	4
Iron Wedges . pairs	1
Hilling Hoes	11
Pitch fork	1
A Wheat Fan	1
Half Bushel	1

The Hogs at all the Plantations running in the Woods after the Mast, no Acct. could be taken of them.

Richard Henry Lee, lately President of Congress; his Son Ludwell, Colo. Fitzgerald, and a Mr. Hunter (Mercht.) of London came here to Dinner & stayed all Night.

The Stock at the Ferry not being got up, Postponed taking the Acct. of them until they shod. be got together.

Richard Henry Lee's son Ludwell Lee lived at Shuter's (Shooter's) Hill near Alexandria.

Mr. Hunter was a son of Robert Hunter, a Scottish merchant living in London and trading primarily with Canada. Hunter's son Robert Jr., or John, as he is identified in some sources (*Pa. Mag.*, 17:76–82), was only 20 years old when his father sent him to America in 1785, at a time when representatives of British mercantile houses were swarming into the country to collect pre-Revolutionary debts. In Montreal young Hunter met Joseph Hadfield, who was also collecting debts for his family's firm, and the two joined forces for part of their journey through the states (see 31 Jan. 1785). Hadfield, who had visited Mount Vernon in January, remained in Baltimore while Hunter went to Alexandria and Mount Vernon. Among the subjects discussed during Hunter's visit was navigation of the Potomac River. GW "gave success to the navigation of the Potomac for his toast, which he has very much [at] heart. . . . He is quite pleased at the idea of the Baltimore merchants laughing at him and saying it was a ridiculous plan and would never succeed. They begin now, says the General, to look a little serious about the matter, as they know it must hurt their commerce amazingly" (WRIGHT, 193).

Thursday 17th. Thermometer at 58 in the Morning—60 at Noon and 62 at Night.

Colo. Lee & all the Company went away after Breakfast.

Mr. Shaw went up to the Assembly in the Afternoon at Alexand.

Morning a little foggy & thick but clear afterwards with the Wind at No. West and cool.

ASSEMBLY . . . AT ALEXAND.: "The Gentlemen of Alexandria, who are desirous to become Subscribers to the Assemblies for the approaching Season, are requested to meet at the Coffee-House this Evening at 6 o'Clock, to form Regulations for the same. It is intended that the Assemblies commence on Thursday the 17th Instant, at Mr. Wises's new Room" (*Va. Journal,* 10 Nov. 1785). John Wise's Fountain Tavern, where the assemblies were held, was located on Royal Street (*Va. Journal,* 16 June 1785 and 17 Aug. 1786).

Friday 18th. Thermometer at 49 in the Morning—54 at Noon and 50 at Night.

Morning clear & serene—a white Frost and ground froze—Ice an eighth of an Inch thick. Wind at No. Wt. & pretty fresh untill the afternoon when it was almost calm.

Began to take up a number of small Pines to replace the dead ones in my wilderness. Got them with much dirt about the Roots.

Took an Account of the Horses, Cattle & Sheep at Home.

viz.

Horses

Magnolia—an Arabian				1
Nelson . Riding Horse	1			
Blewskin . Ditto	1			2
	height	age		
Partner . A Bay	15	12	For the Chariot	
Ajax . lightr. Bay	15	11		
Chatham . dull Bay	15	8		
Valiant . Yellowh. Bay	14¾	16		
English . Bay	15	very old		
McIntosh . Bay	14½	9		
Careless . Bay	14½	5		
Young . Bay				8
Dragon . Black	15	6	Waggn. Hors.	
Jolly . Ditto	15	14		
Chichester . Bay	14½			
Jock . Grey	14¼	5		4
Black . Mare dray	15	old	Cart H.	
Black . Horse Ditto	14	old		
used in Tumblers				2

A Brown Bay . . . . 14 . . 6	Hacks			
Chevalier . dull bay . 14½ . .				
Brown Bay . Muddy hole . . .				
Columbus . br[own] Do. 14				4
Total				21

Cattle

Working Oxen . . .	old	2		
Ditto Do. . . .	young	2	. . . .	4
Cows from Camp		4		
Rivr. Plantn.		8		
Dogue run Do.		6		
Ferry Do.		3	. . . .	21
Bull				1
		In all . . .		26

Note. One of the Cows that came from the River Plantn. (making the above, 9) got mired this Fall and died, and of the above, the 4 Cows from Camp—two from the Ferry—three from Dogue run—and one from the Neck are ordered to be detained here—and all the rest to be sent to their respective places.

Sheep

Weathers		40		
Ewes . . .	sucking Lambs . . .	4		
Lambs . .	for killing . . .	4	. . . .	48

Began to take up my summer Turnips at the House. Got abt. half up to day.

Sent to Mr. Digges for Papaw Bushes to replace the dead ones in my Shrubberies. Coming late I had not time to plant them but put the Roots in the ground until tomorrow.

Planted the two duke Cherries—sent me by Major Jenifer in the two gardens—one under each Wall, abt. 30 feet from the Garden Houses—and planted the Bury & 2 St. Germain Pairs also sent me by him in the No. Garden—new part thereof—one of each kind on the circular Walk and the other two on the Strait walk.

Put the Box with the Magnolia, & other exotics from So. Carolina and that with the Kentucke Coffee tree under a bush cover in the open part of the Green Ho[use] and began to cover the Palmetto Royal at the Front gate with Brush with the leaf on—but got a small part only South of the gate & South part thereof done before night.

Magnolia, or Magnolio, was an Arabian horse which GW had bought for £500 from the estate of John Parke Custis (LEDGER B, 224). He was a five-year-old, "a chesnut colour, near sixteen hands high, finely formed, and thought by all who have seen him to be perfect. He was got by the Ranger Arabian, his dam by Othello son of Crab, her dam by Morton's Traveller, and her dam was Selima by the Godolphin Arabian" (*Va. Journal,* 24 Mar. 1785).

Nelson and Blueskin, two horses that had carried GW during the Revolution, were now in honorable retirement at Mount Vernon. Nelson was, according to George Washington Parke Custis, the chestnut which GW rode at Yorktown. He was named for Gov. Thomas Nelson, Jr., of Virginia, and was probably the horse which Governor Nelson sent GW as a gift in 1778 after hearing of GW's difficulties in finding a suitable animal to replace one he had been riding (CUSTIS, 166; Nelson to GW, 11 Aug. 1778, DLC:GW). Blueskin seems to have been sold or given to GW by Benjamin Dulany or his wife, and GW wrote late in 1785 to Elizabeth French Dulany, presenting the horse to her: "Marks of antiquity have supplied the place of those beauties with which this horse abounded in his better days. Nothing but the recollection of which, & of his having been the favourite of Mr. Dulany in the days of his Court ship, can reconcile her [Mrs. Dulany] to the meagre appearance he now makes" (GW to Elizabeth French Dulany, c.23 Nov. 1785, MdHi).

Saturday 19th. Thermometer at 46 in the Morng. 54 at Noon and [ ] at Night.

Wind at No. West and cold all day, with Clouds which threatned Snow in the evening. Ground very hard frozen.

Finished digging my Summer Turnips and putting them in a Cellar.

Also finished covering the Palmetto royal at the front gate, except a small piece on the south side, nearest the gate, for which brush could not be got in time.

My Ice House Walls except the Pediment over the outer door and the inner Walls of the arch were compleated this day likewise.

Doctr. Craik whom I had sent for to visit York George (in the Neck) who is much afflicted with the gravel came here about Sundown and stayed all Night.

Sunday 20th. Thermometer at 48 in the Morning–54 at Noon and 54 at Night.

Clear and calm all day, but the Air keen notwithstanding.

George Washington & wife & Mr. Shaw went to Lund Washingtons to Dinner & returned in the afternoon.

Colo. Harrison (Judge) came here to Dinner and Doctr. Craik (who went away early this Morning) at Night.

My Nephew Lawe. Washington came here with a letter today from Mr. Bayley respecting their Board &ca.

William Bailey, a Georgetown merchant, boarded GW's nephews George Steptoe and Lawrence Augustine Washington during part of their stay at the Georgetown academy, furnishing them with supplies from his store (GW to Stephen Bloomer Balch, 26 June 1785, Benjamin Stoddert to GW, 21 June 1785, DLC:GW).

Monday 21st. Thermometer at 48 in the Morning–[ ] at Noon and [ ] at N.

Lowering morning, with the wind at No. Et. About half after ten A.M. it began to Snow & continued to do so (of a Wet kind) until Night, when it ceased tho' the ground was not covered more than an Inch thick.

Colo. Harrison & Doctr. Craik left this after Breakfast, and I went up to Alexandria with G. Washington to meet the Directors of the Potomack Coma. and to a Turtle feast (the Turtle given by myself to the Gentlemen of Alexa.).

Returned in the Evening and found the Count Doradour recommended by, & related to the Marqs. de la Fayette here, as also the Revd. Mr. Magowan.

The directors of the Potomac Company met to approve some accounts receivable (PICKELL, 82).

The comte de Doradour, a Frenchman from Auvergne, was "going to look for a settlement in America. His fortune Has Been partly deranged By a law suit, and what Remains of it He intends to fix in some of the United States" (Lafayette to GW, 11 May 1785, PEL). Doradour carried letters of introduction to numerous Virginians from Thomas Jefferson, at this time United States minister to France, and eventually purchased a large tract of land west of the mountains (Jefferson to Nicholas Lewis, 19 Dec. 1786, DLC: Jefferson Papers).

Tuesday 22d. Thermometer at 40 in the Morning–46 at Noon and 52 at Night.

Clear and cold Wind at No. West all day. The Snow, except on the No. side of Hills & Houses had dissolvd.

The Count Doradour and Mr. Magowan went away after Breakfast.

The Reverd. Mr. Keith of Alexandria and a Mr. Bowie of Philadelphia came to Dinner and returned to Alexandria in the Evening.

Gave my People their Cloathing pr. list taken.

Removing Earth to day, as yesterday, to cover my Ice Ho[use].

Isaac Stockton Keith (d. 1813) became minister of the Presbyterian Meeting House in Alexandria in 1780 and was one of the first trustees of the Alexandria academy. He left to go to Charleston, S.C., in 1788. Keith was probably the Isaac Keith, a Pennsylvanian, who received a degree from Princeton in 1778 (MCGROARTY, 17–18; POWELL, 101; HENING, 12:393).

John Bowie asked permission in 1784 to write a biography of GW. Although GW initially agreed to the proposal, he had second thoughts and put so many restrictions on Bowie that it is doubtful that the book was ever completed. GW's foremost worry seems to have been that he would be thought vain for allowing his biography to be written during his lifetime, and he insisted the book not be published until after his death (see GW to James Craik, 25 Mar. 1784, GW to John Witherspoon, 8 Mar. 1785, DLC: GW).

Wednesday 23d. Thermometer at 48 in the Morng. 54 at Noon and [ ] at Night.

Clear, warm, and pleasant, with the Wind at South.

Finished all the Brick work of my Ice House today.

Miss Kitty Washington, Genl. Lincoln, Colonels Hooe & Lyles, Mr. Porter, Captn. Goodwin, Doctr. Swift, Mr. Potts, Mr. Dalby, Mr. Monshur Mr. Williams, Mr. Philips & a Mr. Cramer or Cranmur came here to Dinner and all of them returned in the evening except Kitty Washington.

Sent Mr. Shaw through Alexandria, to agree for the Schooling & Board of my Nephews George & Lawrence Washington now at the Academy at George Town & thence to the latter place to conduct them to the former for the purpose of going to School at the Alexandria Academy.

William Lyles, a merchant from Charles County, Md., who had moved to Alexandria c.1782, had a distillery and a dry goods store there and rented the house formerly owned by George W. Fairfax on Prince Street (*Va. Journal,* 10 June 1784, 30 Nov. 1786; MOORE [1], 87–92).

Capt. Nash Goodwin of the ship *Mary* was a cousin of Thomas Porter and nephew of Josiah Watson. His ship was due to leave for Le Havre, France, on 10 Dec. (*Va. Journal,* 1 Dec. 1785; WRIGHT, 190).

Dr. Foster Swift, of Massachusetts, settled in Alexandria to practice medicine (*Va. Journal,* 7 July 1785). He later moved to New London, Conn., and eventually became resident physician on Governor's Island in New York harbor (BROCKETT, 128). Swift was the brother of the Alexandria merchant Jonathan Swift and a friend of Benjamin Lincoln, who introduced him to GW on this day (BUCHANAN [2], 92, 96).

Mr. Williams is probably Thomas Williams, an Englishman and a partner in the Alexandria firm of Williams, Cary & Williams, which sold European and East Indian goods. In 1784 the business moved from Capt. John Harper's wharf to Fairfax Street, next to Robert Lyle's store (WRIGHT, 191; SPROUSE [2], 19; *Va. Journal,* 3 June and 4 Nov. 1784).

The Alexandria academy was formed in 1785 through the efforts of Dr. William Brown and other Alexandria residents. In November, GW became a trustee of the academy.

Thursday 24th. Thermometer at 48 in the Morng. 56 at Noon and 55 at Night.

Clear, Warm & pleasant, wind being still southerly.

Immediately after Breakfast, rid to my Plantation at the Ferry and took the following Acct. of my Stock–viz.

Horses

	hands	age		
Prince a black Horse	14	20	W.H.	
Ditto–a Sorrel Do.	14¼	old		2
Jenny–bla. Mare	14¼	old	Working Mares	
Peggy–White Do.	14	10		
Fly–Dark Grey Do.	13½	8		
Kitty–Small bay–Do.	13	15		
Bonny–Sorrel–Do.	14	10		
Nancy–black–Do.	sml.	12		6
A Black Mare Steady, likely	13½	4	unb. Ms.	
A sorrel Ditto, Leonidas Do.		1		
A bay–Do. very small		Spring		3
A bla. Horse . unlikely		4	unb. Hors.	
A Small bay Leonidas–likely		1		
A black–bald face		Sprg.		3
Total				14

Cattle

		age	
Darling–a red & W. Ox		6	
Bembo . White & red Do.		9	
Mark black & White Do.		11	
Duke red brindle		very old	4
Cows			14
Heifers	4 Years old	1	
	3 years.	2	
	2 years	2	
	Calves this spg.	5	10
Steers	full grown	2	
	4 years old	2	
	3 years old	5	
	2 years Do.	3	

	1 years Do.	1	
	Spring Calves	7	20
Bulls	2 years old		1
Beeves in Corn field			2
		Total	51

Sheep

Rams	1
Ewes	9
Weathers	5
Total	15

Tools & Implements

A good Cart		
2 Yokes with Rings		
A Cain		
Wheat Fans		1
Wire riddles—course	4	
Sand Sieves	1	
Courser Size	1	6
Plows Bar shears		4
Iron Traces . . pairs		8
Haims, Clevis, Bridles &ca. compleat for them		
Weeding Hoes		1
Hilling Ditto		13
Grubbing Ditto		1
Mattocks		4
Axes		5
Iron Wedge—1½ pair		

From the Ferry, I went to the Plantation at Dogue run and took the following Account of the Tools there—being omitted when I was there last.

Viz.

Oxe Carts	1	
At the Ho[use] for repair	1	2
Oxe Yokes with rings		4
Oxe Chains		2
Wheat Fans		1
Riddles—viz.		
1 Open & tolerable good		
1 Sand Sieve & much worn		
Axes		9

Mattocks		6
Grubbing Hoes		6
Hilling Ditto		16
Iron Wedges—pairs		4
Spades—good		1
Bar shear Plows		4
Iron Traces		8
Haims, Clevis, Bridles &ca. complete		
Spare Colters		3
Adzes	1	
Drawing knife	1	
Handsaws	1	
Froes	1	
Broad Chissels	1	
Narrow Do.	1	
Gouge	1	
Augcr—¾ Inch	1	

Recapitulation of all my Stocks of Horses, Cattle & Sheep.

Horses

Stud Horse. Magnolio		1	
Ditto . . Dray		1	2
Riding Horses			2
Chariot Horses			8
Hack Horses			4
Waggon Horses—Home Ho[use]		4	
Cart Ditto Do. Do.		1	5
Plow Ditto Plantns.			18
Cart Mare Home Ho[use]	1		
Plow Ditto Planns.	28	29	
Broke Ditto, not worked		5	
Unbroke Do. ove[r] 4 yr. old		13	
Ditto 3 yrs.		5	
Ditto 2 yrs.		3	
Ditto 1		8	
Ditto Colts		5	68
Unbroke Horses 4 & upwds.		3	
Ditto Ditto 3 yrs		6	
Ditto Do. 2 Ditto		4	
Ditto Do. 1 Ditto		4	
Ditto Do. Spring Colts		6	23
In all			130

Note, In the above Acct., are included 2 English Mares and their Colts—the one a Horse, and the other a Mare which by being at a Meadow had not been included in any of the foregoing lists.

Of the above Mares 16 may go to Magnolio and 33 to the Jack Ass if he should arrive safe, and both of them be in order at the proper Season for covering.

Cattle

Bulls	aged	2	
	2 yrs. old	2	
	1 yr. old	2	6
Draught Oxen			26
Steers—full grown		35	
4 yrs. old		4	
3 yrs. old		10	
2 yrs. old		14	
1 yr. old		12	
Calves		27	102
Cows			101
Heifers	6 yrs. old	6	
	4 yrs. old	6	
	3 yrs. Do.	20	
	2 yrs. Do.	19	
	1 yr. Do.	10	
Calves		31	92
			327
Beeves fatting			9
		In all	336

Sheep

Rams		19
Ewes		167
Lambs		15
Weathers	59	
Ditto—fatting	23	82
	In all	283

Friday 25th. Thermometer at 50 in the Morng. [ ] at Noon and [ ] at Night.

Wind Westerly & cooler than it had been the two days preceeding. About Noon a black Cloud arose to the Westward out of which came a mixture of Snow and Rain—this disappearing the Sun shone but the day upon the whole was variable & unpleast.

Set out after breakfast, accompanied by Mr. G. Washington, to make Mr. Mason at Colchester a Visit, but hearing on the road that he had removed from thence I turned into Gunston Hall where we dined and returned in the Evening & found Colo. Henry Lee & his Lady here.

Mr. Shaw returned, having removed George & Lawe. Washington to the Alexandria Academy & fixed them at the Widow Dades.

Mrs. Dade was probably Parthenia Alexander Massey Dade, widow of Townshend Dade (d.1781), and the aunt of GW's neighbor, Robert Alexander. GW's two nephews boarded at Mrs. Dade's house in Alexandria until Jan. 1787, when they were moved to the home of Samuel Hanson of Samuel (LEDGER B, 206, 229). Hanson had difficulties with the boys and eventually they were removed to the care of GW's old friend, Dr. Craik (LEDGER B, 301; GW to Hanson, 5 May 1788, GW to George Steptoe Washington, 23 Mar. 1789, DLC:GW).

Saturday 26th. Thermometer at 44 in the Morning—51 at Noon and 50 at Night.

Wind Westerly and rather Cool in the Morning but less of it & warmer afterwards. Day variable—Clouds & sunshine.

Colo. Lee & his Lady went away after breakfast—crossing to Maryland on their Way home.

Sunday 27th. Thermometer at 46 in the Morng. 52 at Noon and 50 at Night.

Very little wind all day but smoaky with some Clouds and rather chilly.

General Lincoln and Colo. Henley Dined here & returned in the Afternoon.

Monday 28th. Thermometer at 46 in the Morning—50 at Noon and [ ] at Night.

Thick Smoak and Clouds in the morning & great appearances of Snow until one Oclock, when the Sun came out and was More pleasant but cold notwithstanding.

Went with G. Washington to dine with Colo. Lyles in Alexandria. Returned in the evening.

Tuesday 29th. Thermometer at 44 in the Morning—54 at Noon and 54 at Night.

A large hoar frost followed by Southerly Wind and some Clouds—but upon the whole tolerably clear & pleasant.

Sent my Boat to Alexandria for a Hhd. of Common Rum and some Articles brought from Boston for me by General Lincoln. Majr. G. Washington went up to receive them.

George Mason of Lexington, eldest son of George Mason of Gunston Hall. (Board of Regents of Gunston Hall)

Went out after Breakfast with my hounds from France, & two which were lent me, yesterday, by young Mr. Mason. Found a Fox which was run tolerably well by two of the Frh. Bitches & one of Mason's Dogs. The other French Dogs shewed but little disposition to follow and with the second Dog of Mason's got upon another Fox which was followed slow and indifferently by some & not at all by the rest until the sent became so cold that it cd. not be followed at all.

ARTICLES BROUGHT FROM BOSTON: Among the items received on this day were eight boxes of "Spermacita Candles" and "68 lbs. New England Cheese" (LEDGER B, 205). YOUNG MR. MASON: GW probably means George Mason, Jr., oldest son of George Mason of Gunston Hall. He and his new wife, Elizabeth Mary Ann Barnes Hooe Mason, lived at Lexington, a plantation on Dogues Neck given him by his father (COPELAND, 238).

Wednesday 30th. Thermometer at 45 in the Morning—52 at Noon and 55 at Night.

Morning very thick with Clouds & Smoak. About 9 Oclock it began to snow very moderately, which neither continued long—nor lay on the ground. At one the Sun came out, and the afternoon became clear & pleasant, the Wind, though not much of it, being Southerly all day.

On the Wheat which was given to me by Colo. Spaight from the Cape of Good hope, and which having been sowed forward had become very forward—full half leg high—and jointed, I determined to try an experiment and accordingly on three Rows next the fencing on the East side the Inclosure I cut it within 4 Inches of the ground just above the Crown of the plant from whence the Shutes had issued. The remainder I suffered to remain in its exuberent state to try the difference.

December

Thursday 1st. Thermometer at [ ] in the Morning—[ ] at Noon and 52 at Night.

White frost, and clear morning—very little wind all day, and that Southerly.

Took the Hounds out before Sun rise and about 8 Oclock, after being upon several drags, or the same drag several times, put up a Fox which the Dogs run very indifferently—being very much dispersed and often at Cold Hunting until about 12 or between that and one when the Scent had got so cold that they could follow it no longer. 3 or 4 of the French Hds. discovered no greater disposition for Hunting today than they did on tuesday last.

Miss Kitty Washington went from this After Breakfast, to Alexandria and Mr. Shaw who with G. Washington went out a Hunting with me meeting her in the Road accompanied her to that place.

In order to try the difference between burning Spermaciti and Tallow Candles—I took one of each—

The 1st. weighing . . . 3 oz. 10 p[enny] w[eight] 6 g[rams]
2 Ditto 5 2

and lighted them at the same instant. The first burnt 8 hours and 21 Minutes; when, of the latter, their remained 14 penny weight; which continued to burn one hour and a quarter longer, making in all 9 hours & 36 Minutes. By which it appears (as both burnt without flairing) that, estimating Spirmaciti Candles at 3/. pr. lb. & Tallow Candles at 1/. pr. lb. the former is dearer than the latter as 30 is to nearly 13. In other words more than 2¼ dearer.

Friday 2d. Thermometer at [ ] in the morning—56 at Noon and 56 at Night.

Colo. & Mrs. Macarty came here to Dinner—as did Colonels Fitzgerald and Gilpin and Mr. Chas. Lee & Doctr. Baker.

Wind Southerly all day—clear & pleasant.

Dr. Baker is probably Dr. William Baker of Alexandria.

Saturday 3d. Thermometer at 50 in the Morning—56 at Noon and 61 at Night.

The day very pleasant until the afternoon, when it began to lower. The Wind in the morning was Westerly, & in the Evening Easterly but not much of it.

Employed all day at my writing Table on business of the Potomack Company. Brot. 2 Hounds fm. Colo. McCarty.

George Washington & wife went up to Abingdon after Breakfast.

Doctr. Brown dined here and went away afterwards.

Finished covering my Ice House with dirt, & sodding of it.

Sunday 4th. Thermometer at 53 in the Morng. 56 at Noon and 59 at Night.

A thick fog, or rather mist in the morning, without any Wind until about 10 Oclock when it turned to a slow rain—which ceased about Noon and assumed the appearance of fair Weather —but about 4 Oclk. it began to drip again.

Last Night Jno. Alton, an Overseer of mine in the Neck—an old & faithful Servant who had lived with me 30 odd years died of an imposthume in his thigh after lingering for more than 4 Months with it, and being reduced to a mere skeleton—and this evening the wife of Thos. Bishop, another old Servant who had lived with me an equal number of years also died.

Thomas Bishop's wife, Susanna, had served as midwife for slaves and servants on the Mount Vernon plantations.

Monday 5th. Thermometer at [ ] in the Morning—58 at Noon & 58 at Night.

Lowering all day—with very little wind and that Northerly.

It being a good scenting morning I went out with the Hounds (carrying the two had from Colo. McCarty). Run at different two foxes but caught neither. My French Hounds performed better to day; and have afforded hopes of their performing well, when they come to be a little more used to Hunting, and understand more fully the kind of game they are intended to run.

When I returned home, wch. was not until past three Oclock found a Doctr. Baynham here—recommended to me by Colo. Fairfax of England.

George Washington and his Wife returned in the Evening from Abingdon.

My Overseer Fairfax also returned this Evening with Jack Ass, and his Keeper, a Spaniard from Boston.

William Baynham (1749–1814), from Caroline County, Va., was introduced by George W. Fairfax as "a young Gent. of a most worthy character, held in the highest Esteem by all that know him, in Scotland, where he lived many years, prosecuting his Studies in Surgery, also in London, where I understand he was in considerable practice sometime past" (Fairfax to GW, 23 June 1785, DLC:GW). Baynham was returning to his native country after 16 years abroad. He settled in Essex County, where he practiced surgery and medicine, enjoying a national reputation as one of the ablest surgeons in the United States.

Tuesday 6th. Thermometer at 52 in the morng. 57 at Noon and 59 at Night.

Morning clear & very pleasant with but little wind. Before Noon it sprang up from the Westward and afterwards became cloudy but the Sun set clear.

Finished getting in the Woods the Posts & railing for the fencing of my paddock.

Made another experiment of the difference in expence between burning Spirmaciti & Tallow Candles which stand thus:

A Tallow Candle weighing 3 oz. 11 py. Wt. burned 5 Hrs. 48 M.

A Spirma Citi Do. weighing 3 oz. 9 P.W. 18 grms. burned 7 Hrs. & 28 M.

Which is an hour and 40 mints. longer than the Tallow Candle & of which when the latter was burnd out there remained 14 penny Wt. 6 grs. Hence, reckoning as in the former instance Tallow at 1/. pr. lb. & Spirma Citi at 3/. pr. lb. the latter is dearer than the former as 31½ is to ten & an half or [ ]

Wednesday 7th. Thermometer at 52 in the Morning & 59 at Noon—but removing it afterwards out of the room where the fire was, into the East Entry leading in to my Study, this circumstance with the encrease of the cold fell the Mercury to 42.

Morning clear calm & pleast.; but the wind coming out violently from the No. West about half after eight Oclock, it turned cold & uncomfortable.

Doctr. Baynham went away after breakfast.

Sent Mr. Shaw to Alexandria, to discharge Lieutt. Governor Cushings draft on me for 300 Silver Dollars in favor of Mr. [ ] the Order being in the hands of Mr. Tayler—and to do other business.

Took away the supports to the Arch over my Ice house.

CUSHINGS DRAFT: This was for money that Gov. Thomas Cushing had expended for the care of the Spanish jackass after its arrival in Boston and before GW's overseer arrived to take it to Mount Vernon (see entry for 26 Oct. 1785). Cushing wrote that he had "at present taken the liberty to draw a sett of bills of exchange dated November 16th. 1785 for the sum of three hundred dollars in favour of Messrs. Isaac & William Smith merchants of this Town or their order, payable at sight" (Thomas Cushing to GW, 16 Nov. 1785, DLC:GW).

MR. TAYLER: probably Jesse Taylor, Sr., a Belfast merchant who immigrated to America in 1779. He had a store in Alexandria which dealt in imported goods (*Va. Journal,* 3 June 1784; BROCKETT, 95).

Thursday 8th. Thermometer at 30 in the Morning–38 at Noon and [ ] at Night.

Wind to the Eastward of North, in the Morning, and Cold–ground hard frozen. Afterwards it died away in a great Measure and Shifted more to the westward backing.

Finished removing the Earth for covering of, and the way in to my Ice House. And again set the People to taking up & planting small Pines in the Wilderness on the Right of the lawn.

Also sent to Colo. Masons Quarter, and got young Crab trees for the Shrubberies–but not getting them home in time to plant, the Roots were buried until they could be planted in the places designed for them to morrow or &ca.

Captn. Sullivan, of a Ship at Alexandria, agreeably to my request, came here to dinner, to interpret between me and the Spaniard who had the care of the Jack Ass sent me. My questions, & his Answers respecting the Jack, are committed to writing. Captn. Sullivan returned after dinner & Captn. Fairley of New York came here in the afternoon.

Capt. Giles Sullivan's ship *Union* was lying in Alexandria harbor awaiting a cargo of tobacco for L'Orient (*Va. Journal,* 24 Nov. 1785). Sullivan was connected with the firm of Hooe & Harrison in Alexandria.

CAPTN. FAIRLEY: James Fairlie (d. 1830), a major and aide-de-camp to Baron von Steuben during the Revolution, had brought GW letters from Alexander Hamilton (25 Nov. 1785, DLC:GW) and Henry Knox (22 Nov. 1785, DLC: GW). Hamilton requested GW's help in getting financial relief through Congress for Steuben, whose affairs were in serious difficulties. He also, as did Knox, informed GW of problems in getting the state chapters of the Society of the Cincinnati to accept the recommendations of the general meeting held at Philadelphia on 12 May 1784. These recommendations had been designed to quiet the widespread fear and criticism of the society.

Friday 9th. Thermometer at 36 in the Morning–39 at Noon and [ ] at Night.

Not much wind–thick and Misting all day. Towards Night it began to rain fast & continued to do so until day.

Planted the Crab trees which were brought home yesterday and more young pines.

Saturday 10th. Thermometer at 36 in the Morning—38 at Noon and 40 at Night.

Little or no wind all day but thick and Mizling as yesterday till Night when it began to rain fast again.

Opened a drain into the Shoar that goes from the Cellers, to receive the water from the Gutters, and spout from the House top that it may be carried of under ground.

Flooring the Ice House. Preparing with the Negros for Killing Hogs on Monday.

SHOAR: shore, an open sewer or drainage ditch.

Sunday 11th. Thermometer at 38 in the Morng. 50 at Noon and 58 at Night.

A heavy mist all day with little or no wind. At or before dusk it began to rain fast and about 9 at Night it cleared with a puff of Wind from the Southward and the Moon & Stars appeared.

Mr. Wilson, Mr. Sanderson and a Mr. Hugh Mitchel dined here and went away in the afternoon.

Hugh Mitchell is probably a member of the large Mitchell family of Maryland, whose members were intermarried with the Hansons and Jenifers. A Hugh Mitchell was listed as a juror in Fairfax Court in 1786 (Fairfax County Order Book, 1783–88, 277, Vi Microfilm). In 1790 there was a Hugh Mitchel living in Anne Arundel County, Md. (HEADS OF FAMILIES, MD., 12).

Monday 12th. Thermometer at [ ] in the Morning—[ ] at Noon and 58 at Night.

Morning cloudy and soft without any wind. In the Evening it began to Mizzle, and after dark to rain fast and continued to do so until I went to bed and how much longer I know not.

Majr. Farlie went away before breakfast, with 251 Diplomas which I had signed for the Members of the Cincinnati of the State of New York, at the request of General McDougall Presedent of that Society.

After an early breakfast George Washington, Mr. Shaw & my self went into the woods back of Muddy hole Plantation a hunting and were joined by Mr. Lund Washington and Mr. William Peake. About half after ten Oclock (being first plagued with the Dogs running Hogs) We found a fox near Colo. Masons Plantation on little Hunting Creek (West fork) having followed on his

"The Death of the Fox," one of a series of hunting prints which hung at Mount Vernon during Washington's lifetime. (Mount Vernon Ladies' Association of the Union)

Drag more than half a Mile; and run him with Eight Dogs (the other 4 getting, as was supposed, after a second Fox) close and well for an hour—When the Dogs came to a fault, and to cold Hunting until 20 Minutes after 12 When being joined by the missing Dogs they put him up a fresh and in about 50 Minutes killed [him] up in an open field of Colo. Mason's—every rider & every Dog being present at the death.

Two Hounds which were lent, and sent to me yesterday by Mr. Chichester—viz.—a Dog named Rattler, & a Bitch named Juno—behaved very well. My French Dogs also come on—all, except the Bitch which raized Puppies, running constantly whilst the Scent was hot.

Mr. Peak & Lund Washington came home to dinner with us.

Alexander McDougall (1732–1786), a Scottish emigrant, was a prosperous New York merchant. He had been a leading radical in New York before the Revolution, and became a brigadier and major general in the Continental Army. He served in the Continental Congress in 1781–82, 1784–85 and was president of the New York chapter of the Society of the Cincinnati from its organization until his death.

Tuesday 13th. Thermometer at [ ] in the Morng. 47 at Noon and [ ] at Night.

Wind Westerly, fresh, & air turning cold. Flying Clouds all day, but clear at Night, and still.

Finished killing my Hogs—The Number & weight of which are as follow.

	No.	Wt.
River Plantn.	44	6814
Dogue run Do.	28	4003
Muddy hole Do.	30	3638
Ferry—Do.	26	2930
Total	128	17385

Out of the above Thos. Bishop & Thos. Green are each to have 500. Hezekiah Fairfax has had 480 & Morris 416 and Davy 414—leaving for family use 15075 lbs. which with 4 Hogs killed for early Bacon (in October) Weighing 810 lbs. make in all 15,885 lbs. laid up for the consumption of my Table—use of my People—and the poor who are distressed for it.

Mr. Baldwin, formerly a Chaplain in the Army from Connecticut—now a Lawyer in the state of Georgia called here on his way to the last but would not stay [to] dinner.

A Mr. Douglas came here to rent my Land on Difficult run for which I asked him £50 pr. Ann. and to which he is to give an Answer after consulting his Brothers in Alexanda.

Thomas Green, overseer of the plantation carpenters, was working at Mount Vernon as a joiner by Jan. 1783 and stayed until late 1793. He was a drunken incompetent, and although GW often threatened to fire him, his compassion for the man's family restrained him. Green finally ran away or was fired and left his wife Sarah (Sally), daughter of GW's old servant, Thomas Bishop, and several small children destitute (LEDGER B, 170, 209, 239, 243, 252, 279, 350; THANE, 246, 328–30).

Morris and Davy, two of GW's slaves, were at this time in charge of Dogue Run and Muddy Hole farms, respectively.

Abraham Baldwin (1754–1807) was a tutor at Yale during the early years of the Revolution and then served as chaplain of the 2nd Connecticut Regiment. He later studied law and in 1784 settled in Georgia where he became a member of the Georgia Commons House of Assembly. He was influential in setting up an educational system in Georgia and was the first president of Franklin College (later the University of Georgia). Baldwin was a member of the Continental Congress 1785, 1787–88, and of the Federal

Convention in 1787. He was in the United States House of Representatives 1789–99 and the United States Senate 1799–1807. He was undoubtedly on his way home from the Continental Congress at this time.

MR. DOUGLAS: This may have been Hugh Douglass (Douglas) of Garrallan in Loudoun County (WISE, 292–96). GW's 300-acre tract on Difficult Run in Loudoun County was of value chiefly for its location at Difficult Bridge on the road from Alexandria to Leesburg and Winchester (WRITINGS, 37:295).

Wednesday 14th. Thermometer at 36 in the Morng. [ ] at Noon and 42 at Night.

Morning and day clear & pleasant—wind at So. East. Ground a little froze in the Morning.

Mr. George Washington and his Wife set off to visit her friends in New Kent &ca.—Mr. Bassetts Carriage & Horses having come up for them on Sunday Night last.

Rid to the Ferry Plantn. The Mill, and Dogue run Plantation and went & came by the place (in front of the Ho[use]) where Muddy hole [people] were at Work.

Thursday 15th. Thermometer at 40 in the Morng. 45 at Noon and [ ] at Night.

Moderate & clear all the fore part of the day with the Wind at So. East, but not fresh. In the Afternoon it began to lower—at Dusk turned very cloudy and in the Night set in to a constant rain.

Mr. Shaw went up to Alexandria, after dinner, to a Ball I presume. And in the Evening Joseph Winzor & Willm. Kirchwall 2 of my tenants from Frederick came in & stayed all Night.

TENANTS FROM FREDERICK: GW had bought two lots totaling about 570 acres at George Mercer's 1774 sale of a 6,500-acre tract in Frederick County. The land, now in Clarke County, was on the Shenandoah River near the present town of Berryville. Late in 1784 Joseph Winzor of Maryland bargained with Edward Snickers, who was acting as GW's agent in the matter, for a 14-year lease on 172 acres of the land. Although GW preferred a shorter lease, he honored Snickers's agreement with Winzor for a lease commencing 1 Jan. 1785 and ending 31 Dec. 1798, at a rent of £17 4s. per year. William Kirchwall's (Kercheval) lease for 172 acres was for 13 years, commencing 1 Jan. 1786 and ending 31 Dec. 1798 at a rental of £17 6s. per year. Both men had their rent increased slightly after the 1789 resurvey, when their farms were discovered to total 174½ acres each (CHAPPELEAR [3], 33–36; GW to Battaile Muse, 28 July 1785, DLC:GW; GW's rental accounts, 1788–90 and 1791, ViMtV).

Friday 16th. Thermometer at 50 in the Morng. 56 at Noon and 56 at Night.

Rainy Morning and an Easterly wind, but not much of it.

Drizzling all day and towards Night it began to rain again and threatned a wet Night. Very light wind all day.

Before dinner Joseph Hickman, another of my Tenants from Frederick came in, to whom and those that came yesterday and [ ] Williams, I passed Leases for the Land on which they live. All went away after it.

Mr. Shaw returned before dinner from Alexandria.

Joseph Hickman and John Williams seem to have been living on GW's Frederick lands before the leases were made out. Both were given 14-year leases, retroactive from 1 Jan. 1785 to 31 Dec. 1798. Hickman's tenement was 116 acres, for which he paid £11 12s. per year. Williams leased 100 acres for £10. GW wrote his rental agent, Battaile Muse, on this day, instructing Muse to use his own judgment in making decisions about whether the tenants were complying with the terms of the leases. Since Williams did not come to Mount Vernon on this day, GW sent his lease to Muse for completion. GW also requested that Muse send him a list of his tenants, with an account of the lots they leased, the rents due, and the amounts paid (GW to Muse, 28 July and 16 Dec. 1785, DLC:GW; CHAPPELEAR [3], 33–36; GW's rental accounts, 1788–90 and 1791, ViMtV).

Saturday 17th. Thermometer at 56 in the Morng. [ ] at Noon and [ ] at Night.

Rainy Morning, wind though not fresh at No. West which afterwards more to the No. & East & continued raining off & on all day.

Went to Alexandria to meet the Trustees of the Academy in that place and offered to vest in the hands of the said Trustees, when they are permanently established by Charter, the Sum of One thousand pounds, the Interest of which only, to be applied towards the establishment of a charity School for the education of Orphan and other poor Children—which offer was accepted. Returned again in the Evening—Roads remarkably wet & bad.

GW wrote the trustees: "It is not in my power at this time to advance the above sum; but that a measure which may be productive of good may not be delayed—I will until my death, or until it shall be more convenient for my Estate to advance the principal, pay the interest thereof (to wit, Fifty pounds) annually" (GW to Trustees of the Alexandria Academy, 17 Dec. 1785, DLC:GW). In his will, GW left 20 shares of stock in the Bank of Alexandria, valued at $4,000, to fulfill this promise. The charity school was incorporated as an integral part of the academy, to be governed by the same board of trustees. In 1786 there were 20 charity children attending the school.

Sunday 18th. Thermometer at 44 in the Morning—54 at Noon and 52 at Night.

Morning perfectly clear & pleasant, with but little wind and continued so through the day. Serene moderate and pleasant.

Monday 19th. Thermometer at 42 in the Morng. 56 at Noon and 52 at Night.

Calm and pleasant all day, especially in the Morning. Towards evening the wind, though very little of it, came from the Eastward & the weather lowered.

Rid to the Mill, and to Dogue run Plantation. Took the Hounds with me, and in the Pincushion found a fox, which the Dogs run very well for an hour—after which, coming to a fault—they took (as I presume) the heel, & in Muddy hole found a fresh Fox, which was only run by part of the Dogs. The others did not seem inclined to hunt.

Davy a Mulatto Man who has for many years looked after my Muddy hole Plantation, went into the Neck to take cha[rge] of the River Plantation in the room of Jno. Alton deceased. And Will (Son of Doll) was sent to Muddy hole as an Overseer in his place.

Both my Mills stopped & repairing.

THE PINCUSHION: The Devil's Pincushion was a large rock near the Alexandria-Colchester road about halfway between Dogue Run and Little Hunting Creek. The land around the rock was called the Pincushion (MUIR, 51–52).

Tuesday 20th. Thermometer at 42 in the Morng. 47 at Night and 45 at Noon.

Morning tolerably clear; but a red sky at the place of the Suns rising (which is an indication of dirty weather) and the wind (tho not fresh) at No. East. The day continued tolerably clear and pleasant, until the Evening when it began to lower.

Dispatched at his own reqt. the Spaniard who had the cha[rge] of my Jack from Spain. Sent him with Mr. Shaw to Alexandria to go in the Stage to New York.

Brought some Carts and Cutters from my Plantations to assist in laying in a Stock of Fire wood for Christmas.

Mr. Shaw returned in the evening accompanied by my Nephew Ferdinando Washington.

THE SPANIARD: Pedro Tellez, who had accompanied the Spanish jackass to Mount Vernon (see entry for 26 Oct. 1785), had asked to return to Spain by way of New York, where he would see the Spanish minister, Don Diego de Gardoqui. He refused any payment from GW, asserting that he was being paid by the king, but GW did prevail upon him to take £21 "as an acknowledgment of the obligation I am under to him, for his care of the animal on which I set the highest value" (GW to Francisco Rendon, 19 Dec. 1785, DLC:GW; LEDGER B, 205). GW also gave the Spaniard two certificates. One, for the benefit of the king, acknowledged Tellez's care and attention to the animal; the other, addressed to the public at large, identified Tellez and solicited aid in his behalf: "Not being able to speak any other language than that of his native tongue, it is requested as a favor of the good people on the road to assist & direct him properly" (19 Dec. 1785, DLC:GW).

Ferdinand, or Ferdinando, Washington (1767–1788) was the oldest son of GW's brother Samuel and Anne Steptoe Washington. In 1783 GW had written his brother John Augustine about the possibility of a berth in the navy or on a merchant ship for their nephew but nothing seems to have come of this inquiry. Ferdinand, by extravagance and bad conduct, incurred GW's displeasure, and GW later refused to assist in settling the young man's estate (GW to Robert Chambers, 28 Jan. 1789, DLC:GW).

Wednesday 21st. Thermometer at 44 in the Morning—44 at Noon and 46 at Night.

Lowering all day with but little Wind and that Easterly.

Mr. Danl. Dulany (son of Danl.) Mr. Benja. Dulany, Messrs. Saml. & Thos. Hanson, Mr. Philp. Alexander, and a Mr. Mounsher came here to Dinner and Stayed all Night.

Finished measuring my Corn at the several Plantations, which stand thus.

	Barrels	
River Plantation viz.		
Large end of Corn Ho[use]	203	
Small end of Ditto.	135	
Fatting Hogs have eat	44	
For Mrs. Alton	6	
		388
Muddy hole Plantn. viz.		
In the Corn House	112	
Given to the fattg. Hogs	28	
		140
Dogue Run Plantn. viz.		
In Corn House	85	
Given to the Hogs	30	
		75
Ferry Plantation—viz.		
In the Corn House	85	
Fatting Hogs	28	
Overseers Share	14	
		127
Total		730

Deduct		
Corn already expd. on Hogs	130	
Overseers Shares	20	
		150
Remaining for all my purps., only		580

Daniel Dulany, Jr. (1750–1824), had come back to America to try to settle problems arising from the confiscation of his family's estates during the Revolution. He sailed for England a few months later, never to return to his native land.

This Alexander was either Philip Alexander (died c.1790), son of Gerard Alexander (d. 1761), of the "Robert" Alexanders, or Philip Alexander (b. 1742), son of Philip Alexander of the "Philip" branch. The second Philip served Fairfax County on the committee of safety (1774) and in the House of Delegates (1777).

[Thursday 22d.] Went a Fox hunting with the Gentlemen who came here yesterday–together with Ferdinando Washington and Mr. Shaw, after a very early breakfast. Found a Fox just back of Muddy hole Plantation and after a Chase of an hour and a quarter with my Dogs, & eight couple of Doctor Smiths (brought by Mr. Phil. Alexander) we put him into a hollow tree, in which we fastned him, and in the Pincushion put up another Fox which in an hour & 13 Minutes was killed. We then after allowing the Fox in the hole half an hour put the Dogs upon his Tracks & in half a Mile he took to another hollow tree and was again put out of it but he did not go 600 yards before he had recourse to the same shift. Finding therefore that he was a conquered Fox we took the Dogs off and all came home to Dinner except Mr. Danl. Dulany who left us in the Field after the first Fox was Treed. Lund Washington came home with us to dinner.

Doctr. Brown who had been sent for to Philip Bateman came to Dinner and returned afterwards as did all the Gentlemen except the two Mr. Hansons and Mr. Alexander.

The Morning of this day indeed all the forenoon was very lowering but the Evening was clear & very pleasant.

Lund Washington by this time was winding up his long tenure as manager at Mount Vernon. He had told GW in November that he wished to leave his employment as soon as convenient, and by 20 Dec., GW had made definite arrangements for the change. "Having come to a fixed determination . . . to attend to the business of my plantations; and having enquired of Geo: [Augustine] Washington how far it would be agreeable to him & his wife to make this place a permanent residence, (for before it was only considered as their temporary abode, until some plan could be settled for them) & finding it to comport with their inclinations, I now inform you that it will be in my power to comply with your wishes with less inconvenience than appeared when you first proposed to leave my employment" (DLC:GW). GW did request that Lund continue to help with the mill and some business matters until George Augustine Washington became familiar with these. "Nothing else occurs to me at this time in which it is essential to give you any trouble after the present year; for if I should not be able to visit the plantations as often as I could wish . . . I am resolved that an account of the stock & every occurence that happens in the course of the week shall be minutely detailed to me every saturday. Matters cannot go much out of sorts in that time without a seasonable remedy" (GW to Lund Washington, 20 Nov. and 20 Dec. 1785, DLC:GW).

Friday 23d. Thermometer at [ ] in the Morng. 44 at Noon and 42 at Night.

Morning cloudy, with the Wind at West; which shifting to the No. Et. produced strong, and encreasing appearances of falling weather before the Evening.

Went out with the two Mr. Hansons & Mr. Alexander, when they set out on their return after breakfast, with the Dogs; just to try if we could touch on a Fox as we went along the Road–they homewards and I to my Plantation in the Neck. This we did, but the Scent being Cold, and seeing no great prospect of making it out the Dogs were taken off and the Gentlemen Went home and I to Muddy hole Plantation instead of the Neck–it being too late to go to, and return from the former before Dinner.

Saturday 24th. Thermometer at 38 in the Morng. 34 at Night and 36 at Noon.

Wind at No. East with rain in the Morning (a good deal of wch. appeared to have fallen in the Night). About 10 Oclock it began to Snow & continued to do so untill about 2 Oclock when it ceased–just covering the ground the Snow being wet.

Sunday 25th. Thermometer at 34 in the Morng. 42 at Noon and 42 at Night.

Morning perfectly clear and fine without Wind. About 9 Oclock it sprung up from the Southward and blew fresh with various appearances of weather sometimes much like rain & then clearing. At Night the Wind Shifted to the Westward and before Morning got to No. West blowing hard all the while.

Count Castiglioni, Colo. Ball, and Mr. Willm. Hunter came here to dinner–the last of whom returned to Alexandria afterwards.

Count Luigi Castiglioni (1757–1832) of Milan, a student of natural sciences, arrived in America in May 1785 and spent two years traveling throughout the states, studying various aspects of American life, especially the political institutions and the flora and fauna. He was a great admirer of GW and an impartial observer of American life. His *Viaggio negli Stati Uniti dell' America Settentrionale* was published in Milan in 1790.

Burgess Ball (1749–1800), formerly of Lancaster County, served in various Virginia regiments throughout most of the Revolution, retiring in 1781 as a lieutenant colonel. He was at this time married to Frances Washington (1763–1815), sister of George Augustine Washington, and was living in Spotsylvania County.

Monday 26th. Thermometer at 32 in the Morning—40 at Noon and 38 at Night.

Clear and cold in the Morning with the wind high at No. West which moderated a little towards Night.

Tuesday 27th. Thermometer at 38 in the Morning—44 at Noon and [ ] at Night.

Clear with the wind very high from the Southward until the Evening when it shifted to the Westward & blew equally hard but did not get to be very cold.

Wednesday 28th. Thermometer at 36 in the Morning—38 at Noon and [ ] at Night.

Colo. Ball went away yesterday, after breakfast—tho' it was unnoticed in the occurrances of the day.

Wind exceedingly high from the No. West & clear.

A Mr. Israel Jenny of Loudoun County came here in the Afternoon, respecting some Land which he has been endeavouring to obtain under an idea of its being waste, but which he finds to be within the lines of my Chattin run tract in Fauquier County, though claimed by Mr. Robert Scott who has put a Tenant upon it of the name of Jesse Hitt, who has now been upon it three years and thereafter to pay Rent.

Mr. Muse my Collector to be written to on this Subject as also concerning my Land in Ashbys Bend part of wch. is claimed by Mr. Landon Carter.

Israel Janney (died c.1823) was a son of Jacob Janney (d. 1786) of Loudoun County. He was interested in agricultural experimentation and was a pioneer in the use of gypsum (plaster of paris) to improve his lands.

GW's Chattins Run tract in Fauquier County was on the eastern slope of the Blue Ridge near Rector Town. The land in question amounted to 170–80 acres, and the suit brought against GW by Robert Scott ran on for years and was still unsettled in 1791. For further details of the dispute, see GW to Battaile Muse, 5 Jan. and 4 Feb. 1786, Muse to GW, 7 Feb., 21 Mar. 1789,

22 Aug. 1791, DLC:GW. GW's Ashby's Bent land, amounting to approximately 2,500 acres, was located in both Fauquier and Loudoun counties on the eastern slopes of the Blue Ridge. Both this and the Chattins Run land was subdivided into small farms, or tenements, of about 100–200 acres each, which were rented out for periods of time varying from ten years to three lives.

It is uncertain which of the three Landon Carters then living in Virginia claimed the Ashby's Bent land.

Thursday 29th. Thermometer at 29 in the Morning–[ ] at Noon and 40 at Night.

Morning clear with very little wind and that from the South. Pleasand all day until the evening when it began to lower and about eight at Night set in to raining with a strong Southerly wind wch. continued through the Night.

Count Castiglioni went away after breakfast, on his tour to the Southward.

Mr. Jenny also left this at the same time.

After which I went to my Dogue run Plantation to measure, with a view to new model, the Fields at that place. Did not return until dark nor finish my Survey.

Mr. Shaw went to Alexandria to the Assembly.

Friday 30th. Thermometer at 46 in the [morning]–[ ] at Noon and [ ] at Night.

A good deal of rain fell in the Night which ceased about day break but the Wind from the Southward continued to blow very hard all day with flying Clouds.

Went to Dogue run again to compleat my Surveys of the Fields which I did about 2 Oclock and upon my r[e]turn

Found Miss Sally Ramsay Miss Kitty Washington–Mr. Porter and Doctr. Craik Junr. here.

Mr. Shaw also returned from Alexandria before Dinner.

Saturday 31st. Thermometer at [ ] in the Morning–[ ] at Noon and 37 at Night.

A Raw Wind from the Eastwd. blew in the forenoon. Afternoon Calm, but chilly with appearances now & then of a change in the weather.

Rid to my Plantations in the Neck Muddy hole, and Ferry. George Steptoe Washington came here to dinner and after it went away the Company that came yesterday.

Landed 230 Bushels of Oats today from an Eastern shore Vessel and by her had brought from Alexandria the Pictures drawn by Mr. Pine of Fanny Bassett now Washington and the young Custis.

BUSHELS OF OATS: GW's Indian corn crop for 1785 was very poor and did "not amount to one third of what I made last year; which is insufficient to feed my negroes, much more to afford support for my Horses" (GW to David Stuart, 24 Dec. 1785, DLC:GW). He was forced to buy grain to supplement his own supply.

Visitors and Planting

1786

January 1786

Sunday 1st. Thermometer at 36 in the Morng. [ ] at Noon and [ ] at Night.

Lowering day, with but little Wind, and that Easterly.

Lund Washington and Wife dined here & returned in the Afternoon.

Mr. Shaw went up to Alexandria and stayed all Night.

Monday 2d. Thermometer at 34 in the Morng. 35 at Noon and 35 at Night.

Heavy lowering Morning with the wind at East. About 9 Oclock it began to rain and continued to do so, slowly, all day.

Immediately after an early breakfast I went out with the Hounds but returned as soon as it began to rain, without touching upon the drag of a Fox.

Mr. Shaw returned from Alexandria this Morning before Breakt.

Tuesday 3d. Thermometer at 39 in the Morning–46 at Noon and 42 at Night.

Clear and pleasant morning without wind at Sun rising but it soon sprung up from the Southwesterly quarter and veering more to the westward blew hard until the evening when it again turned calm & very pleasant.

Wednesday 4th. Thermometer at 35 in the Morning–42 at Noon and 40 at Night.

Morning calm and clear with very little wind all day.

After breakfast I rid by the places where my Muddy hole & Ferry people were clearing–thence to the Mill and Dogue run Plantations and having the Hounds with me in passing from the latter towards Muddy hole Plantation I found a Fox which after dragging him some distance and running him hard for near an hour was killed by the cross road in front of the House.

Having provided cutting Knives, and made the Boxes at my own Shop, I directed my Overseers at the several Plantations at which I had been to cut Straw and mix three 4ths. of it with one fourth Bran (from my Mill) to feed their out lying Horses—whilst their work Horses is also to be fed with this and Oats mixed.

I also directed that my Chariot Horses and all others about my home Ho[use] except the Stud horse and three horses which will be frequently rid a hunting to be fed with Bran & chopped Hay

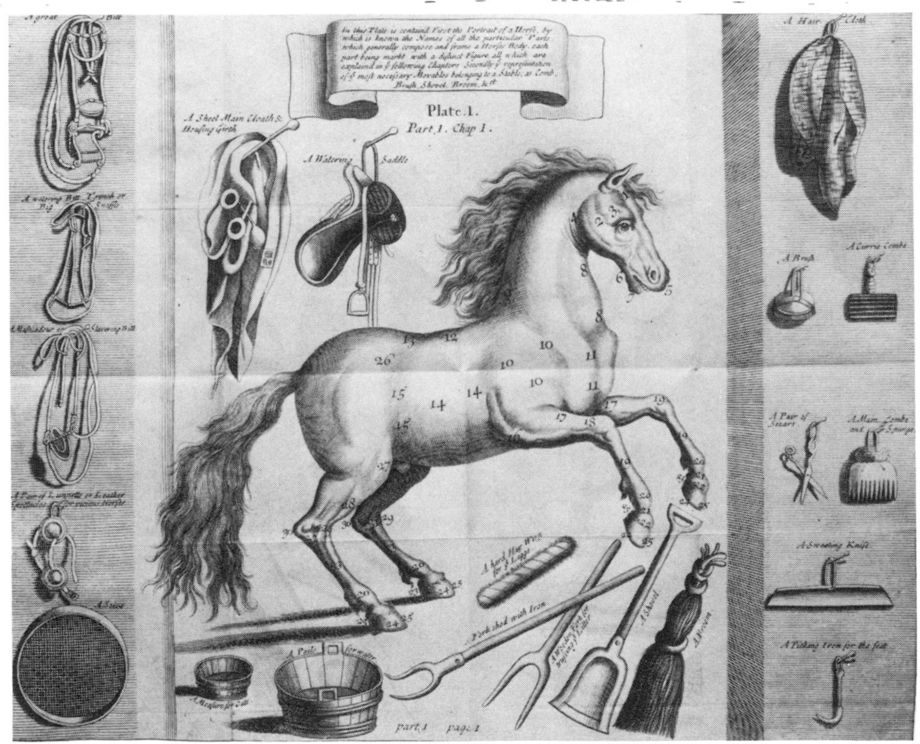

Plate from Washington's copy of Jacques de Solleysell's *Compleat Horseman,* London, 1729. (Boston Athenaeum)

in the above proportion and that my waggon & Cart Horses should be fed with chopped Rye & chopped Hay in the same proportion of one to 4.

Mr. Bushrod Washington and his wife came here in a Chariot 4 Horses & 3 Servants just after we had dined.

Thursday 5th. Thermometer at 33 in the Morning—42 at Noon and 32 at Night.

Morning clear and cold—ground hard froze—as it was yesterday

Morning. Wind at No. West, blowing pretty fresh all day. Went into the Neck.

A Daniel McPherson from Loudoun came here with some money from my Loudoun Tenants—sent by the Widow of Lewis Lamart.

The Cape Wheat which (on the 30th. of November) was cut, not as I thought and had ordered, that is within 4 Inches of the ground; but between 6 and 8 from it; having grown a good deal I ordered (and 6 or 8 days ago tho not noticed before, it was in par[t] done) that it should be again cut. Part of 2 Rows of the No. Et. Corner were, by mistake of orders, cut within 1 or 2 Inches of the ground; so as to shew the Crown of the Wheat quite bear & white. I thereupon stopped the cutting of any more, resolving to attend to the effect of this close shearing, at this season. About 12 feet of these Rows, were all that received the second cutting.

Took an Acct. of the Tools about the home house which are as follow

7 Spades	7 Axes
4 Mattocks	8 Butchrs. Knives
5 Weedg. Hoes	3 Hillg. Do.
1 Cuttg. Knive	1 Hay Ditto

Lewis Lemart (Lamart), GW's rent collector in Loudoun County, had probably died sometime in 1785, and his widow, Anne, sent to Mount Vernon the £27 12s. owed by GW's tenants in that county (LEDGER B, 68).

Friday 6th. Thermometer at 30 in the Morng. 28 at Noon and 30 at Night.

Wind at No. Et. in the Morning, which was Cloudy, with intervals of Snow through the day and very cold. The wind towards Night getting to the No. Westward blew h[ar]d.

My Boat went up with a load of Flour to Alexandria from my Mill for Mr. Hartshorne. A distressing time It is to be feared the people must have had of it & probably would not, after all, reach the Port.

Saturday 7th. Thermometer at 26 in the Morning—34 at Noon and 32 at Night.

Morning clear with the Wind at No. West. Fresh, and Cold, all day. The little Snow which fell yesterday had disappeared except in places where the influence of the Sun could not be felt.

The Boat which was sent off yesterday with flour got no further than Johnsons Ferry & there by neglect suffered to get aground. Sent and ordered it to be got off, and to proceed, or to return, as circumstances might dictate. The last of which was done.

Sunday 8th. Thermometer at 27 in the Morng.—38 at Noon and 35 at Night.

Day clear, with the wind pretty fresh at No. West in the forenoon which moderating as the Sun rose backed to South West and grew calm towards the evening.

Mr. Bushrod Washington and his Wife went away after Breakfast and about 11 Oclock Betcy & Patcy Custis returned to Abingdon in my Chariot—accompanied by their Brother & Sister, Nelly & Washington Custis.

Sent my Boat of this afternoon with the Flour for Alexandria, with which she returned last Night on Acct. of the weather.

Monday 9th. Thermometer at 28 in the Morng. 38 at Noon and [ ] at Night.

Wind Southerly all day. Clear but a chilly air.

Saturday, yesterday, and this day morning, the flats and Creeks were froze, but that on the former dispersed with the tide when the Winds blew. The latter remained.

Sent Mr. Shaw to Alexandria to dispatch my Boat which went up yesterday and to pur⟨cha⟩se & send down a ton of Iron in ⟨it⟩ wch. was accordingly [done]. He and the Boat both, returned at Night.

Rid over my ferry plantation—thence to the Mill, & thence to my Dogue run & Muddy hole Plantations before dinner—as also to the place where my Negro Carpenters were at Work and directed them to get me a stick for a heavy roller, and scantling for Plow stocks—Harrows &ca. &ca.

Tuesday 10th. Thermometer at [ ] in the Morning—[ ] at Noon and 38 at Night.

Wind Southerly all day & at times pretty fresh, and in the forenoon cold—but warmer & much pleasanter afterwards.

Rid to my Plantation in the Neck, and took the hounds with me. About 11 Oclock found a fox in the Pocoson at Sheridens point and after running it very indifferently and treeing it once caught it about one Oclock.

In the evening one William Barber from the lower end of

Fauquier came here to rent some Land I have in that quarter and stayed all Night.

Wednesday 11th. Thermometer at 34 in the morning—36 at Noon and 33 at Night.

Morning very thick and heavy. About 8 Oclock it began to Snow moderately with the Wind at So. Et. and continued to do so until 12.

Agreed to let William Barber have 50 (or more acres of Land if he chooses it) at the rate of Ten pounds pr. Hundred Acres; for the term of fourteen years: and to allow him one year free from Rent in consideration of the improvements he may make.

Sent Mr. Shaw to my Mill to get the Mill Book, and to take a state of the flour in the Mill.

And sent my Overseer to forwarn some persons who were hunting upon my land from the like practice.

Thursday 12th. Thermometer at 28 in the Morning—39 at Noon and 40 at Night.

The Snow which fell yesterday had not covered the ground more than ¾ of an inch thick.

A very heavy hoar frost this Morning. Day calm, and the evening clear, and remarkably pleasant & warm.

Mr. Shaw went up to the Ball at Alexandria.

Friday 13th. Thermometer at 32 in the Morning—38 at Noon and 35 at Night.

But little wind all day and that from the No. West. Evening quite calm.

Laid out the ground behind the Stable, formerly a Vineyard, for a fruit Garden.

Mr. Shaw returned about 12 Oclock from Alexandria.

Saturday 14th. Thermometer at 26 in the Morng.—35 at Noon and 36 at Night.

Went out with the Hounds, & run a fox from 11 Oclock untill near 3 Oclock when I came home and left the Dogs at fault after which they recovered the Fox & it is supposed killed it.

Before the Chase, I visited my Ferry & Dogue run Plantations.

Sunday 15th. Thermometer at 34 in the Morning 42 at Noon and 40 at Night.

Little or no Wind all day. Clear and very pleasant.

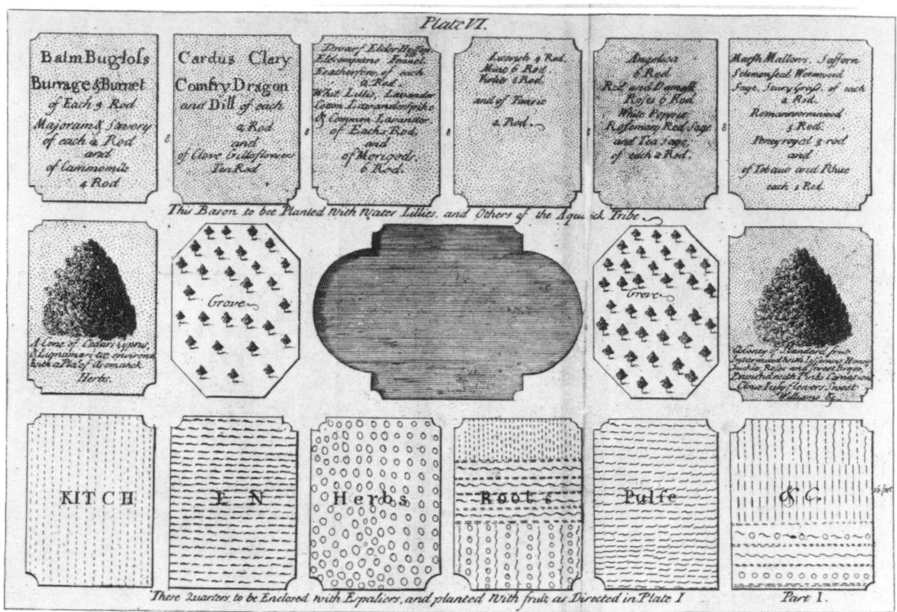

"Design of a Complete Fruit, Kitchen, and Physick Garden," from Batty Langley's *New Principles of Gardening,* London, 1728. (Beinecke Rare Book and Manuscript Library, Yale University)

Nelly & Washington Custis returned home to day.

Doctr. Stuart came here to Dinner & returned in the Afternoon.

Monday 16th. Thermometer at 35 in the Morng. [ ] at Noon and 38 at Night.

Lowering Morning with theatnings, & spittings of Snow till about Noon when the wind (for before it was calm) came out at No. West tho' not hard dispelled the Clouds.

Run round my Plantation at the Ferry and on my return found a Mr. Armstrong here on business of Mr. Balch's respectg. my Nephews—who after dining returned.

Began, from an appreh[ensio]n that there would not be much frost to put Ice in to my Ice Ho[use] tho there was but little of it.

Sent my Stone Mason—Cornelius McDermott Roe, to the Proprietors of the Quarries of free Stone along down the River to see if I could be supplied with enough of a proper kind to repair my Stone Steps & for other purposes.

Along the right bank of the Potomac River below Occoquan Creek lay large reserves of sandstone that were quarried for constructing buildings in the Potomac Valley, including George Mason's Gunston Hall (MILLER, 47).

January 17th. Thermometer at 27 in the Morning—30 at Noon and 28 at N.

Wind at No. West all day, and Cold. Thawed but little, altho' it was clear.

Employed as yesterday, in collecting Ice, but under many disadvantages, being obliged to go over to the Maryland shore and pick up the floating Ice in the River—which I was disposed to do, rather than run the risk of not laying up a store.

Cornelius McDermott Roe returned, having had the offer of Stone [from] Mr. Brent.

Sandstone quarries along the lower reaches of Aquia Creek were owned in the eighteenth century by the Brent family of Woodstock and Richland, Stafford County. Stone from these quarries was later used in the construction of the Capitol and the president's house in Washington (BRYAN, 1:169).

Wednesday 18th. Thermometer at 20 in the Morning—22 at Noon and 26 at Night.

Day very cold—no thawing and the afternoon threatning of Snow. A fine mist of it falling—Wind Northerly.

Colo. Fitzgerald called here on his way from Dumfries & dined and then proceeded. Fixed with him, and requested that he would give the Board of Directors of the Potomack Company notice of the meeting intended to be held at the Great Falls on Monday the 30th. Instt.

Getting Ice this day also.

Thursday 19th. Thermometer at 19 in the Morning—20 at Noon and 22 at Night.

Morning Cloudy—Wind Northerly and weather cold. Snow about an Inch deep fell in the Night. After ten oclock it began again, & continued Snowing fine till bed time with the wind Northerly.

Discontinued getting Ice, the river not being in a State to get it from the other shore and the prospect such as to get it any where in the course of a day or two.

The Negro Shoemaker belonging to Mr. Lund Washington came to work here in the forenoon of this day.

Friday 20th. Thermometer at 18 in the Morng.—24 at Noon and 26 at Night.

A Mixture of Snow and hail fell all the fore part of the day and hail & rain the latter part, which consolidated the Snow which in the Morning might be about 6 or 8 Inches deep. Wind Northwardly all day, but not much of it in any part of it.

Saturday 21st. Thermometer at 26 in the Morning–[ ] at Noon and 34 at Night.

Cloudy and hazy till betwn. eleven & 12 oclock when the Suns feeble efforts to shine were overcome. About one oclock a heavy mist came on. About two it grew very dark–thundered and rained–after whch. it continued misling till bed time.

Rid to my Plantations at Muddy hole and Dogue run–from thence to the Mill. Upon my return found Mr. Jno. Dandridge here.

MR. JNO. DANDRIDGE: either John Dandridge (d. 1799), son of Mrs. Washington's brother Bartholomew, or John Dandridge (b. 1756), son of Nathaniel West Dandridge and grandson of Mrs. Washington's paternal uncle, William Dandridge of Elsing Green.

Sunday 22d. Thermometer at 40 in the Morning–42 at Noon and 48 at Night.

Raining more or less all day, and a close thick fog the whole day proceeding from the dissolution of the Snow which by Night was almost gone. Wind tho' not much of it Southerly and warm–the damps in the house being also very great the damps upon the walls being to be swept of.

Monday 23d. Thermometer at 38 in the Morning–46 at Noon and 40 at Night.

Clear all day with the Wind at No. West but neither hard nor cold.

Snow entirely gone, except in places hid from the influence of the Sun & the Southwardly wind which blew yesterday.

Tuesday 24th. Thermometer at 31 in the Morning–36 at Noon and 34 at Night.

Morning clear & pleasant: Lowering afterwards; with appearances of Snow–little or no Wind all day.

Began my work of Ice-getting again to day but it was not in a proper State being rather a mixture of Snow & Ice and not hard enough.

Wednesday 25th. Thermometer at 34 in the morning [ ] at Noon and 40 at Night.

Morning calm and very foggy till after 8 oclock when the fog dispersed and was very pleasant. About one oclock the Wind sprung up at No. West but blew neither hard nor cold.

Mr. Jno. Dandridge set off on his return home after breakfast.

I rid to Morris's, Muddy hole and Neck Plantations between Breakfast and dinner.

The State of the Ice was such that I was obliged to disist from getting more until the next freezing spell.

And set about the Banks round the Lawn, in front of the gate between the two Mounds of Earth.

Thursday 26th. Thermometer at 33 in the Morng.—[ ] at Noon and 39 at Night.

Clear and pleasant all day and more especially in the afternoon —Not much wind, but that from the No. West.

Renewed my Ice operation to day, employing as many hands as I conveniently could in gettg. it from the Maryland shore, carting, and pounding it.

Mr. Shaw went up to the dancing assembly at Alexandria after Dinner.

Friday 27th. Thermometer at 30 in the Morning—[ ] at Noon and [ ] at Night.

Clear and pleasant all day; Wind at No. West in the forenoon and Eastwardly afterwards, but not much of it.

Mrs. Washington set out after breakfast for Abingdon—to see Mrs. Stuart who is ill.

I rid to my Mill and to the Plantation at Dogue run—also to the places where the Muddy hole & ferry people were at Work.

Mr. Shaw returned home an hour or two within Night.

Getting Ice again to day.

Saturday 28th. Thermometer at 34 in the morning—43 at Noon and 44 at Night.

Morning calm & clear but the [ground] hard frozen. About 10 oclock the wind sprung up at South, but did not blow hard. Thawed the ground a good deal.

Went out after breakfast with my hounds. Found a Fox in the Branch within Mr. Thomson Masons Field and run him sometimes hard and sometimes at cold hunting from 11 oclock till near two when I came home and left the huntsman with them who followed in the same manner two hours or more longer, and then took the Dogs off without killing. In the course of the chase, & at the upper end of the cover in which the above Fox was found I see two run out at once neither of which appeared to be the chased Fox. This shews how plenty they are on that side the Creek.

When I came home found Colo. Gibson a Mr. Pollock (of Richmond) and Colo. Allison here, who dined and stayed all night.

Getting Ice again to day.

George Gibson (1747–1791), born in Lancaster County, Pa., joined the Virginia service at the beginning of the Revolution and held the rank of colonel in the 1st Virginia State Regiment from 5 June 1777 to Jan. 1782. After the war he returned to his home in Cumberland County, Pa. (*Va. Mag.*, 18:24–25, n.1; HEITMAN [1], 189).

Oliver Pollock (c.1737–1823), born near Coleraine in northern Ireland, came to Philadelphia in 1760. He went into the West India trade and before the Revolution settled in New Orleans, where he developed a prosperous trading business. During the war Pollock served as commercial agent both for Virginia and the Continental Congress. His financial assistance to George Rogers Clark's army in the West was vital to its success. Gibson's association with Pollock dated from Aug. 1776 when the two men collaborated in securing a supply of gunpowder for Virginia from Don Luis de Unzaga y Amézaga, governor of Louisiana (JAMES [2], 1, 3, 4, 61, 143–45). Pollock carried a letter of introduction from Patrick Henry (Henry to GW, 18 Jan. 1786, DLC:GW).

Sunday 29th. Thermometer at 40 in the Morning—54 at Noon and 50 at Night.

The morning remarkably fine & pleasant, with little or no wind—the afternoon a little lowering and at Night it began a mizzling rain which encreased and continued raining all night.

After breakfast the Gentlemen who came yesterday returned.

In the afternoon Colo. Grayson & his Nephew Mr. Benjn. Orr, came in and stayed all Night.

Col. William Grayson's sister married John Orr (b. 1726); Benjamin Grayson Orr was one of their three sons.

Monday 30th. Thermometer at 54 in the Morning—56 at Noon and 50 at Night.

The Morning foggy, with showers at intervals till near 11 oclock after which it cleared, with a brisk Southwardly wind.

Mrs. Washington with Betcy & Patcy Custis came home, from Abingdon before dinner and after it Colo. Greyson & Mr. Orr left this.

Planted the Hemlock Pine wch. was brought to me by Cornelius McDermot Row from Colo. Blackburns, in my shrubberies —and—on sixteen square rod of ground in my lower pasture, I put 140 Bushels of what we call Marle viz—on 4 of these N. Wt. corner were placed 50 bushels—on 4 others So. Wt. Corner 20 bushels—On 4 others So. Et. Corner 40 bushels and on the remaining 4: 20 bushels. This marl was spread on the Sod, in these proportions—to try—first whether what we have denominated to be marl possesses any virtue as a manure—and secondly—if it does, the quantity proper for an acre.

Transplanted (after dividing it into two) the French honeysuckle in my North garden to the Lawn—one half in front of ea. garden gate.

Tuesday 31st. Thermometer at 42 in the Morning—40 at Noon and 34 at Night.

The morning was a little cloudy but the weather soon cleared with a brisk No. Wester which occasioned a great change in the air.

Planted a few pine trees in my Wildernesses.

February 1786

Wednesday first. Thermometer at [ ] in the Morng.—[ ] at Noon and [ ] at Night.

Ground very hard froze, Wind Eastwardly in the Morning, and So. Et. the remaining part of the day; but clear, & tolerably pleasant notwithstanding.

Not being able to leave here yesterday (as I intended) for the appointed meeting of the Directors of the Potomack Navigation at the Great Falls this day, I set out this Morning at the first dawning of day, for this purpose, and after as disagreeable a ride as I ever had for the distance, arrived, at the Falls at half after 11 Oclock where I found Colo. Gilpin (who had been there since Sunday Night) levelling &ca. and Colo. Fitzgerald who got there just before me.

Spent the remainder of this day in viewing the different grounds along which it was supposed the Canal might be carried and after dining at the Huts went in the evening accompanied by Colo. Fitzgerald & Mr. Potts to a Mr. Wheelers in the Neighbourhood (abt. 1½ Miles off) to lodge.

THE HUTS: The Potomac Company made its construction headquarters on the Virginia side of the Great Falls, where in 1790 the town of Matildaville was authorized. In 1786 this settlement, which was never more than a construction town, probably consisted of little more than "huts" for the workers (HENING, 13:171; BACON-FOSTER, 87).

Thursday 2d. Thermometer at [ ] in the Morning—[ ] at [noon] and [ ] at Night. A very remarkable hoar frost, with but little Wind; day pleasant till the evening when it clouded up and abt. 8 oclock began to Snow.

Spent this day in examining the ground more attentively, and levelling the different ways we had discovered yesterday but on acct. of the swolen state of the river, & rapidity of the currant we could not determine, absolutely, upon the best cut and therefore directed Mr. Stuart, the Assistant Manager to have all of them opened, accurately measured, levelled, & their bottoms sounded by the day of March when the Directors are to be requested pointedly to meet for the final choice.

Dined again at the Hutts; some little time after which, Govr. Lee (who had been detained by high waters) and Mr. Rumsey came in—the first concurred in sentiment with us on these measures.

After 7 Oclock at Night, Colo. Fitzgerald Mr. Potts & Myself left the Hutts, & came to Mr. William Scotts about 6 Miles on this side of the Falls where we lodged.

Friday 3d. Thermometer at [ ] in the Morng.—[ ] at Noon and [ ] at Night.

The Snow that fell last Night did not cover the ground an Inch. The Wind was at So. West, and the day overhead was pleasant. Snow soon disappeared.

After an early breakfast we left Mr. Scotts; and about noon I reached home; where I found an Eastern shore man delivering the Oats which Doctr. Stuart had engaged on my behalf of a Mr. George Savage of Northampton—viz. 800 Bushels.

Soon after I arrived Miss Sally Ramsay, Miss Kitty Washington, Doctr. Craik Junr. & Mr. Porter came in and Dined, and stayed all Night. After Dinner Mr. Rumsey arrived and stayed the evening also.

George Savage, of Northampton County, Va., was a planter descended from an established Eastern Shore family. In a letter to Dr. David Stuart on 24 Dec. 1785, GW thanked Stuart for contracting on his behalf with Savage for 800 bushels of oats. In addition, GW asked Stuart to try to procure for him another 1,200 bushels because his corn crop had been less than one-third of the previous year (DLC:GW). Early in February, GW acknowledged the delivery of the 800 bushels by Savage's skipper John Whitney (GW to George Savage, 8 Feb. 1786, DLC:GW) and later that month, Savage wrote GW to expect shortly a shipment of corn from him via the schooner *Molly and Betsey* (18 Feb. 1786, DLC:GW). Since about 1782 Savage had held the position of commissioner of wrecks in Northampton. After becoming president, GW appointed Savage collector of the port of Cherry Stone, also in that county.

Saturday 4th. Thermometer at 46 in the Morng.–[ ] at Noon and 40 at Night.

Clear morning with very little wind–after which it sprung up but not fresh, from the Eastward, and lowered.

Sketch of a garden house at Mount Vernon. From Benson J. Lossing's *Mount Vernon and Its Associations,* New York, 1859. (University of Virginia Library)

Mr. Porter and Doctr. Craik went away before Breakfast and Mr. Rumsay after dinner.

Having assembled the Men from my Plantations, I removed the garden Houses which were in the middle of the front walls to the extreme points of them; which were done with more ease, & less damage than I expected, considering the height one of them was to be raised from the ground.

Sunday 5th. Thermometer at 34 in the morning–36 at Noon and 37 at Night.

Wind Northerly. About 9 oclk. last Night it began to Snow which turned soon to rain which continued through the Night and more or less all day, intermixed now & then with spittings of Snow. Abt. Noon the Wind shifted to the No. West and blew pretty fresh but the weather in other respects did not change.

Monday 6th. Thermometer at 36 in the Morning—40 at Noon and 38 at Night.

Flying Clouds in the morning with a brisk No. West wind all day and cold though clear after ten oclock.

The largest of my Buck fauns which had been missing since friday last came home after dinner with its left hind knee broke & much shivered—supposed to be by a shot.

Planting pines in the wilderness on the left of the lawn and spading the ground there to day.

Tuesday 7th. Thermometer at 34 in the Morning—[ ] at Noon and 54 at Night.

Morning clear & very pleasant, as it continued to be all day. Wind Southerly, but not fresh.

Mrs. Washington, Kitty Washington, Miss Ramsay, Mr. Shaw and myself went to Colo. McCartys to the funeral of Mrs. Peers (one of his daughters). I took my ferry & dogue run plantations in the way. We returned home to dinner—after which Doctor Griffith came in and my overseer from the Plantation on Rappahannock.

The funeral was for Mary McCarty Peers, whom GW called Molly upon her childhood visits to Mount Vernon.

Wednesday 8th. Thermometer at 42 in the Morng.—52 at Noon and 44 at Night.

Day rather variable, but upon the whole pleasant; In the morning there were flying clouds with the wind pretty fresh from the No. West—after which it was clear and still, till the evening, when the Wind came out at So. East.

After Breakfast Mr. Griffith went away, and before dinner Mr. Wm. Craik came in and stayed all Night.

Finished planting all the young pine trees in the Wilderness on the left.

Thursday 9th. Thermometer at 43 in the Morng.—54 at Noon and 50 at Night.

Clear morning, with a remarkable white frost. Wind Southerly all day.

Went early in the Morning to my river Plantation. Took the Dogs with me and on my return hunted, but never got a fox a foot tho I dragged one to Mr. Robt. Alexanders Pocoson at whose house I called.

In my way home I took Muddy hole plantation. Found Mr. Willm. Craik gone and Mr. Fendall and Mr. Hipkins here who went away at Night by which Doctr. Craik Senr. came in.

Friday 10th. Thermometer at 52 in the Morning—62 at Noon and 66 at Night.

Wind Southerly & pretty fresh all day, till evening, when it shifted to the No. West and turned cold—a large circle round the Moon. This day was remarkably fine & promotive of vegitation. The buds of the lylack were much swelled & seemed ready to unfold.

Doctr. Craik went away after Breakfast.

I began to hand weed the drilled wheat from the Cape behind the Stables. The part which was cut so close by mistake appeared to be quite dead to, if not at the roots. The top of the blades of the other, in some places, had turned red as if singed with the frost; and the bottom blades were, in many places grown yellow. The last sowed wheat had, within these few days, vegitated a good deal, and was stooling very prettily.

Making up the banks round the serpentine walks to the front gate.

Saturday 11th. Thermometer at 34 in the Morning—34 at Noon and 30 at Night.

Wind at No. East all day—very raw, and cold—a red angry sky at Sunrising; lowering about Noon and snowing afterwards, by intervals, towards night.

A Mr. Wooldridge (an English gentleman) and a Mr. Waddell of No. Carolina—together with Mr. Murray, Mr. Wilson, & Mr. Maize came here to dinner & stayed all night.

Transplanted the following trees, to the following places in the North garden—viz.—the first on the left, looking eastward from the garden house, along the walk in front of it, is a peach tree transplanted the 14th. of last March from the Gardeners nursery, to the South side of the walk, by the Englh. Walnuts. The 2d. & 4th. on the same side, are burgamy Pears, grafted the first of April last yr. by the green House. The 3d. on the same side, is a black May heart cherry, grafted at the same time, in the same place. The 5th. on the same side is a Duke cherry, Do. Do. The 3d. tree from the same house, on the *right* side (looking the same way) is also a Duke cherry, grafted as above. By the stumps of the Cornation Cherry, and apricot, which were removed in to the same garden on the 26th. of last October (not expecting either of them to live) I planted a white heart cherry; and one of the small cherries that used to grow in the walk, in front of the House; the white heart was placed by the stump of the Cornation Cherry.

Brought a Goose & Gander of the Chineese breed of Geese, from the reverend Mr. Griffiths and also two of the large white (or Portugal) Peach trees; and 2 Scions from a tree growing in his garden, to which he could give no name—the last for my Shrubberies.

In 1775 the merchants of London appointed a committee to consider the importance of American trade to Britain. They chose Thomas Wooldrige, a British merchant, and two others to report on the situation in North Carolina (*Va. Gaz.*, D&H, 8 April 1775). Residing in New York City after the war, Wooldrige belonged to the firms of Wooldrige & Kelly and Kelly, Lot & Co., which engaged in West Indian trade. Wooldrige was in financial straits in 1786, for on 20 July 1786 Alexander Hamilton wrote to him concerning ways to satisfy his creditors. The following year Wooldrige was imprisoned in New York City for debts (HAMILTON [2], 3:678, n.1).

Edmund Waddell (Waddill), a prosperous planter of Randolph County, N.C., represented that county in the state House of Commons in 1787 and in the Senate from 1793 to 1798. In 1788 Waddell attended the state convention called to ratify the Constitution.

Sunday 12th. Thermometer at 30 in the Morng.—32 at Noon and 34 at Night.

Snow about half an inch deep in the Morning but soon disappeared afterwards—cloudy for the most part and but a feeble Sun at any time of the day—not much Wind and that about So. Et.

Messrs. Wilson, Murray, and Mease went away before breakfast—Mr. Wooldridge and Mr. Waddell after it and Miss Ramsay & Kitty Washington some time after them in my Chariot.

Monday 13th. Thermometer at 34 in the Morning—34 at Noon and 32 at Night.

Cloudy Morning but tolerably clear afterwards till Noon when it lowered and sprinkled fine Snow by intervals till Night by which the ground was not covered more than half an inch. Wind Southerly but raw and cold notwithstanding.

Planted the two peach trees which were brought on Saturday from Doctr. Griffiths in my fruit garden behind the Stable (the two uppermost ones at the No. Et. Corner of it). Also planted [ ] others from the Nursery in the Garden.

Began to raise the Mound of earth on the right of the gate (coming in).

Rid to my Plantations at Muddy hole—Dogue Run and Ferry and also to the Mill. Found Doctr. Craik here on my return, who dined with us and proceeded to Mr. Littles at Cameron to whose wife he was sent for.

Charles Little (c.1744–1813) emigrated from Scotland to Virginia in 1768, married Mary Manley, a sister of Penelope Manley French, and settled near Cameron at Cleesh, which he bought from the estate of the late Thomas Colvill (POWELL, 202; HARRISON [1], 285).

Tuesday 14th. Thermometer at 32 in the Morning—36 at [noon] and 38 at Night.

In the course of last night there fell 8 Inches Snow and it continued snowing slightly till 10 or 11 Oclock when it cleared & became a fine afternoon and evening—Not much wind and that variable sometimes at So. Et. then at No. West and then calm.

Employed all the women and Weak hands (who on acct. of the Snow) could not work out, in picking the Wild Onion from the Eastern shore Oat for seed.

Doctr. Craik came in whilst we were at Dinner and stayed all Night.

Wednesday 15th. Thermometer at 34 in the Morning—36 at Noon and 36 at Night.

Morning lowering. Towards Noon it became clear and warm, after which it clouded up again. Between 4 and 5 it began to Rain wch. turned to snow in a little time soon after which it ceased. Wind for the most part of the day was Southerly.

Doctr. Craik went away after Breakfast.

Began with some of the Men abt. the House to bundle faggots for filling up gullies; as they could not on acct. of the Weather remove earth.

Thursday 16th. Thermometer at 36 in the Morning—46 at Noon and 46 at Night.

Morning cloudy and not pleasant, wind being at No. West, but not fresh. Afterwards it became clear, calm, and exceedingly agreeable.

The warm & pleasant afternoon almost carried of the Snow.

Put one of Doctr. Gordons Subscription Papers (yesterday) in the hands of Doctr. Craik to offer to his acquaintance.

Rev. William Gordon. (Massachusetts Historical Society)

Dr. William Gordon (1728–1809), a dissenting minister in England, migrated to America in 1770 and settled in Roxbury, Mass., where he soon became active in the independence movement. As the Revolution progressed Gordon began copying and collecting documents with which to write a history of the struggle, and in 1784 he visited at Mount Vernon for 2½ weeks while he copied and abstracted Revolutionary documents from among GW's papers (FREEMAN, 6:36). Before he returned to England (1786) to find a publisher, Gordon circulated subscription papers for his history, which was first published in four volumes as *The History of the Rise, Progress, and Establishment of Independence of the United States of America* (London, 1788). Besides this subscription paper given to Dr. Craik, GW forwarded copies to correspondents in Alexandria and Fredericksburg. GW subscribed to two sets himself, for a total of £2 (GW to James Mercer, 20 Jan. 1786, DLC:GW; LEDGER B, 223; see also PILCHER).

Friday 17th. Thermometer at 38 in the Morning—52 at Noon and 48 at Night.

A thick fog till 9 oclock A.M. when it dispelled; was clear and pleasant till towards Sunsetting when the western horison seemed to cloud & lower. Wind Southerly all day but the ground very wet—Snow all dissolved where the Sun had access.

Rid to my Mill, and the Plantations at Muddy hole, Dogue Run & ferry.

Sent for Doctr. Brown, who visited my Negro Overseer (Will) and Gabriel at Muddy hole who were both sick—the first since this day week & was visited by Doctr. Brown on Tuesday last.

Saturday 18th. Thermometer at 45 in the Morning—56 at Noon and 50 at Night.

The morning lowered—cleard at Noon and about two it rained a little; with appearances of a good deal, at first—however it soon ceased, though it continued cloudy till night, when the Wind, which had blowed pretty fresh from the Southward all day, shifted to the No. West.

Began the yards back of the Green house designed for the Jack Ass & Magnolia.

The Bitch Stately was lined by the Dog Vulcan. Jupiter had been put to her and Venus but never seemed to take the least notice of them but whether he ever lined either of them is not certain. The contrary is supposed.

Rid to the Plantation in the Neck and returned home by Muddy hole and visited the sick men there whom I found better.

Took a list to day of all my Negroes which are as follows at Mount Vernon and the plantations around it—viz.—

Home House.

Will	Val de Chambre	1
Frank *Austin	Waiters in the House	2
Herculus Nathan	Cooks	2
Giles *Joe Paris—boy	Drivers, & Stablers	3
*Doll *Jenny	almost past Service	2
*Betty *Lame Alice *Charlotte	Sempstresses	3
*Sall *Caroline	House Maids	2
Sall Brass *Dolly	Washers	2
*Alce Myrtilla *Kitty Winny	Spinners old & almost blind	4
*Schomberg	past labour	1
Frank Cook Jack	Stock keeper old Jobber	2

Name	Occupation	Number
Gunner Boatswain Sam Anthony *Tom Davis *Will *Joe	Labourers	7
Jack	Waggoner	1
*Simms	Carter	1
Bristol	Gardener	1
Isaac James Sambo *Tom Nokes	Carpenters	4
Natt George	Smiths	2
*Peter–lame	Knitter	1
	grown	41

Children

Name	House	Age	Number
*Oney	Betty's House	12 yrs. old	
*Delphy	Ditto	6 do.	2
*Anna	little Alice's	13 do.	
*Christopher	Do.	11 do.	
*Judy	Do.	7 do.	
*Vina	Do.	5 do.	4
*Sinah	Kitty's	14 do.	
*Mima	Ditto	12 do.	
*Ally	Ditto	10 do.	
*Lucy	Ditto	8 do.	
*Grace	Ditto	6 do.	
*Letty	Ditto	4 do.	
*Nancy	Ditto	2 do.	7
*Richmond	Lame Alce	9 do.	
*Evey	Do.	2 do.	
*Delia	Do.	3 mo.	3
Lilly	Myrtilla's	11 yrs. old	
Ben	Ditto	8 do.	
Harry	Do.	3 do.	
Boatswain	Do.	6 do.	
Lally	Do.	3 mo.	5
*Cyrus	Sall's	11 do.	1
*Timothy	Charlottes	1 do.	1

*Wilson	Caroline	1 do.	1
*Moll *Peter	Mr. Custis's Estate		2
		In all	67

Mill

Ben	Miller	1
Jack Tom Davy	Cowpers	3
	In all	4

River Plantn.

*Davy	Overseer	1
*Breechy Nat Ned Essex Bath *Johny Adam *Will Robin *Ben	Labourg. Men dead	10
*Molly	Overseers Wife	1
Ruth *Dolly Peg Daphne Murria *Agnus Suck Sucky Judy–M Judy–F *Hannah *Cornelia *Lidia *Esther Cloe *Fanny *Alice	labourg. Women	17
	grown	29

February 1786

Children

Will	Mill Judy's	——— 13 yrs. old		1
*Joe	Hannahs	——— 12 Do.		1
Ben	Peg's	10 Do.		
Penny	Ditto	——— 8 Do.		2
Joe	Daphne's	8 do.		
Moses	Ditto	6 do.		
Lucy	Ditto	4 do.		
Daphne	Ditto	——— 1 do.		4
*Ned	Lidia's	7 do.		
*Peter	Ditto	5 do.		
*Phoebe	Ditto	——— 3 do.		3
Cynthia	Suckey's	6 do.		
Daniel	Ditto	——— 4 do.		2
*James	Ferry Doll's	8 do.		1
*Bett	Neck Dolls	7 do.		
*Natt	Ditto	4 do.		
*Dolly	Ditto	3 do.		
*Jack	Ditto	——— 1 do.		4
Rose	Suck-Bass	12 do.		1
*Milly	House Sall's	7 do.		1
*Billy	Do. Charlottes	4 do.		1
*Hukey	Agnus's	1 do.		1
*Ambrose	Cornelia's	1 month		1
			In all	52

Dogue Run—Plantn.

*Morris	Overseer	1
Robin Adam Jack Jack—long Dick Ben *Matt *Morris	Labourg. Men	8
*Brunswick	Ruptured	1
Hannah	Overrs. wife	1

*Lucy Moll Jenny Silla Charity *Betty *Peg *Sall *Grace *Sue	Labourg. Women old	10
	grown	21

Children

Sarah	Charity's	6 yrs. old	
Billy	Ditto	5 do.	
Hannah	Ditto	3 do.	
Elly	Ditto	6 mo.	4
*Jesse	Salls	6 yrs. old	
*Kitty	Do.	4 do.	
*Lawrence	Do.	1 do.	3
*Jenny	Lucy's	9 do.	
*Daniel	Do.	3 do.	
*Ned	Do.	6 Mo.	3
Aggy	Jones (dead)	9 yrs. old	
Simon	Do.	4 do.	
Bett	Do.	3 do.	3
Sophia	Sylla's	3 do.	
Sabra	Ditto	6 Mo.	2
*Andrew	Bettys'	1 yr. old	1
*Crager	Pegs	6 Mo.	1
		In all	38

Ferry–Plantn.

*Sam Kit London *Caesar *Cupid *Paul	labourg. Men	5
*Betty *Doll *Lucy	labourg. Women	3

*Lucy Flora *Fanny *Rachel *Jenny Edy *Daphne	Labouring Women		7
		grown	15

Children

Name	Mother	Age	
*Godfrey	Betty's	12 yrs. old	
*Beck	Ditto	11 do.	
*Hanson	Ditto	7 do.	
*Lucretia	Ditto	6 do.	
*John	Ditto	3 do.	
*Bill langston	Ditto	6 Mo.	6
*Patt	Doll's	11 yrs. old	
*Milly	Ditto	4 do.	
*Daniel	Ditto	3 do.	
*Silvia	Ditto	1 do.	4
*Edmund	Lucy	6 do.	
*Mike	Ditto	3 do.	
*Phill	Ditto	8 Mo.	3
Joy	Flora	8 yrs. old	
Jacob	Ditto	5 do.	2
		In all	30

Muddy hole Plann.

*Will	Overseer		
*Will Charles Gabriel *Jupiter	Labourg. Men		5
Kate Nanny Sarah Alice Peg Sackey Darcus Amy Nancy	labourg. Women		9
		grown	14

Children

Molly	Kates	14 yrs. old	
Virgin	Ditto	11 do.	
Will	Ditto	8 do.	
Kate	Ditto	4 do.	4
Moses	Darcuss	8 do.	
Townshend	Do.	6 Mo.	2
Letty	Peg's	7 yrs. old	
Forrister	Ditto	2 do.	2
Uriah	Sackey's	10 do.	1
Kate	Alice's	4 do.	1
Isbel	Sarah's	3 do.	1

Muddy hole . . .	In all	25
Home House		67
River Plantation		52
Dogue Run Plantn.		38
Ferry Plantation		30
Mill		4
	Total	216

N.B. Those marked with asterisks are Dower Negros.

Sunday 19th. Thermometer at 35 in the morning—38 at Noon and 38 at Night.

Morning clear and tolerably pleasant, though the horison was red & angry at the place of the Suns rising. After noon it lowered a good deal and at Night there fell a mixture of Snow and Rain—which turned to a kind of misling rain that continued through the Night. But little wind in the fore part of the day—at So. Et. and East afterwards.

Monday 20th. Thermometer at 35 in the Morning—38 at Noon and 38 at Night.

Missling all day intermixed at times with Rain with but little wind.

Began, though the ground was too wet, to set the Posts of my Paddock fence.

Mr. Lawrence Washington of Chotank, Mr. Wm. Thompson Mr. Willm. Stuart and Mr. Lund Washington came here to dinner—all of whom except the first went away after it.

William Thompson, of Colchester (see entry for 16 April 1775), in 1785 married Ann Washington, daughter of Lund Washington's brother Robert Washington (b. 1729). William Stuart (b. 1761) was a younger brother of David Stuart.

Tuesday 21st. Thermometer at 40 in the Morning—40 at Noon and 38 at N.

Clear, with the wind pretty fresh at No. West in the forenoon calm afterwards.

A Mr. McPherson of Alexandria came & returned before dinner. His business was, to communicate the desires of a Neighbourhood in Berkeley County, to build a School & Meeting House on some Land of mine there, leased to one [ ]. My answer was, that if the tenant's consent could be obtained, and the spot chosen was upon the exterior of my Land, so as that no damage would result from Roads &ca. to it, mine should not be wanting.

Colo. Carrington, Doctr. Brown, and a Mr. Scott of Maryland (a liver with Colo. Fitzhugh) also Mr. Lawe. Washington (of this County) came here to dinner; all of whom except Colo. Carrington went away after it. In the evening Mr. Crawford and his wife—child and nurse came in and stayed all night.

Edward Carrington (1749–1810) was the son of George and Anne Mayo Carrington of Goochland County, Va. He served in the Revolutionary War as a lieutenant colonel in the 1st Continental Artillery and was a member of the Continental Congress 1785–86; in 1789 GW appointed him marshal of the United States District Court of Virginia. In 1791 he was made supervisor of the revenue for Virginia. Carrington served as the foreman of the jury in the Aaron Burr treason trial in 1807.

Wednesday 22d. Thermometer 36 in the Morning—40 at Noon and 40 at Night.

A grey Morning with a red and angry looking horison at the place of the Suns rising. About 10 Oclock it began to lower very much & at Noon to drip Rain which continued with intervals all the remaining part of the day but not so as to drive people from their work. Calm all day.

After breakfast Colo. Carrington & Mr. Crawford [and] his wife left this—the first for Alexandria to pursue his rout to Congress (of which he is a member)—the other on his return home.

Mr. Lawe. Washington went up to Alexandria after breakfast—dined & returned in the Evening.

Thursday 23d. Thermometer at 36 in the Morning—32 at Noon and 32 at Night.

Wind at East all day. By eight A.M. it began to Snow and continued to do so more or less all day, covering the ground by Night 3 or 4 Inches when it became a kind of Sleet.

Mr. Lund Washington came here to dinner, and returned afterwards. A Mr. Rice Hooe came in the afternoon and stayed all Night.

Mr. Shaw went to Alexandria to the Assembly and to do some business in town for me.

The weather early in the Morning obliged me to quit planting Posts for my Paddock.

MR. RICE HOOE: probably Rice Wingfield Hooe (1764–1806), of King George County, the son of Richard and Anne Ireland Hooe. In 1790 he married Susannah Fitzhugh. He was sheriff of King George County 1804–6.

Friday 24th. Thermometer at 32 in the morning—33 at Noon and 29 at Night.

Cloudy about day break—but it soon cleared, and about 8 oclock the wind began to blow very high from the No. Wt. and continued to do so all day—growing very cold & freezing hard especially towards Night.

Mr. Lawe. Washington and Mr. Hooe left this after breakfast, and crossed in my Boat (which could not get back till the wind moderated after Sun down) to Maryland, as the nearest cut home.

After sunset Mr. Shaw returned from alexandria.

Not being able either to remove Earth, set Posts, or plant Trees sent the Men into the New grounds to making faggots and the Women to picking the wild onions from the Oats which I wanted to Sow.

Saturday 25th. Thermometer at 24 in the morning—31 at Noon and 30 at Night.

Clear and calm in the forenoon—wind Southerly afterwards and thawing, the ground being hard frozen.

Renewed the fencing of my Paddock to day.

Went into the Neck and to Muddy hole Plantations to measure the fields which I had plowed for Oats & for experiments—also to Dogue run to divide some fields and to mark the Rows for planting Corn.

In the Afternoon Mr. Willm. Boo⟨th⟩ came in and stayed all Night.

Sunday 26th. Thermometer at 29 in the Morning—42 at Noon and 40 at Night.

Clear & calm all the forenoon, wind Southerly afterwards, & towards sunset lowered a good deal; but cleared again after dark.

Monday 27th. Thermometer at 38 in the morning—46 at Noon and 43 at Night.

Forenoon warm, and variable with but little wind. About noon it sprung up fresh from No. West and blew hard all the afternoon.

Mr. Booth went away after breakfast—and Doctr. Brown came after dinner (and returned) to visit Boatswain a sick Negro man.

Having received, yesterday Evening, a number of fruit trees from my Nephew, Mr. Willm. Washington of Blenheim I planted them in my fruit garden in the following order & places—viz.

In the No. Et. Square of this garden—the Tree at the No. Et. Corner is a Carnation Cherry—and the next to it, below, on the East side, is also a Carnation. The 3d. row, three two pound Pears, east side, next the Carnation—& one, 1 pound ditto. 5th. Row. 2 Cooks pears East, & 2 green Burgamot. 7 Row, 3 Bell pears East & 1 Catharine Ditto. 9th. Row 2 yellow Burgamot East & 2 Boncriton Pears.

No. West Square.

2d. Row 1 popes pear—next the cross walk & 3 of Colo. Richd. Henry Lee's fine winter Pear. 5 Row, four old Ho. Russitans. 6 Row four of the Heath Peach. 7 Row—four of Booth's Genitan. 8 Row, three amber Plumbs next the cross walk and 2 Green gage Do. west of them. 9th. Row, two Booths Genitans next the cross Walk & 2 Newtown pippin west of them.

So. West Square

1st. Row, next the cross Walk, Peaches from the Garden. 2d. Row 4 New town pippin. 3d. Row, Peaches from the Garden. 4th. Row, 4 Gloucester white apple—5 Row Peaches from the garden. 6 row 2 Glostr. whe. Ap. on the West side, & next these, adjoining the cross walk, are 2 apple trees taken from the middle walk in the No. Garden—said to be Vandiviers—7 Row, Peach trees from the Garden—8 Row, 1 apple tree next the cross walk, taken from the border in the No. garden, by the English Walnut trees & the other 3 trees are from Stratford, given to me by Colo. Henry Lee 1 of which he calls the Medlar Russitan—another the Chantilly pear—and the 3d. the Carnation cherry but this being a mistake, the others are not to be depended upon.

The 3d. and 7th. Trees in the outer or East row, next the fencing are May duke Cherry from Blenheim.

So. East Square

2d. Row, next the cross walk, are two Golden, and two New Town Pippins from Major Jenefirs—4th. Row four of the Maryland

Red strick from the same place. 6th. Row—next the cross walk, two more of the same—that is Maryland red strick.

Fruit trees not previously mentioned in the diaries are listed here. The Pound pear was used only for cooking, a very common "kitchen" variety. The Bell may be the Windsor, often called Summer Bell, a summer pear not highly regarded. The Catherine pear was listed in the first catalogue of fruits issued in the colonies, William Prince's 1771 catalogue. Boncriton is GW's rendering of Bon Chretien. DOWNING, 406, lists two Pope's pears, the Scarlet Major and the Quaker, both from Long Island. Colonel Lee's winter pear is not further identified. The Russitan apple is GW's rendering of Russeting, an alternate form of Russet. The Heath peach was a late-ripening clingstone developed in Maryland from a stone brought from the Mediterranean. "Booths Genitans" means the Jenneting, an early apple which folk etymology often corrupted into "June-eating." It was probably brought to GW by William Booth, of Westmoreland and later the Shenandoah Valley, who left Mount Vernon this day. The Amber plum may be the Amber Primordian, an early variety from the south of France. The Green Gage is still a universally popular variety (all plums are *Prunus domestica*). The Vandervere apple was a winter variety said to have been named for a family in Wilmington, Del., where it originated (DOWNING, 141). The medlar, *Mespilus germanica,* no longer considered to be an apple, is a crooked tree or large shrub bearing fruit which is eaten after frost. The Chantilly pear is one of the seemingly endless number of French pears, not further identified. The Golden Pippin is a variety of the Newtown Pippin already discussed.

Tuesday 28th. Thermometer at 30 in the Morng.—[ ] at Noon and [ ] at Night.

A hard frost, and very cold morning, Wind being still at No. West. The forenoon clear—afternoon lowering and about eight oclock in the evening it began to Snow.

Set out, by appointment, to attend a meeting of the Board of Directors of the Potomack Company at the Great Falls. Dined and lodged at Abingdon, to which place Mrs. Washington and all the Children accompanied me. Mr. Shaw also set out on a visit to Dumfries.

March 1786

Wednesday 1st. Thermometer at [ ] in the Morning—[ ] at Noon and [ ] at Night.

The Snow which fell in the night was little, if any over an inch deep this Morning. The forenoon of the day was variable and foggy—the afternoon clear, warm, and pleasant till the evening, when it lowered and threatned a disagreeable change.

After a very early breakfast at Abingdon I set off for the meeting at the Great falls & passing near the little falls arrived at the former about 10 Oclock; where in a little time, assembled Govr. Johnston Colo. Fitzgerald, and Colo. Gilpin.

Little or no business done to day—& seperating in the evening for the purpose of procuring Quarters, I went to Mr. Fairfax's (about 3 Miles off) where I lodged.

Thursday 2d. Thermometer at [ ] in the Morning—[ ] at Noon and [ ] at Night.

A little Snow fell in the Night. About Sun rise there were some appearances of fair weather but about 8 Oclock it began to Snow fast. By 10 it was intermixed with hail & Rain—which, about Noon, became wholly Rain and towards Sun down all Snow, and storming; indeed the day through it blew hard from the No. East quarter.

Accompanied by Mr. Fairfax I repaired again to the Falls where we arrived about 8 oclock & where we found Colo. Gilpin, who remained there all Night. About two hours afterwards, Govr. Johnson, Colo. Fitzgereld and Mr. Potts arrived but the day was so stormy that we could neither level, nor Survey the different tracks talked of for the Canal—which, & to determine on the most eligable one were the principle objects of the meeting. Unable to do any business without doors, we returned to the Huts—resolved on the next advances—considered some other Matters—dined there as we did yesterday and again seperated for lodgings. Colo. Fitzgerald & Mr. Potts accompanied Mr. Fairfax & myself to Towlston.

THE NEXT ADVANCES: Although almost all of the 500 shares had been subscribed, many of the subscribers (including the state of Maryland, which held 50 shares) were delinquent in paying the first two "advances" (which were also called "dividends") of 5 and 2½ percent. The board resolved to press these delinquents and to call for payment by subscribers of two more dividends of 10 percent each (PICKELL, 84–87).

Friday 3d. Thermometer at [ ] in the Morning—[ ] at Noon and [ ] at Night.

The Snow which fell yesterday & last night covered the ground at least a foot deep and continuing snowing a little all day, & blowing hard from the No. West. We were obliged tho' we assembled at the huts again to relinquish all hopes of levelling & Surveying the ground this trip; & therefore resolved on the Rout for the Canal from the best view we could take, & information

List of Workmen Employed at the Great Falls for the Potomack Company Under Richardson Stuart from the 2d Octor. to the 12th Novr. 1786 and Certified by the Subsribers Overseers

Mens Names	Occupation	No. of days	At pr. month or day	Inches Bored a 6/8 pr. hundred	Rations deducted a 1/3	Total Amount in Virginia Currency £ S D	
Thomas Boylan	Overseer	31	£5	.....	.....	5 .. 19 .. 3	
James Rennells	do.	36	£4	....	....	5 .. 10 .. 8½	
Thomas Sturgis	do.	22	£3	....	..	2 .. 10 .. 6	2.10.9¾
Ignatious Wheeler	do.	18	£4			2 .. 15 .. 5	
William Fanna	do.	17	£3		1	1 .. 18 .. 0	[illegible]
James Hamilton	do.	13	£3			1 .. 10 .. 0	
Edward McGinn	do.	4	£3	....		9 .. 3	
John Radcliff		36	33/4			2 .. 7 .. 7	£2.6.3
Owen Dawly	Borer	13	40/	800	8	3 .. 3 .. 4	
James Lampard	do.	8	do.		2	9 .. 10	
John Buttler	do.	25	do.		9	1 .. 7 .. 2½	

Payroll for workmen employed at the Great Falls. (Library of Congress)

get; and after doing some other business, as a board—particularly resolving to advertize a Contract for the Supply of our labourers with provisions, we broke up the Meeting; and I again returned (first dining at the Hutts) with Colo. Fitzgerald to Towlston, in a very severe evening.

The provisions per man per day were advertised as consisting of 1½ pounds of fresh meat, or 1¼ pounds of salt beef, or 1 pound of salt pork, plus 1½ pounds of flour or bread and "3 gills of good spirituous liquor, per day; also, 1 gill of salt and 1 of vinegar per week, to each ration" (*Va. Journal,* 23 Mar. 1786).

Saturday 4th. Thermometer at [ ] in the Morng.—[ ] at Noon—30 and at Night.

The Wind blew hard all last Night at No. West, and it was as cold this Morning as at any time this winter; but not havg. the thermometer to apply to, I could only judge from appearances, & my own feelings.

After breakfast Colo. Fitzgerald and myself set off on our return home, & parted at 4 Mile Run. About half after four I got to Mount Vernon, where Mrs. Washington, Nelly, and little Washington had just arrived—as also Mr. Shaw from Dumfries.

Sunday 5th. Thermometer at 24 in the Morning—32 at Noon and 34 at Night.

Miniature of Richard Bland Lee, by James Peale. (Mr. John W. Davidge, Jr.)

Elizabeth Collins Lee, wife of Richard Bland Lee. From a copy attributed to Alice Reading. (Virginia Historical Society)

Wind pretty fresh from the No. West all day, and much appearance of Snow; but none fell.

Mr. Richd. Bland Lee came here to dinner and stayed all Night.

Richard Bland Lee (1761–1827) was the third son of Henry Lee of Leesylvania, and younger brother of Light Horse Harry and Charles Lee. He lived in Loudoun County, which he represented in the Virginia House of Delegates 1784–88 and 1796. He later moved to Alexandria and served as a delegate from Fairfax County 1799–1800.

Monday 6th. Thermometer at 36 in the morng.—37 at Noon and 37 at Night.

Cloudy & heavy all day, with little wind & that soft.

Mr. Lee went away about 10 Oclock and Mr. Thornton Washington came in after we had dined and stayed all night.

Mr. Lund Washingtons Negro Shoemaker left working here on saturday last.

Returned to the erection of my deer paddock, which the bad weather had impeded. Brought carts from the plantations to assist in drawing in the Materials for the Work.

Thornton Washington lived at Cedar Lawn, near Harewood, in Berkeley County. He was married twice, first to Mildred Berry and then to Frances Townshend Washington.

Tuesday 7th. Thermometer at 34 in the Morning—⟨4⟩6 at Noon and 42 at Night.

Morning clear & calm—grd. a little frozen. Wind pretty fresh afterwards from the Northwest—notwithstanding which it lowered a good deal towards evening.

I rid to Muddy hole and Dogue run Plantations and by the grd. where the ferry hands were at work.

Wednesday 8th. Thermometer at 38 in the Morning—43 at Noon and [ ] at Night.

Morning clear and calm; but very strong appearances of Snow afternoon, not enough how[eve]r to cover the ground—The Wind all the latter part of the day blowing pretty fresh from the No. West.

A Mr. [ ] Nisbett brother to J. M. Nisbett accompanied by Colo. Fitzgerald, Mr. Herbert and Mr. Potts came here to dinner and stayed all Night.

Alexander Nesbitt (d. 1791) and John Maxwell Nesbitt (c.1730–1802) were sons of Jonathan Nesbitt of Loughbrickland, County Down, Ireland. The brothers established themselves as merchants after emigrating to Philadelphia: Alexander with Walter Stewart in the dry goods house of Stewart & Nesbitt, and John with a distant relative, Redmond Conyngham, in the mercantile firm of Conyngham, Nesbitt & Co., which during the Revolution became known as J. M. Nesbitt & Co. Both Alexander and John served during the war as members of the First Troop Philadelphia City Cavalry. John was prominent in Philadelphia financial circles, serving as a director of the Bank of North America 1781–92 and as the first president of the Insurance Company of North America 1792–96 (CAMPBELL [3], 126–27).

Thursday 9th. Thermometer at 36 in the Morning—41 at Noon and 38 at Night.

Clear all day, & for the Season cold, the wind being fresh from the No. West.

After breakfast the Gentlemen who came yesterday returned to Alexandria and after candles were lighted Doctr. Jenifer came in and stayed all Night.

Friday 10th. Thermometer at 32 in the Morning—44 at Noon and 44 at Night.

Ground very hard froze in the Morning, which was cold—the wind being fresh all day at No. West. In the evening it became calm. The day was clear.

Lund Washington came here to Breakfast—after which he and Doctr. Jenifer both went away.

Between breakfast and Dinner, a Mr. Rollins, who has undertaken to finish my new Room came here settled a plan with my joiners & returned before dinner.

John Rawlins, a stucco worker, or plasterer, was originally from England. Recommended by GW's former aide, Tench Tilghman, now a Baltimore merchant, Rawlins had come to Mount Vernon in Sept. 1785 to make an estimate of the cost of decorating the New Room and in November sent GW a drawing of his design for the room and an estimate of £168 Maryland currency plus traveling expenses for "Ornaments in Ceiling, Cove, Cornice & moulding at top of cove, with pannels on the walls plaine" (Rawlins to GW, 15 Nov. 1785, NjMoNP; GW to Tilghman, 14 Sept. 1785, Tilghman to GW, 31 Aug. 1785, DLC:GW). Although GW declared this price to be exorbitant, he let Tilghman make an agreement with Rawlins for the work (GW to Tilghman, 30 Nov. 1785, DLC:GW). Articles of agreement were signed by Rawlins and Tilghman on 25 Feb. 1786 and Rawlins was to start work by 15 April. GW was to provide food and lodging for Rawlins and his workers and transportation for them and for "such of the Stucco as it shall be necessary to mould at Baltimore" (DLC:GW). In order not to delay the work on the room, GW's own joiners and carpenters were to do any work necessary to prepare for Rawlins's arrival (GW to Tilghman, 30 Nov. 1785, DLC:GW).

Saturday 11th. Thermometer at 34 in the Morning—44 at Noon and 40 at Night.

Weather clear and cool, Wind at No. West, and ground hard froze in the Morning. Rode to all my Plantns. and to the Mill. On my Return found a Mr. James Hains, the Manager of the James River Canal here—sent by the Directors to me—and to proceed with Letters from me to the Potomack and Susquehanna Works which being given, he proceeded after dinner to the former.

Brought a Load of Salt in my Boat from Alexandria, for Fishing.

MR. JAMES HAINS: James Harris, who carried a letter dated 2 Mar., to GW from Edmund Randolph introducing Harris as "a mechanic, formed by nature for the management of water, when applied to mills," and asking GW to aid Harris's inspection trip to the two navigation projects (DLC: GW). SUSQUEHANNA WORKS: In 1783 Maryland chartered a company similar to the Potomac and James river navigation companies to make the Susquehanna River navigable through Maryland. By 1786 the company was cutting a canal along the left bank of the river beginning at Port Deposit, just below the Pennsylvania line, and eventually running almost to its mouth. After 20 years of work the canal was officially open but was never successful; it was later superseded by the Susquehanna and Tidewater Canal, the Maryland portion of which ran along the right bank of the river (SCHARF [4], 2:524; LIVINGOOD, 34, 71–73).

Sunday 12th. Thermometer at 36 in the Morng.—53 at Noon and 50 at Night.

Very clear and pleasant, all day, till towards sunset, when the western horison became thick. The Wind in the forenoon was at No. West but not hard. Afterwards it was at East and variable

—a large circle round the Moon at 8 and 9 Oclock in the Evening.

About dusk, Mr. William Harrison (a delegate to Congress from the State of Maryland) and his Son came in on their way to New York.

William Harrison was the brother of Robert Hanson Harrison, a close friend and wartime secretary of GW's. The former was a delegate to Congress 1785–87.

Monday 13th. Thermometer at 38 in the Morning—49 at Noon and 48 at Night.

Clear and pleasant with but little Wind, and that variable. In the forenoon it was Northerly and in the afternoon easterly and towds. Sun set lowering—the sun setting in a bank.

Mr. Harrison and son went away after breakfast and Mr. Lund Washington came immediately afterwards and stayed till the afternoon.

The ground being in order for it, I set the people to raising and forming the mounds of Earth by the gate in order to plant weeping willow thereon.

Sent my Boat to Alexanda. for Salt with the Overseer in it who by my order, engaged my Fishing landing at Johnsons ferry to Mr. Lomax in Alexandria—who is to put doors and windows to the house and pay Twenty five pounds for the use of it during the fishing Season.

MOUNDS OF EARTH: GW's plan for the landscaping of the west front of Mount Vernon called for two artificial mounds, one on each side of the gate at the end of the bowling green. A weeping willow was to be planted on each mound.

Tuesday 14th. Thermometer at 38 in the Morning—50 at Noon and 42 at Night.

A Red horison in the East at Sunrising; but tolerably clear till towards Noon, with a large circle round the sun. After noon it turned cloudy, and towards night there were strong appearances of rain—Wind at East all day.

Rid to my Plantations at Dogue Run, Muddy Hole, and in the Neck. At the former had begun to sow Oats in ground that was intended for, and had been added to my upper Meadow but after sowing the narrow slipe at the lower end I ordered the plowmen to stop and forbid any more harrowing as the ground was too wet & heavy to be worked to any advantage.

That ground in the Neck wch. I was cross plowing, for Oats also, was too wet and heavy; but the lateness of the season induced me to continue plowing as I wanted to bring it into fine tilth on acct. of clover seed which I meant to sow with the Oats.

Planted the intervals between the forest trees in my serpentine roads, or walks to the House from the front gate, with Weeping Willow. Note, part of these (nearly all on the right side going to the gate) were planted on Wednesday the first day of this Month, whilst I was on the business of the Potomk. Company at the great Falls.

Sent my Overseer, and Boat to Alexandria for another load of Salt.

Wednesday 15th. Thermometer at 38 in the morning—41 at Noon and 46 at Night.

Misting *all* day, and now and then raining pretty smartly, wind constantly at East.

The wet obliged me to discontinue my working on the Mounds and set the people to picking the wild onions out of the Oats which I am abt. to sow.

In the afternoon, the Vessel wch. I sent to york river for Corn from the Plantations of the deceased Mr. Custis arrived with 1000 bushels.

THE VESSEL WCH. I SENT TO YORK RIVER: This was the shipment of corn which GW had employed George Savage's skipper, John Whitney, to bring to Mount Vernon (see entry for 3 Feb. 1786). In addition to the Indian corn, Whitney brought six bushels of peas, all from John Parke Custis's plantation on the Pamunkey River (GW to Savage, 17 Mar. 1786, owned by Mr. Randolph P. Barton, Salem, Mass.).

Thursday 16th. Thermometer at 48 in the Morning—57 at Noon and 50 at Night.

Misling morning. About 9 Oclock it cleared and was warm and pleasant overhead but very wet under foot, occasioned by the quantity of Rain that fell last Night—but little wind and that from the Westward. About 4 oclock a pretty heavy shower of Rain fell.

Finished the Mound on the right and planted the largest weeping willow in my nursery in the centre of it—ground too wet to do any thing to the other Mound on the left.

Landed 450 Bushels of Corn to day—more might have been got up but for the badness of the road occasioned by the late rains made it difficult passing with Carts.

Friday 17th. Thermometer at 49 in the morning—52 at Noon and 48 at Night.

Cloudy all day, and sometimes dripping rain—Wind at No. West but not fresh nor cold.

Finished landing Corn—viz. 1000 Bushels which had swelled 13 bushels over.

Had every species of stock turned off my Muddy hole Wheat field except two English Colts and [ ] with young.

Saturday 18th. Thermometer at 44 in the Morning—56 at Noon and 52 at Night.

Morning a little cloudy, and the Wind at No. West with appearances of blowing hard; but towards noon it cleared, the wind moderated, and in the afternoon it became calm and very pleasant.

Rid to my Ferry, Dogue Run, Muddy hole, and Neck plantations. On my return before dinner found a Mr. Charton (a french Gentleman) here introduced by a letter from Governr. Henry.

Got the Mound on the left so far compleated as to plant the next largest of my weeping Willows thereon the buds of which were quite expanded, and the leaves appearing in their unfolded state—quaere, how much too far, in this state of the Sap, is the Season advanced? Also planted the cuttings from, or trimming, of these trees in a nursery they being in the same forward State.

Spaded up some of the ground in my botanical garden for the purpose of planting the scaly bark hiccory nut of Gloucester in.

Also a piece of ground No. West of the green House, adjoining thereto, the garden Wall, & Post & rail fencing lately erected as yards for my Stud horses in order to plant the Seed of the Honey loccust &ca. &ca.

About Noon this day finished crossing the ground in the Neck —designed for Oats and clover—and nothing but the lateness of the Season could (if that will) justify my doing it whilst the ground is so wet—or beginning to inlist Corn ground which I did at the same place whilst the ground was in this condition.

Henry L. Charton was introduced to GW a week before his visit to Mount Vernon by a letter from Patrick Henry. Henry wrote that Charton, Albert Gallatin, and Savary de Valcoulon proposed "to settle (a large body of land, on the waters of Ohio near to some of yours) by white people, chiefly from Europe" (excerpt, Patrick Henry to GW, 11 Mar. 1786, sold by Mercury Stamp Co., Inc., 5 June 1970, Item 3079). Apparently Charton discussed the possibility of purchasing some of GW's land in the west during this visit. In early May there was further correspondence concerning the property, but the western settlement negotiations never got beyond this stage (GW to Henry Charton, 20 May 1786, InHi).

Sunday 19th. Thermometer at 46 in the morning–50 at Noon & 46 at Night.

Wind moderate in the forenoon, and the morning exceedingly pleasant; but blowing fresh from the Eastward after twelve o'clock. It lowered in the afternoon and threatned an unfavourable change.

A Gentleman calling himself the Count de Cheiza D'arteignan Officer of the French Guards came here to dinner; but bringing no letters of introduction, nor any authentic testemonials of his being either; I was at a loss how to receive, or treat him. He stayed dinner and the evening.

Mr. Charton went away after dinner.

The comte de Cheiza d'Artaignan had just arrived in Alexandria from Cap Français in Santo Domingo (see d'Artaignan to GW, 18 Mar. 1786, DLC: GW).

Monday 20th. Thermometer at 42 in the Morning–48 at Noon and 46 at Night.

Wind fresh from the No. East all day–misling and raining, more or less, till eveng. At times it fell pretty heavily.

Planted in that square of my Botanical garden, adjoining to the Servants & spinning House in two and an half rows, 95 of the gloucester hiccory nut. They are on that side of the square next the House–between the Walk, and a locust tree standing within the Square.

Trimmed all the Weeping willow trees which had been planted in the serpentine Walks both sides & which had begun to display their leaves.

Tuesday 21st. Thermometer at [ ] in the morning–60 at Noon, and 58 at Night.

Wind brisk from the No. West all day (drying the ground finely)–in the morning it was a little cloudy but clear afterwards.

The Count de Cheiza D'Artingnon (so calling himself) was sent, with my horses, to day, at his own request, to Alexanda.

Mr. Shaw went to town to day on my business.

In the So. West square of my fruit Garden, beginning with the upper row, next the cross walk, the following trees were planted–viz.–1st. row 4 damisons–3d. Row 4 common plumbs–5th. row 4 damisons–7 Row 4 common Plumbs–9th. row 4 damisons; according to my Gardiners account–all from Mr. Manleys place–And in the So. East square, at the east side of the 3d. Row (counting from the cross Walk) are 2 Pears (common) from the same place.

A Captn. Hite came here between breakfast and dinner to see if I would join him in an Iron work on the So. Branch wch. proposition I rejected—and

Captn. W. Brooke came here to dinner and returned afterwds.

Mr. Shaw returned from Alexandria abt. 9 Oclock at Night.

Wednesday 22d. Thermometer at 50 in the morning—58 at Noon and 58 at Night.

Wind rather variable, but chiefly from the Westward. About noon it lowered and a large circle appeared round the Sun—but the Sun set clear and the evening was red.

Had the intervals between my Cape Wheat hoed. Cut the top of every other row of the first sowed of it about 8 Inches from the ground it being not less than 12 or 14 Inches high and many of the blades, in places, appearing to be dying. Left the alternate rows untouched, to see what effect this cutting will have. The second sowing of this Wheat appears very lively & thriving. Having a few grains of it left I had it planted in the missing places.

Hoed the ground behind the Garden again and planded therein, in three Rows 177 of the wild, or Cherokee plumb; (sent me by Mr. Geo. A. Washington) 8 inches a part in the rows with 18 inch intervals.

Also hoed up, under the Pines, in the inclosure near H[ell] hole abt. 4 Rods of ground wch. is much shaded, and poor, to try whether it will bring the orchard grass.

Rid to all my Plantations; directed the Overseer at Dogue Run to harrow the ground wch. had been sometime plowed for Oats, in order to get it ready for sowing, though it was much wetter than were to be wished. Did the same in the Neck, or River plantation, where the ground intended for the same purpose was in like condition.

CHEROKEE PLUMB: possibly *Prunus angustifolia,* Chickasaw plum.

Thursday 23d. Thermometer at 51 in the Morning—[ ] at Noon and 50 at night.

Wind very fresh the whole day at No. West, and weather clear.

Along side the Cherokee plumb (planted yesterday) I planted in a Row and piece, the Spanish chesnuts sowed last fall.

And next these 43 rows, one foot apart & about an inch asunder in the row between 17 and 18,000 seed of the honey locust.

Next these, in three rows, planted 160 of the Portugal peach stones.

And adjoining these are 3 other rows of the common chestnut.

In the Evening Doctr. Craik came in.

Muddy hole hands finished grubbing their side of the New ground, in front of the House, & went about their fencing at home.

Friday 24th. Thermometer at 46 in the morning–56 at Noon and 55 at Night.

Wind at No. West in the Morning, and rather cool. After noon it was at South west and blew pretty fresh–looking hazy.

Rid to my Plantations at Dogue run, Muddy hole and in the Neck. Began again to sow Oats at the first and last of these, though the ground was yet too wet.

Sowed the ground which was prepared on Wednesday last under the Pine trees with about 1 quart of Orchard grass seeds, and a gill of red Clover seeds mixed.

Doctr. Craik went up to Alexandria after breakfast.

Saturday 25th. Thermometer at 53 in the Morning–68 at Noon and 64 at Night.

Clear, warm, and pleasant all day–wind southerly, and pretty fresh–smoaky, the sun, consequently, looking red.

Rid to all the Plantations, and to the Mill.

Finding the ground both at Dogue run and River plantation (which had been twice plowed at each) for Oats, too much consolidated & baked (the last plowings being when it was too wet) for the harrow to make much impression in it, and the lateness of the Season not allowing time to give it another plowing before sowing, I directed the Seed to be sown on it as it now is, and to be *plowed* in, smoothing it afterwards with the harrow–but the ground in *many* places breaking up in large clods, & flakes, more so indeed than at the first plowing, it is to be feared the seed will be irregularly sown–burried too deep–and the Crop (after all the pains I intended to take with it) be indifferent and in bad condition to receive the grass seeds which were intended to be sown therewith.

In removing the planks about the Venetian Window, at the North end of the house, the Sill, and ends of the Posts, and studs, were found decayed; and were accordingly, the first renewed, and the other repaired.

Doctr. Craik came here to dinner, & returned to Maryland after it.

Sunday 26th. Thermometer at 57 in the morning—67 at Noon and 67 at Night.

Clear and very smoaky all day, with the wind brisk from the Southwest. Towards sundown it began to lower a little.

The warmth of yesterday and this day, forwarded vegetation much; the buds of some trees, particularly the Weeping Willow & Maple, had displayed their leaves and blossoms & all others were swelled, and many ready to put forth. The apricot trees were beginning to blossom and the grass to shew its verdure.

Monday 27th. Thermometer at 46 in the Morning [ ] at Noon and 56 at Night.

Cloudy all the forenoon—Wind at No. Wt.

Rid to all my Plantations. Finished plowing in the Oats at Dogue Run—ground much too wet; but not to be avoided, as nothing could be well worse than a longer delay of getting them sowed. Ordered the ground to be harrowed, to smooth and prepare it for the Timothy seed which I mean to sow with the Oats when they are up and require rolling.

What from the wetness of the above ground, and the last plowing (after sowing) being deeper than I chose, it is to be feared the Seed will come up badly.

The same apprehension I have concerning the Oats in the Neck, which are plowed in in the same manner, and the ground equally wet. The harrow at this place follow the plows close. At Dogue Run the whole was first plowed in before the harrow moved.

Tuesday 28th. Thermometer at 42 in the morning—50 at Noon and 52 at Night.

Clear all day with the Wind at So. It should have been noted, that in the Night of the 26th. there fell Rain—tho' not a great deal—enough however to wet the top of the ground.

Finished sowing my Oats in the Neck and plowing them in, but not the harrowing of the ground after the Plows.

Finished the Land sides of my Paddock fencing, and as a temporary expedient, set about Water fences at each end, to serve till the fishing season is over.

Also finished the Mound on the left side (going out) of the front gate.

Sowed in [ ] rows in my botanical garden, one foot as-sun⟨der,⟩ and about 3/4 of an inch a part, in the rows, all the seed I had of the palmetto royal.

Replaced the following trees in my Shrubberies which were dead or supposed to be so—viz.—

10 swamp Magnolio
4 red buds
5 black haws
3 locusts
1 swamp red berry.

Sent Mr. Shaw to Alexandria to settle some accts. and receive money. He returned in the evening.

Wednesday 29th. Thermometer at 48 in the Morning—60 at Noon and 62 at Night.

Lowering in the forenoon, and sometimes dropping Rain—clear afterwards—Wind Southerly all day and at times fresh.

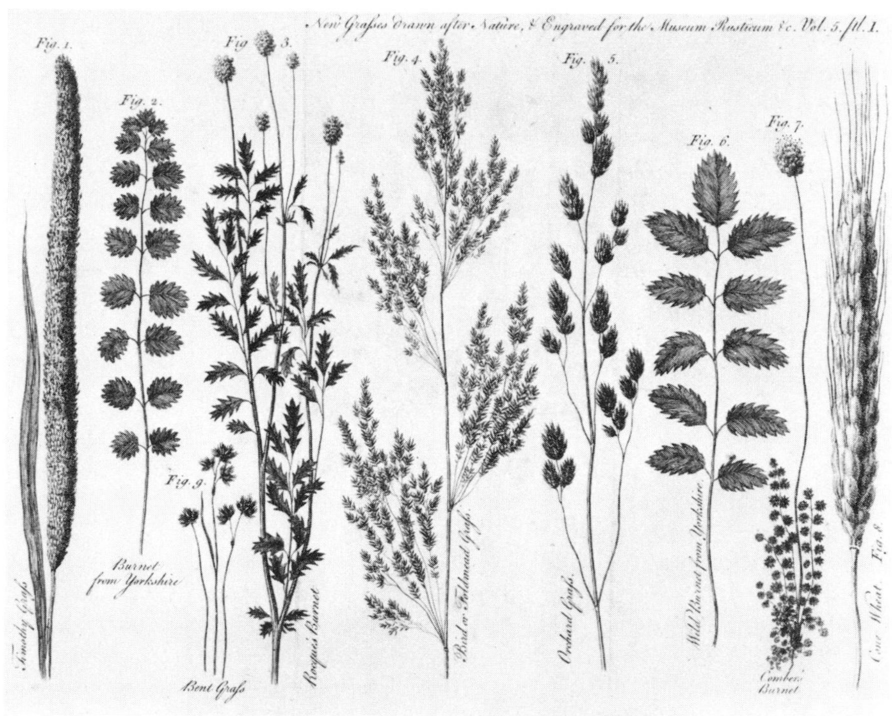

Some varieties of burnet, from *Museum Rusticum et Commerciale,* London, 1764. (Beinecke Rare Book and Manuscript Library, Yale University)

Finished crossing the ground at Muddy hole plantation, intended for experiments.

Began to plow a piece of grd. in the Neck for Burnet, Saintfoin and Rib grass, in front of the overseers house.

Rid to all my Plantations and to the fish house at the ferry where my Carpenters were at work. In the afternoon a Mr. Brindley, manager of the Susquehanna canal and Mr. Hanes manager of the James River Navigation came in and stayed all night.

RIB GRASS: *Plantago lanceolata,* plantain or ribwort. Arthur Young said he had long recommended it as a forage crop (ANNALS, 6:47), but it is now a common weed in grasslands.

James Brindley was a nephew of James Brindley (1716–1772), the talented Englishman who had initiated the dry-land canal era in England in the 1760s under the auspices of the duke of Bridgewater. Coming from the Susquehanna canal works Brindley and Harris "took the great Falls in their way down, & both approve of the present line for our Canal," wrote GW to John Fitzgerald and George Gilpin, adding, "no person in this country has *more* practical knowledge than Mr. Brindley" (31 Mar. 1786, DLC:GW). Brindley was on his way to Richmond to consult and advise on the James River project and GW hoped he would do the same for the Potomac project on his way back to the Susquehanna.

Thursday 30th. Thermometer at 58 in the Morning–63 at Noon and [ ] at Night.

Lowering more or less all day, with the wind at South.

Rid to the ferry, Dogue run, and Muddy hole plantations & to the Mill.

On my return home, found a Mr. Wallace, an Irish Gentlemen—some time since recommended to me by Mr. Edward Newenham, here.

The Corn which I had lately received from York River having got very hot, I was obliged to send part of it to be spread in my Mill loft—part to be spread on the Barn floor at Muddy hole—part I spread above stairs in the servants Hall and part I spread on Carpets in the yard the last of which from the appearance of the Weather I was obliged soon to take in again.

Finished harrowing the ground in which Oats had been sowed at Dogue Run, and in the Neck; and set a number of Hoes at the former to breaking the clods wch. the harrow could not effect. The ground in the Neck in many places was left very lumpy also but on acct. of other jobs there I could do no more to it at present.

Perceived the Oats which had been sown, at Dogue run on the 14th. instt. to be generally up. On Monday last they were beginning to peep out of the ground.

Planted in the holly clumps, in my shrubberies, a number of small holly trees which some months ago Colo. Lee of Stratford sent me in a box with earth—also in the same shrubberies some of the slips of the Tree box. I also planted several holly trees which had been sent to me the day before by a Neighbour Mr. Thos. Allison.

Mr. Brindley and Mr. Hains or Harris, went away after breakfast.

Sir Edward Newenham (1732–1814), the Irish politician who represented Dublin in Parliament at this time, had recommended Wallace to GW. GW and Newenham corresponded from at least 1781 until a few years before GW's death. Wallace returned to Mount Vernon early in June and left soon after for Bordeaux (see entries for 8, 9, and 17 June 1786).

Thomas Allison (Alliston) lived in the lower Accotink Creek area on the road leading to GW's mill (SPROUSE [2], 16).

Friday 31st. Thermometer at 56 in the Morng.—[ ] at Noon and [ ] at Night.

Raining a little before day with thunder & lightning—after which it misted till towds. Noon when there were appearances of its clearing; but in the afternoon it rained pretty smartly, and continued threatning. Wind No. & No. West sometime No. E.

Walked to my Plantation in the Neck where, tho' the ground was nearly prepared for my grape Seeds I could not sow them on acct. of the Weather.

Got my Paddock fence quite inclosed except along the margin of the Rivr.

In the afternoon, George Washington and his wife arrived in Colo. Bassetts Chariot.

April 1786

Saturday 1st. Thermometer at 34 in the Morning—34 at Noon and 32 at Night.

A very disagreeable mixture of Rain and fine hail fell all day, with a fresh and cold No. easterly wind. Towards night and in the Night it snowed. Few days or Nights this year have been more inclemt. and disagreeable than this.

Sunday 2d. Thermometer at 31 in the morning—40 at Noon and 41 at Night.

A very hard frost this Morning; Water & wet Ice frozen and

day cold—Wind hard at No. West and weather clear—Snow which fell in the Night had drifted so as not to tell the depth of it easily. All the blossoms & young foliage much injured, and the forward fruit (if no more) entirely destroyed.

Just after dinner Mr. Fendall came in, and about Sun down a Doctr. Middleton—both of whom stayed all night.

April 3d. Thermometer at 36 in the Morng.—50 at Noon and 50 at Night.

A hard frost this morning & a good deal of Ice—Wind Southerly and clear till the afternoon, when it shifted to the East and lowered.

Mr. Fendall went away before Breakfast and Mr. Wallace & Doctr. Middleton soon after it.

Lund Washington dined here. Snow chiefly dissolved—ground very wet and unfit to stir.

Planted [ ] stocks of the imported haw thorn—brought by Mr. G. A. Washington from Mr. Lyons—in the inclosure below the Stable—also, 4 of the yellow Jessamine by the Garden gates.

Tryed my Jack to day to a Mare that was horsing but he would not cover her. Mr. Griffith came.

Tuesday 4th. Thermometer at 45 in the morning—49 at Noon and [ ] at Night.

Little wind, but very cloudy in the morning, and before 10 oclock it began to Rain; and continued to do so moderately all day and till we went to bed from the East.

Sent my Seins and People to the Fishing landing at the ferry, but no hand was made of Fishing.

Planted 6 of the pride of China brought from Mr. Lyons by G. A. Washington in my shrubberies in front of the House—3 on each side the right & left walks between the Houses & garden gates and also the two young trees sent me some time ago by Mr. Griffith, to which no name had been given. These latter were planted, one on each side of the Right & left walks—near the garden gates on the hither or Et. side.

Wednesday 5th. Thermometer at 45 in the Morning—45 at Noon and 44 at Night.

Wind at No. West or more northerly all day and raining and mizzling without intermission—being very disagreeable and the ground very wet.

Fanned all the heated Corn to day. The trouble this Corn has occasioned to preserve it from entire destruction is equal to the worth of it. To prevent its receiving some damage & getting musty I have not been able to do.

Hauling the Sein again to day to no great effect.

Thursday 6th. Thermometer at 42 in the Morning—52 at Noon and 54 at Night.

Very clear all day and upon the whole pleasant though the Wind blew pritty fresh and cool in the Morning from the No. West—but shifting to the Southward it grew calm in the afternoon.

Mr. Griffith went away after breakfast and I rid to my Plantations at the ferry Dogue run & Muddy hole.

Transplanted 46 of the large Magnolio of So. Carolina from the box brought by G. A. Washington last year—viz.—6 at the head of each of the Serpentine Walks next the Circle—26 in the Shrubbery or grove at the South end of the House & 8 in that at the No. end. The ground was so wet, more could not at this time be planted there.

Took the covering off the Plants in my Botanical garden, and found none living of all those planted the 13th. of June last, except some of the Acasce or Acacia, flower fence, and privy & of these it was doubtful.

The Guinea grass shewed no signs of vegitation, and whether the root is living, is questionable.

None of the plants which were sowed with the seeds from China (a few of which had come up last year) were to be seen.

Whether these plants are unfit for this climate or whether covering & thereby hiding them entirely from the Sun the whole winter occasioned this to Rot, I know not.

Cut two or three rows of the Wheat of good hope, within 6 Inches of the ground, it being near 18 Inches high (the first sowing) and the blades of the whole singed with the frost.

Friday 7th. Thermometer at 50 in the morng.—[ ] at Noon and 52 at Night.

Rid to Muddy hole Plantation and finding the ground which had been twice plowed to make my experiments in there middling dry in some places, though wet in others, I tried my drill or Barrel plow; which requiring some alteration in the harrow, obliged me to bring it to the Smiths shop. This suspended any further operation with it to day.

No fish caught to day, of neither Herring or shad.

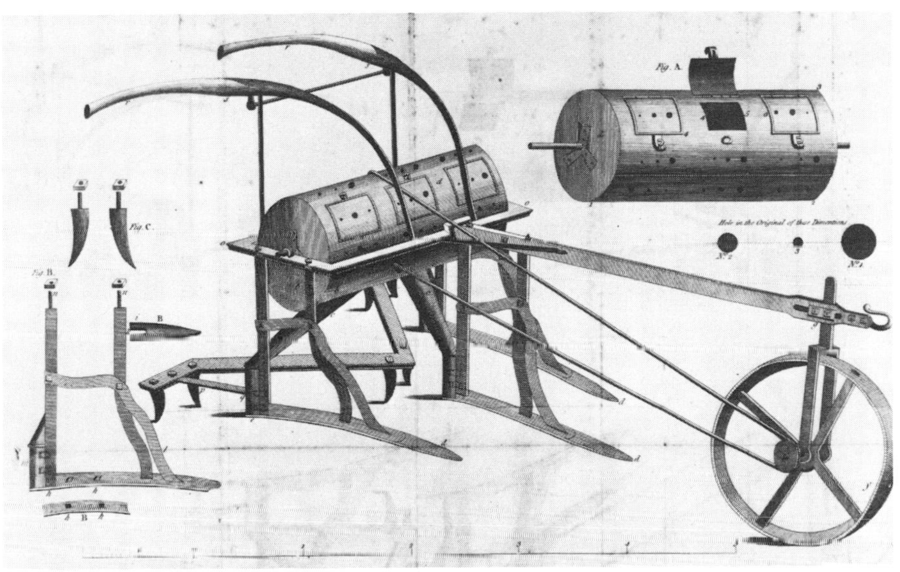

A drill plow, from Arthur Young's *Annals of Agriculture,* London, 1785. (Sterling Memorial Library, Yale University)

Set my Brick layer to getting sand & preparing for laying brick on Monday.

Mr. George Washington went to Alexandria and engaged 100,-000 Herrings to Smith and Douglas (if caught) at 5/ pr. thousand.

Saturday 8th. Thermometer at [ ] in the Morng.–[ ] at Noon and 44 at Night.

Lowering more or less all day and sometimes dropping. Wind South, So. Et., & more Easterly and at times pretty fresh. Towards Sun down the appearances of fair weather was more favourable.

Rid a little after Sun rise to Muddy to try my drill plow again which with the alteration of the harrow yesterday I find will fully answer my expectation and that it drops the grains thicker, or thinner in proportion to the quantity of Seed in the Barrel. The less there is in it the faster it issues from the holes. The weight of a quantity in the barrel, occasions (I presume) a pressure on the holes that do not admit of a free discharge of the Seed through them—whereas a small quantity (sufficient at all times to cover the bottom of the barrel) is, in a manner sifted through them by the revolution of the Barrel.

I sowed with the barrel today, in drills, about 3 pints of a white well looking Oat, brought from Carolina last year by G. A. Washington in 7 rows running from the path leading from the Overseers Ho[use] to the Quarter to the West fence of the field where the ground was in the best order. Afterwards I sowed in such other parts of the adjoining ground as could at any rate be worked the common Oat of the Eastern shore (after picking out the Wild Onion) but in truth nothing but the late Season could warrant sowing in ground so wet.

None of the ground in wch. these Oats were sown had received any improvement from manure—but all of it had been twice plowed, and then listed—after which the harrow had gone over it twice before the Seed harrowing. This, had it not been for the frequent rains &ca. which has fallen would have put the ground in fine order.

Transplanted as many of the large magnolio into the Grove at the No. end of the Ho[use] as made the number there [ ]

Also transplanted from the same box, 9 of the live Oak—viz., 4 in the bends of the lawn before the House and five on the East of the grove (within the yard) at the No. end of the House.

Plowed up my last years turnip patch (at home) to Sow Orchard grass Seeds in.

No fish caught to day.

Sunday 9th. Thermometer at 44 in the Morning–[ ] at Noon and [ ] at Night.

Lowering more or less all day. In the morning there were great appearances of Rain. About Noon it brightened up a little but in the evening it grew cloudy again and a large circle appeared round the Moon between 9 and 10 Oclock at Night. The Wind was at So. Et. and E.So. Et. all day and at times pretty fresh.

Mr. Dalby of Alexandria came here to dinner, and returned afterwards. In the Afternoon Doctr. Stuart and his Sister arrived and stayed all night.

Philip Dalby came to enlist GW's support in recovering a slave. While visiting in Philadelphia, Dalby's servant had been lured away by a group of Quakers organized for the purpose of freeing slaves brought to that city. Dalby inserted a long notice in the Alexandria newspaper warning the general public of this "insidious" practice of the Quakers (*Va. Journal,* 30 Mar. 1786) and was at this time going to Philadelphia to petition the Pennsylvania assembly for the return of his property. GW wrote to Robert Morris: "If the practice of this Society of which Mr. Dalby speaks, is not discountenanced, none of those whose *misfortune* it is to have slaves as attendants, will visit the city if they can possibly avoid it" (12 April 1786, DLC:GW). He added that although he deplored the institution of slavery, its abolition must come through legislative authority. Dalby's suit was successful and he recovered his slave (Robert Morris to GW, 26 April 1786, DLC:GW).

Monday 10th. Thermometer at 42 in the Morning—50 at Noon and 46 at Night.

Cold and raw Northerly wind blew all the forenoon, and in the afternoon shifted Easterly & was not much pleasanter.

Began my brick work to day—first taking away the foundations of the Garden Houses as they were first placed, & repairing the damages in the Walls occasioned by their removal. And also began to put up my pallisades (on the Wall).

Compleated Sowing with 24 quarts the drilled Oats in the ground intended for experiments at Muddy hole; which amounted at 38 Rows ten feet apart (including the parts of rows sowed on Saturday last). In the Afternoon I began to sow Barley, but finding there were too many Seeds discharged from the Barrel, notwithstanding I stopped every other hole, I discontinued the sowing until another Barrel with smaller holes cd. be prepared. The ground in which these Oats have been sowed and in which the Barley seeding had commenced—has been plowed, cross plowed, listed (as it is called, that is 3 furrow ridges) and twice harrowed before the drill plow was put into it. With this the furrow is made & the seed harrowed in witht. manure afterwds.

Began also to sow the Siberian Wheat which I had obtained from Baltimore, by means of Colo. Tilghman, at the Ferry Plantation in the ground laid apart there for experiments. This was done upon ground which, sometime ago, had been marked off by furrows 8 feet apart, in which a second furrow had been run to deepen them. 4 furrows were then plowed to these, which made the whole 5 furrow Ridges. These being done some time ago, and by frequent rains prevented Sowing at the time intended had got hard. I therefore before the Seid was sowed, split these Ridges again, by running twice in the same furrow—after wch. I harrowed the ridges and where the ground was lumpy run my spiked Roller with the Harrow at the tale, over it—wch. I found very efficacious in breaking the clods & pulverizing the earth; and wd. have done it perfectly if there had not been too much moisture remaining of the late rains: after this harrowing, & rolling where necessary, I sowed the Wheat with my drill plow on the reduced ridges in rows 8 feet apart—but I should have observed that, after the ridges were split by the furrow in the middle, and before the furrows were closed again by the harrow—I sprinkled a little dung in them. Finding the barrel discharged the Wheat too fast; I did, after sowing 9 of the shortest (for we began at the furthest corner of the field) rows, I stopped every other hole in the barrel, and in this manner sowed 5 Rows more, & still thinking the seed too liberally bestowed, I stopped 2, & left one hole open, alternately, by which 4 out of 12 holes only, discharged Seeds; and this, as I had taken the strap of leather off, seemed to give Seed enough (though not so regular as were to be wished) to the ground.

Doctr. Stuart and his Sister left this after breakfast (passing through Mary land) to his fathers from whence the Doctor is to proceed to Richmond.

FOUNDATIONS OF THE GARDEN HOUSES: GW was in the process of enlarging his upper and lower gardens. The north and south walls of each garden were extended westward in an inward curve to a point where they converged. At this point in each garden, GW rebuilt an octagonal garden house.

Tuesday 11th. Thermometer at 40 in the Morning—52 at Noon and 52 at Night.

Wind at No. Et. all day, and at times pretty fresh—raw and disagreeable. Towards evening it lowered a good deal, & the Sun set in a bank.

Sowing the Siberian Wheat to day, as yesterday, at the ferry.

And sowed 26 rows of Barley (except a little at each end wch. was too wet for the ground to be worked) at Muddy hole; below, & adjoining to the Oats. This was done with 12 quarts of Seed, and in the manner, and in ground prepared as mentioned yesterday. The ends of these rows are to be sowed as soon as the ground is in order for it.

Rid to the Fishing Landing, where 30 odd shad had just been caught at a haul. Not more than 2 or 3 had been taken at one time before, this spring. And from hence I went to Muddy hole & river Plantations; at the last of which the Overseer after 3 plowings & 3 harrowings—had begun to sow in drills three feet apart, & abt. nine Inches asunder in the Rows, the Seed (without name) saved from those given to me by Colo. Archibd. Cary last year.

In the Section in my botanical garden, next the House nearest the circle, I planted 4 Rows of the laurel berries in the grd. where, last year I had planted the Physic nuts &ca.—now dead & next to these in the same section are [ ] rows of the pride of China. The Rows of both these kinds are 16 inches asunder & the Seeds 6 inches apart in the Rows.

Perceived, the last Sowed Oats at Dogue Run and those wch. had been sowed in the Neck, were coming up.

Wednesday 12th. Thermometer at 42 in the Morng.—55 at Noon and 50 at Night.

A Brisk wind all day from the No. Et.—cold & raw, with appearances of a change of Weather especially towards evening when it lowered very much.

Rid to the fishing Landing, ferry, Dogue Run, and Muddy hole plantations.

Finished at the first, Sowing the ground intended for experiments, with the Siberian Wheat. This spot contained 16 a[cres] 1 R[od] 24 P[erches]—Including the fodder Ho[use] &ca. which would reduce the cultivated Land to 10 acres at most. To sow these it took about 18 quarts of Wheat. [ ] of the last rows had no dung in them and those adjoining for [ ] back were only manured in the poorest parts. The last rows were listed wholly as they were too hard baked for the harrow & roller notwithstanding the middle furrow, to make much impression on them.

At Dogue Run I set the plows to listing the ground which had before been listed, in order to commence my experiments there on Friday. Began in the first long row by Wades houses.

At Muddy hole, I sowed two rows of the Albany Peas in Drills 10 feet asunder (the same as the Oats and Barley) but conceiving they could not, for want of support, be kept [pre]vented from falling when they shd. come near their growth I did not incline to sow any more in this way but to put all the ground between these two rows and the fence along the Road in broadcast. The ground in which these Peas were sowed was managed exactly as that had been in which the Barley & Oats (at this place) was.

Next, adjoining the Oats, on the upper, or South side, I plowed 10 Rows for Tarrots two deep furrows in the same place for each over and above all the plowings, & harrowings which the Barley &ca. had received—In the alternate rows—beginning at the second from the Oats—I sprinkled dung all along in the bottom of the furrows, and covered it with the earth which had been thrown out of them, with Hoes. The same was done with the rows in which there was no dung. This was done to try: first, how this kind of land; and management would do for Carrots and next the difference between manuring in this manner which was pritty liberal and without. On the top of the ridge, made over the furrow, I directed 2 or 3 Seeds to be dropped in a place at the distance of 10 Inches from each other and to be scratched in with a thorny bush.

Planted in the No. West section of my Botanical Garden 5 rows more of the seeds of the pride of China in the same manner those were done yesterday.

ROWS FOR TARROTS: GW inadvertently wrote "tarrots" for carrots. He had a choice of two varieties of *Daucus carota,* the orange and the red horn, and used both varieties as a field crop important in his rotation plan to produce feed for livestock.

Thursday 13th. Thermometer at 44 in the Morning—56 at Noon and 52 at Night. A high, cold, and disagreeable wind from the No. East blew all day and the Sun for the most part hid.

Rid to Muddy hole and river Plantations. The Carrots at the first were sowed as directed yesterday and at the latter I began to Sow Oats in Rows ten feet a part in grd. managed in the following manner. 1 Marked off with single furrows. 2 another, and deep furrow in this. 3. four bouts to these. 4. plowed agn. in the same manner. 5. a single furrow in the middle of these. 6. Dung sprinkled in this furrow—7 the great harrow over all these and 8th. the Seed sowed after the harrow with the drill or barrel plow, & harrowed in with the harrow at the tale of it. Note—It should have been observed that the field intended for experiments at this Plantation is divided into 3 parts, by bouting Rows running crossways and that dung and the *last* single furrow are (at least for the present) bestowed on one of these only—viz. that part which is most westerly, or nearest the Barn.

Doctr. Craik, & Mr. & Mrs. Lund Washington dined here—the first stayed all Night.

Friday 14th. Thermometer at 42 in the Morning—64 at Noon and [ ] at Night.

Clear Morning with the wind at No. East, but neither very fresh nor cold. Afterwd. Southly. & warm.

Doctr. La Moyeur sent for his Black horse & Chaise which his Servant carried away to day.

Doctr. Craik went to Alexanda. after breakfast & returned again at Night.

Rid to my Plantations at Muddy hole, Dogue Run, and ferry in the forenoon and walked to that in the Neck in the Afternoon. At the first I finished sowing the Barley rows and harrowed the ground intended for the Albany Peas in broadcast. At the next I began to sow the remainder (14 qts.) of the Siberian Wheat, which was left at the Ferry and began to Run deep furrows in the Middle & to make five furrow ridges in a piece of the corn grd. for Carrots. At the ferry I ordered a piece of ground to be plowed for Corn & Potatoes and in the Neck after sowing 24 rows of Oats upon a Dunged furrow, I ordered the discontinuance, and to begin sowing Barley adjoining.

Sowed, or rather planted at this place, 11 Rows of the Seeds saved from those had last year from Colo. Archd. Cary and 35 rows (next to them) of Rib-grass Seed. These rows were 3 feet asunder, and the Seeds (3 or 4) dropped at about 1 foot apart, in the rows.

Dr. Jean Pierre Le Mayeur wrote GW, 10 April 1786, that his servant was coming to relieve GW "from the trouble of my Black horse" which was being kept at Mount Vernon (DLC:GW).

Saturday 15th. Thermometer at 56 in the Morning–[ ] at Noon and [ ] at Night.

Clear all day–Wind Easterly in the Morning, & Southerly in the Evening & rather cool.

Rid to Alexandria to a meeting of the Directors of the Potomack Company, who had advertised their intention of contracting on this day with whomsoever should bid lowest for the Supplying the Companys Servants with Rations for one year. A Mr. Abel Westfall of Berkeley having done this the Contract was made with him accordingly. Dined at Mr. Lyles's tavern and returned in the Evening, when I found Mrs. Stuart and her Children and Mr. Arthur Lee here.

In my way to town, I passed through Muddy hole & Dogue Run Plantations. At the first I ordered the ground which was harrowed yesterday for Pease to be sowed with 6 Bushels–which was accordingly done, and harrowed it. The qty. was but little more than an acre & an half.

Finished at the latter, sowing the Siberian Wheat in 34 rows. This ground had been only twice plowed into 5 furrow ridges and then harrowed, before seeding; 8 of the first rows, counting from Wades Houses had been rolled; but wanting the Oxen to Cart dung I was obliged to discontinue the rolling. These workings, with the harrowing at the tale of the barrel plow, did not put the ground by any means in such order as it ought to be for this grain–but the wet Spring, and late Season, would not allow me to do more to it.

Sowed in the Neck, 23 rows of Burnet Seed, in part of what was intended there, along side the rib grass. This was put in exactly as the rib-grass & other grass were–that is in rows 3 feet asunder & about 1 foot apart in the rows.

Plowed a piece of ground containing two acres, at the ferry plantation, for the purposes of drilling Corn, & planting Irish Potatoes in it. This was plowed flush & intended to be cross plowed.

Abel Westfall served in 1776 and 1777 as a captain in Rev. Peter Muhlenberg's 8th Virginia Regiment, which was made up mostly of Germans from the Shenandoah Valley (WUST, 80). MR. LYLES'S TAVERN: Henry Lyles had died 12 days earlier (*Va. Journal,* 6 April 1786).

Sunday 16th. Thermometer at 46 in the Morning–64 at Noon and 67 at Night.

A brisk Southerly wind all day and at times much appearances of rain, but none fell.

Mr. Lee went away after breakfast.

Very few fish caught yet at my fishery at the ferry.

Monday 17th. Thermometer at 58 in the Morning–[ ] at Noon and 58 at Night.

Morning clear and warm, with very little wind. About 10 Oclock it began to lower, and about 2 there were great appearances of rain but the Wind getting to No. West & blowing pretty fresh they all vanished.

Went up to Alexandria to an election of Delegates to represent this County; when the suffrages of the people fell upon Colo. Mason and Doctr. Stuart–on the first contrary to, and after he had declared he could not serve and on the other whilst he was absent at Richmond. Captn. West who had offered his Services & was present, was rejected. The votes were–for Colo. Mason 109–for Doctr. Stuart 105 and for Captn. West 84.

Returned home in the evening.

Tuesday 18th. Thermometer at 52 in the Morning–58 at Noon and [ ] at Night.

Wind at No. West–pretty fresh & cool–cloudy also without much signs of Rain.

Rid to Muddy hole–Dogue Run & ferry plantations; & to the fishing Landing. At the first they had begun to plant the Irish Potatoes in drills; 4 rows were allotted for this purpose 2 whereof had a handful of dung put upon each set–which were at the distance of one foot in the rows. The other 2 Rows were planted at the same distance, and in the same manner excepting in the article of manure there being none in the Rows. At Dogue Run I began to sow barley in drills, next the Siberian Wheat and had (beginning at the meadow fence, & extending towards the old Houses) sowed 11 Rows (long & short) in Carrots; 6 of which, beginning with the first and so on alternately, were dunged; the others not. At the Ferry plantation little progress had been made in breaking up the ground for Potatoes &ca. it being hard occasioned by the late drying & baking winds. At the Fishing landing little success had attended the Seins.

One of Mr. Rawlins workmen (who came here on Saturday last in the Baltimore packet) began lathing my New Room.

In the evening Mr. Danl. Brent and Mr. Wm. Stuart came in and stayed all night.

Sent my Boat to Alexandria this evening in order to bring down Flagstones & Fish Barrels &ca.

Mr. Daniel Brent is probably Daniel Carroll Brent (1759–1814), of Prince William County, a son of Elizabeth Carroll Brent and William Brent (1733–1782), of Richland, Stafford County. FLAGSTONES: These were the flagstones for the piazza, procured for GW by John Rumney (see 9 May 1785).

Wednesday 19th. Thermometer at 50 in the morning—62 at Noon and 60 at Night.

Calm and warm in the forenoon. What little [wind] there was came from the Southward. In the afternoon the wind sprung up —but not fresh from the East.

Rid to my Ferry Plantation, and walked into the Neck. At the first few fish were caught. At the latter I found (including what was sowed yesterday and Saturday) 50 rows of Burnet Seed planted along side, and in the same manner of, the rib grass & that they had begun to sow the Sainfoin Seed. Sowing Barley yesterday & this day, at this plantation 30 Rows of which had been put in before I got there every other one of which had a slight sprinkling only of dung not being able to get it out fast enough to manure every row.

Mrs. Stuart and her Children went away immediately after breakfast—as did Mr. Brent & Mr. Stuart.

A Mr. Chavillie & another Gentleman (the first introduced by the Governor) came just as we had done breakfast & after one had been got for them proceeded on their journey to the Northward.

Before dinner, Mr. Rollins and a Mr. Tharpe came here; the first being the undertaker of my New Room intended to commence the Work, and then to leave it under the conduct of the latter which I objected to for reasons which I assigned him; he therefore determined to return & come back prepared to attend to it himself.

My Muddy hole People having compleated all the work that was to do except with the Plows before Corn planting in the common way, came to get the New ground in front of the House in order for that grain by fencing &ca.

Major Washingtons Charles returned from New Kent with the Calves & Jenny he went for.

Jean Auguste Marie Chevallié (1765–1838), born in Rochefort, France, was the son of Pierre François and Jeanne Esther Charlot Chevallié. The elder Chevallié was an agent for Beaumarchais in furnishing supplies for Virginia during the Revolution. After he failed to receive full payment for his services, he sent his son, Jean Auguste, to America, armed with letters from the French government and from prominent Frenchmen, to press his claims (Jean Auguste Marie Chevallié to James Madison, 27 Aug. 1785, MADISON, 8:358). Eventually Jean Auguste was successful in collecting the debt (Chevallié to Jefferson, 19 Jan. 1787, JEFFERSON [1], 11:55). A few years later, he left France and settled permanently in Richmond where he became a partner in the Gallego Mills (RICHMOND, 36–37).

Richard Tharpe (Thorpe), a stucco artisan, was the "principal workman of the ornamental parts" of the New Room (GW to Sir Edward Newenham, 10 June 1786, DLC:GW). He had probably recently arrived from Ireland. Tharpe's name had been first mentioned to GW by Sir Edward Newenham of Ireland in 1785, at which time GW had not heard of his arrival in this country. Tharpe's work was satisfactory, and GW later hired him to do additional plaster work on the mansion and to repair the lathing (GW to Newenham, 25 Nov. 1785 and 10 June 1786, DLC:GW; see entry for 9 June 1786).

Thursday 20th. Thermometer at 50 in the Morning—50 at Noon and 48 at Night.

Wind fresh but not hard at No. Et. all day and very cloudy, sometimes dropping Rain.

Rid to Muddy hole, Dogue run and ferry Plantations and to the fishery at the latter.

Finished Sowing 50 Rows of Barley in drills, at Dogue run, which took 35 quarts of Seed. The ground for this grain was twice plowed into 5 furrow ridges (or twice listed as it is called)—then rolled with the spiked roller—after which it was harrowed, then sowed with the Barrel plow, & the grain harrowed in with the small harrow at the tale of it. Next adjoining to the Barley I left 40 rows for the common country Pea and then began to plow 10 Rows for Potatoes wch. I directed to be managed in the same manner, previous to setting, with those for the Barley with the addition of a furrow after harrowing, to plant the Potatoes which are to be covered with the plow. These Potatoes are to be planted without dung because it could not be got out in time, the Oxen being employed with the Roller.

The Shad began to Run to day, having caught 100, 200 & 300 at a drought.

My Jack covered a she Mule to day—after which two Mares.

My Boat which went up the day before yesterday, returned this evening only—being detained by the north East wind.

Mr. Battaile Muse came here before dinner on business respecting the Collection of my rents and with his accts. wch. were just looked at, but not settled.

My People from the Ferry began to work in the New ground in front of the House to day.

Sowed a Bushel of Orchard Grass seed (given to me by Wm. Fitzhugh Esqr. of Chatham) in my last years Turnip patch at the home house. The qty. of ground might be about [ ] of an acre. The grd. in which these Seeds were sown had been twice plowed—chopped over & the clods broken with Hoes and twice harrowed afterwards: the Seeds were scratched in with a light Bush.

MY RENTS: see entry for 4 Sept. 1784, n.1.

Friday 21st. Thermometer at 48 in the Morning—48 at Noon and 48 at Night.

Drizzling till about 6 Oclock when it began a constant slow & moderate Rain with the Wind from No. Et. all day.

About Noon, one James Bloxham, an English Farmer from Gloucestershire arrived here with letters of recommendation from Colo. Fairfax (& others to him) consequent of my request to him to enquire after such a person.

Brought from England on the recommendation of Fairfax, James Bloxham signed an agreement with GW to serve as "Farmer and Manager" at 50 guineas a year, with house, provisions, and an extra 10 guineas to bring his family from England. Neither party to the agreement seemed entirely satisfied at first. GW wrote Arthur Young that Bloxham seemed to be a plain and honest farmer, but that his ability to manage a large farm was questionable. Bloxham wrote home that the plows were shocking, the farm hands disagreeable, and "it is impossible for any man to Do Bisness in any form" (Bloxham to William Peacey, 23 July 1786, ABBOTT, 188–89).

Saturday 22d. Thermometer at 50 in the Morning—56 at Noon and 56 at Night.

In the Night there fell a great deal of rain, with some thunder & lightning which put a stop to plowing and indeed most other workings of the Earth.

Morning Mizzling till about Noon, when it broke away without much wind which still hung to the Eastward. It was also tolerably warm and pleast.

Rid to the Plantations at Muddy hole, Dogue Run and Ferry. At the first fixed my Barrels for Planting Corn and Pease—but the ground was too wet to use them. The heavy Rain last night had washed all the Albany Pease which had been sowed in broad cast out of the ground. Those which had been sowed a day or two before in Drills were coming up as the Oats & Barley also were.

At the Ferry Plantation the Siberian Wheat was here & there coming up.

At the Neck Plantation finished before the Rain sowing all my Barley [ ] Rows with [ ] quarts. Also finished Sowing the Burnet & Saintfoin [ ] Rows of the former and [ ] of the latter part of which were short and having some of these Seeds and those of the rib grass left I sowed 8 of the Intervals of these with it in broad Cast—11 ditto of the Saintfoin and 3 ditto of the Burnet in the same manner. Very little fish caught to day or yesterday.

Colo. Fitzhugh and his Son Willm. came here in the Afternoon.

Sunday 23d. Set off after breakfast, on a journey to Richmond—to acknowledge in the General Court some Deeds for Land sold by me as Attorney for Colo. George Mercer which, it seems, could not be executed without. Dined at Dumfries and lodged at Stafford Court House.

Very cloudy all day with but little wind and that from the Eastward.

Monday 24th. A good deal of rain having fallen in the Night, and it continuing to do so till after 6 oclk. I was detained till near seven—when I set out, dined at my mothers in Fredericksburgh & proceeded afterwards to, and lodged at General Spotswoods.

Until Noon the day was Missling, & sometime Raining which it also did in the night—but being warm, vegitation was much promoted—Wind Easterly.

Conversing with Generl. Spotswood on the growth, and preservation of the Pumpion, he informed me that a person in his Neighbourhood who had raised of them many years has preserved them by splitting them in two—taking out the inside and then turning the rind part up (placed on rails or poles) for two or 3 days to dry—after wch. they were packed in straw—a layer of one, and a layer of the [other] alternately—by which means they keep well through the Winter.

PUMPION: *Cucurbita pepo,* pumpkin, a field crop which GW used as winter feed for cattle, planted either between rows of corn or along with root crops.

Tuesday 25th. Set out from General Spotswoods about Sun Rising and breakfasted at the Bowling green.

Where, meeting with Mr. Holmes (a neat, and supposed to be a good farmer) I was informed by him that from experience he had found that the best method of raising clover (in this Country) was to sow it on Wheat in Jany. when the ground was lightly covered with snow having never failed by this practice—whereas fall sowing is often injured by wet, and frost and Spring sowing by drought.

Dined at Rawlins and lodged at Hanover Court House.

The forepart of the day was clear and warm, but the latter part was showery and cooler—Wind westerly but not much of it.

In 1774 John Hoomes, a descendant of one of the first families to settle in Caroline County, received a license to operate an ordinary "in his new buildings at Bowling Green" (CAMPBELL [1], 13, 219, 413). One year after this visit by GW, Hoomes entertained Samuel Vaughan, an English agriculturist and a friend of GW's, who noted that "Mr. Homes who furnished the Stages owns the Bowling green. His farm is in small enclosures well fenced a ditch & rows of handsome red ceder in the fence, kept neat & in prime order. The best cultivated of any on the road" (VAUGHAN, 43).

RAWLINS: probably the tavern GW had earlier referred to as "Clarkes" (see entry for 4 May 1785). Rawlins may have been the tavern keeper in 1786. In 1781 a French officer referred to the "very fine and large inn" located at Hanover Court House (RICE, 2:101).

Wednesday 26th. Left Hanover Court Ho[use] about Sun rise; breakfasted at Norvals tavern and reached Richmond about Noon. Put up at Formicalo's Tavern, where by invitation, I dined with the Judges of the General Court.

Morning cloudy & not much wind, but between 8 and 10 Oclk. it came out fresh from the No. Wt.; and died away again about Noon.

Meeting with Mr. Thos. Newton of Norfolk, he informed me that Mr. Neil Jameeson late of that place, now a merchant in New York, was Executor of Jno. Shaw (also of Norfolk) who was possessed of the Books of Messrs. Balfour & Barraud & to whom he advised me to apply, thinking it probable that I might obtain, a list of the Ballances due to that House and thereby recover what was due to me therefrom.

NORVALS: probably the ordinary in Hanover County situated on the stage road about 12 miles north of Richmond. In 1787 Samuel Vaughan referred to this ordinary as "Nevils" (VAUGHAN, 44).

Serafino Formicola (Formiculo, Formicalo, Formicula), reputedly a "Neapolitan who came to Virginia with Lord Dunmore, as the latter's maitre d'hotel," moved his tavern business from Williamsburg to Richmond in 1780, where the next year he "opened TAVERN" on the southeast corner of Main and Fifteenth streets, and where, during assembly days, "Generals, Colonels, Captains, Senators, Assembly-men, Judges, Doctors, Clerks, and crowds of Gentlemen, of every weight and calibre and every hue of dress, sat all together about the fire, drinking, smoking, singing, and talking" (CHASTELLUX, 2:428; *Va. Gaz.*, D&N, 24 Feb. 1781; HEADS OF FAMILIES, VA., 118; SCHOEPF, 2:64). Later in the decade Formicola moved to the Eagle Tavern at Main and Twelfth streets (DUMBAULD, 46).

Thomas Newton, Jr., a merchant, dealt with GW's flour and acted as GW's agent in Norfolk. This meeting was probably prearranged (see GW to Thomas Newton, Jr., 3 Sept. 1785, GW to Neil Jamieson, 20 May 1786, DLC:GW). Neil Jamieson, earlier one of the leading merchants in Norfolk, fled Virginia during the Revolution (SOLTOW, 89–94). In 1793 GW recorded what was due him from Balfour & Barraud as £1,768 17s. (LEDGER C, 3). Before the Revolution, GW had sold flour to James Balfour (d. 1775) and Daniel Barraud, merchants of Norfolk (*Va. Gaz.*, P, 14 April, 14 July, 25 Aug. 1775; and see 4 Jan. 1775).

Thursday 27th. Acknowledged in the General Court a Deed to James Mercer Esqr. for the Lotts he and I bought at the Sale of his deceased Brother Colo. George Mercer and received a reconveyance from him of my part thereof.

Road with the Lieutt. Govr. Randolph, the Attorney General, and Mr. George Webb, to view the cut which had commenced between Westham and Richmond for the improvement of the Navigation of James river. Going late, and returning to dinner left but little time to view the work, or to form a judgment of the plan of it.

Dined, and spent the evening at the attorneys. Lodged again at Formicalos.

As president of the Council of State (1783–88), Beverley Randolph (1734–1797), of Cumberland County, acted as lieutenant governor in the absence or indisposition of the governor. His cousin Edmund Randolph was attorney general of the state 1776–86. George Webb (b. 1723), who lived in the Bassett-Dandridge-Custis neighborhood in New Kent County, served as treasurer of Virginia during the Revolution and was appointed to the Virginia Council of State in 1780 (MCILWAINE, 2:123; *Va. Mag.*, 25:100).

In Aug. 1785 the James River Company was formed to open navigation of that river above the falls at Richmond, for which several canals were cut (HENING, 11:450–62).

Friday 28th. Left Richmond about 6 Oclock–breakfasted at Norvals–Dined at Rawlins and lodged at the Bowling.

This Morning, as yesterday, was perfectly clear, warm and pleasant. Yesterday however, was calm. To day the Wind blew fresh from the So. West & in the afternoon became cloudy with great appearances of Rain a few drops of which fell, but in the evening it cleared and turned cooler.

Saturday 29th. Set out from the Bowling green a little after Sun-rising–breakfasted at General Spotswoods–Dined at my Sister Lewis's in Fredericksburgh and spent the evening at Mr. Fitzhughs of Chatham.

One of my Chariot Horses having got lame going to Richmond, but forced back to Genl. Spotswoods (not however without much difficulty) was left there with a Servant who was ordered to proceed with him or a horse which Genl. Spotswood would lend in two days.

Wind being fresh at No. West it was clear and cool to day.

Sunday 30th. Set off about Sun rising from Mr. Fitzhughs–breakfasted at Dumfries and reached home to a late Dinner.

Where I found 3 of Mr. Rawlins Men; two of whom (one a Mr. Tharpe, director of the work) had been since Sunday last; & had employed many hands in preparing Mortar & other materials for them. That the Fishing (especially at the home house wch. had been discontinued on acct. of the failure of the Sein) had not been successful–That Colo. Gilpins Scow had been sent up on Monday last–That the Rains had retarded the plows a good deal and had prevented Sowing Pease–or planting Corn. That the Irish Potatoes had been planted on Tuesday last at Dogue Run, though the ground was wet, to prevent the rot destroying them all; the wetness of the ground prevented the use of the roller in this operation, but the want of it was supplied by Hoes, to break the clods–That the Timothy Seed intended for the Oat ground at Dogue run had been sowed on it (and for want of the roller had been scratched in with a Bush, which was wrong, as the Oats were thereby torn & injured) –That the Neck people had, on Wednesday last, finished drilling the Barley at that place in 66 rows–every other of which had a sprinkling of Dung in the middle furrow–That my drilled Wheat from the Cape had been propped to prevent its lodging—That the common Chesnut (which it is apprehended are spoiled) was planted below the hops on thursday last—That the Irish Potatoes had been planted at the River plantation on thursday last in ten rows—each alternate one being dunged as those at Muddy hole were—That the ground which had been prepared for Flax was sown therewith on Friday last and harrowed in—then with clover seed and the whole rolled—That 14 rows of the live & Water Oak Acorns had been planted on the same day in my botanical garden but it was not expected that any, or very few would come up—That every other row of Corn in the cut intended for experiments at Muddy hole was planted by the Drill plow with the early Corn from New York and that all the Peas (consisting of two kinds) had been planted at the same place and in the same cut—That When the worked ground was too wet to stir, or touch the plows were employed in listing for Corn and lastly that the Mercury during my absence had stood thus—viz.

		Morng.	Noon	Night
23d.	Sunday	54	60	58
24.	Monday	53	60	59
25.	Tuesday	56	68	66
26.	Wednesday	62	69	66
27.	Thursday	66	69	64
28.	Friday	64	70	68
29.	Saturday	63	67	60
30.	Sunday	52	60	59

BELOW THE HOPS: *Humulus lupulus,* common or European hop used in brewing. GW had a plot set aside for these plants which in his entries for 13 and 18 April 1785 he calls a "hop enclosure." Among his miscellaneous agricultural papers is a page of notes on the cultivation of hops which he had extracted from a printed source (DLC:GW).

May

Monday first. Rid to the Fishing landing and to the Plantations at the Ferry, Dogue run, and Muddy hole; perceived the Siberian Wheat at the two first had come up thinly which I attributed partly to bad seed and partly to too thin sowing as the Oats and Barley at all three were also too thin and where the ground had been wet, and hard baked none appeared.

Set them to drilling the common Corn at Muddy hole and to sowing Clover Seed in the Neck on the Oats—the ground for which, was in bad order; being so hard baked that the roller could make no impression on it. This business has been unseasonably delayed—partly from the late arrival of the Seed from Phila. & partly from neglect & unfavourable weather after it did arrive.

But indifferent luck in fishing to day.

Planted or rather transplanted from the Box sent me by Colo. Wm. Washington of So. Carolina 6 of the Sweet scented, or aromatic shrub in my Shrubberies, on each side the Serpentine walks on this (or East) side of the Garden gate. The rest of these shrubs I suffered to remain in the Box as they were beginning to shoot forth buds & it might be too late to remove them. Wind at No. West.

SWEET SCENTED . . . SHRUB: *Calycanthus floridus,* Carolina allspice.

Tuesday 2d. Thermometer at 60 in the Morning—69 at Noon and 62 at Night.

Wind Easterly, but not very fresh clear and plesant. Rid by Muddy hole plantation into the Neck. At the first finished drilling the common corn, and ordered the plow to be sent to Dogue run. At the latter I began to drill the common corn—in the furthermost cut—next the river, opposite to Mr. Digges's & continued the sowing of clover there. Could perceive no vegetation in the Burnet Saint foin, or other grass which had been sown at this place.

Planted Pumpions at Morris's near the old Houses in which Mrs. Wade lived; in a light sandy soil, 10 feet a part.

Began to harrow the ground at Morris's, that is Dogue run plantation in which the bad clover seed was sown last fall in order to sprinkle Timothy Seed on it.

Planted 140 Seed sent me by Colo. Wm. Washington and said by him to be the Seed of the large Magnolio or Laurel of Carolina in boxes No. 4, 5 & 6 near the green house.

Also 21 of the Illinois Nuts; compleating at the No. end, the piece of a row in my Botanical Garden in which on the [20th] of [March] I put Gloucester hiccory Nuts.

Wednesday 3d. Thermometer at 60 in the Morning—67 at Noon and 62 at Night.

Calm and clear in the Morning. About Noon the wind sprung up from the Southward and towds. Night veered round to the Eastwd. and turned cool. Mid day warm.

Rid to Muddy hole, Dogue run and Ferry plantations—also to the fishing landing.

At the 1st. hoed up the sunken & cold places in which Barley had been sowed and was rotten in order to resow them.

At the next I had the ground which was harrowed yesterday & cross harrowing to day sowed with Seeds from my Hay loft—which I directed to be again harrowed to cover the seed and more effectually loosen the Earth. Also began to drill Peas at this—the large sort, next the Barley.

Caught a good many Fish yesterday—but not many to day.

Planted two rows of the everlasting Peas in my botanical Garden; in the Section which contained the guinea grass that would not stand the Winter.

Also 2 rows of the Acorn of the live & water Oak in the same garden—adjoining the row which has the hiccory & Illinois Nuts.

And in box No. 9 in the Garden by the green House was put a pistatia Nut given to me by Colo. Mead.

Perceived the Seeds of the Honey locust to be coming up, irregularly—whether owing to their being shallowest planted—hardness of the ground—or not I cannot say.

Also observed the clover & orchard grass seed which had been sown under the Pines in the pine grove for an experiment, was coming up pretty thick.

ILLINOIS NUTS: *Carya illinoensis,* pecan. GW also called them Mississippi nuts. They are Illinois nuts in Jefferson's *Notes on the State of Virginia.*

COLO. MEAD: probably Richard Kidder Meade (1746–1805), originally of Nansemond County, who served as an aide to GW in the Revolution and later settled in Frederick County. PISTATIA NUT: *Pistacia vera,* pistachio.

Thursday 4th. Thermometer at 58 in the Morning—68 at Noon and 63 at Night.

Clear and pleasant, with but little wind, and that Easterly. Towards evening it began to lower a little and at Night a circle appeared round the Moon.

Doctr. Craik came here in the forenoon, & crossed the river after Dinner on his return home, at wch. time I set out for Abingdon in Order (to morrow) to Survey my 4 Miles run Tract; on which I had cause to apprehend trespasses had been committed.

Sent Majr. Washington to Town on Business where he and Mr. Lund Washington engaged to Mr. Watson 100 Barrls. of my Flour to be delivered next week at 32/9 pr. Barrl.

Not many fish caught to day at the Ferry.

Made good the missing Barley at Muddy hole.

Friday 5th. Thermometer at 62 in the Morning—67 at Noon and 63 at Night.

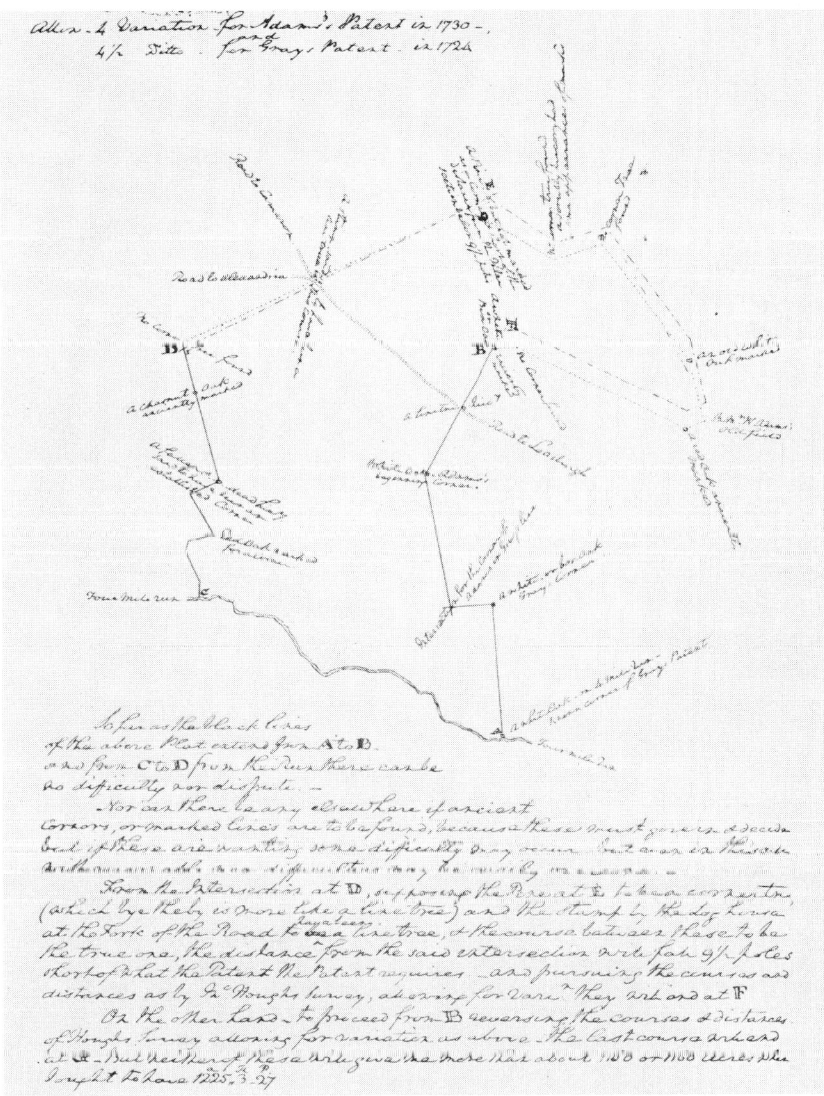

A survey made by Washington in 1799 of his land on Four Mile Run. From *George Washington Atlas*, Washington, D.C., 1932. (Rare Book Department, University of Virginia Library)

The Morning mild and agreeable, as indeed it was through the day till towards evining, when it began to lower pretty much: a large & distinct circle round the Sun before noon & lasted a gd. while.

Set out early from Abingdon, and beginning at the upper corner of my Land (in 4 Miles run) a little below an old Mill; I ran the Tract agréeably to the courses & distances of a Plat made thereof by John Hough, in the year 1766 (Novr.) in presence of Colo. Carlyle & Mr. James Mercer. Not havg. Hough's field Notes, & no Corner trees being *noted* in His *Plat,* I did not attempt to look for lines; but allowing one degree for the variation of Compass since the Survey, above mentioned, was made, I run the courses and distances *only;* & was unable for want of time, to do more than run the lines that brot. me to the run again; the Meanders of wch. must be run at some other time in order to ascertain with precision the quantity of Land which is contained. Upon the whole I found this tract fully equal to my expectations. The whole of it is well wooded–some part is pretty well timbered; and generally speaking, it is level. About the main road, on the South side of the tract, trespasses (on the wood) had been made, but in a less degree than I expected to find and as I run the lines, as set down by Hough, with the variation; I run into the field lately Colo. Carlyle's (now Whitings) so far as to cut off 12 or 15 acres of his inclosure; & made the plat close very well to the run.

Returned at Night to Abingdon being attended in the labours of the day, by Doctr. Stuart.

For background on this land, see entries for 27 Jan. 1775 and 21 and 22 April 1785.

Hough had surveyed the two tracts of land for James Mercer. There were several John Houghs of Loudoun County, and this seems to have been the John Hough who died in 1797. He was probably the one who lived on the Vestal's Gap Road and in 1772 was appointed a trustee for keeping the main roads to Vestal's and Williams' gaps in repair (HARRISON [1], 562, 576). The surveyor and one of the original trustees for the town of Leesburg was John Hough, probably the same man (HENING, 7:235; STEADMAN). He was also a collector of quitrents for the Northern Neck proprietary from 1764 through most of the Revolution (DLC: Toner Collection).

PRESENCE OF COLO. CARLYLE & MR. JAMES MERCER: That is, they were present during the 1766 survey. Col. John Carlyle owned adjoining land. His "field" was inherited by his grandson, Carlyle Fairfax Whiting (1778–1831), in 1784 (STETSON [1], 55; WMQ, 18 [1910], 286).

Saturday 6th. Thermometer at 52 in the Morng.–58 at Noon and 56 at Night.

A fresh wind all Night at No. East. Morning and forenoon

very cloudy, with a mizzling rain, but not enough to wet the ground—wind from the same qtr. or a little more Northerly, continuing all day, which made it cool and disagreeable.

After an early breakfast I set out on my return home, & taking Muddy hole in my way, returned about 10 Oclock.

Found that all the large (Indian) Peas I had, had been sown with the drill plow yesterday, at Dogue run whh. only compleated 8 rows—after which, they proceeded to sow the small black eyed pea & finished with them.

That the drill plow in the Neck had finished planting the common Corn in the Cut in which it had first begun and was pro ceeding in the one adjoining and that the Muddy hole people had just begun to Hoe the New ground (for Corn) in front of the Home House.

That the ferry Plantation had begun to Plant Corn—in the common mode, for want of the drill plow, which was otherwise engaged.

And that an indifferent hd. had been made of Catching Fish since Wednesday last.

Sunday 7th. Thermometer at 56 in the morng.—67 at Noon and 66 at Night.

Clear with the wind fresh, but not cold, from the No. West all day. Towards night it died away, & inclined to the Southward more. Mr. Porter, Mr. Murray, (Young) Mr. Bowen, and a Captain Aitkins came (by invitation) to dine with us today, and returnd to Alexandria in the Evening. Just as we were about to set down to Dinner Doctr. Craik, his Wife, Son William, and daughters (Miss Craik & Miss Nancy) came in—Dined and stayed all Night.

John Murray and Obadiah Bowen (1763–1793), eldest son of Jabez Bowen of Providence, R.I., were partners in the mercantile house of Murray, Bowen & Munford (Montfort) of Alexandria. John Munford, the third partner, was from New York City, where the firm also had a store (WARREN-ADAMS LETTERS, 2:329–30; Alexandria City Hustings Court Deeds, Book B, 366–70, Vi Microfilm).

Joseph Atkins (died c.1787), a sea captain, was a friend and business associate of Thomas Porter. His ship *Hope* had arrived in Alexandria in early April from North Carolina and sailed for Dieppe with a load of tobacco in mid-May (JEFFERSON [1], 10:181; *Va. Journal*, 6 April and 25 May 1786).

Monday 8th. Thermometer at 60 in the Morning—70 at Noon and 65 at Night.

Clear, calm, & warm.

Rid to Muddy hole & Dogue run. Began at the first to cross the lists in order to Plant Corn. The early Corn, & Indian Pease at this place were coming up.

Sent a Carpenter to put a new Axle & do some other repairs to the Barrel plow at Dogue run.

Sowed 3 rows of the Borden grass Seeds in the inclosure behind the Stables, adjoining to, and just below the Cape Wheat, & next the fence. Next to these was near a row of Yellow clover. The first was given to me by Colo. Fitzhugh of Maryland & the other by Colo. Chas. Carter of Ludlow. These rows were two feet apart, and the Seeds sown very thin in the rows, that the more Seeds might be saved from them for the next seasn.

On Saturday last the dead Cedars in my shrubberies were replaced by live ones just taken up.

Doctr. Craik, Wife & family went away after breakfast.

In the Evening a Captn. Whaley from Yohiogany came in on some business respecting the Affairs of the deceased Val. Crawford and Hugh Stephenson; to whom I gave, under cover to Thos. Smith Esqr. (my Lawyer in that Country) a Bill of Sale and the letter wch. inclosed it which the said Vale. Crawford had sent me, in the Mo[nth] of May 1774 as Security for what he owed me, and to indemnify me for my engagements in his behalf—to see if they were valid, & would cover the debt he owed me, as they never had been recorded. I also gave him the Statement of my Acct. with Colo. John, and the deceased Hugh Stephenson, which, in behalf of the latter, he promised to pay, and to obtain the other moiety from the first. He also promised to send in my Negros which had been hired to Gilbert Simpson or bring them in himself. In consequence of this assurance I gave him an order on Majr. Freeman to deliver them.

Valentine Crawford had sent GW a letter dated 6 May 1774 enclosing the bill of sale of his land as security for a £100 debt he owed GW (DLC:GW). Benjamin Whaley, of Fayette County, Pa., delivered this document to Thomas Smith who was to ascertain its validity (GW to Thomas Smith, 8 May 1786, NhD). GW also gave Whaley a statement of his account with John and Hugh Stephenson which indicated that the two brothers owed GW £70 10s. Virginia currency (GW to Thomas Smith, 23 Sept. 1789, DLC: GW).

Thomas Freeman, GW's western agent, had been requested 16 Oct. 1785 to hire "a careful person" to bring the slaves at Washington's Bottom to Mount Vernon, "if the measure can be reconciled to them" (DLC:GW). Of the nine Negroes now there, three apparently were young children, and two, Simon and Nancy, had been among the four slaves sent by GW in

1773 to help start Simpson's plantation (LEDGER B, 87). Despite an absence of nearly 13 years, these last two slaves had some reasons to return to Mount Vernon. "Simon's countrymen, and Nancy's relations," GW had explained to Freeman, "are all here, and would be glad to see them. I would make a Carpenter of Simon, to work with his shipmate Sambo" (16 Oct. 1785, DLC:GW). Nevertheless, none of the slaves, according to Freeman, could be persuaded to go to Mount Vernon "from any Argument I could use" (Freeman to GW, 18 Dec. 1786, DLC:GW). All were sold to various purchasers 5 Oct. 1786, Simon bringing £100 and Nancy together with a young child bringing £80 15s. Total receipts amounted to £418 15s. (DLC:GW).

Tuesday 9th. Thermometer at 60 in the Morng.—66 at Noon and 64 at Night.

Clear & warm, with but little Wind and that did not spring up till about 11 Oclock—first from the No. Et.—shifting afterwards to So. Et.

Rid to all my Plantations between Breakfast and dinner.

Found the Flax in the Neck had come up, and full thick; and that the grass Seeds (rather Millet) obtnd. from Colo. Cary had come up; but none of the Saintfoin Burnet, or rib grass appeared to be springing. Finished planting, with the Barrel plow, the early Corn in the furthest cut in the field for experiments, in the Neck and not having enough to *compleat* another cut in the same field I ordered all the remaining part of it to be drilled with common corn. Accordingly, about Noon, the intermediate rows in the Middle cut which had been left for the early Corn were begun to be planted with the other. At this plantation also the People had begun to break up the Intervals, in the most grassy places between the listed ground—but I set a plough to crossing in order to plant Corn in the common way in the field intended for this purpose.

At Dogue run, the hands there were also hoeing up the intervals between the Corn rows.

The ground, by the heavy rains which fell about 14 days ago, dry weather, and baking Winds since, had got immensely hard; so as that Seeds which were not already up, could not force through it; and those which had come up previously could not grow.

Captn. Whaley went away before breakfast.

Mr. George Digges, and Miss Digges, came to dinner & returned in the Evening—at which time my Brother John came in from Berkeley.

Panicum miliaceum, millet.

Wednesday 10th. Thermometer at 58 in the Morning—[ ] at Noon—and [ ] at Night.

But little wind in the Morning—a red Sky at the sunrising and some clouds and appearances of rain, which soon dispersed.

My Brother and Mr. George Washington went up to Town after Breakfast and did not return till the Evening.

I rid to the Plantations at Muddy hole, Dogue run, and Ferry —also to the fishing landing. At the first I found the early Corn had come up very well, except where the ground was hard, and baked; but that the birds were pulling it up fast. The Peas were also coming up, but not so regular as the Corn and of the Siberian Wheat, Barley & Oats which had come up some were cut off by a bug, & the rest looked indifferently; and in many places very thin; the Barley, which looked strong & of a good colour at first, had got to be yellow, and the ends of the blades in a manner dead. No appearance yet of the Potatoes & Carrots coming up.

Ordered Morris (at Dogue run) to discontinue his 5 furrow lists, and go on with three, as I might (the Season advancing fast) get my Corn in the ground before it was too late.

The Fish appeared to be quite done running—but I ordered my People to continue at the landing trying a haul on every tide untill Saturday and between while's to attempt clearing a landing for sein hauling above the Ferry landing where the Channel approaches nearer the shore and it is thought good for Shad.

Began to plant Corn in the Common way at Muddy hole.

Thursday 11th. Thermometer at 55 in the morning—58 at Noon and 58 at Night.

Morning cloudy, with great appearances of rain. About 11 Oclk. it began to rain; which fell moderately for about ten minutes & ceased but continued cloudy the remainder of the day—Wind at So. East but not very fresh.

My Brother set off on his return home after breakfast, passing through Maryland.

Mrs. Washington and Fanny Washington went up to Abingdon & returned in the Evening.

I rid to the Plantations at Muddy hole, Dogue run and Ferry between Breakfast & dinner and crossed to that in the Neck after dinner. The ground, particularly where they were drilling Corn at the last and indeed at Dogue run, wch. was stiff, & had been plowed when it was too wet was astonish[ing]ly hard & lumpy; and in which it is much to be feared the Corn will never rise.

Friday 12th. Thermometer at 58 in the Morning—67 at Noon and 65 at Night.

Cloudy in the Morning—about Noon the Sun shone but was soon obscured again & it remained cloudy all the latter part of the day—rain exceedingly wanting.

At home all day.

Finished about Noon planting with the Barrel Plow the middle cut in my field of experiments at the River Plantation.

Saturday 13th. Thermometer at 60 in the Morning—64 at Noon and 64 at Night.

Lowering all the forepart of the day with drops of rain (but no more) now and then. Evening clear—Wind variable, but mostly at So. Et.

I rid to Muddy hole, Dogue run & Ferry plantations; and to the fishery at the latter.

Ordered my People to quit hauling, and bring home my Seins.

Finished (yesterday evening) planting Corn with the barrel plow, in the Cut intended for experiments at Dogue run.

Also finished planting Corn in the Middle cut (this day abt. 3 Oclock) at Muddy hole, in the common way—putting a little dung in each hole, in the poor parts of the ground.

The Cotton Seeds, Pumpion Seeds, & Timothy Seeds (which were sowed on the Oats) at Dogue run, were coming up.

THE COTTON SEEDS: *Gossypium.* Cotton was never a part of GW's farming plan. He raised a little on the York River plantation and bought some, apparently for the use of his family, not his slaves. From Philadelphia, GW sent a few Nankeen or Nanking cotton seeds to manager William Pearce 16–17 Mar. 1794. "Let them be planted the first day of May in light and rich ground, well prepared. Put four seeds in a hill" (NBLiHi). These seeds were a gift from John Jay. In thanking Jay 5 Mar. 1794, GW said he feared that Mount Vernon was too high and cold for successful cultivation, as shown by his experience of the effects of frosts on common cotton. He thought the lower parts of Virginia might provide a milder climate and more sandy soil, and said he would send some of the seeds to an acquaintance there (sold by Sotheby, London, 11–12 June 1973, Item 604).

Sunday 14th. Thermometer at 60 in the Morning—70 at Noon and 71 at Night.

Clear all day, with very little Wind and that from So. West.

G. A. Washington and his Wife, and Mr. Shaw went to Pohick Church—dined at Mr. L. Washingtons and returned in the Evening. Colo. Gilpin, The Revd. Mr. McQuir; Mr. Hunter, & Mr. Sanderson came here to dinner and returned afterwards.

Began yesterday afternoon to pen my sheep, & Milch Cattle at the Ho[me] House, in the hurdles which had been made for the former.

THE REVD. MR. MCQUIR: William McWhir (1759–1851) was a Presbyterian clergyman, born in Ireland, who came to Alexandria about 1784. He was in charge of the Alexandria academy where GW's two nephews George Steptoe and Lawrence Augustine Washington were enrolled.

Monday 15th. Thermometer at 64 in the Morning—68 at Noon and 68 at Night.

Clear morning with but little Wind. About 10 Oclock clouds arose to the westward, and at 11 it began to thunder; About 12, a small, & very light sprinkling of rain fell, after which it cleared, but about 4 Oclock in the afternoon another cloud arose from whence we had a slow & moderate rain for about 3 quarters of an hour which softened the top of the ground (before much baked) and must be of great service to vegetation. Wind what there was of it came from the So. West.

I rid to the Plantations in the Neck and to Muddy hole. At the latter perceived the Irish Potatoes to be coming up. At the former the Plows having overtaken the dung Carts (which were carrying out dung to spread in the Corn rows) I set them to plowing and planting the Peas—ordering the alternate Pea rows to be planted at the same distance (viz. 18 Inches) a part, as the Corn is—intending the intermediate ones to be drilled, that is, planted at 6 Inches a part to see which Mode will be most productive.

A [ ] with whom an agreement was made to bring a load of good & clean Shells having brought very bad and dirty ones they were refused.

Majr. G. Washington went up to Alexandria on business. Doctr. Craik returned with him (by desire) in the afternoon to visit Mrs. Washington, who had been troubled for several days with a pain in her Shoulder.

Tuesday 16th. Thermometer at 65 in the Morning—[ ] at Noon and 64 at Night. Morning lowering. About 10 Oclock it thickened and thundered and before eleven began to rain & continued showery till near two Oclock after wch. it ceased but towards [evening] it thickned & began to rain again—Wind for the most part Easterly but not strong. The rain of yesterday & what fell today appear to have wet the ground sufficiently.

Doctr. Craik went away immediately after breakfast. I rid to the Plantations at Muddy hole and Dogue run. Perceived the

Pease at the former had come up very indifferently and looked badly which some of my Negroes ascribed to their being planted too early whilst the earth was too cold for this crop.

The Peas which were planted somewhat later at Morris's (Dogue run) were also coming up, as his Corn was, and much pulled up by the Birds. The Timothy Seed sowed (on the clover field wch. had failed from the badness of the seed and which after harrowing had been laid down in it) at Dogue run, appeared to be coming up thick.

Began to plant Corn at this Plantation yesterday in the common method.

When I returned home I fd. Moses Ball, his Son John Ball, & Wm. Carlin here—the first having his effects under execution wanted to borrow money to redeem them. Lent him ten pounds for this purpose.

In the Afternoon a John Halley (of Maryland) applied to rent a fishing shore of me at Sheridins point. Requested him to make his proposals in writing and I would consider of them and as he was the first who had applied wd. give him the preference upon equal ground.

Wednesday 17th. Thermometer at 62 in the Morning—63 at Noon and 56 at Night.

Morning calm, warm and pleasant. Between 10 and 12 Clouds arose, and showers fell around us, but none here. Between one & 2 Oclock the Wind came out hard at No. West and turned cold—after which it moderated, and shifted to the Eastward; but still continued cold.

At home all day; writing the best part of it.

Began where Oats had been sowed in the Neck, and the grd. had got hard bound, and the clover seed unable to penetrate the earth and to vegitate to harrow and roll it, to see if the Clover & Oats both, would not be benefitted thereby.

Thursday 18th. Thermometer at 58 in the Morning—65 at Noon and 60 at Night.

Wind at So. West with Showery Clouds around us all day; about 7 Oclock it began to rain, and continued to do so powerfully, for 20 or 30 Minits when it cleared again.

Rid to all the Plantations between breakfast & dinner. At the Ferry I found my people had finished planting corn in the common way yesterday & were preparing the small piece near the Fish House to plant with the drill (or Barrel); in which they were also beginning to plant Irish Potatoes. This piece contains a few rod over two Acres. At Dogue run, finding they would be late planting & replanting Corn (for that which was first planted with the drill plow had either come up very badly, or had been destroyed by Birds) I directed, after the Cut (round Barrys houses) in which they were planting, was finished, to run a single furrow in the remainder of the other each way, and to plant it in that manner, hoeing the ground well where the Corn was dropped. Perceived the Irish Potatoes to be coming up at this Plantation. At Muddy hole they finished planting corn about 10 Oclock. At this place I tried a 3 hoed harrow which I had just made, with a single horse. Upon the whole it answered very well. The draft seemed rather hard for one horse but the late rains had made the ground heavier than usual. Ordered my Overseer at this place to take into the Barn & thresh out, the only stack of Wheat remaining at the Plantation and to carry the grain to the Mill. In the Neck every other Pea Row had been planted with the barrel, dropping the Peas at 18 Inches a part in the rows; and five othr. rows (intermediate) on the South, were planted at 6 Inches asunder in the Rows but finding this would take more Seed than I cd. Spare I discontinued sowing more in this manner and return to the 18 Inch distance agn.

A Mr. Thos. Moody came here in the afternoon and paid me some money in discharge of his fathers Bond to Colo. Thos. Colvils Estate to which I am an Exr.

John Knowles came here to work at £5 pr. month and a pint of Rum pr. day.

Thomas Moody was making a payment for a parcel of land bought in 1768 by his father, Benjamin Moody, from the estate of Thomas Colvill. The elder Moody, who protested the executor's survey, had never made payment and thus never received a title. In 1779 Moody sold the land and went to court to force a settlement in the current inflated currency and to gain his title. Under an agreement finally reached in Nov. 1781, the payment today was the first of five payments to be made over the next three years (Washington's reply to bill of complaint executed against him by Benjamin Moody, 22 Aug. 1780, NjMoNP; LEDGER B, 135).

Friday 19th. Thermometer at 55 in the Morning—65 at Noon and 60 at Night.

Wind at No. West in the Morning and indeed through the day—the forepart of which was cool—the Middle and latter part moderate—the whole pleasant.

Rid to Muddy hole, Dogue Run, & Neck Plantations; the harrow plow was stopped at the first, by the Rain which fell yesterday and which had made the grd. too wet, & too heavy to use it in. At the latter, they would have finished drilling the Corn, and planting the Potatoes (the doing of which begun yesterday) but for the Rain which had fallen in the afternoon. It was done however early this morning; and the other spot, in which the Siberian Wht. had been Sowed, was set out; to get it in order for corn. To Dogue run I sent the remains of the Barley about half a peck to be pricked in where missing in the rows (beginning next the wheat) at the distance of eight Inches.

Mr. Porter & Doctr. Craik Junr. came down the River in a Ship bd. to France. Landed & dined here & returned to Alexandria in the afternoon.

Thomas Porter and Dr. James Craik, Jr., came to Mount Vernon aboard Joseph Atkins's ship *Hope* (see 7 May 1786).

Saturday 20th. Thermometer at 56 in the Morning—60 at Noon and 59 at Night. Morning clear with the Wind at South West. About 8 oclock it began to thicken to the westward which increased with distant thunder. By ten o clock it was quite overcast and began to rain moderately & continued to do so without wind for more than two hours when it ceased & the Sun came out but was more [or] less cloudy all the Afternoon, and cool, the wind having shifted to the South East and got fresher.

Rid to Muddy hole and the Neck. The ground at the first having got drier, the harrow plow was again set to work in the drilled ground. Finished planting (yesterday evening) corn in the Neck with the Barrel plow and set about sowing pease there again.

Finished planting with corn the cut at Dogue Run, which includes the Houses that were Barrys and began in that nearest the Overseers House.

Having received from Holt of Williamsburg through the hands of Mr. Dandridge, about 6 gills of the Eastern shore Peas (or as he calls them beans) so celebrated for fertilizing Land I began, & before the rain fell, planted 3 Rows in the inclosure below the Stables adjoining the row of yellow clover, & in a line with the Cape Wheat, being a continuation of those rows (2 feet apart). The Seeds were placed a foot asunder in the rows.

William Holt (d. 1791), an influential citizen of Williamsburg, was a Presbyterian who joined with Rev. John J. Smith of Long Island, N.Y., in establishing a settlement in New Kent County, Va., where they had a forge and mills. GW had several business transactions with Holt at this time.

EASTERN SHORE PEAS: Later in his diaries, and in his correspondence, GW will call this crop the wild bean or the Maggity Bay pea. It was widely called the Magothy Bay or Eastern Shore bean, and farmers had high hopes for it as a fallow crop for soil replenishment. GW paid a large price for a small quantity of seed, had little luck with it, and later reported that it was simply a variety of *Cassia chamaecrista,* the partridge pea which grew wild on his Mount Vernon farms. Its fame persisted, however; calling it the Magadaba bean, the *Farmers' Register,* 1 (1833–34), 285, described it as an annual with black pods, very durable in hot weather.

Sunday 21st. Thermometer at 60 in the Morng.–70 at Noon and 66 at Night.

A good deal, and heavy rain fell in the Night; with thunder & lightning; day warm, with sun shine & clouds alternately. Calm in the forenoon, & wind at East in the afternoon with thunder and great appearances of rain a little only of which fell.

Monday 22d. Thermometer at 64 in the Morning–60 at Noon and 60 at Night.

Wind Easterly, and very cloudy, with drops of Rain now and then.

Rid to Muddy hole, Dogue Run & Ferry Plantations–replanting Corn at the first. Begun to day, & not on Saturday as I have noted, to plant Corn in the cut next the Overseers house at Dogue run–where by a mistake of the Overseer, they had begun, and had planted Barley in the rows of Siberian Wheat and had done [ ] of them before I got there. Stopped and set them to replanting the missing parts of the Barley rows. Finished drilling the Corn at the Ferry Plantation.

Planted 10 more rows of the Eastern shore Peas, along side of those which were put in on Saturday last and all that section with them in my Botanical garden which had the Guinea grass last year–except the 2 Rows which had been before planted on the 3d. Instt. with everlasting Peas.

Seperated my rams from the Ewes at the home house and ordered the same to be done at the Plantations.

Began to take up the pavement of the Piaza.

Tuesday 23d. Thermometer at 60 in the Morng.–60 at Noon and 58 at Night.

Misting in the Morning and very cloudy & cold all day with the Wind at No. Et.

Rid to Muddy hole and Neck Plantations. Ordered the grd. allotted for Cabbages, to be prepared at both places; and plants to be taken from my garden to set it with. This preparation consisted of another listing (or plowing with three furrows) of the ground which had been before listed; leaving an intermediate row at each place for Turnips, to try which would yield most, & be most profitable—replanting the common Corn which had been drilled at Muddy hole. Finished planting Peas with the Barrel in the Neck on Saturday last and listing the Corn ground at the same place this day for planting in the common way.

Began yesterday, with the Ferry people, to list the New ground in front of the House for Corn—with Hoes.

And this day began to lay the Flags in my Piaza—Cornelius and Tom Davis assisting.

ALLOTTED FOR CABBAGES: *Brassica capitata,* cabbage, grown as a soil conditioner and livestock feed. GW called one variety "Drumhead & Cattle Cabbage" when writing to Anthony Whitting, 25 Nov. 1792 (DLC:GW). George Lee wrote GW, "I have sent you a small quantity of the great longsided scots cabbage seed" (28 April 1787, DLC:GW).

Wednesday 24. Thermometer at 56 in the Morng.—56 at Noon and 58 at Night.

Still drizling and cloudy, all day, with the Wind at No. East.

At home all day. About 11 Oclock Doctr. Stuart and Mr. Lund Washington came in, dined, & returned afterwards and in the afternoon Colo. Robt. Stith arrived (from Alexandria) and stayed all night.

Planted yesterday evening at Muddy hole about 1300 Cabbage plants and this morning finished the ground allotted for them at that place—to do which, took in all, abt. [ ] Plants.

Also planted this day, in the Neck, two compleat rows of the Cabbages and the other two rows from the river fence up to the bushy pond by the other fence running Westerly and sent plants over this evening to compleat them in the Morning.

Col. Robert Stith, of Chotank, was the son of Buckner Stith (1722–1791), of Brunswick County, and thus a nephew of Buckner's brother John of Chotank, whom GW had visited on 3 Sept. 1768. He married Mary Townsend Washington, daughter of GW's cousin and boyhood companion Lawrence Washington of Chotank.

Thursday 25th. Thermometer at 59 in the Morning—58 at Noon and 58 at Night.

Drizling in the Morning, after which, about 9 Oclock, it began to rain, and continued to do so, moderately all day. At Night, and in the Night, it rained a good deal—Wind at No. Et.

At home all day. Colo. Stith set off after breakfast, but turned back when it began to rain, and stayed all day & Night.

Finished planting Cabbages in the Neck; and transplanted Carrots from my garden, to two of the Rows at Muddy hole, which had been sowed, or rather planted, with seed which was either put in too deep, or never vegitated. One of these rows had dung in the furrow, and the other not.

Put a Coller on a large Bull in order to break him to the draft. At first he was sulky & restive but came to by degrees.

Friday 26th. Thermometer at 58 in the Morning—60 at Noon and 60 at Night.

Raining with little or no intermission through the day—a great deal having also fallen in the Night—Wind still at No. East.

Sent 50 Barrels of Superfine flour by the sloop Tryal Peter Kirwin to Thos. Newton junr. Esqr. to be disposed of on my Acct.

Half of this flour was shipped uninspected because Capt. Peter Kerwin, "calling unexpectedly, and being in a hurry, would not allow time to get the Inspectors from Alexandria" (GW to Thomas Newton, Jr., 26 May 1786, DLC:GW).

Saturday 27th. Thermometer at 62 in the Morng.—66 at Noon and 68 at Night.

Wind Easterly all day—raining in the morning, clear about Noon with Clouds, mists, and Sunshine afterwards, alternately.

Rid about 11 Oclock to visit the Plantations at Muddy hole and Dogue run. At the latter & in the Neck, the rain which had fallen in such quantities since Wednesday last had stopped their planting of Corn and left a little ground at each of those places unfinished.

Colo. Stith crossed the river after dinner on his return home.

Finished laying 28 courses of the pavement in the Piaza—Weather very unfavourable for it.

Sunday 28th. Thermometer at 66 in the Morning—66 at Noon and 68 at Night.

The forenoon very rainy with high Wind from the No. Et. About Noon it ceased raining. The Wind moderated and veered round to the Southward and then died away.

The continual, and excessive rains, has so surcharged the Earth with Water, that abt. 40 feet of my sunk wall, near the Ice house fell down and the greater part of my cape Wheat lodged.

Monday 29th. Thermometer at 68 in the Morng.—72 at Noon and 70 at Night.

Thunder, Lightning, and a good deal of rain last Night with

Portrait of Tobias Lear, attributed to one of the Sharples family. (Anonymous donor)

mists & rain till nine Oclk. this Morning and Wind fresh from the Eastward most part of the day.

About 9 Oclock, Mr. Tobias Lear, who had been previously engaged on a salary of 200 dollars, to live with me as a private Secretary & precepter for Washington Custis a year came here from New Hampshire, at which place his friends reside.

Rid to the Plantations at Dogue Run & Muddy hole passing by the New ground where my ferry and Muddy [hole] people were Hoeing for Corn.

Found my Mill race broke in 3 or 4 places and nearly half my Tumbling dams at the head of it, carried away by the fresh, occasioned by the immoderate rains, which had fallen and my Corn field both here & at Muddy hole in all the low places, and in the furrows covered with water. At both they were plowing, at the first to plant corn, and at the latter breaking up, but the water in many places followed the plows & it is to be feared that more hurt than good would result from the measure but the backwardness of Corn planting in one instance and rapid growth of grass in both Scarcely left a choice.

On my Return found Colo. Mead here.

Found, when I was at Dogue Run that Richard Burnet and wife had been living in the House formerly Barrys, since Wednesdy. last.

Agreed this day with James Bloxham, who arrived here the [21st] of April from England, to live with and superintend my farming business upon the terms mentioned in a specific agreement in writing.

Benjamin Lincoln recommended Tobias Lear (1762–1816), a Harvard graduate from New Hampshire, to GW for the position of secretary and tutor, describing him as having the "character of a Gentleman & a schoolar" (Lincoln to GW, 4 Jan. 1786, DLC:GW). Lear asked for $200 a year and GW agreed to it in April (GW to Lincoln, 10 April 1786, MH; Lear to GW, 7 May 1786, DLC:GW). What started as only a one-year appointment developed into a close association and an enduring friendship.

Tuesday 30th. Thermometer at [ ] in the Morning–[ ] at Noon and [ ] at Night.

Wind tho' not much of it, was still at East. Morning Misty and threatning till dinner time after which it cleared.

Accompanied by Colo. Mead, I rid to muddy hole and Neck Plantations to shew him my experiments in the drill husbandry –with which he seemed to be pleased.

G. A. Washington went up to Alexandria on my business & did not return till the Evening.

Wednesday 31st. Thermometer at 68 in the Morning–[ ] at Noon–and 69 at Night.

Wind still at No. East, and the day heavy & lowering, without rain.

Colo. Mead left this after a very early Breakfast.

I rid to the Plantations at Muddy hole & Dogue run, by the New ground; and also went to the Mill.

At both places the Plows were at Work in ground much too wet. At the first, that is Muddy hole, they were breaking up ground, and at the other (Dogue Run) they were crossing for the purpose of planting Corn, which would be all in to day and in miserable order, as the ground was little other than Mortar, & hills obliged to be raised to keep the grain out of the Water.

My Mill People, and Cowper, were employed in Repairing the breaches made by the Rain and in preventing the Water of Piney Run going up the Race in to Dogue Run, at the Tumbling dam as it has done since the mishap to the latter.

June

Thursday 1st. Thermometer at 68 in the Morning–72 at Noon and 70 at Night.

Misting in the Morning and at Intervals all day with the wind at No. Et. and at times fresh.

Rid to my Plantations at Muddy hole and in the Neck; at the

latter the People were setting Corn in the field of experiments, furthest cut. The Peas at this place have come up very indifferently, and looked badly. The Barley also did not assume the best appearance but the Oats looked well. Breaking up at both these places altho' the grd. was vastly too wet for it.

Removed my Cow pen & Sheep fold at home.

Doctr. Craik was sent for to a Negro man named Adam in the Neck & to a Negro woman Amy at Muddy hole. After visiting these People & dining here he returned home.

Mr. Shaw was sent to Alexandria on my business to day and returned in the Night.

Friday 2d. Thermometer at 68 in the Morning—70 at Noon and 70 at Night.

A good deal of rain fell in the Night and this Morning with the wind at No. Et. Afterwards it continued Misting and the Sun to shine, alternately through the day.

More clouds and wet weather, and less Sunshine never happened, it is thought in the same time, in this Country before. Waters run from the Hills, and stand in hollows, as in the depth of Winter; & except where there is a great mixture of Sand the ground when plowed, is little other than Mortar. Yet, such is the progress of the grass, that plowing must go forward, or the Corn get smothered and lost by means of it.

Cut the young grass in the levelled part of the Lawn, before the west front of the House, with intention to Roll it, but the ground was too wet and soft to do it.

In the afternoon a Captn. Aitkinson of the Caesar, & another Gentleman came on Shore and drank Tea. The first was furnished with a horse to go to his employer Mr. Sanderson at Alexandria. The other Gentleman returned to the Ship.

Sent to Doctr. Craik informing him how Adam in the Neck did & receiving fresh directions & Medicines for him—soon after which an acct. came of his death.

Capt. J. Atkinson's brig *Cesar,* arriving from Whitehaven, Eng., brought a letter to GW from John Rumney (16 April 1786, DLC:GW) regarding the piazza flagstones he had received in the spring (see entry for 18 April 1786). The brig must have remained at Mount Vernon wharf for several days, for its arrival at Alexandria was not announced until the 15 June edition of the *Va. Journal.*

Saturday 3d. Thermometer at 69 in the Morning—72 at Noon and 71 at Night.

Morning very heavy, sometimes misting, and then raining till 9 oclock—lowering afterwards till the afternoon, when it became calm & clear with a good horizon at the Suns setting. The wind was at No. Et. all the fore part of the day, & pretty fresh.

Rid to the Plantations at the Ferry, Dogue run, and Muddy hole. At the first and last they were plowing, but the grd. was very heavy—at the other it was too wet to plow at all.

The Corn at all these places I found very much pulled up and destroyed by the Birds. The Rains had so softened the ground that to do this was very easy for them.

Of the Siberian Wheat scarce any (of the little that came up) remains in the ground and the appearance of the Barley is very indifferent—not being either of a good colour or vigorous growth; whether owing to the quantity of rain or other Causes I do not undertake to decide. It did not, in the first instance, come up well—the drouth at first hurt it and the water, in many places covered it afterwards; this also happened to the Pease which cut but a poor figure. The Potatoes in low places either never came up, or is destroyed. The Cabbage plants in general stand well, tho' in some low places these also are covered with water, and appear to be dead. The Oats seem to be in a more thriving way than any other species of the Crops and where they came up well at first have a promising look.

Sunday 4th. Thermometer at 70 in the Morning 72 at Noon and 75 at Night.

An exceeding heavy fog in the Morning, and quite calm all day and clear.

Received from on board the Brig Ann, from Ireland, two Servant Men for whom I had agreed yesterday—viz.—Thomas Ryan a Shoemaker, and Caven Bowe a Tayler redemptioners for 3 years Service by Indenture if they could not pay, each, the Sum of £12 Sterg. which sums I agreed to pay.

Geo. A. Washington set off early this morning for Fredericksburgh. His wife & Washington Custis went to Church at Alexandria intending from thence to Abingdon. Mr. Shaw also went to Alexandria & returned in the Night.

On 8 June, William Deakins, Jr. (1742–1798), a Georgetown merchant, announced the arrival at Georgetown of "the brig Anne, Capt. Tolson, with one hundred and fifty very healthy indented servants; among them are several valuable tradesmen—Their indentures will be disposed of on reasonable terms for cash or tobacco" (COL. FRANCIS DEAKINS, 129–30; *Va. Journal,* 8 June 1786).

Monday 5th. Thermometer at 72 in the Morning—78 at Noon and 74 at Night.

Morning, and generally thro' the day, clear, and very pleasant, but warm. Very little Wind, and that Southerly.

Before breakfast, Mrs. Jenifer the widow of Doctr. Jenifer came, & returned in the afternoon. Soon after breakfast Messrs. Sanderson, Wilson, Murray & McPherson came in; all of whom, except the latter, went away before dinner. Mr. Sanderson dined & crossed the river afterwards on his way to embark at Leonard town, Saint Marys, for England.

LEONARD TOWN: Leonardtown, St. Mary's County, Md., about 45 miles south-southwest of Washington.

Tuesday 6. Thermometer at 72 in the Morning—76 at Noon and 74 at Night.

Thick Morning, and more or less cloudy all day, but no rain—but little Wind—that which was came from the No. Et.—rather more Easterly.

Rid to the Plantations at the Ferry, Muddy hole, & Neck. At the first & last the people were setting and planting of Corn. The ferry people finished listing with the hoes their part of the New ground in front of the House on Saturday last and the hands belonging to Muddy hole will do the same to day.

Sheared my Sheep in the Neck this day and rid through the Wheat and rye at that Plantation. Found the first to stand generally sufficiently thick on the ground but the heads appeared very short. They were full in blossum. The lower blades almost generally had turned quite red, and were dead but I did not perceive any signs of rust on them, or that the head, or Straw was injur'd thereby. The Rye was much better than I ever expected it would be. Except being rather too thin (especially in places, tho' much thicker than I had any idea it ever would be) it might, upon the whole, be called a good field.

The ground at all the Plantations plowed very heavily and wet.

Began to cut the clover at the Home House (sowed Aprl. was [a] year) which lay in the upper part of the field & unmixed with Orchard grass.

Had the ground which had been lately listed at Dogue Run for Cabbages chopped fine with the Hoes and intended to put the plants in the ground this evening but it was so late before the Overseer sent to my Gardener for them that there was only time left to draw and carry them to the Plantation this evening.

Mr. Shaw (with my newly purchased Shoemaker to provide

Frontispiece of *Museum Rusticum* depicts various aspects of agriculture, including sheep shearing. (Beinecke Rare Book and Manuscript Library, Yale University)

himself with Tools) went up to Town on my business & returned in the Afternoon.

Wednesday 7th. Mercury at 72 in the Morning—78 at Noon and 74 at Night.

Morning a little cloudy—in the afternoon light showers around us, with thunder and lightning at a distance—light breezes from the Southward.

Rid to the Ferry, Dogue run, and Muddy hole Plantations and through the Wheat and Rye at the first—neither of which answered my expectations. The first, besides having a small head generally, was mixed exceedingly with cheat and the latter was much broken down with the winds and rain which had happened and abounded in white heads deficient of grain—occasioned I presume by the heavy rains which happened while the ear was in bloom. The Wheat, it is to be hoped, will escape this disaster as there has been little or no wind or rain since it began to bloom which is now pretty well over.

The people at the Plantations above mentioned, were all replanting & setting Corn according to circumstances, in their drilled ground. At Muddy hole, setting took place altogether and here also they began to replant Peas, but had not enough of the large kind to make good the deficiency—but plenty of the small, black eyed Peas.

Sheared the few sheep I had at the Ferry to day.

Fanny Washington and the two Children, Nelly, & Geo. Washington, together with Miss Nancy Craik came home yesterday whilst we were at dinner.

Ann (Nancy) Craik, daughter of Dr. James Craik, later married Richard Harrison.

Thursday 8th. Mercury at 72 in the Morning—76 at Noon and 73 at Night.

Clear in the forenoon and calm. About One o'clock a cloud arose in the No. West quarter wch. spread extensively; and before 3 began to Rain fast and continued to do so near half an hour. During this flurry the Wind blew fresh from the Westward, but after the rain ceased it came back to the Southwest and continued moderate till sometime in the Night when it got to the No. Wt. & blew pretty fresh.

Rid to the Plantations at Dogue Run and Muddy hole and to the tumbling dam of Dogue Run, where I had begun with two hands from each Quarter, and two Carpenters, to repair the breaches which had been made by the late rains. After having got the Water stopped, in order to lay the Wooden frame, the run swelled so much (occasioned by the rain which fell this afternoon) as to carry away the greatest part of the earth and rendered the labour of the day of little effect.

Still setting, & replanting corn at Dogue run and Muddy hole in the Drilled fields—the last of which with replanting pease in the same would be compleated this day.

Rid through my rye at Muddy hole which would have been fully equal to what might have been expected from the grd. had it not been for the rains which had broken down & tangled the straw and occasioned a number of white, & unfilled heads.

The Eastern shore Peas (according to the information of my Overseer in the Neck) were sowed yesterday (by the barrel plow) in the ground which had been put in rib wort (that never came up). There were 10 Rows of the Peas and a little being left I ordered him to dibble in what remained in additional rows.

Cut all the Clover at the Ho[me] House to day, & the small spots of grass round the Sweet brier Circles; also some under the Trees at the No. end of the House by the Smiths shop to day and put the clover in wind Rows except the part last cut.

Mr. Wallace came here to dinner & stayed all night.

Friday 9th. Mercury at 70 in the Morning—77 at Noon and 74 at Night.

Morning clear and pleast. with the Wind at No. West but not fresh, nor had it changed the air cooler.

Mr. Wallace went away after breakfast and I rid to Muddy hole & river Plantations. The heaviness of the Plowing, and wetness of the land had encreased by the late Rains. Nothing indeed but the backwardness of the season and rapid growth of the grass & Weeds could justify working ground in the condition the plowed land is.

Passed through the Wheat at Muddy hole this day—found it, upon the whole as good as was to be expected from the impoverished state of the land—Though there is a good deal of cheat in the freshest part of the ground and the spick, (blasted grains) more or less in all. Finished replanting the corn & Peas in the drilled ground at Muddy hole this Morning about nine oclock, and not yesterday as was expected & began to replant Corn in the Cut adjoining.

The drilled corn in the Neck had also been gone over, and the people were replanting in the other field tho' by much too wet for such business.

Agreed this day with Mr. Tharpe to do my Plaistering in any of the Rooms in, or abt. the house & to repair the lathing at 7d. pr. Square yard.

Got all the clover hay into small cocks this afternoon.

Mr. Shaw went up to Town today on my business & returned in the Evening.

Saturday 10th. Mercury at 66 in the Morning—72 at Noon and [ ] at Night.

A heavy lowering Morning with the wind at East. At times the Sun appeared for a few momts. but generally the clouds were heavy with distant thunder in the So. Wt. quarter in the Afternoon tho' no rain fell here.

Rid to the Plantations at Muddy hole, Dogue run, and Ferry. Took the Mill in the way. Finished replanting Corn this morning at the Ferry wholly and yesterday at Dogue run in the ground which was drilled. Began to hoe Corn at the Ferry (on the hill) which is the first plantation in order for it and here it ought to have followed the plows; the work of which is backward on acct. of their having been stopped.

Turned the Cocks of clover hay to day and put all the rest of the grass except that which was cut this afternoon late into Cocks.

Major Washington returned in the afternoon from Fredericksburgh.

In my ride to day I visited the Labourers at the Tumbling dam. Find it will employ them the greatest part of next week. Wed with the hoes, the Millet, or Corn grass in the Neck to day.

Sunday 11th. Thermometer at 68 in the Morning—80 at Noon and 75 at Night.

A heavy fog in the morning, and cloudy most part of the day with great appearances of rain but none fell. Wind at East in the Morning tho not much of it fresh afterwards from the So. West till 6 oclock when it came out at No. Wt.

Sometime after Candles were lighted Colo. Senf came in.

During the Revolution, John (Jean) Christian Senf, a native of Sweden, served as an engineer for South Carolina and Virginia. In describing him to Jefferson, Gen. Horatio Gates called Senf "the best Draughtsman I know, and an Excellent Engineer" (Gates to Jefferson, 24 Sept. 1780, JEFFERSON [1], 3:662). After the war Senf returned to Europe but came back to America in 1785. It was during this year that legislation was passed in South Carolina authorizing construction of the Santee canal to connect the Santee and Cooper rivers. Senf became the chief engineer for that project. In 1789 Senf discussed with GW the possibility of conducting a survey of inland navigation from New York to East Florida (GW to Senf, 12 Oct. 1789, DLC:GW).

Monday 12th. Mercury at 68 in the Morning—72 at Noon and 69 at Night.

Morning early was calm, but about 7 Oclock the Wind sprung up at No. West and blew pretty fresh till late in the Afternoon when it became calm.

I rid to the Ferry, Dogue run and Muddy hole Plantations, and to the People who were working at the Tumbling-Dam.

Finished replanting Corn at Muddy hole on Saturday last & began late in the Afternoon of that day to hoe the drilled Corn at that place. Also finished breaking up the cut of drilled Corn nearest the Barn, which compleated the last breaking up of the whole corn ground at that Plantation.

Began to cut the Meadow near the wood, at Dogue run about 10 Oclock to day and got all the clover & other Hay into large Cocks this afternoon.

Tuesday 13th. Mercury at 68 in the Morning 75 at Noon and 73 at Night. Rid to the River, Muddy hole & Dogue run Plantations. At the first found the plows in the Eastermost cut of drilled Corn; where they had begun yesterday morning and were going over it the 2d. time. The hoes, which had got into it yesterday about 2 Oclock (after having finished replanting Corn) were following in the same cut. The plows would get through it about Noon, and the hoes nearly, if not quite, by night.

Found the Flax just beginning to blossum at this place where it was rankest.

At Muddy hole the plows had, this morning, finished breaking up and were beginning to cross plow in the cut next the drilled Corn.

At Dogue run the people would but just finish replanting corn by Night and would begin to weed with the hoes the drill Corn on the East side of the field where the Potatoes were planted.

Finished cutting the Meadow (into which 5 mowers went yesterday) 3 or 4 Oclock.

Stopped the water of Dogue run at the Tumbling dam to day and turned it into the race.

On my return home found Judge Harrison of Maryland and Mr. Rawlins both here—the last of whom went away after dinner.

Detail of John Trumbull's "Capture of the Hessians at Trenton" depicts GW's aides-de-camp Robert Hanson Harrison (in foreground) and Tench Tilghman. (Yale University Art Gallery)

Wednesday 14th. Mercury at 68 in the Morning—74 at Noon and 76 at Night.

After an early breakfast Judge Harrison left this for his own house and in Company with Colo. Senf, I set out for our Works at the great falls; where we arrived about 11 Oclock and after viewing them set out on our return & reached Colo. Gilpins where we lodged.

Mr. Rumsey was not there (at the Falls) having gone that Morning to Seneca but Mr. Stuart the assistant was present.

This day was clear and warm with but little wind from the Southward.

Thursday 15th. Mercury at 70 in the Morning—82 at Noon and 82 at Night.

Clear with little wind and very warm.

Took Alexandria—My Mill dam Meadow at Dogue run and

the Plantation there—as also the Ferry Plantation in my way home.

Found the tumbling dam all but new laying the sheeting, and filling below it, compleated. Directed all the Breaches in the race & the leak at Piney branch dam, to be thoroughly repaired before the hands should quit.

Found the Hay which had been cut in the upper Meadow nearly cured and 4 Mowers in the meadow next the Overseers House.

About 7 Oclock in the afternoon, Doctr. La Moyeur came in with a Servant, Chaise, & 3 Horses.

Friday 16th. Mercury at 74 in the Morning—82 at Noon and 80 at Night.

Clear with little wind in the Morning. About 10 or 11 oclock a breeze sprung up from the Eastward but died soon afterwards—rising again in the afternoon at So. West.

Finished my Mill race and Dam this Afternoon.

Began about 10 Oclock to put up the Book press in my study.

Saturday 17th. Mercury at 76 in the Morning—85 at Noon and 83 at Night.

Calm and very warm all day with but little wind and that Southerly—at times it was a little cloudy and at night there were thunder & lightning but no rain.

Rid to all the Plantations to day. In the Neck the Hoes and Plows were in the last (Westermost) cut. The first got to work in it about noon yesterday and the latter about 3 or 4 oclock in the Afternoon; both having passed through the middle cut, compleating as they went. The three hoed harrow was about got through the Eastermost cut (alternate rows) by Noon. The Oats were beginning to shoot forth the heads. At Muddy hole Plantation, the Hoes having overtaken the Plows that were crossing went to weeding the drilled Peas and I directed them to replant both Potatoes and Cabbages where missing in the same field. At Dogue run the Hoes appeared to have made little progress in weeding the drilled field—first because it was tedious among the Cabbages, Potatoes & Pease but principally because the ground had got so rough & matted with grass as to require much labour. At the Ferry, the Hoes had weeded the Corn in the cut on the Hill and about 10 O clock had begun in the flat below next the meadow fence & adjoining the drilled Corn. Examined the Wheat again to day, & concluded that at least half of it is destroyed.

Doctr. La Moyeur & Majr. Washington went up to Alexandria to day—The latter on my business. They dined there & returned in the evening. Just as we had dined, Captn. Smith of Mr. Ridouts Brig, Mr. Wallace a passenger in it for Bordeaux, and Doctr. Mortimer (going as far as Norfolk in her) came in and had dinner set for them.

Mr. Hough, Butcher in Alexandria, came here this afternoon, & purchased from me three fatted Beeves (2 in the Neck, & 1 at Dogue run) for which he is to pay next week £42—also the picking of 12 Weathers from my flock at 34/[ ]. pr. head. If upon consulting my Farmer & they could be spared, he was to have 20.

Sometime in late June the brig *Fanny* under Capt. W. B. Smith left Alexandria en route eventually for Bordeaux (*Va. Journal,* 22 June 1786). Thomas Ridout (1754–1829), born in Dorsetshire, Eng., and a resident of Annapolis before the Revolution, was a commission merchant in Bordeaux at this time. GW had business dealings with Ridout in the 1780s until the latter, burdened with debts, left France for the American West (RIDOUT, 215–35; GW to Ridout, 20 May 1786, Ridout to GW, 10 Sept. 1786, DLC: GW).

Dr. Charles Mortimer, Jr., was probably going to Norfolk to set up practice (BLANTON, 56, 346). MR. HOUGH: Lawrence Hooff, cartwright and butcher (Fairfax County Deeds, Book M-1, 70–74, Vi Microfilm).

Sunday 18th. Mercury at 78 in the Morning—84 at Noon and 78 at Night.

Calm, clear, and very warm in the forepart of the day; abt. 2 Oclock a cloud arose to the Westward; and a pretty heavy shower of rain fell with some thunder & lightning; after which it cleared; but another shower came on about sun down tho' it was very moderate & of short continuance.

Monday 19th. Mercury at 73 in the Morning. 79 at Noon and 78 at Night.

Morning cloudy, but clear afterwards, with the wind at So. West.

Rid to Muddy hole, Dogue run, and Ferry Plantations; and to the Meadows (where people were at Work) at the two latter.

Finding my Corn was in danger of being lost by Grass & weeds, I stopped Brickmaking, and sent Gunner, Boatswain, Anthony, and Myrtilla to assist at Dogue run in weeding it.

The grass at the Ferry being forwarder, and better than that at Dogue Run, where the Scythmen began last to cut, I removed them (tho' the grass was not half down) to the former place. 4 Cutters at work.

Mr. Herbert & wife—Mr. Throcmorton & his Wife—Miss Hannah, & Miss Kitty Washington, & Mr. Willm. Craik came here to dinner & all stayed the Evening except Mr. Herbert who returned to Alexandria.

A Monsr. Andri Michaux—a Botanest sent by the Court of France to America (after having been only 6 Weeks returned from India) came in a little before dinner with letters of Introduction & recommendation from the Duke de Lauzen, & Marqs. de la Fayette to me. He dined and returned afterwards to Alexandria on his way to New York, from whence he had come; and where he was about to establish a Botanical garden.

Albion Throckmorton (died c.1795), of Frederick County, son of John Throckmorton (1731–c.1795), of Gloucester County, married Warner Washington's oldest daughter, Mildred Washington (c.1766–1804), in Dec. 1785, apparently against the wishes of her family (WAYLAND [1], 177; GW to George William Fairfax, 10 Nov. 1785, DLC:GW; STANARD [2], 50–52). Throckmorton served as cornet in the 1st Continental Dragoons during the Revolution. Hannah and Catharine Washington, usually called Katy or Kitty, were Mrs. Throckmorton's sisters.

André Michaux (1746–1802) was a French botanist whose work in America would later produce *Flora Boreali-Americana* (1803). He sent a note to GW the day after his visit, enclosing some seeds and promising to send live plants. In 1793 GW subscribed a small sum to assist the American Philosophical Society in financing an expedition Michaux planned to make to the Pacific. Thomas Jefferson collected the money on behalf of the society and wrote an elaborate set of instructions to guide Michaux in his research, just as he would do for Meriwether Lewis ten years later. While the objectives of the expedition were ostensibly scientific, Michaux was in reality acting as the agent of the French minister Edmond Genet in a scheme to mount an assault on Spanish possessions beyond the Mississippi. After Genet's recall Michaux's expedition was terminated by Genet's successor in Mar. 1794.

Tuesday 20th. Mercury at 71 in the morning—77 at Noon and 78 at Night.

Morning clear and pleasant with but little wind. In the afternoon the Wind blew from the Eastward, & a cloud arising in the contrary direction it began about 9 Oclock to rain very powerfully and continued to do so, more or less through the Night.

Mr. Craik went away before Breakfast, and the rest of the Company about 11 Oclock, at which time I rid to the Plantations at Dogue Run & ferry and to the Meadows where People were cutting & making Hay. Stopped the cutters at the ferry, and set them to making hay; having too much grass down & exposed for the numbers employed in this business to execute in time without.

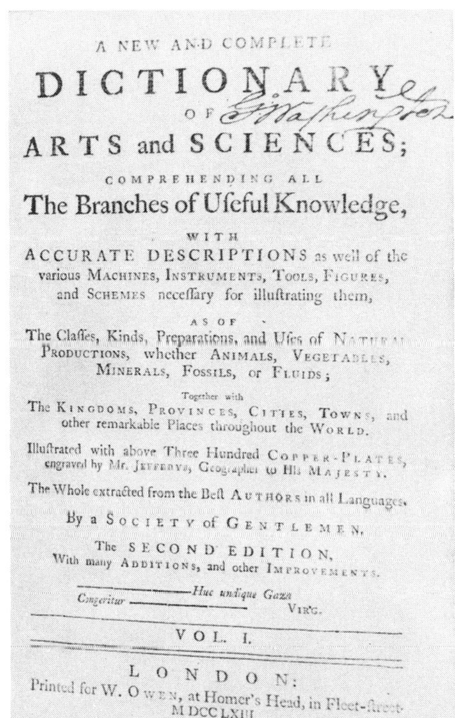

A NEW AND COMPLETE

DICTIONARY

OF

ARTS and SCIENCES;

COMPREHENDING ALL

The Branches of Uſeful Knowledge,

WITH

ACCURATE DESCRIPTIONS as well of the various MACHINES, INSTRUMENTS, TOOLS, FIGURES, and SCHEMES neceſſary for illuſtrating them,

AS OF

The Claſſes, Kinds, Preparations, and Uſes of NATURAL PRODUCTIONS, whether ANIMALS, VEGETABLES, MINERALS, FOSSILS, or FLUIDS;

Together with

The KINGDOMS, PROVINCES, CITIES, TOWNS, and other remarkable Places throughout the WORLD.

Illuſtrated with above Three Hundred COPPER-PLATES, engraved by Mr. JEFFERYS, Geographer to His MAJESTY.

The Whole extracted from the Beſt AUTHORS in all Languages.

By a SOCIETY of GENTLEMEN.

The SECOND EDITION, With many ADDITIONS, and other IMPROVEMENTS.

——*Hinc undique Gaza Congeritur* —— VIRG.

VOL. I.

LONDON: Printed for W. OWEN, at Homer's Head, in Fleet-ſtreet. M DCC LXIII.

Title page of Washington's copy of *Dictionary of Arts and Sciences.* (Mount Vernon Ladies' Association of the Union)

Mr. Shaw went up to Alexandria on my business and returned in the afternoon.

Wednesday 21st. Mercury at 66 in the Morning—66 at Noon and 66 at Night. Wind at No. Et. and raining more or less till near Noon, after wch. it continued cloudy till sun down with the wind in the same quarter.

A stop put to out doors work till near noon.

About sun down Mr. Fendall came here.

Thursday 22d. Mercury at 63 in the Morning—68 at Noon and 68 at Night.

Calm, clear, cool and pleasant all day.

Mr. Fendall went away after Breakfast.

I rid to all the Plantations, and to the Hay makers at the Ferry.

The Plows finished the drilled Corn in the Neck on Monday afternoon and the hoes got over it on Tuesday Morning, and both went into the cut of common Corn by the Barn.

Friday 23d. Mercury at 66 in the Morning–76 at Noon and 74 at Night.

Very little wind all day, but clear & pleasant notwithstanding.

Finished Hoeing the drilled corn at Dogue run about 9 oclock this forenoon and began to weed the Corn in the dunged ground at that place wch. had got very foul.

Doctr. La Moyieur came here this afternoon.

Saturday 24th. Mercury at 69 in the Morning–76 at Noon and 80 at Night.

Clear in the forenoon with but little wind. In the afternoon clouds arose and a smart shower of rain fell.

Rid to all the Plantations and to the Hay Makers at the Ferry. In the Neck, both Plows & Hoes would have finished the cut of Corn by the Barn had not the Rain prevented. The Ferry hands would also have finished the cut of common corn on the Flat but for the same cause.

Major Washington & his wife went up to Alexandria and were detained there all Night by the rain and appearances of the Clouds afterwards.

Sunday 25th. Mercury at 75 in the Morng.–80 at Noon and 80 at Night.

Clear all day with little or no Wind and very warm.

Majr. Washington and fanny came home before Breakfast.

Munday 26th. Mercury at 74 in the Morning–78 at Noon and 78 at Night.

The forenoon was clear and calm–as was the Afternoon except a cloud which rose to the westward and produced rain and a very high wind in the Night.

Rid to Muddy hole, Dogue run and Ferry Plantations. Found the Muddy hole people in the Eastermost cut of Corn having finished (with the hoes) the Middle cut on Saturday. The Plows however were yet in the Middle cut. At Dogue Run the Plows had finished breaking up, and had begun crossing the cut in which Barrys houses stand–into which they went about dinner time on Saturday. About 11 Oclock to day the hoes finished weeding the Cowpened ground, and had got into the Swamp corn which was more weedy than the rest. At the Ferry, the plows finished about 9 Oclock the drilled corn by the Fish house and went into the other drilled corn by the Meadow. About the same time the hoes having finished weeding the Corn in the flat, planted in the common way, had begun to weed the drilled corn by the Fish house and to replant the Irish Potatoes therein.

Finished cutting the meadow at the Ferry this afternoon.

Tuesday 27th. Mercury at 69 in the Morning—70 at Noon and 70 at Night.

Lowering (rather cloudy) in the morning, with the wind brisk, but not cold from the No. West. Afternoon clear & pleasant.

Rid to all my Plantations. Found the Plows & Hoes in the Neck had gone over the cut by the Barn. The first finished it yesterday about breakfast, & the other about dinner time and were in the Cut adjoining. Finding the Hoe Harrow did not do good work in the drilled Corn, I ordered it to desist and the Bar share plow to be used, till the common Corn was all crossed; after which to use it, when the ground was worked the other way. Cut down the clover at Muddy hole this forenoon (whilst it was moist from the Rain of last night) and put it into Wind rows—3 swaiths in a Row. The Dogue run hands had not got over the Corn in the Swamps. At the Ferry the People had just finished weeding the drilled Corn by the Fish House, & replanting the Patatoes therein; not having quite enough of the latter to replant the whole—the deficiency was supplied with Corn. Making the hay that was cut yesterday at the Ferry, with the small gang.

Doctr. Craik dined here, and returned home afterwards.

Mr. Shaw went up to Alexa. on my business and returned late in the evening.

Wednesday 28th. Mercury at 68 in the Morning—72 at Noon and 70 at Night.

Clear & pleasant all day. In the forenoon the Wind was at N. Wt.—in the afternoon it was at So. West.

Rid to the Plantations at Muddy hole Dogue Run and the Ferry and to the Hay fields. At the first I sowed turnips in Drills in the ground which had been sowed with Oats that never came up (by the Negro Quarters). There were 7 rows, running from 180 to 200 Steps of these (averaging 190 yards) wch. were sowed with about a gill or little more seed. The first row, Southerly, was harrowed with the little harrow at the tail of the barrel; but gathering earth and burying the Seed too deep, I took out every other tooth and with it in this order harrowed the next row. This also appeared to cover too deep. I therefore took the harrow off altogether & tied brush in its place which did much better. The

Seed used here was of the first recd. from Mr. Chichester and was of the last year. The hands at Dogue run having just weeded their Swamp Corn as I got there, about Noon, I directed, finding there was no prospect of getting over the Corn there with hoes before harvest that the whole shd. be immediately succoured and then between this and Sunday the forwardest which was also the most weedy should be gone over with the Hoes.

The Mowers after cutting down the Clover yesterday (wch. was done by noon) went into the Meadow at Morris's wch. had been left, & were cutting there to day. The grass at the Ferry was all got into cocks this afternoon.

Doctr. Le Moyuer came in before Dinner.

Mr. Shaw went out after breakfast to day, to see if he could engage any Mowers for me. He returned in the afternoon, having partly engaged 2 or 3.

Thursday 29th. Mercury at 68 in the Morning–71 at Noon and 70 at Night.

Cool & pleasant–the Wind being at No. West & Westerly all day.

At home all day. In the evening Major Gibbs came in.

Planted in one Row, between the Cherokee Plumb, & the honey locust, back of the No. Garden adjoining the green House (where the Spanish chesnuts had been placed and were rotten) 25 of the Paliurus, very good to make hedges and inclosures for fields. Also in the section betwn. the work House & Salt house adjoining the Pride of China Plants, & between the rows in which the Carolina Laurel seeds had been sowed, 46 of the Pistatia nut in 3 rows and in the places where the Hemlock pine had been planted and were dead, Et. & W. of the Garden gates, the Seeds of the Pyramidical Cyprus 75 in number–all of which with others were presented to me by Mr. Michaux Botanist to his most Christn. Majesty.

Mr. Shaw went out again to day to procure if to be had scythemen for Corn & grass–of which he engaged two for the latter to be at Work at Dogue run to morrow and 4 of the latter to be at this place on Monday.

Caleb Gibbs (c. 1748–1818) was born in Newport, R.I., but lived much of his life in Massachusetts. During the Revolution he was adjutant in the 21st and 14th regiments of the Continental infantry before GW appointed him captain in command of the commander in chief's guard on 12 Mar. 1776. In July 1778 Gibbs was promoted to major. He continued to command the guard until Jan. 1783, and resigned his commission in June 1784.

Plants not previously named are *Paliurus spina-christi,* Jerusalem thorn, and *Cupressus sempervirens,* a pyramidical form of the cypress often planted as an ornamental. CHRISTN. MAJESTY: Louis XVI (1754–1793) ruled France from 1774–92.

Friday 30th. Mercury at 65 in the Morning—68 at Noon and 70 at Night.

Clear and pleasant all day the wind being at No. West and west all day, though not fresh.

Rid to the Plantations at Muddy hole, Dogue run, & Ferry; & to the Hay makers at the second. At Dogue, found the Corn had all been succoured, and the hoes had got into the fresh & weedy ground along the wood side—about 3 oclock yesterday. The Meadow near the Overseers House, at this place would all be cut down about dinner time—The two white men, viz., Tayler & Hill, engaged by Mr. Shaw yesterday, having got to work there this Morning. The Plows at the ferry finished the drill Corn yesterday about 2 O clock and the hoes got over it about breakfast. Began to cut my Rye at the Ferry about 12 Oclock to day—employed three Negro Cradlers—viz.—Caesar, Sambo & Boatswain—the greater part of which appeared to me to be blighted and the rest very ripe, & much beat down. Both Rye & Wheat at this place had the appearance of greater ripeness than at any other and might have been safely cut Six or eight days ago if I could have left my corn to do it.

Mr. Bushrod Washington came in whilst we were at Dinner.

CORN HAD ALL BEEN SUCCOURED: That is, the suckers, or sprouts springing up from the roots at the ground line, had been pulled off.

Repository Symbols and Abbreviations

Bibliography

Index

Repository Symbols and Abbreviations

CSmH — Henry E. Huntington Library, San Marino, Calif.
DLC — Library of Congress
DLC:GW — George Washington Papers, Library of Congress
DNA — National Archives
DNA:PCC — National Archives, RG 360, Papers of the Continental Congress
DSI — Smithsonian Institution
InHi — Indiana University, Bloomington
InU — Indiana University, Bloomington
MdHi — Maryland Historical Society, Baltimore
MH — Harvard University, Cambridge
MHi — Massachusetts Historical Society, Boston
MnHi — Minnesota Historical Society, Saint Paul
NBLiHi — Long Island Historical Society, Brooklyn, N.Y.
NhD — Dartmouth College, Hanover, N.H.
NjMoNP — Morristown National Historical Park, Morristown, N.J.
NjP — Princeton University
NN — New York Public Library
NNebgGW — Washington's Headquarters, Jonathan Hasbrouck House, Newburgh, N.Y.
PHi — Historical Society of Pennsylvania, Philadelphia
PEL — Lafayette College, Easton, Pa.
PPAmP — American Philosophical Society, Philadelphia
PSC — Swarthmore College, Swarthmore, Pa.
RPJCB — John Carter Brown Library, Brown University, Providence, R.I.
ViBCtH — Bath County Historical Society, Bath, Va.
ViHi — Virginia Historical Society, Richmond
ViMtV — Mount Vernon Ladies' Association of the Union

Bibliography

ABBOTT — Wilbur Cortez Abbott. "James Bloxham, Farmer." Massachusetts Historical Society *Proceedings,* 59 (1925–26), 177–203.

ADAMS [1] — Lyman Butterfield, ed. *Diary and Autobiography of John Adams.* 4 vols. Cambridge, Mass.: Belknap Press, 1961–62.

ADAMS [3] — Henry Adams. *The Life of Albert Gallatin.* 1879. Reprint, New York: Peter Smith, 1943.

ALLEGHENY — *History of Allegheny County Pennsylvania.* In two parts. Chicago: A. Warner & Co., 1889.

ALLEN — Benjamin Allen. "John D. Shane's Interview with Benjamin Allen, Clark County." *Filson Club Historical Quarterly,* 5 (1931), 63–98.

AMBLER — Charles H. Ambler. *Francis H. Pierpont: Union War Governor of Virginia and Father of West Virginia.* Chapel Hill: University of North Carolina Press, 1937.

ANNALS — Arthur Young, ed. *Annals of Agriculture & Other Useful Arts.* 46 vols. London: various publishers, 1784–1815.

AREY — Hiram C. Arey. "The Public Career of Thomas Lewis." Master's thesis, University of Virginia, 1933.

BACON-FOSTER — Corra Bacon-Foster. *Early Chapters in the Development of the Potomac Route to the West.* Washington, D.C.: Columbia Historical Society, 1912.

BALDWIN [2] — Leland D. Baldwin. *Whiskey Rebels: The Story of a Frontier Uprising*. Rev. ed. Pittsburgh: University of Pittsburgh Press, 1939.

BARTON — R. T. Barton. "Gabriel Jones 'The Lawyer.'" *West Virginia Historical Magazine Quarterly*, 2, no. 2 (1902), 19–30.

BERKELEY [2] — "Soldiers of Berkeley County, W.Va." *William and Mary Quarterly*, 1st ser., 13 (1904), 29–36.

BERRY'S FERRY — "Berry's Ferry, and Old Roads Leading to That Ferry." *Proceedings of the Clarke County Historical Association*, 6 (1946), 8–13.

BETTS [2] — Edwin M. Betts, ed. *Thomas Jefferson's Garden Book, 1766–1824*. Philadelphia: American Philosophical Society, 1944.

BIOGRAFISCH WOORDENBOEK — P. C. Molhuysen, P. J. Blok, and K. H. Kossman, eds. *Nieuw Nederlandsch Biografisch Woordenboek*. 10 vols. Leiden: A. W. Sijthoff's Uitgevers-Maatschappij N.V., 1911–37.

BLANTON — Wyndham B. Blanton. *Medicine in Virginia in the Eighteenth Century*. Richmond: Garrett & Massie, 1931.

BLUE COAT BOYS — "The Blue Coat Boys." *Tyler's Quarterly Historical and Genealogical Magazine*, 1 (1919), 43–45.

BLUM — Mrs. Willetta Baylis Blum and Dr. William Blum, Sr., eds. *The Baylis Family of Virginia*. Washington, D.C.: Shenandoah Publishing House, 1958.

BOATNER [1] — Mark Mayo Boatner III. *Encyclopedia of the American Revolution*. New York: David McKay Co., 1966.

BOND [2] — Beverley W. Bond, Jr. *The Foundations of Ohio*. Columbus: Ohio State Archaeological and Historical Society, 1941.

BROCKETT — Franklin Longdon Brockett. *The Lodge of Washington: A History of the Alexandria Washington Lodge, No. 22, A.F. and A.M. of Alexandria, Va.* Alexandria, Va.: George E. French, 1876.

BROWN [2] Alexander Crosby Brown. "America's Greatest Eighteenth Century Engineering Achievement." *Virginia Cavalcade,* 12 (1963), 40–47.

BROWN [3] Alexander Crosby Brown. *The Dismal Swamp Company*. Chesapeake, Va.: Norfolk County Historical Society, 1970.

BROWNE Fairfax Harrison. "With Braddock's Army: Mrs. Browne's Diary in Virginia and Maryland." *Virginia Magazine of History and Biography,* 32 (1924), 305–20.

BRYAN Wilhelmus Bogart Bryan. *A History of the National Capital, from Its Foundation through the Period of the Adoption of the Organic Act*. New York: Macmillan Co., 1914.

BUCHANAN [2] Roberdeau Buchanan. *Genealogy of the Roberdeau Family*. Washington, D.C.: Joseph L. Pearson, 1876.

BUCK Solon J. and Elizabeth Hawthorne Buck. *The Planting of Civilization in Western Pennsylvania*. Pittsburgh: University of Pittsburgh, 1939.

BULLTOWN *The Bulltown Country, 1764–1940*. Charleston, W.Va.: West Virginia Writers' Project, 1940.

BURNABY Rufus Rockwell Wilson, ed. *Burnaby's Travels through North America*. Reprint. New York: A. Wessels Co., 1904.

BUSHONG Millard K. Bushong. *Historic Jefferson County*. Boyce, Va.: Carr Publishing Co., 1972.

CALLAHAN [2] James Morton Callahan, *History of the Making of Morgantown, West Virginia: A Type Study in Trans-Appalachian Local History*. Morgantown, W.Va.: West Virginia University, 1926.

CAMPBELL [1] Thomas Elliott Campbell. *Colonial Caroline: A History of Caroline County, Virginia*. Richmond: Dietz Press, 1954.

CAMPBELL [3] John H. Campbell. *History of the Friendly Sons of St. Patrick and of the Hibernian Society for the Relief of Emi-*

grants from Ireland*. Philadelphia: Hibernian Society, 1892.

CARTMELL Thomas Kemp Cartmell. *Shenandoah Valley Pioneers and Their Descendants: A History of Frederick County, Virginia.* Winchester, Va.: Eddy Press Corp., 1909.

CHALFANT Ella Chalfant. *A Goodly Heritage: Earliest Wills on an American Frontier.* Pittsburgh: University of Pittsburgh Press, 1955.

CHALKLEY Lyman Chalkley. *Chronicles of the Scotch-Irish Settlement in Virginia, Extracted from the Original Court Records of Augusta County, 1745–1800.* 3 vols. 1912. Reprint, Baltimore: Genealogical Publishing Co., 1974.

CHAPPELEAR [2] Curtis Chappelear. "A Map of the Original Grants and Early Landmarks in Clarke County, Virginia, and Vicinity." *Proceedings of the Clarke County Historical Association,* 2 (1942), facing p. 56.

CHAPPELEAR [3] Curtis Chappelear. "Early Landowners in the Benjamin Harrison and Robert Carter Nicholas Tracts." *Proceedings of the Clarke County Historical Association,* 7 (1947), 33–48.

CHASTELLUX François Jean de Beauvoir, Marquis de Chastellux. *Travels in North America in the Years 1780, 1781, and 1782.* 2 vols. Ed. Howard C. Rice, Jr. Chapel Hill: University of North Carolina Press, 1963.

CLINKENBEARD William Clinkenbeard. "Reverend John D. Shane's Interview with Pioneer William Clinkenbeard." *Filson Club Historical Quarterly,* 2 (1928), 95–128.

COLLES Christopher Colles. *A Survey of the Roads of the United States of America, 1789.* Ed. Walter W. Ristow. Cambridge: Harvard University Press, 1961.

COL. FRANCIS DEAKINS "Colonel Francis Deakins." *Glades Star,* 1 (1941–49), 129–30.

CONGRESSIONAL DIRECTORY — *Biographical Directory of the American Congress, 1774–1971.* Washington, D.C.: U.S. Government Printing Office, 1971.

COPELAND — Pamela C. Copeland and Richard K. MacMaster. *The Five George Masons: Patriots and Planters of Virginia and Maryland.* Charlottesville: University Press of Virginia, for the Regents of Gunston Hall, 1975.

CRAIK [2] — James Craik. "Boyhood Memories of Dr. James Craik, D.D., L.L.D." *Virginia Magazine of History and Biography,* 46 (1938), 135–45.

CRUMRINE [1] — Boyd Crumrine, ed. "Minute Book of the Virginia Court Held at Fort Dunmore (Pittsburgh) for the District of West Augusta, 1775–1776." *Annals of the Carnegie Museum,* 1 (1901–2), 525–68.

CRUMRINE [2] — Boyd Crumrine. *History of Washington County, Pennsylvania, with Biographical Sketches of Many of the Pioneers and Prominent Men.* Philadelphia: L. H. Everts & Co., 1882.

CRUMRINE [3] — Boyd Crumrine. "The Boundary Controversy between Pennsylvania and Virginia, 1748–1785." *Annals of the Carnegie Museum,* 1 (1901–2), 505–24.

CUSTIS — George Washington Parke Custis. *Recollections and Private Memoirs of Washington.* New York: Derby & Jackson, 1860.

DANDRIDGE — Danske Dandridge. *Historic Shepherdstown.* Charlottesville: Michie Company, 1910.

DECATUR — Stephen Decatur, Jr. *Private Affairs of George Washington, from the Records and Accounts of Tobias Lear, Esquire, His Secretary.* Boston: Houghton Mifflin Co., 1933.

DELAPLAINE — Edward S. Delaplaine. *The Life of Thomas Johnson, Member of the Continental Congress, First Governor of the State of Maryland, and Associate Judge of the United States Supreme Court.*

New York: Frederick H. Hitchcock, Grafton Press, 1927.

DIARIES John C. Fitzpatrick, ed. *The Diaries of George Washington, 1748–1799*. 4 vols. Boston and New York: Houghton Mifflin Co., 1925.

DONEHOO George P. Donehoo. *A History of the Indian Villages and Place Names in Pennsylvania*. Harrisburg, Pa.: Telegraph Press, 1928.

DOUGLASS Ephraim Douglass. "Pittsburg and Uniontown, Pennsylvania: Letters from Ephraim Douglass to Gen. James Irvine." *Pennsylvania Magazine of History and Biography*, 1 (1877), 44–54.

DOWNING Andrew Jackson Downing. *The Fruits and Fruit Trees of America*. New York: Wiley & Putnam, 1845.

DUMBAULD Edward Dumbauld. *Thomas Jefferson, American Tourist*. Norman: University of Oklahoma Press, 1946.

DURNBAUGH Donald F. Durnbaugh, ed. *The Brethren in Colonial America: A Source Book on the Transplantation and Development of the Church of the Brethren in the Eighteenth Century*. Elgin, Ill.: Brethren Press, 1967.

EARLY Ruth H. Early. *The Family of Early Which Settled upon the Eastern Shore of Virginia and Its Connection with Other Families*. Lynchburg, Va.: Brown-Morrison Co., 1920.

EATON David W. Eaton. *Historical Atlas of Westmoreland County, Virginia: Patents Showing How Lands Were Patented from the Crown & Proprietors of the Northern Neck of Virginia*. Richmond: Dietz Press, 1942.

ECKER Grace Dunlop Ecker. *A Portrait of Old George Town*. 2d ed. Richmond: Dietz Press, 1951.

EDGAR Lady Matilda Edgar. *A Colonial Governor in Maryland: Horatio Sharpe and His Times, 1753–1773*. London: Longmans, Green and Co., 1912.

EGLE — William Henry Egle. "The Constitutional Convention of 1776: Biographical Sketches of Its Members." *Pennsylvania Magazine of History and Biography*, 3 (1879), 96–101, 194–201, 319–30, 438–46; 4 (1880), 89–98, 225–33, 361–72.

ESPENSHADE — A. Howry Espenshade. *Pennsylvania Place Names*. State College: Pennsylvania State College, 1925.

EVANS — Griffith Evans. "Journal of Griffith Evans, 1784–1785." Ed. Hallock F. Raup. *Pennsylvania Magazine of History and Biography*, 65 (1941), 202–32.

EXECUTIVE JOURNAL, 1 — *Journal of the Executive Proceedings of the Senate of the United States of America*. Vol. 1. Washington, D.C.: Duff Green, 1828.

FAYETTE COUNTY STATE TAX — "Return of State Tax for the County of Fayette, 1785 and 1786." *Pennsylvania Archives*, 3d ser., 22 (1898), 541–641.

FITHIAN [2] — Philip Vickers Fithian. *Journal, 1775–1776, Written on the Virginia-Pennsylvania Frontier and in the Army around New York*. Ed. Robert Greenhalgh Albion and Leonidas Dodson. Princeton, N.J.: Princeton University Press, 1934.

FOORD — James Foord. "To the West on Business in 1804, an Account, with Excerpts from His Journal, of James Foord's Trip to Kentucky in 1804. Ed. Bayrd Still. *Pennsylvania Magazine of History and Biography*, 64 (1940), 1–21.

FOTHERGILL — Augusta B. Fothergill and John Mark Naugle. *Virginia Tax Payers 1782–87 Other than Those Published by the United States Census Bureau*. 1940. Reprint, Baltimore: Genealogical Publishing Co., 1974.

FREDERICK — Millard Milburn Rice. *New Facts and Old Families, from the Records of Frederick County, Maryland*. Redwood City, Calif.: Monocacy Book Co., 1976.

FREDERICK COUNTY — "Journal of the Committee of Observation of the Middle District of Frederick County, Maryland. September 12, 1775–

October 24, 1776." *Maryland Historical Magazine,* 10 (1915), 301–21; 11 (1916), 50–66, 157–75, 237–60, 204–21; 12 (1917), 10–12, 142–63, 261–75, 324–47.

FREEMAN — Douglas Southall Freeman. *George Washington.* 7 vols. New York: Charles Scribner's Sons, 1949–57.

FRIEND — "The Friend Family of Garrett County, Maryland." *Glades Star,* 1 (1941–49), 53–55, 61–62.

FRONTIER FORTS — *Report of the Commission to Locate the Site of the Frontier Forts of Pennsylvania.* 2 vols. N.p.: Clarence M. Busch, 1896.

GARDINER — Mabel Henshaw Gardiner and Ann Henshaw Gardiner. *Chronicles of Old Berkeley, a Narrative History of a Virginia County from Its Beginnings to 1926.* Durham, N.C.: Seeman Press, 1938.

GARRETT COUNTY SURVEYS AND PATENTS — "Early Land Surveys and Patents in Garrett County, Maryland." *Glades Star,* 1 (1941–49), 117–19, 125–28.

GARRISON — Hazel Shields Garrison. "Cartography of Pennsylvania before 1800." *Pennsylvania Magazine of History and Biography,* 59 (1935), 255–83.

GERALD — Herbert P. Gerald. "Marshall Hall Burying Ground at Marshall Hall, Md." *Maryland Historical Magazine,* 24 (1929), 172–76.

GIBBS — Patricia Ann Gibbs. "Taverns in Tidewater Virginia, 1700–1774." Master's thesis, College of William and Mary, 1968.

GIPSON — Lawrence Harvey Gipson. *Lewis Evans.* Philadelphia: Historical Society of Pennsylvania, 1939.

GREEN — Bennet Wood Green. *Word-Book of Virginia Folk-Speech.* Richmond: William Ellis Jones' Sons, 1912.

GRIFFITH — Dennis Griffith. *Map of the State of Maryland . . . June 20th. 1794.* Philadelphia: Thackara & Vallance, 1795.

GRIGSBY — Hugh Blair Grigsby. *The History of the Virginia Federal Convention of 1788, with Some Account of the Eminent Virginians of That Era Who Were Members of the Body.* 2 vols. Richmond: Virginia Historical Society, 1890–91.

GROOME [3] — H. C. Groome. "The Parishes and Their History." Fauquier Historical Society, *Bulletin,* 1st ser., (1921–24), 246–71.

GWATHMEY — John Hastings Gwathmey. *Historical Register of Virginians in the Revolution: Soldiers, Sailors, Marines, 1775–1783.* Richmond: Dietz Press, 1938.

GW ATLAS — Lawrence Martin, ed. *The George Washington Atlas.* Washington, D.C.: United States George Washington Bicentennial Commission, 1932.

HADFIELD — Joseph Hadfield. *An Englishman in America, 1785: Being the Diary of Joseph Hadfield.* Ed. Douglas S. Robertson. Toronto, Can.: Hunter-Rose Co., 1933.

HAMILTON [2] — Harold C. Syrett et al., eds. *The Papers of Alexander Hamilton.* New York: Columbia University Press, 1961—.

HAMMOND — John Martin Hammond. *Colonial Mansions of Maryland and Delaware.* Philadelphia and London: J. B. Lippincott Co., 1914.

HARDY — Stella Pickett Hardy. *Colonial Families of the Southern States of America.* Baltimore: Southern Book Co., 1958.

HARRISON [1] — Fairfax Harrison. *Landmarks of Old Prince William.* Reprint. Berryville, Va.: Chesapeake Book Co., 1964.

HARRISON [7] — J. Houston Harrison. *Settlers by the Long Grey Trail: Some Pioneers to Old Augusta County, Virginia, and Their Descendants, of the Family of Harrison and Allied Families.* 1935. Reprint, Baltimore: Genealogical Publishing Co., 1975.

HEADS OF FAMILIES, MD. — *Heads of Families at the First Census of the United States Taken in the Year 1790: Maryland.* 1907. Reprint, Baltimore: Genealogical Publishing Co., 1965.

HEADS OF FAMILIES, PA. *Heads of Families at the First Census of the United States Taken in the Year 1790: Pennsylvania.* 1908. Reprint, Baltimore: Genealogical Publishing Co., 1970.

HEADS OF FAMILIES, VA. *Heads of Families at the First Census of the United States Taken in the Year 1790: Virginia.* 1908. Reprint, Baltimore: Genealogical Publishing Co., 1970.

HEDGES James B. Hedges. *The Browns of Providence Plantations: Colonial Years.* Providence: Brown University Press, 1968.

HEITMAN [1] Francis Bernard Heitman. *Historical Register of Officers of the Continental Army during the War of the Revolution, April 1775, to December, 1783.* Washington, D.C.: F. B. Heitman, 1893.

HEITMAN [2] Francis Bernard Heitman. *Historical Register of Officers of the Continental Army during the War of the Revolution, April, 1775, to December, 1783.* Rev. ed. Washington, D.C.: Rare Book Shop Publishing Co., 1914.

HENING William Waller Hening, ed. *The Statutes at Large: Being a Collection of All the Laws of Virginia from the First Session of the Legislature, in the Year 1619.* 13 vols. New York, Philadelphia, Richmond: various publishers, 1819–23.

HESTER Mary Foy Hester. "The Public Career of John Harvie." Master's thesis, University of Virginia, 1938.

HIGGINBOTHAM Don Higginbotham. *Daniel Morgan, Revolutionary Rifleman.* Chapel Hill: University of North Carolina Press, 1961.

HILLIER Richardson Hillier. "The Hite Family and the Settlement of the West." Master's thesis, University of Virginia, 1936.

HOLMES Oliver W. Holmes, ed. "The Colonial Taverns of Georgetown." *Records of the*

Columbia Historical Society of Washington, D.C., 51–52 (1951–52), 1–18.

H.B.J. — H. R. McIlwaine and John Pendleton Kennedy, eds. *Journals of the House Burgesses of Virginia.* 13 vols. Richmond: Virginia State Library, 1905–15.

HULBERT [1] — Archer Butler Hulbert. *Braddock's Road and Three Relative Papers.* Cleveland, Ohio: Arthur H. Clark Co., 1903.

HULBERT [2] — Archer Butler Hulbert, ed. *Washington and the West.* New York: Century Co., 1905.

HUME — Edgar Erskine Hume, ed. *General Washington's Correspondence concerning the Society of the Cincinnati.* Baltimore: Johns Hopkins Press, 1941.

JAMES [2] — James Alton James. *Oliver Pollock: The Life and Times of an Unknown Patriot.* New York: D. Appleton-Century Co., 1937.

JEFFERSON [1] — Julian P. Boyd, ed. *The Papers of Thomas Jefferson.* Princeton, N.J.: Princeton University Press, 1950—.

JOHNSTON — Ross B. Johnston, ed. "West Virginians in the American Revolution." *West Virginia History,* 7 (1945–46), 54–64.

JCC — Worthington Chauncey Ford et al., eds. *Journals of the Continental Congress, 1774–1789.* 34 vols. Washington, D.C.: U.S. Government Printing Office, 1904–37.

KEGLEY — Frederick Bittle Kegley. *Kegley's Virginia Frontier.* Roanoke, Va.: Southwest Virginia Historical Society, 1938.

KEYES — "More about Keyes of Keyes' Ferry." *Magazine of the Jefferson County Historical Society,* 8 (1942), 18.

KING [6] — J. Estelle Stewart King, comp. *Abstracts of Wills, Inventories, and Administration Accounts of Loudoun County, Virginia, 1757–1800.* Beverly Hills, Calif.: J. Estelle Stewart King, 1940.

KOONTZ — Louis K. Koontz. *The Virginia Frontier, 1754–1763.* Baltimore: Johns Hopkins Press, 1925.

LACOCK — John Kennedy Lacock. "Braddock Road." *Pennsylvania Magazine of History and Biography*, 38 (1914), 1–38.

LAND — Aubrey C. Land. *The Dulanys of Maryland: A Biographical Study of Daniel Dulany, the Elder (1685–1753) and Daniel Dulany, the Younger (1722–1797)*. Baltimore: Maryland Historical Society, 1955.

LEDGER A — Manuscript Ledger in George Washington Papers, Library of Congress.

LEDGER B — Manuscript Ledger in George Washington Papers, Library of Congress.

LEDGER C — Manuscript Ledger in Morristown National Historical Park.

LEE [5] — Edmund Jennings Lee. *Lee of Virginia, 1642–1892*. Philadelphia: privately printed, 1895.

LEE [6] — Charles Lee. *The Lee Papers*. 4 vols. *Collections of the New-York Historical Society*. Vols. 4–7. New York: New-York Historical Society, 1872–75.

LIPPINCOTT — Horace Mather Lippincott. *George Washington and the University of Pennsylvania*. Philadelphia: General Alumni Society, 1916.

LIVINGOOD — James Weston Livingood. *The Philadelphia-Baltimore Trade Rivalry, 1780–1860*. New York: Arno Press & the New York Times, 1970.

LMCC — Edmund C. Burnett, ed. *Letters of Members of the Continental Congress*. 8 vols. 1921–38. Reprint, Gloucester, Mass.: Peter Smith, 1963.

LOWDERMILK — Will H. Lowdermilk. *History of Cumberland Maryland*. 1878. Reprint, Baltimore: Regional Publishing Co., 1971.

LYONS — "Judge Peter Lyons' Letters to His Granddaughter." *Tyler's Quarterly Historical and Genealogical Magazine*, 8 (1926–27), 184–94.

MCALLISTER — John Meriwether McAllister and Lura Boulton Tandy, eds. *Genealogies of the Lewis and Kindred Families*. Columbia,

Miss.: E. W. Stephens Publishing Co., 1906.

MCCULLOUGH'S PATH "McCullough's Pack Horse Path." *Glades Star*, 1 (1948), 297–99.

MCGROARTY William Buckner McGroarty. *The Old Presbyterian Meeting House at Alexandria, Virginia, 1774–1874.* Richmond: William Byrd Press, 1940.

MCILWAINE H. R. McIlwaine, ed. *Official Letters of the Governors of the State of Virginia.* Vol. 2. *The Letters of Thomas Jefferson.* Richmond: Virginia State Library, 1928.

MCWHORTER Lucullus Virgil McWhorter. *The Border Settlers of Northwestern Virginia from 1768 to 1795.* Dayton, Va.: Ruebush-Elkins Co., 1915.

MACKENZIE [1] George Norbury Mackenzie, ed. *Colonial Families of the United States of America.* 7 vols. Baltimore: Genealogical Publishing Co., 1966.

MADISON William T. Hutchinson et al., eds. *The Papers of James Madison.* Chicago: University of Chicago Press, 1962–75; Charlottesville: University Press of Virginia, 1977—.

MARSHALL [2] Herbert A. Johnson et al., eds. *The Papers of John Marshall.* Chapel Hill: University of North Carolina Press, for the Institute for Early American History and Culture, Williamsburg, Va., 1974—.

MASON [1] Frances Norton Mason, ed. *John Norton & Sons, Merchants of London and Virginia.* New York: Augustus M. Kelley, 1968.

MASON [2] Robert A. Rutland, ed. *The Papers of George Mason, 1725–1792.* 3 vols. Chapel Hill: University of North Carolina Press, 1970.

MATHEWS Catherine Van Cortlandt Mathews. *Andrew Ellicott: His Life and Letters.* New York: Grafton Press, 1908.

MAXWELL Hu Maxwell. *History of Tucker County, West Virginia, from the Earliest Explorations and Settlements to the Pres-*

ent Time. Kingwood, W.Va.: Preston Publishing Co., 1884.

MD. COUNCIL, 1778–79 — *Journal and Correspondence of the State Council of Maryland, April 1, 1778–October 26, 1779*. Ed. William Hand Browne. *Archives of Maryland*. Vol. 21. Baltimore: Maryland Historical Society, 1901.

MD. COUNCIL, 1781–84 — *Journal and Correspondence of the State Council of Maryland, 1781–1784*. Ed. J. Hall Pleasants. *Archives of Maryland*. Vol. 48. Baltimore: Maryland Historical Society, 1931.

MEADE [1] — William Meade. *Old Churches, Ministers, and Families of Virginia*. 2 vols. Philadelphia: J. B. Lippincott Co., 1910.

MEADE [3] — Robert Douthat Meade. *Patrick Henry: Practical Revolutionary*. Philadelphia and New York: J. B. Lippincott Co., 1969.

MERCER COUNTY — "Mercer County, Kentucky: Abstracts of Will Books 3 and 4." *Register of the Kentucky State Historical Society*, 37 (1939), 94–115.

MERCHANTS — "Merchants and Mills: from the Letter Book of Robert Carter, of Nominy, Westmoreland County." *William and Mary Quarterly*, 1st ser., 11 (1902–3), 245–46.

MERENESS — Newton D. Mereness, ed. *Travels in the American Colonies*. New York: Macmillan Co., 1916.

MILLER — Helen Hill Miller. *George Mason: Gentleman Revolutionary*. Chapel Hill: University of North Carolina Press, 1975.

MINTZ — Max M. Mintz. *Gouverneur Morris and the American Revolution*. Norman, Okla.: University of Oklahoma Press, 1970.

MOORE [1] — Gay Montague Moore. *Seaport in Virginia: George Washington's Alexandria*. Charlottesville: University Press of Virginia, 1949.

MORDECAI — Samuel Mordecai. *Virginia, Especially Richmond, in By-Gone Days; with a Glance at the Present.* 2d ed. Richmond: West & Johnston, 1860.

MORGAN [2] — French Morgan. *A History and Genealogy of the Family of Col. Morgan Morgan, the First White Settler of the State of West Virginia.* 1950. Reprint, Parsons, W.Va.: McClain Printing Co., 1966.

MORTON [2] — Oren Frederic Morton. *A History of Preston County, West Virginia.* 2 vols. Kingwood, W.Va.: Journal Publishing Co., 1914.

MUIR — Dorothy Troth Muir. *Potomac Interlude: The Story of Woodlawn Mansion and the Mount Vernon Neighborhood, 1846–1943.* Washington, D.C.: Mount Vernon Print Shop, 1943.

MULKEARN AND PUGH — Lois Mulkearn and Edwin V. Pugh. *A Traveler's Guide to Historic Western Pennsylvania.* Pittsburgh: University of Pittsburgh Press, 1954.

MVAR — Mount Vernon Ladies' Association of the Union *Annual Report.*

NASATIR AND MONELL — Abraham P. Nasatir and Gary Elwyn Monell. *French Consuls in the United States. A Calendar of Their Correspondence in the Archives Nationales.* Washington, D.C.: U.S. Government Printing Office, 1967.

NESS — George T. Ness, Jr. "A Lost Man of Maryland." *Maryland Historical Magazine,* 35 (1940), 315–36.

NEWBRAUGH — Frederick T. Newbraugh. *Warm Springs Echoes about Berkeley Springs and Morgan County.* 2 vols. 2d ed. Hagerstown, Md.: Automated Systems Corp., n.d.

NORFLEET [1] — Fillmore Norfleet. *Saint-Mémin in Virginia: Portraits and Biographies.* Richmond: Dietz Press, 1942.

NORFLEET [2] — Fillmore Norfleet. *Suffolk in Virginia, c.1795–1840: A Record of Lots, Lives, and Likenesses.* Richmond: privately printed, 1974.

NORRIS [1] — J. E. Norris, ed. *History of the Lower Shenandoah Valley.* 1890. Reprint, Berryville: Virginia Book Co., 1972.

NUSSBAUM — Frederick L. Nussbaum. *Commercial Policy in the French Revolution: A Study of the Career of G. J. A. Ducher.* New York: AMS Press, 1970.

NUTE — Grace L. Nute. "Washington and the Potomac: Manuscripts of the Minnesota Historical Society, (1754) 1769–1796." *American Historical Review,* 28 (1922–23), 497–519, 705–22.

OLD STATE ROAD — "The Old State Road thru Garrett County." *Glades Star,* 1 (1941–49), 313–15, 318.

PA. ARCH. — Samuel Hazard et al., eds. *Pennsylvania Archives.* 9 ser., 138 vols. Philadelphia and Harrisburg: various publishers, 1852–1949.

PA. ARCH., COL. REC. — *Colonial Records of Pennsylvania, 1683–1800.* 16 vols. Philadelphia: various publishers, 1852–53.

PA. IN 1800 — John "D" Stemmons, ed. *Pennsylvania in 1800: A Computerized Index to the 1800 Federal Population Schedules of the State of Pennsylvania.* Salt Lake City, Utah: John "D" Stemmons, 1972.

PA. RANGERS — "List of Soldiers Who Served as Rangers on the Frontiers, 1778–1783." *Pennsylvania Archives,* 23 (1898), 193–356.

PARKER — John C. Parker. *The Dismal Swamp: Memoranda concerning Its History and Ownership from 1762 to 1962.* Franklin, Va.: Union Bag–Camp Paper Corp., 1962.

PICKELL — John Pickell. *A New Chapter in the Early Life of Washington, in Connection with the Narrative History of the Potomac Company.* New York: D. Appleton & Co., 1856.

PILCHER — George W. Pilcher. "William Gordon and the History of the American Revolution." *The Historian,* 34 (1972), 447–64.

POWELL — Mary G. Powell. *The History of Old Alexandria, Virginia, from July 13, 1749 to May 24, 1861.* Richmond: William Byrd Press, 1928.

PRESTON — John Preston. "Some Letters of John Preston." *William and Mary Quarterly,* 2d ser., 1 (1921), 42–51.

REESE — Lee Fleming Reese, comp. *The Ashby Book: Descendants of Captain Thomas Ashby of Virginia.* San Diego, Calif.: Reese, 1976.

RICE — Howard C. Rice, Jr., and Anne S. K. Brown, eds. *The American Campaigns of Rochambeau's Army, 1780, 1781, 1782, 1783.* 2 vols. Princeton, N.J., and Providence: Princeton University Press and Brown University Press, 1972.

RICHMOND — *Richmond Portraits in an Exhibition of Makers of Richmond, 1737–1860.* Richmond: Valentine Museum, 1949.

RIDOUT — Thomas Ridout. "Reminiscences of Thomas Ridout." *Maryland Historical Magazine,* 20 (1925), 215–35.

ROCKS — "The Rocks." *Magazine of the Jefferson County Historical Society,* 10 (1944), 16–17.

ROHRBAUGH — Lewis Bunker Rohrbaugh. *Rohrbaugh Genealogy: Descendants of Nine Rohrback Immigrants to Colonial America, 1709–1754, and More than One Hundred Rohrback Immigrants to America, 1825–1900.* Philadelphia: Dando-Schaff Printing and Publishing Co., 1970.

ROSENTHAL — Gustavus Baron de Rosenthal. "Journal of a Volunteer Expedition to Sandusky, from May 24 to June 13, 1782." *Pennsylvania Magazine of History and Biography,* 18 (1894), 129–57, 293–328.

ROWLAND [1] — Kate Mason Rowland, ed. *The Life of Charles Carroll of Carrollton, 1737–1832, with His Correspondence and Public Papers.* 2 vols. New York: G. P. Putnam's Sons, 1898.

SABINE — Lorenzo Sabine. *Biographical Sketches of Loyalists of the American Revolu-*

tion, with an Historical Essay. 2 vols. Boston: Little, Brown & Co., 1864.

SALLEE Helen Hite Sallee. "The Descendents of Colonel Abraham Hite." *Kentucky Ancestors,* 6 (1971), 186–91.

SARGENT [2] Charles Sprague Sargent. *The Trees at Mount Vernon*. Reprinted from the *Annual Report* for 1926 of the Mount Vernon Ladies' Association of the Union. N.p., 1927.

SCHARF [3] John Thomas Scharf. *History of Western Maryland*. 2 vols. Philadelphia: Louis H. Everts, 1882.

SCHARF [4] John Thomas Scharf. *History of Maryland, from the Earliest Period to the Present Day*. 3 vols. Baltimore: John B. Piet, 1879.

SCHEEL Eugene M. Scheel. *The Guide to Loudoun: A Survey of the Architecture and History of a Virginia County*. Leesburg, Va.: Potomac Press, 1975.

SCHOEPF Johann David Schoepf. *Travels in the Confederation*. Ed. and trans. Alfred J. Morrison. 2 vols. Philadelphia: William J. Campbell, 1911.

SHAW Ronald E. Shaw. *Erie Water West: A History of the Erie Canal, 1792–1854*. Lexington: University of Kentucky Press, 1966.

SHELBY "Excerpts from Executive Journal of Governor Isaac Shelby." *Register of the Kentucky State Historical Society,* 28 (1930), 203–13.

SIMS Edgar B. Sims. *Sims Index to Land Grants in West Virginia*. Charleston: State of West Virginia, 1952.

SNOWDEN William H. Snowden. *Some Old Historic Landmarks of Virginia and Maryland*. N.p.: Washington-Virginia Railway Co., 1904.

SOLECKI Ralph S. Solecki. "An Archeological Survey of Two River Basins in West Virginia." *West Virginia History,* 10 (1949), 189–212, 319–432.

SOLTOW — James H. Soltow. *The Economic Role of Williamsburg*. Williamsburg, Va.: Colonial Williamsburg, 1965.

SPROUSE [1] — Edith Moore Sprouse, ed. *A Surname and Subject Index of the Minute and Order Books of the County Court, Fairfax County, Virginia, 1749–1774*. Fairfax, Va.: Fairfax County History Commission, 1976.

SPROUSE [2] — Edith Moore Sprouse, ed. *A Surname and Subject Index of the Minute and Order Books of the County Court, Fairfax County, Virginia, 1783–1802*. Fairfax, Va.: Fairfax County History Commission, 1976.

STANARD [2] — William G. Stanard. "Throckmorton of England and Virginia." *William and Mary Quarterly,* 1st ser., 3 (1894–95), 46–52, 192–95.

STANARD [3] — William G. Stanard. "Abstracts of Virginia Land Patents." *Virginia Magazine of History and Biography,* 3 (1896), 177–88.

6 STAT. — *The Public Statutes at Large of the United States of America.* Vol. 6. Boston: Little & Brown, 1846.

9 STAT. — *The Statutes at Large and Treaties of the United States of America.* Vol. 9. Boston: Little & Brown, 1851.

STEADMAN — Melvin Lee Steadman, Jr. *Historic Leesburg, Virginia: A Walking Tour*. Leesburg, Va.: Potomac Press, 1967.

STETSON [1] — Charles W. Stetson. *Four Mile Run Land Grants*. Washington, D.C.: Mimeoform Press, 1935.

STETSON [2] — Charles W. Stetson. *Washington and His Neighbors*. Richmond: Garrett and Massie, 1956.

STEVENS [5] — Henry N. Stevens. *Lewis Evans: His Map of the Middle British Colonies in America*. 1920. Reprint, New York: Arno Press & The New York Times, 1971.

TAGGART — Hugh T. Taggart. "Old Georgetown." *Records of the Columbia Historical Society,* 11 (1908), 120–224.

TERRELL — I. L. Terrell. "Courthouses of Rockingham County." *Virginia Cavalcade,* 23, no. 2 (1973), 42–47.

THANE — Elswyth Thane. *Potomac Squire.* New York: Duell, Sloan and Pearce, 1963.

TOMLINSON — "Jesse Tomlinson of the Little Meadows" and "More about the Tomlinsons." *Glades Star,* 1 (1941–49), 69–71, 96.

TORBERT — Alice Coyle Torbert. *Eleanor Calvert and Her Circle.* New York: William-Frederick Press, 1950.

TURNER — Ella May Turner. *James Rumsey: Pioneer in Steam Navigation.* Scottsdale, Pa.: Mennonite Publishing House, 1930.

TYLER [1] — Lyon G. Tyler. "Original Records of the Phi Beta Kappa Society." *William and Mary Quarterly,* 1st ser., 4 (1895–96), 213–59.

UMBLE — R. E. Umble. "Mount Washington, Fort Necessity and Shrine." In *Fort Necessity and Historic Shrines of the Redstone Country.* Uniontown, Pa.: Fort Necessity Chapter, Pennsylvania Society of the Sons of the American Revolution, 1932.

VA. COUNCIL JLS. — H. R. McIlwaine et al., eds. *Journal of the Council of the State of Virginia.* 4 vols. Richmond: Division of Purchase and Printing, Virginia State Library, 1931–67.

VAN VOORHIS — John S. Van Voorhis. *The Old and New Monongahela.* 1893. Reprint, Baltimore: Genealogical Publishing Co., 1974.

VA. EXEC. JLS. — H. R. McIlwaine, Wilmer L. Hall, and Benjamin Hillman, eds. . *Executive Journals of the Council of Colonial Virginia.* 6 vols. Richmond: Virginia State Library, 1925–66.

VA. REG. — William Maxwell, ed. *The Virginia Historical Register.* 6 vols. 1848. Reprint, Spartanburg, S.C.: Reprint Co., 1973.

VAUGHAN — Samuel Vaughan. "Minutes Made by S. V. from Stage to Stage on a Tour to Fort Pitt or Pittsbourg in Company with Mr. Michl. Morgan Obrian, from Thence by S. V. Only through Virginia, Maryland, & Pensylvania (18 June to 4 Sept. 1787)." Manuscript diary in the collection of the descendants of Samuel Vaughan.

VEECH — James Veech. *The Monongahela of Old; or, Historical Sketches of South-Western Pennsylvania to the Year 1800.* Pittsburgh: Mrs. E. V. Blaine, 1892. Reissued 1910.

VICKERS — John Vickers. *Thomas Coke: Apostle of Methodism.* Nashville and New York: Abingdon Press, 1969.

VSP — William P. Palmer et al., eds. *Calendar of Virginia State Papers and Other Manuscripts.* 11 vols. Richmond: various publishers, 1875–93.

WALKER — Thomas Walker. "Journal of Dr. Thomas Walker." *First Explorations of Kentucky.* Ed. Josiah Stoddard Johnston. Louisville, Ky.: John P. Morton and Co., 1898.

WALKINSHAW — Lewis Clark Walkinshaw. *Annals of Southwestern Pennsylvania.* 3 vols. New York: Lewis Historical Publishing Co., 1939.

WARREN-ADAMS LETTERS — *Warren-Adams Letters: Being Chiefly a Correspondence among John Adams, Samuel Adams, and James Warren.* 2 vols. Boston: Massachusetts Historical Society, 1917–25.

WASHINGTON COUNTY SUPPLY TAX—1781 — "Washington County Supply Tax—1781." *Pennsylvania Archives,* 3d ser., 22 (1898), 699–782.

WASHINGTON COUNTY WARRANTEES — "Warrantees of Land in the County of Washington, 1784–1892." *Pennsylvania Archives,* 3d ser., 26 (1898), 529–624.

WASHINGTON PAPERS INDEX — *Index to the George Washington Papers.* Index series. Library of Congress. Washington, D.C.: U.S. Government Printing Office, 1964.

WATSON [2] Winslow C. Watson, ed. *Men and Times of the Revolution, or Memoirs of Elkanah Watson.* New York: Dana and Co., 1856.

WAYLAND [1] John Walter Wayland. *The Washingtons and Their Homes.* 1944. Reprint, Berryville: Virginia Book Co., 1973.

WAYLAND [2] John Walter Wayland. *Historic Homes of Northern Virginia and the Eastern Panhandle of West Virginia.* Staunton, Va.: McClure Printing Co., 1937.

WAYLAND [3] John Walter Wayland. *The Lincolns in Virginia.* Staunton, Va.: McClure Printing Co., 1946.

WAYLAND [4] John Walter Wayland. *A History of Rockingham County, Virginia.* Dayton, Va.: Reubush-Elkins Co., 1912.

WELLFORD Robert Wellford. "A Diary Kept by Dr. Robert Wellford, of Fredericksburg, Virginia, during the March of the Virginia Troops to Fort Pitt (Pittsburg) to Suppress the Whiskey Insurrection in 1794." *William and Mary Quarterly,* 1st ser., 11 (1902–3), 1–19.

WESTCOTT Thompson Westcott. *The Life of John Fitch, the Inventor of the Steamboat.* Philadelphia: J. B. Lippincott & Co., 1857.

WESTERN MD. "Journeys of George Washington thru Western Maryland." *Glades Star,* 1 (1941–49), 289–95.

WESTMORELAND MILITIA "Muster Rolls Relating to the Associators and Militia of the County of Westmoreland." *Pennsylvania Archives,* 6th ser., 2 (1907), 295–410.

WHARTON Francis Wharton, ed. *The Revolutionary Diplomatic Correspondence of the United States.* 6 vols. Washington, D.C.: U.S. Government Printing Office, 1889.

WILLIAMS [2] Thomas John Chew Williams. *A History of Washington County, Maryland, from the Earliest Settlements to the Present Time.* 2 vols. 1906. Reprint, Baltimore: Regional Publishing Co., 1968.

WISE — Jennings Cropper Wise. *Col. John Wise of England and Virginia (1617–1795): His Ancestors and Descendants.* Richmond: privately printed, 1918.

WMQ — *The William and Mary Quarterly: A Magazine of Early American History.* Williamsburg, Va.: published by the Institute of Early American History and Culture.

WORMELEY — "The Wormeley Family." *Virginia Magazine of History and Biography,* 35 (1927), 455–56; 36 (1928), 98–101, 283–93, 385–88; 37 (1929), 82–86.

W.P.A. [1] — W.P.A. Writers' Project. *Prince William: The Story of Its People and Its Places.* Manassas, Va.: Bethlehem Good Housekeeping Club, 1941.

W.P.A. [2] — W.P.A. Writers' Project. *Maryland: A Guide to the Old Line State.* New York: Oxford University Press, 1940.

W.P.A. [4] — W.P.A. Writers' Project. *West Virginia: Guide to the Old Dominion.* New York: Oxford University Press, 1940.

W.P.A. [5] — W.P.A. Writers' Project. *West Virginia: A Guide to the Mountain State.* New York: Oxford University Press, 1941.

W.P.A. [6] — W.P.A. Writers' Project. *Pennsylvania: A Guide to the Keystone State.* New York: Oxford University Press, 1940.

W.P.A. [7] — W.P.A. Writers' Project. *New York: A Guide to the Empire State.* New York: Oxford University Press, 1940.

WRIGHT — Louis B. Wright and Marion Tinling, eds. *Quebec to Carolina in 1785–1786.* San Marino, Calif.: Huntington Library, 1943.

WRITINGS — John C. Fitzpatrick, ed. *The Writings of George Washington from the Original Manuscript Sources, 1745–1799.* 39 vols. Washington, D.C.: U.S. Government Printing Office, 1931–44.

WUST — Klaus Wust. *The Virginia Germans.* Charlottesville: University Press of Virginia, 1969.

Index

Individuals and places mentioned for the first time in this volume have been identified in the footnotes; identification notes for those which previously appeared in the first three volumes may be located by consulting the indexes for those volumes. A cumulative index will be included in the last volume of the *Diaries*.

Index

Index